WORKS ISSUED BY
THE HAKLUYT SOCIETY

———

NEWFOUNDLAND DISCOVERED

SECOND SERIES
NO. 160

HAKLUYT SOCIETY

COUNCIL AND OFFICERS, 1980–81

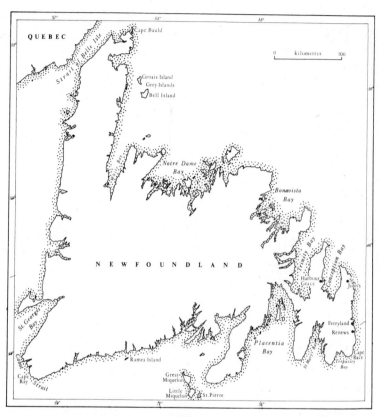

Fig. 1. The island of Newfoundland

NEWFOUNDLAND DISCOVERED

ENGLISH ATTEMPTS AT COLONISATION, 1610–1630

edited by
GILLIAN T. CELL

THE HAKLUYT SOCIETY
LONDON
1982

ISBN 0 904 180 13 1

Printed in Great Britain at the
University Press, Cambridge

Published by the Hakluyt Society
c/o The Map Room,
British Library Reference Division
London WC1B 3DG

CONTENTS

CHAPTER III

LORD FALKLAND'S COLONY

CHAPTER IV

SIR GEORGE CALVERT AND THE FERRYLAND COLONY

ACKNOWLEDGEMENTS

I should like to acknowledge the help which has been so generously afforded me during the preparation of this volume. Lord Middleton has kindly allowed me to print letters from the Middleton Manuscripts which are deposited at the University of Nottingham. From Lord Lothian I received permission to print letters from the Cowper Manuscripts at Melbourne Hall in Derbyshire. The staffs at both the University of Nottingham Manuscripts Office and Melbourne Hall were most gracious during my visits. The New York Public Library was good enough to copy and to permit me to print a letter from the Arents Tobacco Collection. I should like to express my thanks for their assistance to the staffs at the Public Record Office, the British Library, the Wilson Library at the University of North Carolina at Chapel Hill, and Duke University Library.

The Honorary Secretary of the Hakluyt Society, Professor E. M. J. Campbell, has been unfailingly helpful and Dr. Kenneth R. Andrews of the Council has read the manuscript and aided greatly in its preparation. For many years Professor David B. Quinn has given me the benefit of his unrivalled knowledge as well as his unstinted help and support; my debt to him is boundless. Professor Raymond Lahey of Memorial University, Newfoundland, scrambled over the Cupids Cove site with me; I am grateful for his kindness and that of Professor Frederick Aldrich, also of Memorial University. Thomas Farr helped with the collation of the texts of Whitbourne's *Discourse and discovery*.

Finally, and very importantly, I wish to recognise the patient support and interest of my children, Thomas, Katherine, and John, and of my husband, John W. Cell.

GILLIAN TOWNSEND CELL

CHAPEL HILL, N.C.

ix

ILLUSTRATIONS AND MAPS

ABBREVIATIONS USED IN THE FOOTNOTES

APC	*Acts of the Privy Council*
APC Col.	*Acts of the Privy Council, Colonial*
B.L.	British Library
CSP Col.	*Calendar of State Papers, Colonial*
CSP Dom.	*Calendar of State Papers, Domestic*
CSP Ire.	*Calendar of State Papers, Ireland*
CO	Colonial Office
DCB	Dictionary of Canadian Biography
DNB	Dictionary of National Biography
DWB	Dictionary of Welsh Biography
HCA	High Court of Admiralty
N.L.W.	National Library of Wales
PC	Privy Council
P.R.O.	Public Record Office
SP	State Papers
STC	*Short title catalogue*

A NOTE ON EDITING

Texts printed directly from manuscripts are given as nearly as possible as they read, with a minimum of alterations in spelling and punctuation, except that contractions have been expanded and italicised.

BIBLIOGRAPHY

I. MANUSCRIPT SOURCES

1. PUBLIC RECORD OFFICE
   Chancery Patent Roll, James I, 8°, pt viii. C 66/1826.
   Exchequer, King's Remembrancer. E 190/822/9.
   High Court of Admiralty, Oyer and Terminer Examinations. HCA 1/4, 47.
   High Court of Admiralty, Examinations, Instance and Prize. HCA 13/42, 65.
   High Court of Admiralty, Exemplifications. HCA 14/42.
   High Court of Admiralty, Libels. HCA 24/110.
   Privy Council Registers. PC 2/27, 29, 30, 31, 39.
   State Papers, Colonial. CO 1/1, 2, 4, 5, 9, 14.
   State Papers, Domestic, Elizabeth. SP 12/237.
   State Papers, Domestic, James I. SP 14/141.
   State Papers, Domestic, Charles I. SP 16/31, 84, 100, 150.
   State Papers, Sign Manual Warrants. SP 39/15.
   State Papers, Ireland. SP 63/246.

2. BRITISH LIBRARY
   Additional Manuscripts. 4756, 11033.
   Cotton Manuscripts. Otho E VIII, 3.
   Egerton Manuscripts. 2395, 2451.
   Sloane Manuscripts. 170, 3662, 3827.

3. LAMBETH PALACE, LONDON
   MS 250. Journal of John Guy, 1612 (ff. 406–12v).

4. BODLEIAN LIBRARY
   Malone Manuscripts. 2.

5. TRINITY HOUSE, LONDON
   Transactions, 1609–1625.

6. NATIONAL LIBRARY OF SCOTLAND, EDINBURGH
   Advocates Manuscripts. 17.1.19.

7. NATIONAL LIBRARY OF WALES, ABERYSTWYTH
   MS 1595 E.
   MS 5390 D.

8. BRISTOL CITY RECORD OFFICE
Book of Charters, I.
Great Orphans Book, III.
MS Calendar, 07831.

9. UNIVERSITY OF NOTTINGHAM
Middleton Manuscripts. Mi X 1/1-66.

10. MELBOURNE HALL, DERBY
Cowper Manuscripts. Bundles 24, 29.

11. MARYLAND HISTORICAL SOCIETY, BALTIMORE
Calvert Papers.

II. PRINTED SOURCES[1]

Acts of the privy council, 1613–14, 1616–17, 1618–19, 1619–21, 1621–23, 1921–32.
Acts of the privy council, colonial, 1613–80. 1908.
ALEXANDER, SIR WILLIAM. *An encouragement to colonies.* William Stanley, 1624.
ANSPACH, LEWIS A. *A history of the island of Newfoundland.* 1819.
BAGWELL, RICHARD. *Ireland under the Stuarts and during the Interregnum.* 3 vols. 1909–16.
BROWN, ALEXANDER. *The genesis of the United States.* 2 vols. Boston, 1890.
BROWNE, WILLIAM H. *George Calvert and Cecilius Calvert, barons Baltimore of Baltimore.* New York, 1890.
C., T. *A short discourse of the New-found-land: Contaynig [sic] diverse reasons and inducements, for the planting of that country.* Dublin, Society of Stationers, 1623.
Calendar of State Papers, Colonial, America and West Indies, 1574–1660. 1860.
Calendar of State Papers, Domestic, 1611–18, 1619–23, 1623–25, 1625–26, 1627–28, 1628–29, 1629–31, 1631–33, Add. 1635–49. 1856–62.
Calendar of State Papers, Ireland, 1603–6, 1611–12, 1615–25, 1625–32, Add. 1625–60. 1872–1903.
CARR, CECIL T., ed. *Select charters of the trading companies, A.D. 1530–1707.* (Selden Society, XXVIII.) 1913.
CELL, GILLIAN T. *English enterprise in Newfoundland, 1577–1660.* Toronto, 1969.
CLARK, ANDREW, ed. *Registers of the University of Oxford, 1571–1622.* 2 vols. Oxford, 1885–89.
CLARKE, AIDAN. *The Old English in Ireland, 1625–41.* Ithaca, N.Y., 1966.
COAKLEY, THOMAS M. 'George Calvert and Newfoundland.' *Maryland Historical Magazine*, LXXI (1976), 1–18.
COLBY, FREDERIC T., ed. *The visitation of the county of Devon in the year 1620.* (Harleian Society, VI.) 1872.
DEAN, JOHN W., ed. *Captain John Mason, the founder of New Hampshire.* (Prince Society.) Boston, 1887.

[1] Unless otherwise stated, the place of publication of all printed works is London.

Dictionary of Canadian biography, vol. I. Toronto, 1966.

Dictionary of national biography. 63 vols. 1885–1900.

Dictionary of Welsh biography. 1959.

EBURNE, RICHARD. *A plaine path-way to plantations: that is, a discourse in generall, concerning the plantation of our English people in other countries…with certaine motives for a present plantation in New-found land*. G. P[urslow] for John Marriott, 1624.

FOSTER, JOSEPH, ed. *Alumni Oxonienses, 1500–1714*. 4 vols. Oxford, 1891–2.

FULLER, THOMAS. *The history of the worthies of England*, ed. P. A. Nuttall. 4 vols. 1840.

FULLERTON, LADY GEORGIANA C. *The life of Elisabeth, lady Falkland*. 1883.

GALLOWAY, DAVID. 'Robert Hayman (1575–1629): some materials for the life of a colonial governor and first "Canadian" author.' *William and Mary Quarterly*, 3rd ser., XXIV (1967), 75–87.

GARDINER, SAMUEL R. *A history of England from the accession of James I to the outbreak of the civil war, 1604–42*. 10 vols. 1884.

GILLOW, JOSEPH, ed. *A literary and biographical history of the English Catholics*. 5 vols. n.d.

HAKLUYT, RICHARD. *The principal navigations, voyages, traffiques and discoveries of the English nation*. 12 vols. (Hakluyt Society, extra ser., I–XII.) Glasgow, 1903–5.

HAKLUYT, RICHARD. *The original writings and correspondence of the two Richard Hakluyts*, ed. E. G. R. Taylor. 2 vols. (Hakluyt Society, 2nd ser., LXXVI–LXXVII.) 1935.

HARP, ELMER. *The cultural affinities of the Newfoundland Dorset Eskimo*. (National Museum of Canada, Bulletin no. 200.) Ottawa, 1964.

HARPER, J. RUSSELL. 'In quest of lord Baltimore's house at Ferryland.' *Canadian Geographical Journal*, LXI (1960), 106–13.

H[ARRISON], F[AIRFAX]. *The Devon Carys*. 2 vols. New York, 1920.

HARRISSE, HENRY. *Découverte et évolution cartographique de Terre-Neuve et des pays circonvoisins*. Paris, 1900.

HAVRAN, MARTIN. *Caroline courtier: the life of lord Cottington*. 1973.

HAYMAN, ROBERT. *Quodlibets, lately come over from new Britaniola, old Newfoundland*. Elizabeth All-de for Roger Mitchell, 1628.

HOWLEY, JAMES P. *The Beothucks or Red Indians, the aboriginal inhabitants of Newfoundland*. Cambridge, 1915.

INNIS, HAROLD A. *The cod fisheries*. Rev. ed. Toronto, 1954.

JENNESS, DIAMOND. *The Indians of Canada*. 3rd ed. (National Museum of Canada, Bulletin no. 65.) Ottawa, 1955.

JENNINGS, FRANCIS. *The invasion of America*. Chapel Hill, N.C., 1975.

JONES, J. J. 'The golden fleece.' *The National Library of Wales Journal*, III (1943–4), 58–60.

JUDAH, CHARLES B. *The North American fisheries and British policy to 1713*. (Illinois Studies in the Social Sciences, XVIII.) Urbana, Illinois, 1933.

KENNEDY, JOHN P. *Discourse on the life and character of George Calvert, the first lord Baltimore*. Baltimore, 1845.

KENNY, HAMILL. 'New light on an old name.' *Maryland Historical Magazine*, XLIX (1954), 116–21.

KRUGLER, JOHN D. 'Sir George Calvert's resignation as secretary of state and the founding of Maryland.' *Maryland Historical Magazine*, LXVIII (1973), 239–54.

KRUGLER, JOHN D. '"Our trusty and welbeloved councillor": the parliamentary career of Sir George Calvert, 1609–1624.' *Maryland Historical Magazine*, LXXII (1977), 473–87.

KRUGLER, JOHN D. '"The face of a protestant and the heart of a papist:" a reexamination of Sir George Calvert's conversion to Roman Catholicism.' *Journal of Church and State*, XX (1978), 507–31.

LAHEY, RAYMOND J. 'The role of religion in lord Baltimore's colonial enterprise,' *Maryland Historical Magazine*, LXXII (1977), 492–511.

LATIMORE, JOHN. *The annals of Bristol in the seventeenth century*. Bristol 1900.

LATIMORE, JOHN. *The history of the society of merchant venturers of the city of Bristol*. Bristol, 1903.

LEVACKE, BRIAN. *The civil lawyers in England, 1603–41*. Oxford, 1973.

Lincoln's Inn, The records of the honourable society of. 2 vols. 1896.

LLOYD, DAVID. *State-worthies, or, the states-men and favourites of England since the reformation*. 1671.

LOUNSBURY, RALPH G. *The British fishery at Newfoundland, 1634–1763*. (Yale Historical Publications Miscellany, no. 27.) New Haven, 1934.

MCGRATH, PATRICK V., ed. *Records relating to the society of merchant venturers in the city of Bristol in the seventeenth century*. (Bristol Record Society, XVII.) Bristol, 1952.

MCGRATH, PATRICK V., ed. *Merchants and merchandise in seventeenth-century Bristol*. (Bristol Record Society, XIX.) Bristol, 1955.

MCGRATH, PATRICK V. *The merchant venturers of Bristol: a history of the society of merchant venturers of the city of Bristol from its origins to the present day*. Bristol, 1975.

MASON, JOHN. *A briefe discourse of the New-found-land*. Andro Hart, Edinburgh, 1620.

METCALFE, WALTER C., ed. *The visitation of Hertfordshire in 1572 and 1634*. (Harleian Society, XII.) 1886.

MOODY, THEODORE, MARTIN, F. X. and BYRNE, F. J., edd. *A new history of Ireland*, vol. III. Oxford, 1976.

MORANDIÈRE, CHARLES DE LA. *Histoire de la pêche française de la morue dans l'Amérique septentrionale des origines à 1789*. 2 vols. Paris, 1962.

MORRIS, JOHN G. *The lords Baltimore*. Baltimore, 1874.

MUSGRAVE, SIR WILLIAM. *Obituary prior to 1800*, ed. Sir George J. Armytage. 6 vols. (Harleian Society, XLIV–XLIX.) 1899–1901.

ORPHEUS JUNIOR pseud. See Sir William Vaughan.

PARKER, JOHN. *Books to build an empire: a bibliographical history of English overseas interests to 1620*. Amsterdam, 1965.

Parliaments of England, 1213–1702, vol. I. 1878.

PEDLEY, CHARLES. *The history of Newfoundland from the earliest times to the year 1860*. 1863.

PERRET, ROBERT. *La géographie de Terre-Neuve*. Paris, 1913.

POWELL, JOHN W. DAMER. 'The explorations of John Guy in Newfoundland.' *Geographical Journal*, LXXXVI (1935), 512–18.

POWELL, JOHN W. DAMER. 'John Guy: founder of Newfoundland.' *United Empire*, XXIV (1933), 323–7.

POWELL, JOHN W. DAMER. 'John Guy's voyage in the *Endeavour*.' *United Empire*, XXVIII, (1937), 16–17.

PRESTON, RICHARD A. *Gorges of Plymouth fort*. Toronto, 1953.

PRINCE, JOHN. *Damonii orientales illustres: or the worthies of Devon*. Exeter, 1701.

PROWSE, DANIEL W. *A history of Newfoundland*. 1895.

PURCHAS, SAMUEL. *Purchas his pilgrimage*. First three editions. William Stansby for Henry Fetherstone. 1613, 1614, 1617.

PURCHAS, SAMUEL. *Hakluytus posthumus or Purchas his pilgrimes*. 4 vols. William Stansby for Henry Fetherstone, 1625. Another edition. 20 vols. (Hakluyt Society, extra ser., XIV–XXXIII.) Glasgow, 1905–7.

QUINN, DAVID B., ed. *The voyages and colonising enterprises of Sir Humphrey Gilbert*. 2 vols. (Hakluyt Society, 2nd ser., LXXXIII–LXXXIV.) 1940.

QUINN, DAVID B. *The Roanoke voyages*. 2 vols. (Hakluyt Society, 2nd ser., CIV–CV.) 1955.

QUINN, DAVID B. *Raleigh and the British empire*. Rev. ed. New York, 1962.

QUINN, DAVID B. *England and the discovery of America, 1481–1620*. New York, 1974.

QUINN, DAVID B., ed. *New American world: a documentary history of North America to 1612*. 5 vols. New York, 1979.

QUINN, DAVID B. 'The argument for the English discovery of America between 1480 and 1496.' *Geographical Journal*, CXII (1961), 277–85.

RABB, THEODORE K. *Enterprise and empire: merchant and gentry investment in the expansion of England, 1575–1630*. Cambridge, Mass., 1967.

RICH, E. E. 'Colonial settlement and its labour problems.' *Cambridge Economic History*, edd. E. E. Rich and C. H. Wilson, vol. IV. Cambridge, 1967. Pp. 302–73.

ROE, SIR THOMAS. *The negotiations of Sir Thomas Roe, in his embassy to the Ottoman porte, from the year 1621 to 1628 inclusive*, ed. S. Richardson. 1740.

SHAW, WILLIAM A., ed. *The knights of England*. 2 vols. 1906.

SLAFTER, EDMUND F., ed. *Sir William Alexander and American colonisation*. (Prince Society.) Boston, 1865.

SMITH, JOHN. *Travels and works*, edd. E. Arber and A. G. Bradley. 2 vols. 2nd ed. Edinburgh, 1910.

STOCK, LEO F., ed. *Proceedings and debates of the British parliaments respecting North America, 1582–1688,* vol. I. Washington, 1924.

STRAFFORD, THE EARL OF. *Letters and despatches,* ed. W. Knowler. 2 vols. 1739.

TAYLOR, EVA G. R. See Richard Hakluyt.

THOMAS, SIR DAVID LL. 'Iscennen and Golden Grove.' *Trans. Honourable Society of Cymmrodorion* (1940), 115–29.

VAUGHAN, SIR WILLIAM. Ἐρωτοπαιγνιον *pium: continens canticum canticorum Salomonis, et psalmos aliquot selectiores.* pt 1. ap R. Johnesum, 1597.

VAUGHAN, SIR WILLIAM. *Poematum libellus; Erotopainion pium,* pt. 2; *Speculum humanae condicionis.* (Three works in one). G. Shaw, 1598.

VAUGHAN, SIR WILLIAM. *The golden grove.* 1st ed. S. Stafford, 1600.

VAUGHAN, SIR WILLIAM. *Naturall and artificiall directions for health, derived from the best philosophers, as well moderne as ancient.* 1st ed. R. Bradocke, 1600.

VAUGHAN, SIR WILLIAM. *The spirit of detraction conjured and convicted in seven circles.* W. Stanley for G. Norton, 1611.

VAUGHAN, SIR WILLIAM. *Cambrensium Caroleia.* William Stansby, 1625.

VAUGHAN, SIR WILLIAM. *The golden fleece...transported from Cambrioll Colchos, out of the southermost part of the island, commonly called the Newfoundland, by Orpheus Junior, for the generall and perpetuall good of Great Britaine.* Francis Williams, 1626.

VAUGHAN, SIR WILLIAM. *The Newlanders cure.* N. O[kes] for T. Constable, 1630.

VAUGHAN, SIR WILLIAM. *The church militant.* T. Paine for H. Blunden, 1640.

VAUGHAN, SIR WILLIAM. *The soules exercise.* T. and R. Cotes for H. Blunden, 1641.

VIVIAN, J. J. and DRAKE, H. H., edd. *The visitation of the county of Cornwall in the year 1620.* (Harleian Society, IX.) 1874.

WALPOLE, HORACE. *A catalogue of the royal and noble authors of England.* 2 vols. Strawberry Hill, 1758.

WHITBOURNE, RICHARD. *A discourse and discovery of New-found-land, with many reasons to proove how worthy and beneficiall a plantation may there be made, after a far better manner than now it is.* Felix Kyngston for William Barret, 1620. Bound with: Bishops' letter instructing parishes to collect money for Whitbourne. By G. Montaigne, bishop of London. 16 Sept. 1622. [F. Kingston, 1622]; and with *The copy of a reference* [from king James and others concerning collections of money; also granting Whitbourne a 21-year privilege to print his books.] [F. Kingston, 1622.]

WHITBOURNE, RICHARD. *A discourse and discovery of Newfoundland...as also an invitation and likewise certain letters sent from that countrey.* Felix Kingston, 1622. Bound with: Bishops' letter instructing parishes to collect money for Whitbourne. By S. Harsnet, bishop of Norwich. 2 Dec. 1622. [F. Kingston, 1622]; and with *The copy of a reference* [from king James and others concerning collections of money; also granting Whitbourne a 21-year privilege to print his books.] [F. Kingston, 1622.] Another edition, 1623, but without the bishops' letter.

WHITBOURNE, RICHARD. *A discourse containing a loving invitation both honourable and profitable to all such as shall be adventurers, in the New-found-land.* Felix Kyngston, 1622.

WILHELM, LEWIS W. *Sir George Calvert, baron of Baltimore.* (Maryland Historical Society, Fund Publication, no. 20.) Baltimore, 1884.

WILLIAMS, E. ROLAND. 'Cambriol: the story of a forgotten colony.' *Welsh Outlook*, VIII (1921), 230–3.

WILLIAMSON, JAMES A., ed. *The voyages of the Cabots and the English discovery of North America.* 1929.

WILLSON, DAVID H. *The privy councillors in the house of commons, 1604–1629.* Minneapolis, Minnesota, 1940.

WINNE, EDWARD. *A letetr [sic]...to the right honorable, Sir George Calvert, Knight...from Feryland in Newfoundland, the 26. of August, 1621.* [B. Alsop], 1621.

WOOD, ANTHONY A. *Athenae Oxonienses.* 2 vols. 1721.

WROTH, LAURENCE C. 'Tobacco or codfish: lord Baltimore makes his choice.' *Bulletin of the New York Public Library*, LVIII (1954), 523–34.

INTRODUCTION

By the beginning of the seventeenth century no part of the New World was more familiar to the English than the island of Newfoundland. For more than a hundred years – since John Cabot's voyage of 1497 if not before[1] – English fishermen had frequented the fishery in company with French, Basques, Portuguese and Spaniards. In fact two separate industries had developed side by side. The continental fishermen, with their more plentiful supplies of salt, fished on the Banks and put their catch, heavily salted, directly into the holds of their ships. They came to the island at the end of the season only to pick up fresh water and wood for their homeward journey. The English, on the other hand, and some of the continental Europeans used the island as their base during the summer months. Fishing from small boats, they dried their catch gradually with a combination of salt, sun and wind. When the season ended they left behind their huts, stages, flakes and boats to be used another year while they sailed for market.[2]

The trade to Newfoundland thus became not only the first regular trade between Europe and the New World, but one that in many ways was significantly different from those that developed later. First and most obviously, it was a trade that flourished without settlement. Ships plied back and forth each year, those going to the Banks leaving Europe in late January or February, those to the shore fishery a month or two later. In a normal year the summer months sufficed to take and prepare enough fish to fill a fishing ship of seventy or eighty tons, and many made enough to sell to the empty sack ships that came out to collect a cargo. The fleet was back by late October and free to engage in other business during the winter. Secondly, the mechanics of the industry existed before the island was discovered; merchants simply transferred to the rich new grounds the financial practices and the techniques of

---

[1] D. B. Quinn, 'The argument for the English discovery of American between 1480 and 1496,' *Geographical Journal*, CXII (1961), 277–85; reprinted in Quinn, *England and the discovery of America, 1481–1620* (New York, 1974).
[2] For a fuller description of the techniques of the 'dry' and 'green' fisheries, see H. A. Innis, *The cod fisheries* (Toronto, 1954), pp. 48–9, and G. T. Cell, *English enterprise in Newfoundland, 1577–1660* (Toronto, 1969), p. 4.

taking and drying fish that had been worked out in the old-established fisheries such as Iceland or the North Sea. In the case of the English, this meant that Newfoundland merchants continued to own vessels in partnership, to organise voyages under precisely detailed charter-parties, and to share the expense of setting out a fishing ship between owners or charterers and the victualler, the profits being divided among the investors with approximately a third going to the captain and crew. Such customs survived among fishing merchants even when, during the course of the sixteenth century, they began to die out in other branches of the shipping industry. They ensured that each party's investment was kept low and the risk shared. Particularly when the fish was exchanged in the Mediterranean for the wine, fruit and oil of southern Europe, the profits were relatively high in proportion to the initial investment.[1]

To participate in a Newfoundland voyage, then, did not require large reserves of capital or even special shipping; a vessel used for a coastal passage within European waters one year might cross the Atlantic the next. Unlike the mining, ranching or plantation development in Spanish America, the Caribbean or the southern parts of North America, the Newfoundland fishery did not demand drastic economic or technical change, the large-scale permanent movement of people or the exploitation of a non-European labour force. It simply extended across the Atlantic the use of skills, techniques and labour already available. In consequence the new trade slipped easily into existing commercial patterns of Atlantic Europe.

Nevertheless in the climate of an expanding Europe it was inevitable that sooner or later the promoters of settlement would cast their eyes upon Newfoundland. Nor is it surprising that the English showed the greatest interest, for no other nation was as closely identified with the shore fishery. By the end of the sixteenth century they had succeeded in driving many of the continental fishermen out of the south-east corner of the island, the Avalon peninsula, which a hundred to a hundred and fifty English ships now visited every year. The demand for dried fish, as the demand for cloth earlier in the century, seemed insatiable. Europe was desperately short of protein, affordable protein at a time that meat was beyond the pocket of most of the population and durable protein at a time when the armies and navies of the new

---

[1] The organisation of the English fishing industry is described more fully in Cell, *English enterprise*, ch. 1. On the financial arrangements in the French fishery, see Innis, *Cod fisheries*, pp. 16–23.

nation states were growing at an unprecedented rate. During the war with Spain, the victuallers of Elizabeth's army and navy kept vigil in the west-country ports to snap up the English catch. No fish was supposed to be exported, but some was smuggled into Spain by way of France. When there was no war, fish sold easily in the markets of Catholic Europe. English Protestants had a less voracious appetite for dried codfish, which the government tried to stimulate by the legal imposition of fish days.[1]

But it was not English fishermen who thought in terms of settlement. What they wanted – a profitable, uncomplicated trade – they already enjoyed. The first advocates of colonisation in Newfoundland, if one disregards John Rastell in the early part of the sixteenth century,[2] were men connected with Sir Humphrey Gilbert and imbued with the anti-Spanish nationalism of Elizabeth's later years. Upon these sentiments the early proponents of Newfoundland, Anthony Parkhurst and Edward Hayes, played when they suggested that settlement would secure English dominance of the fishing grounds and possibly the exclusion of foreign fishermen.[3] That prospect, however, could not compete with the more glamorous inducements of mines, discoveries of a north-west passage, or raids upon the Spanish treasure fleet. Even though Gilbert, encouraged by.the conviction that he had found silver, did take formal possession of Newfoundland in 1583, it remained the preserve of the annual fishermen throughout the sixteenth century. Their yearly visits, not the grandiose claims of the mercurial Gilbert, marked the island as a place to which Englishmen had a right.

In the early years of James I came a revival of English interest in overseas settlement, with Virginia, New England, Guiana and Newfoundland all being considered as possible sites. The behaviour on the Guiana expedition of 1604 and in Jamestown in the early days indicates that old habits and old illusions died hard; the privateering impulse and the lure of quick wealth still too easily ensnared Englishmen. But as they moved further north so their approach to plantation became more sober and more practical, partly because of the difficulties of the environment but more perhaps because in Newfoundland and, to a lesser extent, in New England the fisheries did provide an obvious commercial possibility. When, in 1610, a company was formed to

---

[1] Cell, *English enterprise*, pp. 24–5, 27, 28, 30.
[2] *Interlude of the four elements* (J. Rastell, 1525?).
[3] R. Hakluyt, *Principal navigations, voyages, traffiques & discoveries of the English nation* (Glasgow, 1903–5), VIII, 9–16, 34–77; E. G. R. Taylor, ed., *The original writings and correspondence of the two Richard Hakluyts* (Hakluyt Society, 1935), I, 123–7.

undertake the settlement of Newfoundland the fishery was at the centre of its plans.[1] Indeed the logic of the situation demanded that it must be. The island's agricultural potential was obviously limited, whatever propagandists might promise or inexperienced settlers hope, and the Newfoundland company does not seem to have deluded itself with dreams of mineral wealth, apart from iron. Fishing must be its source of profit and through settlement the company must have anticipated gaining some advantage over the seasonal fishermen.

What that advantage would be was clearly perceived by John Guy, a Bristol merchant experienced in the trade and first governor of the colony founded at Cupids Cove in 1610. It lay in settlers having first choice of beach space, being able to begin to fish early and to get their catch to market first, and perhaps, though this he dare not say publicly, gradually excluding the annual fishermen from Newfoundland's harbours.[2] What was to Guy and the company an advantage was to the fishing merchants a threat. By this time about two hundred of their ships went to the island each summer and the annual profit from the fishery must have been in the region of £100,000.[3] The industry was managed by hundreds of small merchants in the provincial ports from Bristol to Southampton. They had never yet experienced any interference with their business, other than the occasional disturbance resulting from tensions in Europe, and they had enjoyed the protection of a government very conscious of the fishery's economic worth and its importance as a training ground for the nation's seamen. It was not to be expected that they would welcome any change in their highly conservative business, still less one that endangered their very right to pursue it. The trans-Atlantic fishing grounds had traditionally been open to all comers; there had never been any legal right of exclusion, never any monopoly. Even though, in the charter of 1610 which created the Newfoundland company, the government explicitly guaranteed the continuing freedom of the fishery,[4] the fishermen were not convinced. Too many monopolies already restricted English trade. West-country merchants had only recently been threatened with the closure of their markets in France and Spain. Were the Newfoundland

---

[1] A more detailed account of the Newfoundland company and the settlement at Cupids may be found in Cell, *English enterprise*, ch. IV.

[2] See below, p. 63.

[3] Newfoundland company's petition of incorporation, 9 Feb. 1609/10 (Trinity House, Transactions, 1609–25, ff. I, IV); L. F. Stock, ed., *Proceedings and debates of the British parliaments respecting North America, 1542–1688* (Washington, 1924), I, 55.

[4] P.R.O., Patent Rolls, 8 Jas I, pt viii, C 66/1826, printed in C. T. Carr, ed., *Select charters of trading companies, A.D. 1530–1707* (Selden Society, 1913), pp. 51–62.

fishing grounds to be closed to them, the tightly integrated economy of the south-west would be thrown into chaos.

So from the beginning the lines were drawn: the long-established west-country fishing merchants against the settlement interests, represented first by the London and Bristol company for the colonisation of Newfoundland, organised in 1610. A typical seventeenth century trading venture, the company blended a sprinkling of courtiers and gentlemen who supplied influence and status, with a larger group of merchants who furnished most of the capital and most of the energy.[1] Although the majority of the merchants came from London, the initiative in founding the company probably came from Bristol, a port which had looked west to the North Atlantic fisheries for over a hundred years. Perhaps some proprietary instinct asserted itself now in the move to exploit the fishery more systematically in conjunction with settlement. Certainly it was a Bristol merchant, John Guy, who visited the island in 1608, who subsequently wrote 'a Treatise to animate the English to plant there,'[2] and who served as the colony's first governor.

On 2 May 1610 the Newfoundland company was chartered with an initial membership of forty-eight and shares selling for £25.[3] While the letters patent awarded the whole island to the company, the focus of activity was clearly to be the Avalon peninsula. In that area all settlement between 1610 and 1630, whether sponsored by the company or by independent proprietors, would be clustered. The peninsula possessed the advantage of familiarity, good harbours and beaches for the fishery, and a negative benefit in the absence of native inhabitants. Indeed the charter stated that the whole island was uninhabited, an assertion which, as the company knew, was not true. But the never very numerous Beothuk had retreated from the areas frequented by shore fishermen and, more importantly, must already have suffered serious demographic disturbance as a result of their century of contact with the European.[4] Not only did the charter ignore any native rights but, in a more curious omission, it failed to claim that the English had any right to the island conferred either by first discovery or by Sir

---

[1] *Ibid.*

[2] Unfortunately no copy of this document has survived. S. Purchas, *Hakluytus posthumus: or Purchas his pilgrimes* (Glasgow, 1905–7), XIX, 405; and see below, p. 62.

[3] Carr, *Select charters*, pp. 51–62; Notebook of Newfoundland company records, 1610–13 (University of Nottingham, Middleton MSS, Mi X 1/1, ff. 15v–16).

[4] According to Diamond Jenness, *The Indians of Canada*, 3rd ed. (National Museum of Canada, Bulletin no. 65, Ottawa, 1955), p. 266, there may have been only about five hundred Beothuk Indians at the end of the fifteenth century. This may be a conservative estimate. On the basis of such works as Francis Jennings, *The invasion of America* (Chapel Hill, N.C., 1975), it seems reasonable to asume a degree of demographic change.

Humphrey Gilbert's actions in 1583. Rather it based the right of possession simply upon fifty years of visits by English fishermen.

Some two months after the letters patent were sealed, forty colonists left Bristol, led by John Guy, and sailed straight for Cupids Cove in Conception Bay. The site had been selected by Guy as early as 1608; it had a sheltered harbour and good supplies of fresh water. Only in its agricultural possibilities was Guy seriously misled;[1] the grain which he found sprouting so easily would fail to ripen in the short northern summer. Root vegetables, turnips particularly, seem to have been the colonists' only success.

Nevertheless the founding of the first colony was a strikingly business-like affair. Four years had now passed since the troubled beginnings at Jamestown, and the Newfoundland company, which had a number of members in common with the Virginia organisation, had learned some lessons. What those lessons were is evident both in the instructions given to Guy, which stressed the importance of a site which was not low-lying and swampy, of care in Indian relations, and of keeping the men busy and productive,[2] and in the choice of personnel. The first settlers seem to have been accustomed to manual labour and some at least had experience of the fishery.[3] The governor himself was no impractical gentleman but a shrewd merchant, alert to the need to diversify so as to supplement the income made from fishing. The rapid lading of the ship in which the colonists had come from England, with a cargo of timber and samples of furs highlights the contrast with the lackadaisical behaviour in Virginia. During the following winter the settlers constructed houses and workrooms and protected themselves with guns mounted on a palisade; they cleared and planted land; they built fishing boats and a twelve ton pinnace, the *Endeavour*, which they could use for exploration.[4] Thanks to the rigorous activity coupled with a mild winter and an apparently adequate food supply, the colony stayed unusually healthy; only four men died, an exceptionally low mortality rate compared to that on the James or among the French at Ste-Croix in 1604. As they read Guy's early letters, the shareholders in England must have felt that his confidence in the future self-sufficiency of the colony was entirely justified.

[1] See below, pp. 61, 62–3.
[2] 'Instructions directed by the counsaile...to Iohn Guy', 26 May 1610, Notebook (University of Nottingham, Middleton MSS, Mi X 1/1, ff. 12–14). This long and detailed version differs substantially from the damaged version in B.L., Cotton MSS, Otho E, VIII, 3.   [3] See below, p. 63.
[4] The events of the winter are related in John Guy's letter to the Newfoundland company's council, 11 May 1611, Purchas, *Pilgrimes*, XIX, 410–6.

At the end of the summer of 1611 the governor went home to report
in person. When he returned the following spring he brought more
settlers, including sixteen women. The first English child would be born
in Newfoundland in March 1613, fittingly enough to the wife of
Nicholas Guy who was probably related to the governor.[1] More
newcomers arrived in the summer of 1612, among them a group sent
over by a prominent shareholder, Sir Percival Willoughby, whose
nineteen-year-old son, Thomas, came with them.

By this time the company was making grants of land to its
shareholders according to the size of their investment. Sir Percival
received the northern section of the peninsula between Conception and
Trinity Bays and he pressed the company, albeit unsuccessfully, for Bell
Island which was rumoured to contain iron deposits. Those he sent over
included a surveyor and a man from his Nottinghamshire estate whose
job it was to report on the island's fertility and natural resources. He
sent too a number of young boys as apprentices. To supervise them
and to act as guardian to the unruly Thomas, he chose Henry Crout.
In general Willoughby's colonists were not impressed either with the
island itself or with the amount of hard work expected from them.
Thomas, who had evidently left England in disgrace, found that
idleness at Cupids earned him an unwelcome dip in an icy stream. Only
Crout reported positively, for the good reason that he had already
purchased a half share in the company. There was nothing like having
a financial stake in a colony to help one see potential profit where others
saw only barren wilderness. Crout seems to have had a position of some
standing at the settlement and he was given the responsibility of
keeping the official journal for the winter of 1612–13, a complete copy
of which has survived. It took four years of struggling with a hostile
environment, unwilling labour, and a chronically dissatisfied employer
before Crout lost both his optimism and his investment.[2]

The labour problem was endemic in early settlements. Apprentices
were rarely a success and they were regularly shipped home after a year
or so. Both Crout and Guy criticised the company for its dependence
on this cheap but unreliable source of labour. Company servants,
whether in Virginia or Newfoundland, expected land of their own;
that hope more than any other drove them to quit England. But it is
not clear that the Newfoundland company ever made any provision

[1] Cell, *English enterprise*, pp. 64–5; Henry Crout's journal, 1 Sept. 1612–30 April 1613
(University of Nottingham, Middleton MSS, Mi X 1/66, f. 16).
[2] Cell, *English enterprise*, pp. 65–7.

7

for allotting land to its men. If it did not, then it made a serious mistake for it both increased the likelihood of dissatisfaction and restricted the amount of land brought under settlement. The fact that only a small area had actually been planted would be used against the colonising interests by the annual fishermen. Settlement was further limited when the plans for another company colony at Renews in 1612 were thwarted by the intimidating presence of the pirate Peter Easton. About three years later the company transferred the land around Renews to Sir William Vaughan; from that time on it came to rely increasingly upon private adventurers to extend the area of settlement.[1]

But for the winter of 1612–13 the company had sixty-two people, the largest group of settlers yet, at Cupids. The record of this winter is extraordinarily full, because of the survival of a document unique in the history of early colonisation: a copy of the colony's official journal. With unusual imagination, the company had included in its instructions to John Guy in 1610 the requirement that he 'keepe a Iournall of all accidentes and what wynds and wether everie day especially between September and march', so that 'the memorie of accurantes perrishe not'.[2] Such a record would give the company an intimate knowledge of the settlers' daily life and needs, and suggests an unusually scientific approach to the problems of colonisation. The governor probably kept the first journal himself; in his absence in 1611–12 the second became the responsibility of his deputies, his brother Philip and William Colston, another Bristol man. Samuel Purchas had a copy of the second winter's diary, but because it was, in his opinion, 'very tedious' he chose not to print it in his selection of documents relating to Newfoundland.[3]

The journal for 1612–13 was dutifully if not very imaginatively kept by Henry Crout. He made daily entries from the first of September to the end of April, missing only 1 April for some unexplained reason. Crout observed meticulously the company's stricture concerning the weather. Every day he noted the incidence of rain or snowfall, the direction of the wind, the duration of periods of sunshine, as well as giving some indication of relative temperature. Lacking instrumentation, Crout had to rely on subjective terms: the weather might be 'cold', 'something cold', 'very cold', or 'extremely cold'; the day might bring 'sun shining', or 'fair sun shining', or 'very fair sun shining'. But the overall trends are clear. In the autumn the winds were

[1] *Ibid.*, pp. 67–8.
[2] Notebook (University of Nottingham, Middleton MSS, Mi X 1/1, ff. 12–14).
[3] Purchas, *Pilgrimes*, XIX, 415, 416.

predominantly westerly, with milder temperatures when the wind shifted to the south. Not until 12 October did Crout consider it to be 'very' cold, and six days later he recorded the first showers of snow; heavy snow did not fall until November. In December, with the winds coming from the north and the north west, it froze hard and snowed every day for ten days. But soon it thawed and the weather turned mild and wet. Periodically throughout the winter Crout noted that the weather was no more severe than it might be in England. But in the new year he began to record that the small lake near the settlement had frozen over and, from time to time, the harbour was frozen too. Only once, in March, was it completely blocked by a large iceberg. Typically enough the heaviest snows and the coldest temperatures occurred in February. It was then that he began to report sickness and some deaths. At one point twenty-two men were ill, most with scurvy, and the deep snow made it hard to find the scurvy grass or to dig the turnips which they had found beneficial. The eight who died were either apprentices or craftsmen whom he described as 'hired men for wages'. The first relief ship reached the colony at the end of March and, at about that time, the weather began to moderate and to become very changeable. Cold and snow alternated with rapid thaws and mild temperatures. The last entry that Crout made, on 30 April 1613, recorded another heavy, wet snowfall. While this may have been the coldest winter that the colony had yet experienced, it does not seem to have been particularly severe when compared to modern Newfoundland winters.

Apart from the weather, the journal described in much less detail some of the men's activities, the furs they trapped, the fish they caught. Only once did Crout's brief, laconic style relax and that was in his account of the major event of the winter – the voyage to Trinity Bay, under the command of John Guy.[1] Little is known of any previous explorations of the island by the settlers, although they had used the pinnace in their first winter to explore Conception Bay. The journey to Trinity would have been made during the summer but for Easton; October and November were hardly ideal months. The decision to sail rather than to make the relatively short overland journey to Trinity Bay was perhaps a strange one. More than anything else it may reflect ignorance of the island's geography. Guy evidently had some hopes of discovering a passage from Trinity to Placentia Bay,[2] an illusion nurtured by the heavily fjorded coastline as well as the early cartographic

---

[1] For other narratives of this journey, see below, pp. 68–78, 83–7.
[2] See below, p. 72.

tradition which had depicted Newfoundland as a series of distinct islands. Not until the Wright-Molyneux world map, apparently prepared for the second edition of Hakluyt's *Principal navigations*, had an English cartographer represented Newfoundland as a single, roughly triangular island.[1]

The desire to explore apart, the main purpose of the expedition seems to have been to make contact with the Beothuk Indians. In their instructions given to governor Guy in 1610, the company had cautiously recommended

if any Savige shall come voluntarie to you that you vse him kindly and by no meanes not to detayne against his will not to let him see your house and provissions but if you can vppon ackquaintance made with them and with their good lickinge and consent send over one or to of experience in those Counteys to be kept vntill we could Learne ther langwage or them oures for there farther discoverie of Countrie wee wish you herin to Followe our advise and otherwise not to meddle with them.[2]

In fact no Beothuk, as far as we know, had ventured near to Cupids Cove. When Guy and his party came across a small band of Indians in Bull Arm, it was probably their first sight of the island's indigenous people.

The Beothuk were the easternmost group of the Algonkian-speaking Indians of northeastern America. A people with no agricultural tradition, they migrated between coast and interior according to the season. Those whom Guy met were probably stragglers, preparing to move inland for the winter; therefore, perhaps, the absence of women upon which the English remarked. The accounts of this tentative but friendly meeting are both charming in their details of the dancing, the shared meal, and the laughter at the Indian who alarmed the company by blowing into a bottle, and extremely accurate in their descriptions of the Indians and their way of life. Guy and Crout were struck, as were all European observers, by the Beothuk's liberal use of red ochre, which had a religious significance and may also have warded off insects. The clothing of skin mantles with sleeves, and moccasins was typical; it is not clear upon what experience Richard Whitbourne would base his later statement that the Newfoundland Indians went naked. Guy and Crout noted too the heavy reliance upon birch bark which they used for cooking vessels (for unlike the Algonkians of the mainland they had no pottery), for their summer tipis, and for their canoes. While

[1] Cell, *English enterprise*, pp. 36–8.
[2] Notebook (University of Nottingham, Middleton MSS, Mi X 1/1, ff. 12–14).

the accounts describe the shape and construction of the tipis, the colonists do not seem to have gone inside one for no mention is made of the characteristic sleeping trenches, lined with evergreens. On the other hand they did remark upon the distinctive construction of Beothuk canoes, high at both prow and stern, with a central hump on either side.[1]

Prior contact with Europeans had supplied the Indians both with some goods – a brass kettle and some fishing hooks among other things – and also with some knowledge of the white man's interest in furs. Indeed the Indians may have been more familiar with that trade, as a result of visits from the French, than were the English. Unsure of how to interpret the Beothuk's action in leaving furs behind, the English reacted conservatively and took only a few, carefully leaving payment.

The journey into Trinity Bay also deepened the colonists' knowledge of the island. They noted carefully areas of good land, safe harbours, the presence of caribou, and the likelihood of deposits of iron. On an island near the site of their meeting with the Indians, which they christened Truce Sound, they began to build a house to use as a base for further visits. Apparently Guy intended to return the following summer and may, in some way, have communicated this to the Beothuk. But bad weather was closing in by November; they abandoned their house and left on an adventurous journey home. For the remainder of that winter the colonists stayed at Cupids, attempting only an abortive overland visit back to Trinity Bay in January 1613.

This proved the most trying winter that the English had yet experienced: the weather was more severe, the incidence of sickness and death more frequent. Their livestock suffered and supplies of clothing ran low; while food seems to have held out, they had to dilute their beer with water. Willoughby's apprentices attributed the death of one of their fellows to the fact that he had had to drink water in the winter time. Relief ships reached them early in the spring with supplies and yet more apprentices. But the settlers were dispirited. Letters home expressed more forcefully than ever before disillusionment with the island and resentment at the physical hardships and the harshness of the governor. Even Guy may have been discouraged for suddenly he decided to return to England. He never came back. His

[1] On the Beothuk, see D. Jenness, *The Indians of Canada*, *passim*; E. Harp, Jr., *The cultural affinities of the Newfoundland Dorset Eskimo* (National Museum of Canada, Bulletin no. 200, Ottawa, 1964), pp. 153–4, 156, 165; J. P. Howley, *The Beothucks or Red Indians, the aboriginal inhabitants of Newfoundland* (Cambridge, 1915).

departure left Henry Crout to lead a new expedition to Trinity Bay, but of the Beothuk there was no trace. Twenty years later it was reported that they had been frightened away from the rendezvous when fishermen fired upon them. At the end of the summer of 1613 Crout and Thomas Willoughby sailed for home. Now only thirty people remained at Cupids Cove, the smallest group in the colony's history.[1]

The hard winter of 1612–1613 had been a crisis for both colony and company. Thereafter both struggled to survive. Shareholders and settlers alike had been too sanguine; disappointed, both sides indulged in recriminations. From the relative comfort of London it was easy to condemn the governor and the colonists for their failure to begin a second settlement, their timidity in dealing with pirates, and the lack of a return on the investment. But Guy had undergone too much adversity to be ready to accept blame. He turned upon the company's treasurer, a London merchant named John Slany, and accused him of penny pinching. If the enterprise had gone sour, the fault was Slany's not his, an opinion which Crout shared. To Sir Percival Willoughby, company and settlers alike were at fault: the one for refusing him Bell Island as part of his grant, the other for not moving from Cupids to his own land. As stubborn as he was mean and suspicious, Willoughby sent Crout back to the island in 1616, only to dismiss him a year later. With his second agent, Thomas Rowley, Willoughby's relations were no better and even briefer. Nevertheless, as late as 1631 the determined old man was still trying to find someone he could trust to develop his land.[2]

Meanwhile, in about 1615, the company appointed Captain John Mason to succeed Guy.[3] The choice of a sea captain experienced in dealing with piracy was a logical one, given that pirates had raided the fishery again in 1613, and that the annual fishermen had displayed growing hostility towards the colonists. With these problems Mason might deal more effectively than Guy. Nor unnaturally the merchant and the sailor had different approaches to the role of governor. While Guy had emphasised economic diversity and tried to develop glass and iron works and a trade in naval stores and furs as well as fish, Mason concentrated his energies upon exploration. The summers of 1616 and 1617 he spent in surveying Newfoundland's southern coastline, reaching as far as Placentia Bay and perhaps as far west as St George's Bay, a

[1] Cell, *English enterprise*, pp. 69–70.   [2] *Ibid.*, pp. 71–3, 76–7, 79.
[3] For an account of Mason's life, see J. W. Dean, ed., *Captain John Mason* (Prince Society, Boston, 1887), and *DCB*, I. On his experience in dealing with pirates, see G. P. Insh, *Scottish colonial schemes, 1620–1686* (Glasgow, 1922), p. 34.

region almost unknown to the English.[1] From these expeditions came the first English map of the island to have been compiled from personal experience.[2]

In Mason's mind may have been some thought of moving the colony, perhaps to get away from the area most popular with the fishermen and, therefore, with the pirates. In 1619 it was reported that

master masson is about to cause the Company to enlarge the pattent yf they can;...its large enough yf it be well managed but the company wants corrage hers rome enough for us & Fyshermen two: we want but a little power to writte the rongs they do us: & the greattest want is settelling well; wher we meane to plant, the welch Fooles haue left of...thers now land enoughe to be had...[3]

The Welsh fools were Sir William Vaughan's hapless colonists who had just abandoned their feeble attempt to settle at Renews.[4] Possibly the company had revived their earlier scheme of establishing a colony there. A site at Renews would not have achieved the aim of escaping from the fishermen's aggression, but it would have given notice that the company did not intend to be intimidated, that it was still committed to the future of settlement. Certainly the company sought greater authority over the fishermen who, they claimed, had inflicted serious damage upon the community at Cupids. In 1620 Mason did receive a commission to restore order, and the privy council enjoined all Newfoundland-bound vessels to respect the rights of settlers.[5]

That same year John Mason published in Edinburgh his *Briefe discourse of the New-found-land*. As the place of publication suggests, the tract was written for a Scottish audience and to attract Scottish investment. From this time may date Sir William Alexander's rather desultory involvement with Newfoundland, for he was an acquaintance of Sir John Scott to whom Mason's work was dedicated.[6]

Curiously enough the *Briefe discourse* is the only printed work to derive directly from the Newfoundland company's activities. But Mason chose to say tantalisingly little about the colony itself. He had accumulated an extensive knowledge of the island and he wrote descriptively in an attempt to correct mistaken impressions – whether

[1] Notes for a letter from Crout to Willoughby from Newfoundland, [1616] (University of Nottingham, Middleton MSS, Mi X 1/38); and see below, p. 92.

[2] See below, p. 91.

[3] Thomas Rowley to Willoughby from Cupids Cove, 16 Oct. 1619 (University of Nottingham, Middleton MSS. Mi X 1/51).

[4] See below, pp. 24–5.   [5] Cell, *English enterprise*, pp. 74–5.

[6] See below, p. 90; also Sir William Alexander, *An encouragement to colonies* (William Stanley, 1624), sig. E. IV.

too favourable or too critical – which were based on only a superficial acquaintance. Like the propagandist Richard Whitbourne, who would publish his first book on Newfoundland in the same year, Mason took pains to explain the differences between the continental climate of the Americas and that of England. Newfoundland, he argued, could be inhabited just as comfortably as those parts of Europe which lay in more northerly latitudes. He was eloquent on the subject of the island's bountiful supplies of birds and fishes, fruits and flowers, and emphatic that there were stretches of good land for crops and livestock. In the authority of his apologia he is rivalled only by Whitbourne. Indeed there is some similarity in the two men's arguments on the advantages of planting in Newfoundland rather than in Virginia.

Mason gave up the governorship about 1621 and seems to have had no successor. Yet the colony continued to survive throughout the twenties. Slany and Willoughby kept up their correspondence and their arguments. Slany persisted in trying to hook new investors, most notably Sir Edward Nicholas, one of the secretaries of state. Some level of company support for the settlers was maintained and the company continued to send fishing ships to the island. When Nicholas Guy, who had recently moved from Cupids to Willoughby's land at Carbonear, wrote to his new employer in 1631, he referred to the 'plantation ships that vseialle come'. If by that he meant the Cupids Cove colony and not the more recent, nearby settlement at Harbour Grace, it is the last mention of the original colony that we have. Treasurer Slany died the following year. Without his leadership and his commitment, the company probably withered away. Only a handful of settlers remained, relying for survival upon their own efforts and on supplies from summer fishermen, rather than upon the company.[1]

In this first Newfoundland settlement, as in other ventures on the mainland, the dependence on support from England tended to cripple the settlers' initiative. It was too easy to wait for the arrival of relief ships, particularly once they realised the difficulty of growing most types of crops for themselves. For investors, the expense of continually sending out supplies ate up whatever profits were earned by fishing. The English merchant community still had insufficient experience – not enough colonies had yet failed – to make a realistic appraisal of what was involved in building a viable community on the other side of the Atlantic. The colony must have seemed a hungry maw into which limitless capital could be poured without return. Few shareholders were

[1] Cell, *English enterprise*, pp. 77–9.

prepared to continue their investment indefinitely, and new ones were increasingly hard to find.

There had been one point at which the company had attempted to tap fresh supplies of capital. In 1616 and 1617 they began to grant land not only to their own shareholders, but to others with little or no prior connection with the organisation. The new policy may have evolved in response to the tension within the company that followed John Guy's departure as governor and his quarrels with Slany. The Bristol Society of Merchant Venturers, to which belonged most of the original Bristol members of the Newfoundland company, took land on Trinity Bay and began to develop it on their own account. Shortly afterwards three gentlemen proprietors – William Vaughan, a Welsh scholar and eccentric, Sir Henry Cary, soon to be viscount Falkland and lord deputy of Ireland, and Sir George Calvert, secretary of state and later first baron Baltimore[1] – received independent allotments of land from the company in the southern part of the Avalon peninsula.

The motives of the Newfoundland company in its rapid alienation of land are obvious: pressing financial necessity coupled with the need to strengthen and expand the scale of settlement. Similar concerns had led the Virginia company to try the same solution at about the same time. But the Newfoundland company had also to defend itself against the complaints of the west-country fishermen who would have rejoiced to see colonisation fail. The company had evidently accepted the fact that by itself it could afford nothing more than the colony at Cupids Cove. But with the fishermen becoming vociferous enough in their attacks to force the whole issue of settlement before the attention of the privy council, it must have seemed urgent to company officials to prove that colonisation was both feasible and desirable. The west-country charges that planters monopolised the best beaches and destroyed their equipment were grave even if exaggerated. The government could not afford to sacrifice a trade which supplied a vital reserve of seamen and ships in time of war to a small, struggling colony of far less apparent value. Could it be shown that little of the land awarded in 1610 was now inhabited, the privy council might even decide to withdraw the charter. But could new investors be brought in, a prosperous group of merchants and individuals with the status of Calvert and Cary, then it would not only demonstrate that interest in the plantation still ran

[1] Calvert received his title in 1625, five years after becoming a proprietor in Newfoundland. To avoid confusion he will be referred to as Calvert throughout this volume. There are biographies of all three men in *DNB*, of Calvert and Vaughan in *DCB*, I, and of Vaughan in *DWB*.

high but it would also throw a considerable weight of influence behind the company and perhaps even ensure its continued existence.

Of those who took land, only the motives of the Bristol group are perhaps self-evident. Relations between London and provincial merchants were generally strained in the early seventeenth century because of the tendency of the wealthier London men to engross an increasing share of the nation's trade. More specifically there had been friction between the representatives of the two cities since the foundation of the Newfoundland company. The Bristol merchants had an obvious experience and an obvious financial interest to explain their desire to establish a colony of their own. But Vaughan, Cary and Calvert had no such background. The three men, who seem to have known each other and to have worked more or less closely together, did have certain things in common. All were born in the 1570s to prosperous gentry families, although only the Carys had any claim to social prominence while the Calverts had but recently acquired the status of gentlemen landowners. All attended Oxford colleges in the early nineties and there at least Cary and Calvert may first have become acquainted. Vaughan implies that his connection with Calvert came through his elder brother, John Vaughan,[1] who may well have known Calvert in Ireland. On leaving Oxford Calvert and Vaughan had both taken the Grand Tour. Cary too had seen Europe but from the less pleasant perspective of a soldier in France and the Low Countries and, after the siege of Ostend, a prisoner of war. When he returned to England Vaughan had taken up the study of the law and may for a time have practised as a lawyer before retiring to his native Carmarthenshire.[2] Cary and Calvert had gravitated towards positions at court. We do not know with certainty how any one of the three became interested in colonisation, although in the cases of Cary and Calvert there is some interaction between experience in Ireland and in North America, nor why it was Newfoundland in particular that attracted them. But all three moved in circles – the law, the court, the capital – which provided so much of the investment and the energy for the beginnings of the British empire.

The mixture of a merchant group with the three gentlemen proprietors is typical of the trend of the early seventeenth century. The profit motive was presumably not completely lacking in any of them, and strongest perhaps in the Bristol merchants whose livelihood

[1] W. Vaughan, *The Newlanders cure* (T. Constable, 1630), sig. A5.
[2] B. Levacke, *The civil lawyers in England, 1603–1641* (Oxford, 1973), p. 277.

depended upon success in trade. But none of them seems to have gone into the business expecting or promising quick, spectacular wealth. For merchant and gentleman alike hopes of profit were firmly pinned to the exploitation of the fishery rather than to mining, exploration or even fur trading. Despite the difficulties encountered by the New-foundland company, they must have accepted the company's conviction that fishing could support a settlement and equally that colonists would have an advantage in that industry. As for the three individuals, both their actions and their propaganda suggest that not just profit but a blend of national and personal concerns motivated their efforts. And it was not just the welfare of England that animated them. William Vaughan was eager to relieve the particular social problems of his native Wales, while both Cary and Calvert seem to have envisaged their colonies as alleviating some of the even more acute difficulties of early Stuart Ireland.

The Bristol settlement, begun at Harbour Grace about 1618, is different from the other ventures in a number of ways. It was undertaken by men with personal experience of the fishery and the markets in the Mediterranean. Furthermore, because the settlement was managed by the Merchant Venturers company, it had a natural source of funds and investors and therefore little need of publicity. Not until Robert Hayman had given up· his position as governor did any propaganda directly associated with the Bristol colony appear and, even then, Hayman's book was hardly effective promotion.

The break between the Bristol merchants and the parent company had come about 1616 and, by the following year, the Merchant Venturers were negotiating for land of their own.[1] The two groups of merchants who had originally subscribed to the Newfoundland company in 1610 should have been complementary: the one providing capital, the other expertise. Yet the relationship had never been easy. The London majority jealously guarded their management of the undertaking, while the Bristol men probably resented their total exclusion from the council, which was composed only of London residents, and therefore from the making of policy. Once John Guy left Cupids and the dispute developed between him and treasurer Slany, the Bristol colonists withdrew in 1616 and, a year later, the grant to the Merchant Venturers was made.[2] Their land, christened Bristol's Hope, lay in the southern part of the peninsula between Trinity and

---

[1] John Slany to Willoughby, 10 Feb. 1616/17 (University of Nottingham, Middleton MSS, Mi X 1/44).   [2] Cell, *English enterprise*, pp. 60, 71, 87.

Conception Bays and included the popular fishing harbour, Harbour Grace, which became the site of the colony.[1]

Very little is known about its fortunes, but it seems likely that it was one of the more successful of the offshoot plantations. Its sponsors knew the fishing industry and they had traditionally strong trading links with the Iberian countries where much of the fish coming from Newfoundland was sold. These Bristol merchants evidently continued to reject the attitude typical of their fellow west-countrymen that colonisation restricted and damaged the fishery. More far-sighted perhaps than the rest, they had accepted the argument of Guy and of successive propagandists that a colony could improve the industry's efficiency and profitability by preparing more fish for collection and transportation to the markets of Europe.

According to the accounts of Richard Eburne and William Alexander Bristol's Hope did prosper,[2] though its wellbeing would seem to have owed little to the efforts of its only known governor, Robert Hayman. The choice of Hayman, the Oxford-educated son of a rising Devonshire yeoman family, was a strange one, for Bristol men with Newfoundland experience must surely have been available. Hayman had attended Exeter College where, according to Anthony à Wood, he had known William Vaughan and where he may have met Cary, who was also at Exeter. He had gone on to study for a time at Lincoln's Inn and then at the University of Poitiers. It was while he was in France that his father, Nicholas Hayman, had approached Robert Cecil to find a position for his son. How, or if, Cecil responded we do not know, though Robert Hayman would later claim familiarity with the court of Elizabeth. Nothing then in Hayman's background obviously qualified him to guide the early days of the Bristol colony and his appointment can perhaps only be explained by the fact that his brother-in-law was Master of the Merchant Venturers.[3]

While Hayman spent several summers – but only one winter – at Harbour Grace, his attitude towards his duties seems to have been, to say the least, cavalier. 'Haueing only had the ouerseeing others hard

---

[1] John Mason's map, below, p. 91, exaggerates the size of the Bristol grant. Sir Percival Willoughby held the northern tip of the peninsula between Conception and Trinity Bays, from the northern shore of Carbonear to the harbour of Hearts Content.

[2] Eburne, *A plaine path-way to plantation* (G. P[urslow] for John Marriott, 1624), sig. Q 1–1v; Alexander, *Encouragement to colonies*, sig. E 1.

[3] Anthony à Wood, *Athenae Oxonienses*, 2 vols (London, 1721), I, 576–7; see also D. Galloway, 'Robert Hayman (1575–1629): some materials for the life of a colonial governor and first "Canadian" author', *William and Mary Quarterly*, 3rd ser. XXIV (1967), 75–87.

labour' to distract him,[1] he appears to have devoted far more of his time to his own literary pursuits than to finding ways to make the colony successful or profitable. Unfortunately none of the letters or reports that he presumably sent back to Bristol has survived, but the verses he wrote on a strange miscellany of topics and the works of Rabelais which he translated while in Newfoundland he published in 1628 in the curious *Quodlibets, lately come over from new Britaniola, old Newfoundland.*[2] Many of the poems, if that is not too exalted a word for what is often little more than doggerel, touched on Newfoundland and were addressed to his Bristol sponsors or to others with some connection with the island. Generally they are encouraging in tone if not always felicitous in phrase; William Vaughan's wife, for example, can hardly have been encouraged by the verse dedicated to her, with its casual reference to the ravages of 'scurvy death.' But Hayman does urge those whom he addressed to persist in their commitment, airily dismissing the difficulties and, unlike the other Newfoundland promoters of the sixteen-twenties, hinting at quick and easy profits.

More ambitiously Hayman also tried in 1628 to interest the king in the settlement of the island by proposing that a city, to be named Carolinople in Charles's honour, be built in Newfoundland.[3] Hayman's argument, that colonisation was too onerous a task for any private individual, shows that he was more in touch with reality than his verses would suggest. Charles would echo the same point himself in a letter to Calvert the following year.[4] But in 1628 the king had neither the money nor the attention to spare for any colony and the duke of Buckingham, who Hayman had hoped would advocate the proposal to the king, was assassinated in August. Yet, even as he was blithely exhorting others to sustain their interest in Newfoundland, he himself was turning his attention further south and preparing to join Robert Harcourt's expedition which left for Guiana that summer. He died there the next year.[5] Who his successor was as governor of Bristol's Hope we do not know, but the colony was still in existence in 1631.[6]

Soon after the Bristol men began to negotiate for their grant of land, the first of the gentlemen proprietors, William Vaughan, received his allotment from the Newfoundland company. Vaughan was born in

---

[1] 'A Proposition of Proffitt and Honor Proposed to my Dread and Gratious Soueraigne Lord, Kinge Charles, By his humble Subiect Robert Hayman', [1628] (B.L., Egerton MS 2451, ff. 164–9v).
[2] Elizabeth All-de for Roger Mitchell, 1628.   [3] B.L., Egerton MS 2451, ff. 164–9v.
[4] See below, pp. 296–7.   [5] *DCB*, I.
[6] Nicholas Guy to Sir Percival Willoughby, from Carbonear, 1 September 1631 (Nottingham University, Middleton MSS, Mi X 1/57).

1577, a younger son of Walter Vaughan of Golden Grove in Carmarthenshire. The family were old-established landowners and, William Vaughan would claim, his great-grandfather had served as gentleman usher to king Henry VII. Vaughan's elder brother, John, would be created first earl of Carbery in the Irish peerage in 1628, the same year in which William was knighted in Ireland by Falkland, the lord deputy.[1] At the age of eighteen Vaughan received his B.A. from the Welshman's traditional college, Jesus, and three years later he was awarded the M.A. He then travelled widely on the continent, acquiring the title of doctor of law from Vienna. Vaughan later wrote that, on Christmas day 1602, he narrowly escaped drowning when he fell overboard in rough seas off the coast of France. His preservation he attributed to divine intervention. On no less than three other occasions he believed that the Almighty acted to save his life, so revealing that he, Vaughan, had some special service to perform for 'the Publicke Good'.[2] He later realised that his appointed mission was the colonisation of Newfoundland, but that perception lay some years in the future. Meanwhile, Vaughan returned to England and received the degree of doctor of civil law from Oxford in 1605. The course of his life between then and 1616 is obscure; he published a number of books and he may have practised law.[3] By 1616 he was certainly back in Wales, serving as sheriff of Carmarthen. In that same year he was assigned by the Newfoundland company land in the Avalon peninsula, lying south of a line drawn from Caplin Bay on the east, westwards to Placentia Bay.

One can only speculate as to how and why this scholarly man became involved with the colonisation of Newfoundland. He had not so far joined any of the overseas companies but, through his mother and step-mother, he was connected with Sir Thomas Button, who explored Hudson's Bay in 1612, and with the Perrot and Chichester families, both of which had strong ties with Ireland, so often a stepping stone to an interest in North America.[4] His Oxford acquaintanceship with Robert Hayman is probably not significant, for there is nothing to suggest that

---

[1] Vaughan, *Newlanders cure*, sig. A4v; *DWB*; W. A. Shaw, ed., *The knights of England* (London, 1906), II, 194.

[2] Vaughan, *Newlanders cure*, sig. A6–6v.

[3] Ερωτοπαιγνιον *pium: continens canticum canticorum Salomonis, et psalmos aliquot selectiores*, pt 1 (ap R. Johnesum, 1597); *Speculum humanae condicionis, Erotopainion pium*, pt 2, *Poematum libellus* (three works in one) (G. Shaw, 1598); *The golden grove* (S. Stafford, 1600), 2nd ed. (S. Stafford, 1608); *Naturall and artificiall directions for health derived from the best philosophers, as well moderne as ancient* (R. Bradocke, 1600), a further six editions of this work were published between 1602 and 1633, *STC* (rev. ed.), II; *The spirit of detraction conjured and convicted in seven circles* (W. Stanley for G. Norton, 1611), reissued, 1611, 1630.

[4] *DWB*.

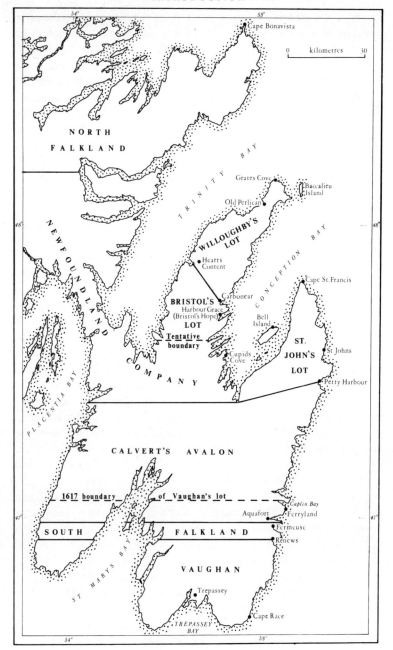

Fig. 2. The Avalon peninsula

Hayman himself had any involvement with the island before the early 1620s. It may have been that, during Vaughan's years in London, he had become acquainted with members of the Newfoundland company. But perhaps the simplest and the most logical explanation lies in his love of Wales, and in the proximity of his county of Carmarthen to Bristol, a port linked to Newfoundland for more than a century. Carmarthen also faces across the Bristol channel to Devon with its major fishing ports of Dartmouth, Plymouth, Barnstaple and Exeter. In his writings Vaughan would contrast the prosperity of Devonshire, with its fleet of ships trading their fish in Spain and Italy, with the depressed state of Wales. The poverty there he blamed not only on the neglect of seaborne commerce but also on the decay of agriculture. Enclosures and rack-renting had driven tenants from their farms and shattered the sense of community which he claimed had once distinguished village life. Particularly in his book *The golden grove* (1600), Vaughan made a plea for a balance between arable and pastoral farming, and for a return to a sense of concern for the well-being of their tenants on the part of landlords. Even these reforms could not take care of that excess of population which he, like so many of his contemporaries, was convinced afflicted Britain; nor could they provide land enough for younger sons lacking a patrimony. For the relief of all these ills Britain must rely upon overseas colonisation.

But where? In *The golden fleece*, Vaughan describes his own process of selection: his consideration of some island that could serve as a halfway house for ships making the long voyage to the East Indies; his contemplation of Virginia and Bermuda. His final choice fell upon Newfoundland, closer at hand, temperate of climate, and free from the complications that would arise from venturing into areas that were the preserve of other powers. With his propensity to see the hand of God in all things, he hails Newfoundland as 'the next land beyond Ireland', divinely 'reserued...for vs Britaines'.[1] The choice made, Vaughan displayed a remarkable degree of energy and perseverance, both in his own attempts to establish a colony there and particularly in the making of propaganda. When the first objective faltered, so he turned to the second the more vigorously.

One year after receiving his land, Vaughan sent out his first settlers to live at the harbour of Aquafort on the east coast of the Avalon peninsula. After one winter there a newly appointed governor, Captain Richard Whitbourne, arrived and moved the colonists to Renews,[2]

[1] William Vaughan (pseud. Orpheus Junior), *The golden fleece* (Francis Williams, 1626), sig. Aaa 3.   [2] See below, p. 211.

a popular harbour with the annual fishermen where the Newfoundland company had once hoped to settle. Traditionally Vaughan's colony has been thought to have been located further south at Trepassey Bay, a belief that appears to have originated at the end of the nineteenth century with D. W. Prowse's standard history of the island.[1] Prowse is often vague about his sources but he seems to have derived the location both from Whitbourne's advocacy of Trepassey as a site and from his interpretation of the John Mason map which Vaughan included in two of his books: *Cambrensium Caroleia*,[2] written to celebrate the marriage of Charles I, and *The golden fleece*, his longest and most ambitious piece of Newfoundland propaganda. But the evidence of the map is inconclusive. Welsh names are scattered across the whole area of William Vaughan's grant, but only one, 'Colchos', is in the vicinity of Trepassey Bay. Most of the place-names are clustered on the east coast between Renews and Cape Race, and 'Golden Grove', which was also the name of the Vaughan family's Welsh estate, is written just inland from Renews.[3] By the time that the map was printed Aquafort had been transferred to lord Falkland and was in the area now called 'South Falkland'. But in *The Newlanders cure*, Vaughan mentions the exact location at which his people lived, and Richard Whitbourne confirms the move to Renews which he supervised in 1618.[4]

Whitbourne seems to have been appointed in an effort to pull the infant colony together. Who those first colonists were, what prior experience they had, and who – if anyone – was in charge of them, we do not know. But the experience of the first year, 1617–18, had not been happy. Whitbourne found them living in abject misery, for they had done nothing more than huddle in the shanties left behind by the summer fishermen, hardly adequate shelter against the severity of a Newfoundland winter. Their negligence contrasts sharply with the care and speed with which both the earlier settlers at Cupids Cove and later Calvert's men at Ferryland built themselves sturdy habitations. Most of the colonists Whitbourne packed home as unsuitable material for pioneers; he sent back even some whom he had brought with him in the summer of 1618. But ill-fate dogged the venture, not only in its choice of men but in the attack made upon one of its ships by prize-hunting deserters from Raleigh's Guiana fleet. With some of his people and much of their provisions lost, Whitbourne was under-

---

[1] *A history of Newfoundland* (London, 1895), p. 110.
[2] Printed by William Stansby, 1625.
[3] See below, p. 91. [4] Sig. F2v, and below, pp. 134–5, 211.

standably discouraged. He moved the settlement to Renews where he left only six men to spend the winter, while he himself returned to make propaganda and to seek a new employer.[1]

Yet Richard Whitbourne would have seemed the ideal choice as governor of a Newfoundland colony. A sea captain used to authority, his experience and knowledge of the island, the fishery, and the continental markets for fish could scarcely have been equalled. Born in Exmouth in Devon, he had gone to sea at the age of fifteen and had first visited Newfoundland in 1579, when William Vaughan was only two years old. On that voyage he had been engaged in whaling and in trading with the Beothuk in the Strait of Belle Isle. Thereafter he had witnessed every important event in the island's history. He was present when Sir Humphrey Gilbert claimed the island for the crown in 1583; two years later he watched as Bernard Drake plundered the Portuguese fishing fleet. He saw the damage inflicted upon English shipping in 1612 by the pirate Peter Easton and again in 1614 by Henry Mainwaring. Because of this background, and perhaps because of his service as captain of his own ship under lord admiral Howard in 1588, he received a commission in 1615 to hold vice-admiralty hearings in Newfoundland to inquire into accusations against the annual fishermen. Although Whitbourne refers repeatedly to this commission, it cannot be traced in the official records. The proceedings may well have formed part of the preliminaries to the privy council's orders of 1618, which charged the Newfoundland company to respect the freedom of the fishery. After that Whitbourne went back to the life of a merchant. In 1616 his ship fell victim to French pirates as he sailed to Lisbon with a cargo of fish. It was on his return from Portugal that he was approached by William Vaughan.[2]

The Welshman appointed Whitbourne governor of his colony for life and the two men, together with some other unnamed adventurers, shared the costs of equipping the expedition of 1618.[3] But the mishaps of that year soured the relationship. When in 1620 Whitbourne published his first piece of propaganda, *A discourse and discovery of Newfoundland*,[4] he gave no indication that he was still connected with Vaughan and professed indifference as to whether new plantations were begun or old ones continued. Whichever it might be, he hoped to encourage more effective settlement than had yet been undertaken, for

---

[1] See below, pp. 115, 134–5.
[2] There are biographies of Whitbourne in *DNB* and *DCB*, I. See also *APC 1616–1617*, pp. 293–4, and below, pp. 111–15.   [3] See below, p. 115.
[4] Printed by Felix Kyngston for William Barrett.

he claimed that little had been accomplished so far. Indeed, by the time that the book appeared, Vaughan's colony no longer existed. The remaining settlers had given up in 1619 and had left for home.[1]

So William Vaughan's brief and unfortunate attempt at colonisation came to an end. There is no evidence that he ever sent out any more settlers to Renews or any other site. In his writings he refers only to the two groups of men and women whom he had despatched in 1617 and 1618, as well as to his hopes of reviving the venture and even of visiting the island in person. There is no good evidence that he ever achieved either of these goals, whether because of ill health, as Hayman suggests, or because of the financial difficulties to which Vaughan himself refers.[2]

It was through his writings rather than his personal activities that Vaughan did most to encourage settlement in Newfoundland. But his were some of the unlikeliest works of propaganda ever published. *The golden fleece* is a monument to the precious style of the seventeenth century. A rambling, discursive work, it hides its argument that fishing and settlement combined will restore Britain's lost prosperity among pages of poetry, history and rabid anti-catholicism. Original in its approach, its discussion of the advantages of colonisation and the descriptions of the island are all strikingly reminiscent of Whitbourne. *The Newlanders cure*, published some four years later, is a collection of medical advice for emigrants, inspired by the suffering of Calvert's colony in 1628.[3]

While Vaughan's reputation as a writer probably guaranteed him an audience, these were not among his more successful works and neither ran to more than one edition. It is doubtful that they attracted many investors. Involvement in overseas ventures was much more likely to follow from personal contacts than from the reading of propaganda, particularly such fanciful propaganda as Vaughan's. Yet the core of his argument was sound. *The golden fleece* promised no sudden fortunes, no spectacular discoveries. Its message was that the success of any settlement would depend upon the trade in fish. If Vaughan's claims that codfish were 'Neptunes sheepe' ready for the fleecing and that Newfoundland was 'Great Britaines Indies' seem ludicrous,[4] it is worth remembering that he was not the first nor the

[1] Thomas Rowley to Sir Percival Willoughby, from Cupids Cove, 16 Oct. 1619 (Nottingham University, Middleton MSS, Mi X 1/51).
[2] Hayman, *Quodlibets*, sig. E4v–F1; Vaughan, *Golden fleece*, sig. B1v.
[3] See below, p. 296.
[4] Vaughan, *Golden fleece*, sig. Bbb1, Bbb2–Ccc1v. *The golden fleece* is not reprinted here as so little of it deals directly with Newfoundland, and because it makes no contribution to geographical knowledge of the island.

last propagandist to point out that England's economy had benefitted far more from the fishery than Spain had from the wealth of Peru or Mexico. It was Vaughan's style, not his thesis, that was exaggerated.

In *The Newlanders cure* Vaughan reveals that, soon after the failure of his colony, he assigned part of his land to Sir Henry Cary and a further portion to Sir George Calvert. Ill-starred though his own attempts were, he was tireless in trying to attract others to settle in Newfoundland. As late as 1630 he was still encouraging, still hoping. But little came of his optimism. While he wrote in 1630 of reviving his plantation, there is no evidence that he ever did so.[1] He even ceased to write about the island. Now a man in his fifties he probably contented himself with his Welsh estates and consoled himself for the failure of his dreams with his meditations and writings upon religion.[2]

No contemporary publicist of Newfoundland could match either Vaughan's style or his imagination, but his works were hardly typical of the propaganda that began to be made for the island in the decade of the twenties. The heavy silence that had shrouded the island, like one of its own fogs, for almost forty years was broken by a series of publications. During the fifteen-seventies and eighties Anthony Parkhurst and Edward Hayes, both associates of Sir Humphrey Gilbert, had praised the island's potential as a site for a colony and, in the tense atmosphere of the years before the Armada, had emphasized its strategic importance. Richard Hakluyt, though not perhaps personally enthusiastic about a settlement so far to the north, had printed some of their writings.[3] But in the fifteen-nineties the spotlight of English attention had swung south to New England and Virginia. Most curiously when the Newfoundland company was formed in 1610 and when it was clearly trying to attract new subscribers later on, it produced no printed propaganda whatsoever. The omission probably reflects more than the island's lack of publicity value. The unusual reticence may well have sprung from a fear that any publicity would arouse yet stronger opposition from the west-country fishermen. Three years after the establishment of Cupids Cove Samuel Purchas did not even acknowledge the existence of the colony in the first edition of his *Pilgrimage*. In the two subsequent editions of 1614 and 1617 he paid it only brief notice,[4] although he had already seen records concerning

---

[1] Sig. A 5, A 7–7v. For a discussion of the long-standing belief that Vaughan did visit Newfoundland himself, see Cell, *English enterprise*, p. 85.

[2] He wrote two more books before his death: *The church militant* (T. Paine for H. Blunden, 1640); *The soules exercise* (T. and R. Cotes for H. Blunden, 1641).

[3] *Principal navigations*, VIII, 9–16, 34–77.

[4] These three editions of *Purchas his pilgrimage* were printed by William Stansby for Henry Fetherstone.

it which were in the possession of Hakluyt and of which he would make limited use in his major work, *Hakluytus posthumus* (1625).[1] Not until 1620 was the silence broken with the publication both of John Mason's *Briefe discourse* and of the first edition of Richard Whitbourne's *Discourse and discovery*.

Improbable though it might seem, Whitbourne, a Devonshire seaman and fishing merchant, was one of the staunchest and most effective proponents of colonisation. Unlike most west-countrymen, he firmly believed that settlement would be of benefit to the industry. The unusual quality of Whitbourne's works, reflecting as they do a life-time's experience, is confirmed by the circumstances surrounding the appearance of the *Discourse* in 1620. The manuscript had formed part of the evidence, which also included testimony by John Guy, considered by the privy council before they issued orders forbidding the fishermen to interfere with the settlers. Its subsequent publication was approved by the council, which ordered that the book be distributed in parishes throughout the country and that a collection be taken up to reward Whitbourne for his services to the nation.[2] Evidently his arguments had swayed the council at least. For the first time in the ten years since the chartering of the Newfoundland company, the government gave official endorsement and encouragement to settlement and came down firmly on the side of the colonisers in their running battle with the fishing interests.[3]

In many respects Whitbourne's books are just what one might expect: straightforward and highly practical, in the tradition of the seamen's narratives preserved by Richard Hakluyt. His style, totally free of the conceits and learned allusions which distinguish Vaughan's works, is infused with the vigour which is characteristic of so much prose written in the sixteenth and seventeenth centuries by men with no great amount of education. While his writing does not have quite the relaxed confidence of John Smith, the contemporary propagandist with whom he has most in common, the fact that the *Discourse and discovery* ran into three editions between 1620 and 1623 suggests that it found a wide and responsive audience.[4]

Whitbourne himself was conscious of the absence of publicity for Newfoundland which, in his opinion, helped to explain the low level

[1] Four volumes, printed by William Stansby for Henry Fetherstone. Purchas, *Pilgrimes*, XIX, 415–24.

[2] See below, pp. 100–1.   [3] *APC Col., 1613–1680*, pp. 30–1.

[4] The second edition of the *Discourse and discovery* (1622) is reprinted below, and collated with the first and third editions. The second edition was chosen as the main text in preference to the first because it is so much fuller.

of public interest in the island. He took it upon himself to rectify that lack and, above all, to prove that settlement would not be 'burdensome, or hurtfull to any of his Maiesties subjects'. So far from damaging the fishing industry, in which after all he had spent his life, a partnership between fishermen and planters would bring new prosperity to both. But the benefits would not be restricted to those directly involved. If the large-scale development of both fishery and settlement which Whitbourne envisaged were to succeed, then the effects would reverberate throughout the nation and the economy as a whole.

The key to success in Whitbourne's eyes was the linkage between fishing and settlement; his advice hinged on ways to make that connection work. Here his suggestions were detailed and sensible, taking nothing for granted. It is as though he had drawn up a list of questions that might be asked by a prospective investor and then set himself to answer them: how much would it cost to equip a ship for the fishery, where might a cargo of fish best be sold, and what profits might be expected? Fishing was an old-established trade, with its own distinctive ways of managing its business. Practices which had died out in other sea-borne trades were still followed by fishermen; for example, the profits of a voyage were still divided among the various parties concerned. The ship owner or charterer, the victualler, and the master and crew all received more or less a third. An outsider would find these customs hard to understand and so might fail to deal successfully with the practitioners of a very traditional industry. Whitbourne recommended that the proprietor of a plantation buy rather than charter a ship of about 100 tons, and use it in conjunction with a smaller vessel. The pinnace should sail first and make preparations both for the settlers and the coming fishing season. In this way the voyage would be more efficient, the first colonists more comfortable, and the extra fish which the crew of the pinnace would catch could be sold to one of the many sack ships which visited the island annually. For the novice, Whitbourne carefully explained the restrictive nature of the charter parties under which ships were hired, as well as the practice of contracting to buy or sell cargoes of fish long before the fishing ships ever left England.[1] The *Discourse* was thus a business manual as well as a piece of propaganda.

There are times when Whitbourne's advice seems almost too obvious, as when he points out that livestock should not be taken to the island until shelter and fodder are available. But the repeated lack of such foresight on the part of inexperienced and impatient promoters

[1] See below, pp. 139–40, 144.

together with his own association with William Vaughan must have convinced him that no advice was too elementary. When Whitbourne recommended that any intending colonial promoter should consult not one but two seasoned advisers, he was probably trying to avoid the kind of fiasco that had occurred at Aquafort in 1617.[1]

Implicit in all of Whitbourne's writing was his answer to the big question: why choose Newfoundland as the site for a colony rather than one of the apparently more hospitable locations further south? For answer he appealed both to the self-interest of the prospective investor and to a sense of national interest. To the individual he held out, and documented, the prospect of immediate returns on the investment. Such quick and sure profits could not be expected anywhere else, for the other English colonies had no readily exploitable staples. It was also cheaper to send settlers and supplies to Newfoundland than, say, to Virginia: not only was the voyage shorter but the sack ships which usually sailed out in ballast would offer reasonable freight charges so as to have an outward cargo. Even the presence of the annual fishermen, which had so far proved a mixed blessing, he viewed positively. Their visits meant that the Newfoundland settlers would never be isolated and they also provided a back-up source of supplies.[2] But to Richard Whitbourne there was far more at stake here than the profits of a handful of investors. The growth of the Newfoundland trade, which he believed settlement would encourage, and the welfare of the nation as a whole were intimately connected.

Ever since Parkhurst and Hayes had pressed for an English plantation in Newfoundland, propagandists had hammered away at the same point: the unique contribution of that trade to the whole economy. None had argued it with as much force and as much irrefutable evidence as Whitbourne. In the expanding overseas commerce of seventeenth-century England, no other trade brought so much wealth into the country while taking so little out. Hard as it might be to accept, a trade in such an unglamorous, every-day commodity as dried codfish was the fulfilment of the mercantilist's dream. With no drain of gold or silver and in return for nothing more than a six months' supply of food and fishing equipment, a cargo of fish could be obtained and exchanged easily for wine, fruits, oil and other desirable and costly products of the Mediterranean and the Levant. The voyages of the two hundred and fifty ships which he estimated had been at the fishery in 1615 would have returned a minimum of £135,000 on the sale of their fish and oil alone; the return would be far higher if those ships went

---

[1] See below, pp. 134–5, 139.　　　　[2] See below, pp. 147–9.

on to secure a second cargo in the Mediterranean. Moreover, ship-building and related trades helped to keep the local economy of the west of England active and healthy.[1]

The fishing lobby, of course, had always maintained that settlement would damage their trade and undermine its vital function as a source of shipping and trained seamen in times of national emergency. That supply, they insisted, would dry up if men abandoned the annual voyage in favour of living on the island. Whitbourne, who had taken his own ship into the English fleet in 1588, recognised the force of this argument. Certainly it was one that government would take seriously. He met it with a series of counter-arguments of his own.

He proposed, for example, that each fishing vessel should leave behind at the end of the season one out of every six crew members. Only ships adopting this practice should have the right to reserved beach space for their fishing in future years. During the winter those who stayed in Newfoundland could build and repair houses, work rooms, fishing equipment and boats so that no time would be wasted the next spring. In the knowledge that their equipment would be safe and ready, fishing ships could leave England later and avoid the dangerous sailing conditions of the late winter. Eventually the colonists could turn to agriculture as well and spread out from the harbours normally frequented by English fishermen into new areas. The existence of stable settlements with some form of civil government would end the disorder that currently prevailed as fishermen, anxious to seize any advantage to get their catch to market first, destroyed the boats and equipment of their rivals. Because fishing merchants routinely employed a certain proportion of inexperienced men, he could argue that this policy would not reduce the availability of trained seamen. Furthermore, by making the industry both more efficient and more profitable, the Newfoundland fleet might increase to as many as four hundred ships and the number of experienced sailors to eight or ten thousand. He was quick to point out that both ships and men engaged in the fishery could be recalled to their country's service far more quickly than those whose voyages took them to the East or West Indies.[2] The flaw in Whitbourne's case lay not in its logic but in his too easy assumption that the fishing merchants shared any commitment to the creation of a permanent community in Newfoundland and that they could be swayed by reasoned argument. The evidence was all to the contrary.

[1] See below, pp. 123–5.   [2] See below, pp. 143–7.

30

A second way in which he tried to meet the fishing interests' objections was deliberately to broaden his appeal for involvement in Newfoundland beyond the fishing ports. Every county, Whitbourne hoped, might outfit and man one vessel and so not only add to the pool of ships and seamen, but also solve the chronic social problems of unemployment, poverty and vagrancy. In effect he was proposing the formation of a kind of national joint-stock with capital raised locally and each parish receiving its share of the profits.[1]

But Whitbourne's vision of the significance of Newfoundland went far beyond the traditional concept of the island's relationship to England alone. For the first time a propagandist set Newfoundland firmly in the context of a developing Atlantic community. In his opening paragraph Whitbourne reminds the reader that the island 'lyes neere the course that ships vsually hold in their returne from the *West-Indies*, and neere halfe the way between *Ireland* and *Virginia*'. For this reason he emphasised the desirability of a settlement at Trepassey Bay, in the south-east corner of Newfoundland. An ideal stopping place for ships going on to Virginia, Bermuda, the St Lawrence and other parts of Canada, there they could pick up wood, fresh water, fish and other supplies as well as carry out the repairs that wooden sailing ships so often needed after an Atlantic crossing. Furthermore, the island was strategically situated to serve as a jumping-off ground for the annexation of new territory in North America or even as a base for voyages in search of a north-west passage.[2] With settlements in New England and in the Caribbean being planned as successive editions of his *Discourse* appeared, Whitbourne seems to have foreseen the pattern of mutual dependency which would soon develop among the English colonies in the New World and which would prove to be so vital to their survival and ultimate success.

The links that were forged among the English possessions were largely economic: Newfoundlanders, as Whitbourne had predicted, would exchange their fish and oil for the agricultural and manufactured products of the colonies to the south. But he thought in terms of strategy too. The island's geographical position would make it crucial should any attack be launched against an English settlement or should the use of force be necessary in the acquisition of further territory. In this context he mentions Virginia specifically. Many Englishmen were still nervous, unjustifiably as it happened, about Spanish tolerance of their presence in the Chesapeake Bay. Whitbourne's sensitivity to that

[1] See below, p. 107.   [2] See below, pp. 116, 119.

supposed threat reflects the fact that his concepts of English policy had been formed during his Elizabethan youth. He knew that the island had been used for raids upon Iberian shipping in 1582 and 1585. He still thought, as Sir Humphrey Gilbert and Sir Francis Walsingham had more than thirty years earlier, that Newfoundland could be one element in any plan to 'annoy the king of Spayne'.[1] Remembering too the embargo that had prevented fish from reaching Spain and France in the fifteen-eighties and nineties, he advocated its renewal should either nation again 'breake league with your Maiesty'. Dried fish was a strategic commodity; its denial could be an important weapon. In this somewhat old-fashioned view of England's international relations, the Low Countries loomed only as a commercial rival. Certainly Whitbourne believed that the English must reduce their reliance upon Dutch merchant shipping and Dutch-caught fish; he even proposed that the sale of all foreign-caught fish in England be prohibited.[2] But to him the Dutch represented an economic success story which his own countrymen should copy. They were not yet the enemy.

Whitbourne had to meet not only the hostility of the fishing interests, but also scepticism that Englishmen really could live in Newfoundland. Like Vaughan and Mason he was aware that disparaging stories were circulating; indeed, he accused the fishermen of spreading them deliberately so as to discourage settlement. The triumph with which representatives of the industry would later reel off the names of those who had tried and failed to establish colonies suggests that his accusation may not have been unfounded.[3] Virginia and New England had suffered the same kind of disparagement from critics of plantation and from disgruntled settlers. Whitbourne may also have been concerned to vindicate Newfoundland after the unfavourable comparisons with New England made by John Smith in his recent works.

Obviously the island's critics would have concentrated upon two factors: its climate and its agricultural limitations. Whitbourne's overestimation of the length of the island by almost two degrees of latitude had the effect of making it seem to extend further to the north, to the fifty-third parallel he said, than was really the case. Nevertheless, he chose to stress, quite correctly, that most of Newfoundland lay further south than England and no more to the north than many populous parts of continental Europe. He pointed out that harbours

[1] Cell, *English enterprise*, pp. 38–9, 47–8.   [2] See below, pp. 127–9.
[3] See below, p. 302.

in Russia and Scandinavia were closed by ice for lengthy periods every winter and that rivers in the Low Countries and even the Thames itself sometimes froze over. That did not prevent a vigorous trade from being pursued during the remainder of the year, nor did it stop people from living comfortably even in the coldest months. Whitbourne correctly perceived the influence upon Newfoundland's climate of the Labrador current which swept ice down off the coast and sometimes into bays and harbours. He misunderstood, however, the cause of the island's frequent fogs, attributing them to tangled and rotting undergrowth which held moisture. In reality, of course, the fogs result from the meeting of cold Arctic air with warmer air from the south-west. It is this combined influence of cold and warm air and currents that makes the climate so very changeable, producing sudden, rapid thaws in January and sharp frosts as late as May. This changeability made it possible for Whitbourne to argue that the winter weather was at times no more severe than that in England. To support this contention he referred to the experiences of John Guy and his colonists at Cupids. Given the low death rate there and among the unfortunates at Vaughan's Aquafort, Whitbourne was on safer ground with his talk of a 'pleasant and healthful' winter climate than were many propagandists.[1] After all, the sequel to George Percy's enthusiasm for the malarial marshes of the James River had been his account of the sufferings of the first Virginian settlers, beset by famine, disease, and Indian attack.

More of a problem even than climate and betraying Whitbourne into an unjustified optimism was the question of fertility. A part of the boreal forest region of North America, much of Newfoundland is covered with conifers, predominantly black and white spruce. The forest is broken by numerous lakes and rivers, and by stretches of 'barrens,' areas of rocky terrain, scrubby growth and thin, stony soil. The land around St George's Bay on the west coast and St John's on the east has proved to be the most suited to mixed farming. Elsewhere, as the settlers at Cupids had discovered, root crops and hay were all that would grow easily.

Not surprisingly, then, Richard Whitbourne sounds most defensive when he describes the island's agricultural prospects. Like John Guy he was deceived about the possibility of successfully growing wheat and other types of grain in most of the island. Nor could he successfully carry off his parallels between the rocky coasts of Newfoundland and

[1] See below, pp. 152–6.

those of Portugal or Italy. Climate made a difference; the terraces of Newfoundland would bear not the vines of southern Europe but only flakes festooned with drying fish. Naturally enough he tends to move on rapidly from explicit accounts of the crops that might be produced to the implicit argument that an island so rich in wild fruits and flowers, in birds and animals, must be potentially fertile. Limited dairy farming is also a possibility in parts of Newfoundland. Whitbourne carefully records areas of good grass land, for example around Renews and Trinity Harbour, which he hoped would support livestock and so reduce the colonists' dependence upon supplies from England.[1]

Apart from setting to rest fears about the island's general habitability, Whitbourne was concerned to acquaint prospective investors with the geography of the island in general, and with those harbours which he considered most suitable for settlement in particular. Whitbourne, unlike Guy, had no doubt that Newfoundland was a single island into which the major bays cut so deeply that a short overland journey would take the traveller from one to another. He had the advantage of having visited the whole island from the northern peninsula and Grand Bay, to St George's Bay (which he called the 'great' bay of St Peter's) on the west coast, and round to Cape Race, Trinity and Bonavista Bays on the east. Like most Englishmen he knew the Avalon peninsula best and described it in the greatest detail. Trinity Harbour earned his highest praise for, as he quite rightly says, it has one of the best natural harbours in the world. Part of Trinity Harbour's attraction lay in its relative remoteness. It was situated at the northernmost edge of the area visited by the English. Beyond it lay what Whitbourne called the Bay of Flowers (Bonavista Bay), where treacherous waters made navigation difficult and the presence of Indians further discouraged fishing.[2]

The other site for settlement which he particularly endorsed was Trepassey Bay on Newfoundland's south coast. Again this was a little removed from the area most frequented by annual fishermen and Whitbourne thought that overland contact between it and Trinity Bay would be easy. Here his knowledge of the interior of the island seems to be a little uncertain. Trinity Bay reaches some eighty miles into the interior and from its base to Placentia or even to St. Mary's Bay is only a short journey by land. From Trinity to Trepassey, however, is at least fifty miles as the crow flies, a considerable distance particularly in bad weather. To Whitbourne the other advantages of Trepassey Bay were its convenience for shipping following the routes to other parts of

[1] See below, pp. 118–21, 152, 156–7.   [2] See below, pp. 116–19.

34

America, its safety as a harbour, and its climate which, he claimed, was the most temperate in the whole island.[1] Despite his enthusiasm, no settlement took place at Trepassey during this period, although the Newfoundland historian Daniel Prowse apparently assumed that Vaughan had followed Whitbourne's advice.[2]

A bonus to Whitbourne as to all other propagandists was the absence of Indians from the Avalon peninsula. He believed that some lived just to the north in Bonavista Bay and that they came down to steal from the fishermen in Trinity Bay. It is probably true that Beothuk did visit Bonavista during the summer, but Whitbourne seems not to have been aware of their camps in Trinity or of John Guy's contact with them there. Most of the Indians, according to Whitbourne, lived in the extreme north and on the west coast, where they helped the French and Basque whalers. It may be, however, that these people were not all Beothuk. Those areas of the island were also inhabited by the Dorset Eskimo and were regularly visited by Montagnais from Labrador and increasingly by Micmac from Nova Scotia.[3] In fact his reference to 'their woolues,' presumably some kind of large dog, suggests positively that they were not Beothuk Indians, for the Beothuk were unusual among Algonkian people in having no dogs. In other respects, as Whitbourne notes, the culture of the Beothuk was very similar to that of the neighbouring Indians on the mainland.[4]

Each mention of the Indians prompted Richard Whitbourne to pay lip-service to the standard propagandist argument that colonisation should be encouraged so that heathens might be brought to Christianity. He also repeats the usual formulae about overseas expansion bringing honour and glory to the crown. But on the whole the *Discourse* is happily free from such stock ideas. What particularly singles Whitbourne out from other writers on Newfoundland, indeed from most writers on other parts of the New World, is the authority which informs every page. This is no armchair propagandist making extravagant and improbable promises. Notice the absence of references to mineral wealth and the scathing comments about those who had believed that gold lay in chunks on the beaches of Guiana or could be found by the barrowful in the West Indies. Only rarely is he credulous, as in his story about mermaids.[5] No propagandist, of course, can be entirely free of exaggeration and inflation. Whitbourne is less culpable than most. He had a lifetime of knowledge and commitment

---

[1] See below, p. 119.   [2] Prowse, *History of Newfoundland*, pp. 110–11.
[3] Harp. *Cultural affinities*, pp. 140, 152, 166–7.
[4] See below, pp. 117, 149, 192–4.   [5] See below, pp. 125–6, 162–3, 169, 194–5.

to reflect upon and the result was, in his own words, 'a Proiect of no fantasie in me, but a truth grounded vpon a well-weighed experience.'[1] He did not promise that the undertaker of a Newfoundland plantation would be rewarded with stupendous wealth but that it would bring greater prosperity to the nation as a whole and respectable profits for the individual. Above all he wanted taken seriously what many too easily dismissed as the 'contemptible trade in fish.'[2]

When Whitbourne wrote the *Discourse* in 1620 he seems to have had no patron. Presumably he hoped the book might attract one, and here he seems to have been successful. Both Sir George Calvert and Sir Henry Cary were among those members of the privy council who studied the manuscript before its publication.[3] Some time within the next two years he formed a connection with Cary.

Soon after the collapse of Vaughan's efforts the Welshman had granted Cary a narrow strip of territory running across the Avalon peninsula from the east coast to Placentia Bay; its northern limit was a point mid-way between Ferryland and Aquafort, its southern boundary the harbour of Renews.[4] This, of course, was the area that Vaughan's people had tried so ineffectually to settle and that Whitbourne had visited in 1618. If there existed a link between Falkland and Whitbourne before 1622 and if Whitbourne had encouraged him to secure this particular piece of land, the proof of it is now lost. While the grant lay in the region most popular with English fishermen, it was extremely small, only six miles from north to south. It would shortly be supplemented by a much larger award on Trinity Bay, granted to Falkland by the Newfoundland company.[5]

Henry Cary was born about 1576, the eldest son of Sir Edward Cary of Hertfordshire who had served as master of the jewel house to both queen Elizabeth and king James. The family was old and well-connected: one branch held the title of lord Hunsdon and was related to Elizabeth through Anne Boleyn, another received the earldom of Monmouth from James I. Cary was educated at Exeter College, Oxford, where according to one account he gained such a reputation as a scholar that his rooms became the haunt of the most distinguished men of his time. After Oxford he fought in France and the Low Countries. His public career began in 1617 with his appointment as comptroller of the royal household and privy councillor. It is hard to justify Cary's sudden rise

---

[1] See below, p. 110.
[2] This was the phrase which, according to John Smith, summed up a common attitude towards the fishing business. Smith, *Travels and works*, edd. E. Arber and A. G. Bradley (Edinburgh, 1910), I, 194.
[3] See below, p. 100.
[4] See below, p. 207.
[5] See below, pp. 211–12.

to prominence; his early career had been unremarkable, his personality was difficult, and he seems to have been continually confused with other members of his extended family and credited with their achievements. The rumour that his advancement resulted from his having been the messenger who carried the news of the old queen's death to the anxious James derived from a confusion between him and his kinsman, Robert Carey. Anthony à Wood believed that the story of his accomplishments at Oxford should be attributed to his son, Lucius, while Thomas Fuller, with yet another Cary in mind, thought that Henry Cary had died in 1620.[1] In fact Cary probably owed his position not to any particular merit but to the favour of the duke of Buckingham, the surest road to success in the later years of James I.

In 1620 Cary was returned to parliament though he made no mark there until, the following year, the king bestowed upon him the title of viscount Falkland in the Scottish peerage. Then a furore arose when Falkland, with characteristic sensitivity, protested at having to continue to sit in the lower house. But in 1622 he received an office which must have satisfied even his sense of his own dignity: he was named lord deputy of Ireland. It was an unfortunate appointment. The early years of his tenure were dominated by the urgent need to raise money for the defence of Ireland. The situation required Falkland to initiate difficult negotiations with an Old English community already alienated by the appropriation of some of their land. If they were to cooperate they demanded concessions. So began the long and bitter debate over the Graces. Falkland was not the man to handle such a delicate situation. It was not so much that he was a bad administrator as that his personality – petulant and easily offended – handicapped him both in his relationships with others and in the implementation of his policies.[2]

Falkland's years as lord deputy coincided with the period of his active involvement with Newfoundland, although he seems to have reversed the more usual sequence of moving from experience in Ireland to an interest in the New World. During his years at court he would have been exposed to the fever of overseas speculation that periodically infected the capital. In 1609, at the time of the first reorganisation of

---

[1] *DNB*; H. Walpole, *A catalogue of the royal and noble authors of England* (Strawberry Hill, 1758), II, 190–1; Wood, *Athenae Oxonienses*, I, 585; T. Fuller, *The history of the worthies of England*, ed. P. A. Nuttall (London, 1840), II, 46–7.

[2] On Falkland's career as lord deputy, see R. Bagwell, *Ireland under the Stuarts* (London, 1909), I, chs. IX, X; A. Clarke, 'Selling royal favours, 1624–1632,' in *A new history of Ireland*, edd. T. W. Moody, F. X. Martin, F. J. Byrne, vol. III, *Early modern Ireland, 1534–1691* (Oxford, 1976), pp. 233–42; A. Clarke, *The Old English in Ireland, 1625–41* (Ithaca, New York, 1966), *passim*.

the Virginia company, he became a member of the council but there is no evidence that he was ever particularly active in its affairs. Three years later he subscribed to the North West Passage company[1] which capitalised upon the excitement generated by Henry Hudson's voyage of 1610 and which, two years later, set out an expedition under the command of Thomas Button, a kinsman of William Vaughan. Possibly Vaughan and Falkland had been acquainted at Oxford. Falkland's wife, Elizabeth, may also have provided a link with Newfoundland for her father, Sir Lawrence Tanfield, had been one of the original shareholders in the Newfoundland company.[2]

Falkland seems to have made no effort to develop his land in the island until two things happened: first he had joined forces with Richard Whitbourne who began to act as his adviser, and secondly he had taken up his Irish appointment. Then it very quickly became apparent that his project was to have an unusual twist, for it was to involve both investment and migration from Ireland as well as from England. Falkland had become convinced that Ireland would benefit from sponsoring a settlement in Newfoundland and also, more perceptively, that there were certain lessons to be drawn from the Irish experience that could be applied to plantations on the other side of the Atlantic.[3]

By December of 1622 a letter from Whitbourne makes it clear that Falkland was actively recruiting investors in Ireland: 'Lords, Knightes, & other gentlemen of that kingdome who shall freely and voluntarily offer themselves with their purses.'[4] But who were these adventurers to be: members of the New or the Old English community? Of the two the latter seem by far the more likely. The Protestant New English had only recently received their estates in Ireland and were already under fire for their failure to settle them. The Old English, on the other hand, found themselves increasingly squeezed between their adherence to the Catholic faith and to the crown. By the sixteen twenties it was becoming more and more difficult to reconcile the two loyalties. Furthermore some long-established Old English landowners in Wexford, Longford and Leitrim had lost their lands because of the assertion of rather dubious royal claims. The Old English saw themselves being treated like the native Irish as their estates became New English plantations, and they resented it. Finally the close cooperation between Falkland and the Catholic George Calvert suggests that the appeal was to

[1] A Brown, *The genesis of the United States* (Boston, 1890), II, 844.
[2] Carr, *Select charters*, p. 52.   [3] See below, pp. 244–5.
[4] See below, pp. 220–5.

the Old English. If so, it was probably not the result of any pro-Catholic sentiments on the lord deputy's part – his notoriously unsympathetic reaction to his wife's conversion would deny that – but rather of a wish to reduce the complications and tensions of Irish politics. The English administration worried lest sooner or later the Old English put aside their English identity and cast their lot with their co-religionists, the native Irish, as indeed they did in 1641. It might well be prepared to encourage some of the disgruntled Old English landowners to emigrate, whereas it would wish the New English to stay and fulfil their responsibility to plant in Ireland. If indeed Falkland was concerned with the problems of the Old English, not so much for their own sake as for reasons of security, then it suggests that he possessed more political acumen than he is usually given credit for.

Propaganda-making for the venture now became intense. In 1622 Richard Whitbourne published two works: a second and much enlarged edition of the *Discourse and discovery* and *A discourse containing a loving invitation*[1] which included some material from the earlier work of 1620 and much that was new besides. Both books reveal the connection with lord Falkland, particularly the *Discourse containing a loving invitation* which was dedicated to the nobleman and designed to attract investors to his scheme. The next year there appeared in Dublin one of the very few promotional tracts to be published outside London. This pamphlet, *A short discourse of the New-found-land*, was aimed far more specifically than were Whitbourne's books at investors in Ireland.[2] The fact that the Stationers company printed it tends to confirm that the intended audience was the Old English; the company would have been unlikely to put out anything that might induce the New English to renege on their Irish plantations. No positive identification can be made of the author who signs himself simply T.C. A Thomas Cary, a kinsman of Falkland's, who was in Ireland during the sixteen twenties and had connections with the English administration seems the most probable author.[3]

Both Whitbourne and T.C. describe precisely what an adventurer could expect in return for an investment of £100 to be paid over a two year period.[4] In the area known as South Falkland, that is the ribbon of land that Falkland had received from Vaughan, an investor would be given a small allotment of land, enough to build a house and fishing rooms to serve a ship of eighty tons, for which he would pay

---

[1] Extract printed below, pp. 207–20.   [2] Reprinted below, pp. 227–37.
[3] *CSP Ire., 1625–1632*, pp. 274–5, 609; Shaw, *Knights*, II, 194.
[4] See below, pp. 214–15, 235–6.

an annual rent of ten shillings. He would be given too a more generous award in the north: one side of a harbour on Trinity Bay and 2,000 acres of adjoining land, the rent being only twenty pence a year. Within three years the investor must plant at least eight people on his southern land or else forfeit it. Greater or lesser investments would be rewarded proportionately. To attract those who had no capital but who were prepared to go to Newfoundland in person, it was provided that any man who stayed in the colony for five years should be given a hundred acres in the south in return for the nominal rent of one penny. A generous grant, it shows that Falkland recognised that one of the most effective recruiting ploys was to promise land to those who had little or no prospect of ever owning land at home. Encouraging too would be the letters from Calvert's colonists at Ferryland which Whitbourne printed and which depicted a busy and flourishing settlement.[1]

As no business records survive for Falkland's colony, all that we know of its organisation comes from the promotional works. Whitbourne and T.C. both make it clear that any money put up by adventurers would be used as common capital to finance the setting out of ships and men. None of it would go directly to Falkland himself. At the end of each year he and the investors would share proportionately in any profits from fishing or from goods produced by colony servants. The venture, then, was to be run as a terminable joint stock. There was to be a council of six or more of the adventurers to manage the business and to report periodically to Falkland. One of the council would act as treasurer and account to the investors.[2]

In other respects, however, the works of Whitbourne and the anonymous T.C. are very different, as presumably were the backgrounds and experience of the two men. Whitbourne had added another question to those he had addressed in the first edition of the *Discourse* – or perhaps this one had been put to him by Falkland himself: what would it cost to send to the fishery a ship with a crew of forty people and enough provisions for ten of them to winter in Newfoundland? He answered the question exhaustively, even to furnishing a list of the supplies that would be needed. From beef to bellows, from nails to pickaxes, no item was too insignificant. He follows his list with an equally full account of the amounts of fish and train oil which might be made in a season, of the price for which the cargo might be sold in the markets of the Mediterranean, and of the profits which could be shared among the investors.[3] The prices which

[1] See below, pp. 195–206. [2] See below, pp. 214, 216, 235.
[3] See below, pp. 173–81.

Whitbourne quotes are conservative; actual profits might well have been greater than those he promises.[1] But, where the fishing business is concerned, Whitbourne's advice always tends towards caution. Nevertheless, his guide to the needs of colonists and the conduct of the trade in fish was so useful that John Smith chose to reprint it in his *Generall historie of Virginia, New England and the Summer Isles* in 1624.[2]

To make the enterprise still more attractive to Falkland and his associates, Whitbourne had further sources of income to suggest. In their long involvement with Newfoundland the English had relied upon the shore fishery and the making of fish dried by sun and salt. The Banks they had left to the Basques, the French and the Portuguese, all of whom had plentiful domestic supplies of the salt needed to make 'green' fish. Whitbourne was now proposing that ships which spent the summer fishing from the shore, sell their catch to sack ships, pick up salt made at the island, and go on to the Banks. Twenty days would suffice to take a new cargo. The ships could then sail directly to the profitable markets of the Mediterranean. Englishmen should also pay more attention to the far north and west of the island and the neighbouring areas of the Canadian mainland. They could break into the whale fishery and the trade in furs so far monopolised by the French.[3]

In the *Discourse* Trinity Harbour and Trepassey Bay had been the two prospective sites for settlement about which Whitbourne had been most enthusiastic. Not unnaturally in the *Discourse containing a loving invitation* he focuses upon Falkland's land. The southern section, which Whitbourne calls Trinity Land, included the favoured Trinity Harbour. But he now adds a detailed description of every harbour on the north side of the Bay, identifying those which were dangerous to shipping or popular with visiting fishermen. This is an area rich in bird life and Whitbourne saw this as one of its attractions, for fishermen commonly killed sea birds for bait. More heavily wooded than the coast to the south, the region might produce timber and naval stores and even iron to supplement the settlers' income from fishing.[4]

In the narrow band of territory known as South Falkland were the two popular fishing ports of Renews, which Whitbourne knew well from his association with William Vaughan, and Fermeuse. Both provided safe anchorages and could be easily defended. The island at

---

[1] For information on the price of fish, see Cell, *English enterprise*, pp. 19, 20, 150.
[2] Smith, *Travels*, II, 277–81.   [3] See below, pp. 183–5.
[4] See below, pp. 146–7, 184–6.

the base of Renews harbour commanded what would be the whole area of settlement; guns placed there could repel any attack, whether by sea or by land. The island was also an excellent place for fishing and might be easily connected to the mainland by a bridge. Between the two harbours lay open land which Whitbourne hoped would produce grain, hemp, flax and, interestingly enough, tobacco. This is the first mention by any propagandist of tobacco as a crop which might be grown in Newfoundland. It was, of course, an optimistic idea but Whitbourne was probably aware of the new but growing export trade from Virginia. The quality of the soil around Renews he praised particularly as unusually deep and free from stones. In his concern to make Englishmen believe that Newfoundland was habitable, he emphasised that Renews lay five degrees further south than London. [1]

In advising Falkland Whitbourne was anxious that the mistakes of Vaughan's colony should not be repeated. Therefore he was particularly insistent about the type of person who should go out to the plantation: they must be skilled and expect to work hard for their livelihood. With his typical attention to detail he suggested the types of craftsmen that would be needed and emphasised that they and their wives must be flexible enough to work in the fishery during the season. The average fishing ship might carry thirty-four persons across the Atlantic, leave fourteen in Newfoundland and still be adequately manned for the voyage home. But the business of choosing settlers and allowing them to prepare for the journey must not be rushed. Those who were recruited in haste were likely to prove unsuited to a way of life which Whitbourne acknowledged to be rigorous. [2] Here he may well have been hinting that Falkland should put him in charge of the recruitment and perhaps of the whole venture. But the lord deputy proved a traditionalist: he named a relative of his wife's, an untried gentleman not an experienced merchant, as governor. Whitbourne he seems to have retained as an adviser.

T.C., on the other hand, obviously had no personal knowledge of the island, but he compensated by having Whitbourne's books to hand and relying heavily upon them for his descriptions of a place which he had never seen. Far more than Whitbourne's writings, the Dublin pamphlet was geared to the gentleman investor who might be attracted by the promise of landed estates. This purpose makes it in many ways a more traditional kind of propaganda than Whitbourne's practical handbooks which assumed that any interested person would approach the problems from the perspective of a merchant rather than simply

[1] See below, pp. 207–11.   [2] See below, pp. 216–17, 219–20.

that of a landowner. T.C. rehearses all the standard arguments in favour of overseas colonisation that had long characterised promotion literature whether it dealt with Newfoundland, New England or Virginia: it would bring honour to the crown and profit both to the individual and the nation. He even dangles the hope of a north-west passage before any prospective adventurers. Different too from Whitbourne is the Irish slant of the *Short discourse*. Old English landowners, feeling insecure in their tenure, might find the offer of land in Newfoundland particularly attractive. But there is also an emphasis on the general benefits that Ireland, in an unusual reversal of roles, would reap as the undertaker rather than the victim of a plantation. The colony would provide Ireland with a market for her exports of foodstuffs and cloth, it would relieve unemployment, and it would create a demand for craftsmen to build and ready the ships and so bring about a beneficial migration of skilled men from England to Ireland. This last point suggests strongly that the author was an Englishman, for it was an Irish grievance that the administration had done so little to encourage the spread of skills among the native Irish. Those whose interest was aroused by the terms and inducements offered in the *Short discourse* were encouraged to put their money in the hands of the plantation's treasurer, Sir Samuel Smith of Dublin, by the beginning of November 1623. Smith had close links with the lord deputy, who had knighted him in 1622 and who would staunchly defend him when Smith's licence to sell spirits in Cork became one element in the feud between Falkland and Adam Loftus, the lord chancellor.[1]

In fact the demands of Falkland's Irish office together with his severe financial difficulties probably destroyed any chance that the colony would succeed. However, for the time being, the business seems to have gone on vigorously enough. Whitbourne, as the letter of December 1622 shows, was providing excellent advice, Leonard Welstead, Falkland's agent in London, was actively recruiting investors on that side of the Irish sea, and a governor, Sir Francis Tanfield, had been appointed. In 1623, following Whitbourne's timetable, a colony was founded in South Falkland under Tanfield. According to T.C. the governor was to have a group of assistants to work with him.[2] This suggests a shared authority which, after the troubles between governor and council at Jamestown, the Newfoundland company had preferred to avoid. The position of assistant harks back to the very beginnings of English settlement in North America and to the incorporation in

---

[1] *CSP Ire.*, *1615–1625*, pp. 532, 547, *1625–1632*, pp. 122, 188–90, 418; Bagwell, *Ireland under the Stuarts*, I, 173.   [2] See below, pp. 235–6.

1587 of the 'Governor and Assistants of the City of Raleigh' which stipulated that the twelve assistants to governor John White were to receive generous grants of land regardless of their financial contribution. We do not know the identity of any of Tanfield's assistants, though it is reasonable to assume that they were gentlemen with some money at stake. Indeed we know very little about the fortunes of Falkland's colony in general. Whitbourne evidently visited it twice as well as making trips to Ireland to consult with the lord deputy.[1] In 1623 Whitbourne brought out a third and slightly revised edition of the *Discourse and discovery*.[2]

But by 1626 Whitbourne evidently thought that the lord deputy's commitment was weakening, even though he could report that a number of prominent west-country gentlemen were showing an interest in the scheme. Clearly the relationship between the two men had become strained and Whitbourne felt the need to defend himself.[3] It is doubtful that Falkland had ever appreciated that in his adviser he had his most valuable resource, a man not of any great vision but with a loving, even obsessive care for detail in practical matters. It may be that Whitbourne's cautious realism worked against him, that his inducements and promises were too unspectacular, his propaganda too balanced for Falkland and the average investor. By November Whitbourne was petitioning Buckingham, the lord admiral, for fresh employment.[4] The petition sounds querulous, a tone new to Whitbourne's writing. Now in his sixties, an old man by the standards of his time, he was faced once more with the failure of his dreams. The connection with Falkland seems to have been his last attempt to realise his goal of a firmly-rooted English settlement in Newfoundland. His insistence upon the need for promoters to have a grasp of the business of the fishing industry had introduced a new professionalism into propaganda.

Probably the South Falkland colony did not long survive Whitbourne's break with it. By 1628 Robert Hayman, whose long suit was urging others to continue the work he himself had played at and then abandoned, counselled Falkland to make a fresh start.[5] However, the small group of documents in the National Library of Wales connected with Sir Henry Salusbury suggests that there was still some activity among Falkland's associates.[6] It is ironic perhaps that the only individual to take land from Falkland whom we can identify should

---

[1] See below, pp. 237–41.
[2] Printed by Felix Kingston.
[3] See below, p. 238.
[4] See below, pp. 242–4.
[5] Hayman, *Quodlibets*, sig. F iv.
[6] See below, pp. 244–9.

be not an Irishman but a Welshman and the brother-in-law of William Vaughan. Salusbury had received, as the promotion literature had promised, land in both South Falkland and on Trinity Bay. He took the trouble to collect a good deal of advice on both colonisation and fishing from such experienced hands as ex-governor John Guy and Nicholas Guy. Whether Salusbury ever put their recommendations into effect is doubtful.

But perhaps the most interesting of these papers is the document that appears to be Falkland's own instructions to planters on his land. There is no similar document for any of the other offshoot colonies, although there are two versions of the instructions given to John Guy before the establishment of the Cupids Cove colony in 1610. Falkland's advice reflects very strongly the English experience in Ireland: the insistence upon keeping the native inhabitants outside the Avalon peninsula, not going to settle among the indigenous people, and maintaining a single language and a single religion. The last two recommendations further support the idea that Falkland intended many of his settlers to come from Ireland but was concerned that they should be English not Gaelic speakers. While it is hardly surprising that he wanted only one religion represented in his colony, it is interesting that he – a Protestant himself – did not specify that that religion should be Protestantism, again perhaps because he envisaged Old English Catholics seizing the opportunity to escape from their predicament in Ireland.

But by the late 1620's Falkland's own predicament was becoming serious. His enemies, and they were many, had repeatedly alleged that the lord deputy had used his position to harass an Irish family, the O'Byrnes, so as to confiscate their lands in Wicklow for himself. This scandal alone did not bring about his recall, but rather an accumulation of failures combined with the death of Buckingham, his defender at court. Falkland left Ireland in 1629 vigorously protesting his innocence. Although he was not replaced until 1632 and was eventually cleared of the charges against him, he never resumed his office and died in retirement in 1633. He may have abandoned the Newfoundland project on his departure from Ireland, which coincided with George Calvert's withdrawal from Newfoundland.

The two men, Falkland and Calvert, had taken land from William Vaughan at the same time and seem to have worked closely together. Calvert's grant lay immediately to the north of South Falkland, making cooperation easy, and reached as far as Caplin Bay, the northern limit of Vaughan's original holding.[1] They must have known each other

[1] See below, pp. 258–60.

well, possibly from their Oxford days and certainly from the time when both had served as privy councillors and members of the Commons. In the mid-twenties both were in Ireland until Calvert left his Irish estate in Wexford in favour of Newfoundland, showing a degree of commitment unequalled by the other proprietors.

The son of Leonard Calvert, a Yorkshire landowner of yeoman stock and a Catholic, George Calvert was born about 1579.[1] After Trinity College, Oxford, and travels on the continent, he attracted the notice of Robert Cecil whose secretary he became.[2] With Cecil as his patron Calvert's career advanced rapidly. His first official appointment was as clerk of the crown in Connacht and Clare in 1606. Two years later he became clerk to the council in England but his links with Ireland continued. In 1611 he was put in joint charge of the musters of the Irish garrisons and in 1613 he was appointed to the commission sent to inquire into the constitutional problems and general grievances in Ireland. The following year he asked, apparently without success, to be named master of the rolls there. Meanwhile he had also become a member of the English parliament. Calvert reached the peak of his career in 1619 when he succeeded Sir Thomas Lake as secretary of state.[3] In that position he was hard-working and capable if uninspired. Among his responsibilities was the correspondence with Spain concerning the proposed marriage between prince Charles and the infanta.

While Calvert himself took a moderate position towards Spain, his identification with this unpopular royal policy damaged his career. Until now he had been able to deal quite effectively with the Commons at a time when the king was notoriously ill-served there by most of his councillors. As rumours, justified or not, of Calvert's own sympathies towards Catholicism began to spread, so his position was still further undermined. The collapse of the marriage negotiations, followed by Buckingham and the prince's mounting antipathy towards Spain, left Calvert high and dry. Sir Edward Conway, technically his junior, was now the favoured secretary and Calvert found himself bypassed. If the duke of Buckingham did not smile upon you it was hard to survive at the court of the ageing James I. By May 1624 Calvert was rumoured to be in poor health and ready to resign. Court gossip had already picked his successor. But not until the following February did he give up the secretaryship, announcing as he did so his conversion

---

[1] J. D. Krugler, 'Sir George Calvert's resignation as secretary of state and the founding of Maryland', *Maryland Historical Magazine*, LXVIII (1973), 239–54.

[2] Cecil may have acted as a link between Calvert and Hayman; see above, p. 18.

[3] *DNB; DCB*, I; *CSP Ire., 1603–1606*, pp. 514–15, *1611–1614*, pp. 183, 426–8, 436, 540.

to Catholicism.[1] In compensation the king conferred upon him the title of baron Baltimore, the name coming from his Irish lands in County Longford.[2] He was also allowed to retain the grant of the subsidy on raw silk which he had received in 1620 and which he finally surrendered in 1631 in return for an annual pension of £1000.[3] Apart from being summoned to court once in February 1627 to be consulted concerning the terms of the peace to be made with Spain, he took no further part in public life in England. For the rest of his life Calvert concentrated upon the business of plantation, whether in Ireland, Newfoundland, or most famously in Maryland.

It is quite clear that the colony in Maryland was intended from the first to be a place of refuge for Catholics and that by 1628, when three priests and many Catholic lay persons were reported to be at Ferryland,[4] the Newfoundland colony had assumed the same purpose. But there is some doubt as to whether that was the original objective in Newfoundland. The timing of Calvert's conversion, therefore, becomes crucial. In a letter of 30 March 1625, a month after Calvert's resignation, the acid-tongued George Abbot, archbishop of Canterbury, wrote that the ex-secretary had been depressed ever since the collapse of the Spanish marriage negotiations and that he had turned 'papist, which he now professeth, this being the third time that he hath beene to blame that way.'[5] The implication is that Calvert had been a Catholic for some time and even that this was not the first time that he had made his beliefs known. Abbot also reported that Calvert had bought a ship and was about to leave for his North American plantation, although the archbishop who claimed to know so much was not sure whether that was in New England or Newfoundland. If it were true that Calvert had long been a Catholic, then he might have acquired the land from Vaughan in 1620 for religious reasons. There are, however, problems with that interpretation, not least among them being Abbot's obvious malice and his well-known hostility towards those whom he regarded as at all pro-Spanish. Furthermore, had Calvert been a Catholic in his early days as secretary, one might have expected to find him

[1] J. D. Krugler, '"Our trusty and welbeloved councillor": the parliamentary career of Sir George Calvert, 1609–1624', *Maryland Historical Magazine*, LXXII (1977), 473–87, and 'Calvert's resignation', *ibid.*, LXVIII (1975), 239–54; D. H. Willson, *The privy councillors in the house of commons, 1604–1629* (Minneapolis, Minnesota, 1940), pp. 87–9, 162; S. R. Gardiner, *History of England from the accession of James I to the outbreak of the civil war, 1603–1642* (London, 1884), III, 194–5, V, 309–10.

[2] H. Kenny, 'New light on an old name', *Maryland Historical Magazine*, XLIX (1954), 116–21.

[3] *CSP Dom., 1619–1623*, p. 142, *1629–1631*, p. 524, *1631–1633*, p. 175.

[4] See below, pp. 284–5.   [5] See below, p. 272.

adopting a far more sympathetic attitude towards Spain from the beginning. But only gradually does Calvert seem to have become fully committed to the wisdom of the Spanish match. It is also not clear why, as early as 1620, Calvert should have thought an American refuge necessary, at least for English Catholics. No Englishman had planned a Catholic colony since Sir George Peckham had taken land under Gilbert's charter in 1582.[1] James I had generally followed a policy of toleration, at least towards the laity, and the pressure upon the king to enforce the Elizabethan penal code was intense only early in the reign, after the exposure of the gunpowder plot, and in his last years, with the parliament of 1621 and the anger at his pro-Spanish policy. Moreover in 1620 Calvert's career had not gone sour; the king liked him and the Commons respected him. It could be that Calvert's Irish experience had already made him sympathetic to the plight of the Old English Catholics, as I will argue he later became. But that is pure speculation. Calvert had not yet gone to live among the dispossessed Old English of Wexford, and the settlers who went to Ferryland in 1621 seem from their names to have been English and Welsh rather than Irish.[2]

In fact George Calvert probably first took land in Newfoundland out of a general interest in the progress of English overseas expansion, which he had already manifested by subscribing to the Virginia and East India companies in 1609 and which he would confirm by joining the New England company in 1622.[3] Only later did he come to see his colony as a place where Catholics could live. His own realisation that he wished to return to the religion of his childhood seems to have come upon him gradually in the early 1620's. Calvert had been forced to conform to the Anglican church at about the age of twelve. Both his education and his career demanded that he adhere to that church and there is no evidence that conformity created any problem for him until about 1622. Serious depression caused by the death of his first wife, Anne, in that year may have caused him to return to his faith, if only temporarily.[4] As he came to see that his career would advance no

---

[1] D. B. Quinn, ed., *The voyages and colonising expeditions of Sir Humphrey Gilbert*, 2 vols (Hakluyt Society, 1940), I, 56–62, 71–5.

[2] See below, p. 204.

[3] L. W. Wilhelm, *Sir George Calvert, Baron of Baltimore* (Maryland Historical Society, Fund Publications, no. 20, Baltimore, Maryland, 1884), pp. 34.

[4] J. D. Krugler, ' "The face of a Protestant and the heart of a papist": a reexamination of Sir George Calvert's conversion to Roman Catholicism', *Journal of Church and State*, XX (1978), 507–31. Krugler suggests this as an explanation of Abbot's statement that Calvert became a Catholic three times: at his birth, at the death of his wife, and in 1625.

further and that his position as secretary of state was becoming untenable, so he could consider seriously the possibility of becoming a Catholic. He may well have reached some decision about his own future and the character of his settlement as a place of religious toleration by April 1623 when he received his royal charter of Avalon. That document is curiously vague on the matter of religion and does not require, as did the Newfoundland company's charter in 1610, that all going to the island take the oath of supremacy.[1] By the time that Calvert was ready to resign, he was also ready to make a public declaration of his conversion.[2]

The argument that, after his resignation, Calvert wanted to encourage migration from Ireland to Newfoundland must remain tentative. His links with Ireland were strong. At some point, perhaps on his visit as commissioner in 1613, he had acquired land in Wexford and one of his daughters had married Sir Robert Talbot of Kildare, a member of the Shrewsbury family, some of whose Irish lands had been claimed by the crown and assigned to New English planters. Contrary to archbishop Abbot's expectation and his own original intentions, it was to Wexford not to Ferryland that Calvert went after leaving office. He had additional estates of over 2,000 acres in Longford, which he had received in 1621 but which, according to a commission of inquiry the following year, he had done little to plant.[3] It may have been pressure to settle on his Irish lands or face losing them that took him to Wexford. Once there he could maintain his ties with Falkland, who had been alerted by the king to his coming and asked to give 'all lawful assistance and good expedition' to Calvert's affairs there. According to James, Calvert intended to remain in Ireland for some considerable time.[4] In fact he stayed for almost two years before going back to England in the spring of 1627 and then, that summer, paying his first visit to Newfoundland.

While George Calvert lived in Ireland it would have been possible for him to meet with the lord deputy to discuss the Newfoundland business, in which they seem to have been cooperating closely. They

---

[1] See below, pp. 258–69. The comparison of this point in the two charters is made by R. J. Lahey, 'The role of religion in lord Baltimore's colonial enterprise', *Maryland Historical Magazine*, LXXII (1977), 492–511.

[2] Krugler, 'Calvert's resignation,' *ibid.*, LXVIII, p. 242, argues that Calvert's resignation and the ruin of his official career triggered his conversion rather than the reverse.

[3] Wilhelm, *Calvert*, pp. 106–7; Moody, *Early modern Ireland*, p. 221; *CSP Ire., 1625–1632*, pp. 95, 117; B.L., Add. MS 4756, f. 126.

[4] *Calendar of patent and close rolls in chancery in Ireland in the reign of Charles I, first to eighth years, inclusive*, ed. James Morrin (Dublin, 1863), p. 36.

shared a headquarters in London where information about their colonies was available,[1] and Calvert had passed on to Richard Whitbourne letters which he had received from Ferryland so that they could be included in the publicity for Falkland's colony in 1622. Leonard Welstead's letter to the lord deputy in January 1623 even makes it sound as though there were to be a joint settlement organised by the two men.[2] There is no doubt that Falkland had been trying to attract Irish investors. He and Calvert may have shared the hope that some Old English landowners would be encouraged to emigrate, men like Sir Robert Talbot, who did accompany his father-in-law to Ferryland in 1628. The events of the sixteen-twenties cannot have reassured the Old English about their future in Ireland. The negotiations over the Graces had stalled, their tenure was still insecure, and there was increasing apprehension that the penalties for recusancy would be reimposed. Nevertheless the pattern of migration from Ireland in the seventeenth century suggests that Falkland and Calvert's recruitment would not have met with great success. While substantial numbers of both Old English and Irish landowners did emigrate, they went to continental Europe rather than to the New World. And once the Calvert family's Maryland settlement got under way, it was not Catholic gentlemen who flocked there attracted by the promise of land and religious toleration, but Irish peasants who went out as indentured servants.[3]

However, the initial moves to develop the land in Newfoundland came while Sir George Calvert was still secretary of state and living in England. After receiving his land from Vaughan in 1620 Calvert acted very quickly. The next year he sent out colonists under the command of Captain Edward Winne, a Welshman recommended to him perhaps by Vaughan. The letters which Winne and later others sent home and which were printed to make propaganda for the Ferryland settlement are the only ones, apart from Calvert's own, to survive from any of the offshoot colonies.[4] Winne's earliest letters, written in August 1621 when the first settlers had just reached the island, are curiously flat, lacking the excitement and immediacy of John Guy's despatches. They may well have been modified for publication, otherwise why print that stale list of abuses allegedly committed by the fishermen. The offences themselves were not new; Guy had

---

[1] See below, pp. 166–7. [2] See below, pp. 226–7.
[3] See John J. Silke, 'The Irish abroad, 1534–1691', in Moody, *Early modern Ireland*, ch. XXIII.
[4] See below, pp. 195–206, 253–8.

introduced 'laws' to deal with them as early as 1611.[1] More convincing is Winne's account of his relationship with several captains of fishing vessels. Clearly the colonists' intrusion into a popular fishing harbour had made the visiting fishermen anxious.

Winne does not explain the choice of Ferryland as a site, but his letter of 26 August implies that it had been selected well in advance. In Calvert's mind there would have been a definite advantage to being so close to Renews and Falkland's people. Winne seems to have had no inkling of Ferryland's reputation as an exceptionally cold harbour, but his reference to the two men who had already suffered from scurvy was a foretaste of the problems of the winter of 1628–29.

There is nothing in Winne's first letter to suggest that he had had any previous experience of Newfoundland, but that deficiency may have been supplied to some extent by the Master Jennings to whose 'helpe and furtherance' Winne refers. This was probably Abraham Jennings, a prominent Plymouth merchant and one of the only two subscribers to the Newfoundland company in 1610 who did not come from London or Bristol. Jennings owned ships which regularly made the Newfoundland voyage. In 1623, his ship the *Abraham* was at St John's and its owner was involved in dealings with John Slany and the Cupids Cove colony. That same year he put money into New England.[2]

After almost twelve months in the island the settlers at Ferryland were still sending home letters which were optimistic and briskly businesslike.[3] They depict a group of men hard at work, building houses, clearing land, cutting timber. Winne's request for women and a surgeon to join the colony had been met, but interestingly enough in light of the later history of Ferryland there was still no clergyman. By 1628 the settlers could choose between a number of Catholic priests and an uncompromising Protestant, Erasmus Stourton, a combination which may have provided well for their spiritual needs but which only complicated Calvert's mounting problems. Already there must have been trouble with some of the younger people for, echoing Guy's and Crout's complaints about apprentices, Winne asked that 'no more boyes and girles be sent...nor any other persons which haue not been brought vp to labour.' Some of the most unsuitable were probably

[1] Cell, *English enterprise*, pp. 64–5.
[2] Carr, *Select charters*, pp. 51–62; Richard Newalls' account book (Bodleian Library, Malone MS 2, ff. 1v–13v, 130–8v); T. K. Rabb, *Enterprise and empire: merchant and gentry investment in the expansion of England, 1575–1630* (Cambridge Mass., 1967), p. 323.
[3] See below, pp. 195–206.

packed home, and in all thirty-two people were to pass the winter of 1622–1623 at the plantation. It was a small but promising beginning. The propaganda works of 1624 judged Calvert's colony to be the most successful yet. According to Sir William Alexander it was even showing a profit.[1] Only Daniel Powell's comment concerning the severity of Ferryland's winter weather would have given Calvert any cause for alarm. Evidently he ignored the warning.

With such favourable omens, Calvert felt sufficiently encouraged to move to strengthen his position and to obtain a larger grant of land. Influence at court he still had. In December 1622 it seemed as though the whole island would be ceded to him and the rights of the Newfoundland company disregarded. But, when the charter was written in April 1623, his grant was restricted to a part of the Avalon peninsula which he was to hold *in capite*. Calvert's holdings now reached from the border with South Falkland north to the boundary of the St John's plantation, held by shareholders in the Newfoundland company, and then across to Conception Bay and west to Placentia.[2] Apparently there were no protests from the company. Its officials, while by no means prepared to surrender all their claims, were probably happy enough to yield to a man who might effectively represent the colonising interests to the crown. Calvert had already emerged as an articulate champion of settlement in the debates in the Commons on the freedom of the New England and Newfoundland fisheries and he had found a ready ally in John Guy.[3] It is possible too that the company realised the futility of opposing a courtier so close to the king. In later years it was rumoured that Calvert coveted the St John's lot, but that may simply have been a story spread to enhance the desirability of that land in the eyes of potential investors.[4] His surviving papers indicate no desire on Calvert's part to extend his lands beyond the limits set in 1623.

By the time that Calvert gave up his official position in 1625, one hundred men and women were living at Ferryland. Only the Cupids Cove colony in its first years ever approached that size. Calvert's greater freedom to concentrate upon his personal affairs shows in the documents from the spring of 1625 when, for the first time, he can be seen actively participating in the management of his settlement. His ships, carrying more settlers and livestock, had been stayed in anticipation of their being needed for service against Spain. Calvert personally corresponded

---

[1] *Encouragement to colonies*, sig. E1.
[2] See below, pp. 258–69.
[3] Stock, *Proceedings and debates*, I, 24–84, *passim*.
[4] See below, pp. 274–5.

with both Buckingham, the lord admiral, and Sir John Coke, secretary of the navy, in an effort to obtain their release. The compromise solution suggested by John Mason, ex-governor of Cupids and now commissary general responsible for victualling the Cadiz expedition, was to release the ships on condition that they return with fish to supply the royal fleet.[1]

Edward Winne had now been replaced as governor by a Catholic gentleman, Sir Arthur Aston.[2] His appointment signalled Calvert's intention to open his settlement to Catholics, fifteen of whom were supposed to accompany Aston to Ferryland in 1625. Father Simon Stock, a Carmelite priest, who may have been at least partly responsible for Calvert's conversion, envisaged the colony as part of a grand design which would not only result in the conversion of the Amerindians but which would be a link in a chain of missionary outposts stretching to China and the East Indies. 'Many Catholic friends of mine will go there to live, if we had religious who would go with them,' wrote Stock to the Congregation of the Propaganda in Rome. But the plans to send a number of Carmelites with the settlers in 1625 and 1626 came to nothing.[3]

Once the war with Spain began and after it broadened to include France, conditions became even more difficult for those with interests in colonisation and maritime trade. Ships were stayed, men impressed, and those vessels which did leave port were threatened by French privateers and Barbary pirates. Aston's departure was delayed again in 1627, but Calvert himself managed to pay a brief visit to the island during the summer, evidently feeling that he must either see to things himself or jeopardise the whole venture.[4] With him went two secular priests, Fathers Smith and Longville.[5] Precisely what had gone wrong between 1622, when his people were sending home such positive reports, and 1627, when the business seemed on the point of collapse, is hard to tell. In Ferryland, as in most young colonies, the early optimism and enthusiasm may have been eroded by the hard reality of day-to-day life. Each settlement had to find out for itself the island's agricultural limitations, each had to find ways to cope with the winter weather and to weed out unsuitable personnel.

Despite the problems Calvert was encouraged enough by what he saw to decide to return the following year with his wife, most of his

---

[1] See below, pp. 269–71.
[2] Lahey, 'The role of religion', p. 500.
[3] Ibid., pp. 497–8, 500–1.
[4] See below, pp. 273–4.
[5] Lahey, 'The role of religion', p. 504.

children and two of his sons-in-law, William Peasley and Robert Talbot of Kildare. With him also went another priest, Father Hacket and about forty settlers, some of whom may well have been Irish, for Charles I, supportive as ever of his father's old minister, asked Falkland to ensure that Calvert could use Irish ports in the movement of his people and their supplies.[1] Calvert had made a remarkable decision, one that distinguishes his seriousness of purpose from the lesser dedication of Falkland or Vaughan. William Vaughan wrote repeatedly of his desire to see Newfoundland for himself, but never did; the lord deputy apparently never had any such intention. But in Calvert's mind a transformation had taken place: Newfoundland was no longer simply a speculation, nor a place where others might be encouraged to settle while the proprietor stayed comfortably at home. It had become a place where the Calverts themselves might 'builde and sett and sowe'.[2]

As it turned out George Calvert would not achieve in Newfoundland the security and stability that he sought. Attacks by the French on the English fishing fleet, verbal abuse of himself and his religion both destroyed his tranquillity. The ex-courtier found himself cast in the uncomfortable role of protector of the fishing industry, leading a raid in reprisal upon the French, and dealing with the government at home about prizes and warships.[3] He may even have asked to be named admiral with responsibility for defending the fishery, a position similar to that granted to John Mason in 1620.[4] Before the winter had set in, when he had spent less than six months on the island, he had already turned his thoughts south.[5]

If he had any hopes left about his future in Newfoundland, his experiences during the winter of 1628–29 must have killed them. Ferryland, a notoriously exposed harbour, was gripped by an intense cold against which even Calvert's stone-built 'mansion house' gave inadequate protection. Too late he may have remembered Powell's warning and regretted Winne's decision to build in 'the coldest harbour of the Land, where those furious Windes and Icy Mountaynes doe play, and beate the greatest part of the Yeare'.[6] Half the settlers, including

[1] See below, pp. 275–6, 284–5. Lahey, 'The role of religion', p. 506, argues that the settlers were probably English, and some of them clearly were. But his contention that they were of English origin because Stock referred to them as his 'spiritual children' seems much too narrow an interpretation of that phrase.

[2] See below, p. 279.   [3] See below, pp. 279–83, 285–9.

[4] P.R.O., State Papers, Colonial, CO 1/1, ff. 178–80; and see below, pp. 283–4.

[5] See below, p. 287.

[6] See below, pp. 292–6; also Vaughan, *Newlanders cure*, sig. F2v–3. Vaughan had recommended that Calvert locate his settlement at Aquafort, Vaughan's old site.

Calvert himself, were sick at one time and nine or ten of them died, probably from scurvy. In the early years of a colony a death rate of one in ten was not particularly high, but on top of the misery caused by the cold, it was more than he was prepared to endure. He was no longer young. For one accustomed to life at court, or even to rural life in southern Ireland, the transition was abrupt indeed. He would leave the island, he said, to those more used to its rigours than he. Calvert's normally flat style becomes lively as he depicts the desolation of the place and the 'sadd face of wynter' that lay upon the land. By August of 1629 he had decided to send some of his family home and to move himself and forty of his people south to Virginia.[1] With some malice it was later reported that 'the Ayre of Newfoundland agrees perfectly well with all Gods Creatures except Iesuits and Scismaticks; A greate mortality amongst the former Tribe so affrighted my Lord of Baltimore, that hee utterly deserted the Country'.[2]

Nevertheless Calvert did not intend to abandon Newfoundland altogether. He had invested too much money – between twenty and thirty thousand pounds his son Cecilius would later claim[3] – and too much effort for that. He had recruited other investors too, of whom only the unhappy George Cottington, a relative of Calvert's close friend Sir Francis Cottington, is known to us by name. He had evidently received land on the island but not the profits he had anticipated.[4] Like Calvert, some of the Ferryland settlers seem to have felt that they also had invested too much to give up, for their investment was personal and, unlike him, they perhaps could not afford to leave. Some had been there since 1621 and if they had come as indentured servants would now be free and in possession of land worth little on the market but capable of supporting them and their families. To protect his interests and his remaining people Calvert appointed a governor named Hoyle, who seems later to have disappeared under rather mysterious circumstances.[5]

From Ferryland George Calvert went directly to Jamestown where he encountered difficulties with the oath of supremacy required to enter Virginia and tendered to him by men hostile to the idea of his settling among them. By the summer of 1630 he was back in England, still soliciting for a grant of land in more southerly latitudes but in an area where he would be free of interference. Not until two months after his

---

[1] See below, pp. 295–6.
[2] David Kirke to Archbishop Laud, 2 Oct. 1639 (P.R.O., CO 1/9, 40).
[3] See below, p. 298.   [4] See below, p. 278.
[5] Cell, *English enterprise*, p. 95.

death, in April 1632, did the charter of Maryland receive the royal seal.

Cecilius Calvert inherited the title and all of his father's estates in England, Ireland and North America. The family's attention now swung south to Maryland, but Baltimore did take the trouble to appoint a new governor of Ferryland in 1633 or 1634, and he was seriously disturbed in 1637 to find that the king was contemplating awarding the island of Newfoundland to a group of courtiers and their associate, David Kirke.[1] His protests had the effect of making Charles I instruct the committee on foreign plantations to be sure that the rights guaranteed to the Calverts in the charter of Avalon were not infringed. Nevertheless in November 1637 a grant was made to Kirke and the rest on the grounds that all the previous patentees, including George Calvert, had abandoned the island. David Kirke proceeded to establish himself in Ferryland, even taking over the house that had been built for the Calvert family. It looked as though the last of the attempts to colonise Newfoundland that had sprung from the charter of 1610 had come to an end. The efforts of the proprietors had been written off as failures.[2]

In fact the Calverts had not given up. Baltimore bided his time and, when the fortunes of the royalist Kirke declined during the civil war, he took the opportunity to renew his claim to the island through an admiralty court suit. The subsequent hearings, held both in London and in Newfoundland, revealed that there were settlers at Ferryland who had been there for thirty years.[3] Not until after the restoration of Charles II was the dispute finally resolved in favour of the Calverts, who continued to maintain their claim to the island well into the eighteenth century.[4]

The charges and counter-charges that Baltimore and Kirke hurled against each other were not as important for their own sake – the institution of lord proprietor had little future in the history of the British colonial empire – as for what the investigation revealed about the character of settlement in Newfoundland. The chartered company of 1610, the Bristol merchants, the gentlemen proprietors had all made their efforts at colonisation, some more seriously and effectively than others. All had passed out of the history of the island. But settlers

---

[1] For a fuller account of the award to Kirke and the subsequent dispute with the Calverts, see Cell, *English enterprise*, pp. 113–16, 121–3.

[2] See below, p. 302.   [3] See below, pp. 300–1.

[4] Petition of Frederick, lord Baltimore, to the privy council, 1753 (Maryland Historical Society, Baltimore, Calvert Papers).

remained. When the men and women who had lived at Ferryland since the early 1620s gave their evidence in 1651 and 1652, they showed no particular affection for George Calvert. They were indifferent as to whether the Calverts or David Kirke won the suit. Indeed they would have preferred to be without any government at all.[1] Their concern was with the business of wresting a living from a harsh environment, and they had won. They had survived, not in any great numbers, surely not in any great comfort. They could do without – in fact they probably did better without – the supervision or the supplies provided by investors in England. Their pursuit of the shore fishery demanded that they should live not clustered in a communal settlement but dispersed along the beaches where they dried their catch. By 1660 the English government reported that about one hundred and fifty families lived scattered in the harbours of the Avalon peninsula.[2]

Considering the money invested, the energy spent, the words printed, it might seem a trifling return. The proprietors themselves can hardly have regarded their experiments as great successes, least of all from the financial point of view. It may be that they had gone into the enterprise with their eyes open and with no great hopes of quick, easy wealth, but few if any were altruistic enough, or rich enough, to be able to ignore the question of profit. As for their other objectives, Vaughan had done little to relieve the agrarian problems of Wales, Falkland and Calvert little to reduce the tensions that would soon kindle revolt in Ireland. But they had demonstrated once again, as did those who invested in the mainland colonies, that the founding of a plantation in the New World was beyond the resources of any one man or any small group. Curiously enough it was Charles I, not generally credited with acute powers of perception, who had pointed this out to Calvert. 'New plantations', he wrote in 1629 '...haue rugged and laborious beginnings, and require much greater meanes in Mannaging them then vsually the power of one priuate subiect can reach into.'[3]

Of course he was right. No individual proprietor from Sir Walter Raleigh onwards had had sufficient resources, nor had any group or chartered company. The needs and demands of settlers continually outran the funds and patience of investors. What in the last resort allowed the early plantations to survive was not so much the funds and leadership of prominent men in England, but the perseverance of those

---

[1] Depositions of James Pratt and Robert Alward, 12 and 29 March 1652 (P.R.O., High Court of Admiralty, Examinations, Instance and Prize, HCA 13/65).
[2] Thomas Povey's report on the state of Newfoundland, 11 May 1660 (B.L., Egerton MS 2395, ff. 263–4).   [3] See below, p. 297.

who had gone to live in the New World, or more often the discovery of a crop such as sugar or tobacco which could be worked with servile labour. It was in the exploitation of a subject labour force that Europeans in the New World showed themselves most ingenious and made the greatest profits.[1] The English colonies in the West Indies or Virginia barely survived until the new plantation economies took root. Among northern settlers those at Massachusetts Bay probably fared best because of the early decision to transfer the whole organisation across the Atlantic and so to free themselves from the control and exaggerated expectations of shareholders in England.

In Newfoundland it did not take long for the faulty assumption that underlay the first settlements to be exposed: settlement could not provide any overwhelming advantage in the exploitation of the fishery. The expenses of collective settlement always exceeded the income gained from fishing, which was not a high profit business. Fishermen, coming to the island in the summer as they had for decades, could work as efficiently and profitably as colonists; indeed, given their greater experience, they must have been far more efficient initially. Nor could they be excluded from the island. It was out of the question that the planters should be given a monopoly. The financial value of the trade aside, the west-country fishing merchants had only to remind the government of the crucial reserve of seamen which their industry supplied in time of war. Economic and strategic factors clearly outweighed the planting interest, even when it was represented by such powerful advocates as a secretary of state or a lord deputy of Ireland.

But when Calvert, Falkland and the rest gave up, settlers remained on the island. That they did so reflected no high-minded concern for the future of English settlement or the national interest, but rather a simple absence of choice. The majority of the men and women who continued to live at Ferryland or Renews or Bristols Hope would have gone out as servants. They had served out their indentures, they had a little land and, while life was not easy, it was probably no harder than existence as labourers, vagrants or orphaned children in England or Ireland would have been. They could fish, grow fodder for their few animals and vegetables for themselves, and trade for other essentials either with the annual fishing fleet or with the steadily growing number of ships from the mainland colonies and the West Indies. By the second half of the seventeenth century Newfoundland was working itself into

---

[1] E. E. Rich, 'Colonial settlement and its labour problems', in *Cambridge economic history*, IV (Cambridge, 1967), edd. E. E. Rich and C. H. Wilson, 302–73.

the interdependent economy of the trans-Atlantic empire as it had earlier slotted into the commercial pattern of England itself. To a limited extent Whitbourne had been proved right. Fishing could not support large-scale settlement, but a combination of fishing with subsistence farming could allow individuals to survive. They could hardly be said to have found 'the golden fleece' as William Vaughan had promised, but then very few inhabitants of the British empire did that.

CHAPTER I

THE FIRST COLONY IN NEWFOUNDLAND

1. 6 October 1610   JOHN GUY TO SIR PERCIVAL WILLOUGHBY[1]

Right worshipfull, yt may please y[ou] to vnderstand, that havinge sett sayle from Kingroade the port of Bristoll The fifte day of Iuly laste, wee were forced with Contrary windes with losse of an ancker, to putt into Myniott[2] from whence departinge the eleventh day of the sayd moneth, we were glad to putt into Milforde, where wee remained vntill the tow and twentieth day of the said moneth: and then proceedinge, the ... day of [A]ugust,[3] we arrived (God be praised) all in safetie in the bay of Conception, in Newfoundland, [in the] harbour here called Cuperres coue; which is a branch of Sammon Coue, and is in the latitude of fortie and seaven degrees, and thirtie and seaven minuites, as I founde by observacion taken on the land. For on the 24th day of September, beinge a hott and most fayre cleare sunshininge day the sunne was elevated aboue the horizon at noone beinge in the meridian, thirtie and eight degrees the declinacion then was in the meridian of London to the southwardes four degrees and twentie minuites but noone beinge here about three hours after, therefore the declinacion was three minuites more so that the Equinoctiall is elevated aboue the horizon here 42 degrees and 23 minuites which deducted out of 90; there resteth 47 degrees and 37 minuites in the elevation of the pole; The windes we had over bound were most southerlie sometimes northerlie and now and then easterly, but very little at west, contrary to the generall opinion of all men, in which manner we haue found it ever since our comminge herevnto All our company was well savinge one which had the smale poxe taken in Bristoll, who is well recovered,[4]

---

[1] Nottingham University, Middleton MSS, Mi X 1/2; printed in D. B. Quinn, ed., *New American World*, 5 vols (New York, 1979), IV, 144–6.   [2] Minehead in Somerset.
[3] The manuscript is torn. A departure date in July differs from the accepted date of early May which is found in Prowse, *History of Newfoundland*, p. 94, and which he implies derives from a Bristol source. I have been unable to find the source in the Bristol archives.
[4] In a letter of 16 May 1611 to John Slany, Guy says that Marmaduke Whittington, who died 15 February 1611, had never really been well since contracting smallpox. Purchas, *Pilgrimes*, XIX, 412.

without that any other was infected with it: for which we are all to
giue greate thankes to God: This harbour is three leagues distance from
Colliers bay to the Northeastward and is preferred by me to beginne
our plantacion before the said Colliers bay, for the goodness of the
harbour the fruitfullnes of the soyle the largenes of the trees, and many
other reasons wee landed here tenne goates, havinge lost one at
Minniott, and one which was killed aboard with the romadginge[1] of
the boate: the residue are all well, stronnge, and lustie, and like well
of the Countrie, except one which was ill aboard, and could not
recover, so that now there are remayninge nine; moreover a boare, and
two sow-piggs, poultrie, cunnies, and pigeons, all which came hether
very well; At our first cominge we saw a Beare now and then, that
haunted this place, makinge accompt the fishermen were gone, but
beinge shott at, we haue not seene nor hard of any these three weeks.
If we had never so many goates here, the would liue as well as in
Fraunce, and be as profitable, and in as little danger of wilde beastes,
for the pasturinge of which sorte of cattle, the land would serue without
riddinge, as also for the Swine//

Att our arrivall here we found the fishinge shippes not departed,
havinge ended there fishinge and expectinge a faire wind, kept in by
easterlie windes, very little Fish hath beene here since our comminge,
some mackerell, and Cods and a greater quantitie of dogfish at Cape
St Fraunces and Bacaleau, after the ship[2] is departed we purpose to send
to fishinge for ou[r] p[ro]vision We haue spent the time since our
arrivall much in landinge of our victualls, and provision, and makinge
safe places for it and our selues to shroude vs in vntill our house coulde
[be] builte, but moste of all in ladinge the shipp backe againe with trees
and sparrs, th[e] quantit[ie w]hereof appeareth in the bill of ladinge
inclosed[3] We haue found the weather ever since our comminge, soe
temperate as in England and rather better, otherwise we should not
haue attended almost alltogeather the ladinge of the shipp, we haue
digged a saw-pitt hard by the sea side, and put a timber house over
it [co]vered with pine bordes; there are tow paire of Sawyers workinge
in it, the pyne trees make good and large bordes and is gentle to saw,
they be better then the deale bordes of norway, there is now a pine
tree at the saw-pitt, that is about tenne feete about at the butt, and thirtie

[1] Used here to mean the rough motion or tossing of the boat, rather than the more
usual meaning of searching or ransacking.
[2] Here and elsewhere in this letter Guy indicates that the colonists came over in a single
ship rather than in the three to which Prowse refers. *History of Newfoundland*, p. 94.
[3] The bill of lading has not survived.

feete longe is eight feete about; our companie is much confirmed in
a good conceipt of this Climate, seeing the weather proue contrary to
the fame, and especially for y^t a fisherman lefte with vs by one Master
Alexander Sanford of Lime that was bound to the Ilands,[1] that had
the disease of the scurvy confirmed in him, to be sent home in the
flemminge,[2] is by our Surgeon very well amended, the scurvy grasse
groweth here hard by vs, I haue seene it and tasted of it since my
commonge hether there is also hearbe yarrow, or nose bleed that is good
for it, likewise the peason of the Country and many other hearbs here
are good for it; the sixte of September the said Master Sanford gaue
me wheate which he found growinge by his stage that was ripe, and
sprang vp of graines of wheate that fell out of the mats used under
the salte which I send you to haue a sight of, He tolde me likewise
of a brooke towardes the south of Reanose, with in tow leagues, that
hath a kind of shelfish, in it which he calleth Clammes in which were
found the last yeare faire and orient pearles, and that some were solde
for 20 crownes, and that this yeare if the fishinge had not proved good
there abouts they woulde haue sought there for more, the same kind
of shelfish tow yeres agoe I saw in Colliers bay[3] which, as also that
to the Southwardes of Renose, I purpose (God willinge) after our house
is built to make search for; such manner of pearls, as the muskles y^t
growe in this harbour yeelde, I send you to haue the sighte of, they
may happen proue better when we dragg for them in deepe water,
The turpentine that commeth from the firr and pine and frankincense
of the spruce is likewise sent, I doubt not but that it will proue that
shippinge may come hether at all times of the yeare, and that the worst
time is when the fishermen come to fishinge, because the drifte Ice from
the northern Countries, at that time only troubleth them, I haue heard
credibly since my comminge heather, That one Master Hutchins of
Salteash was in S$^{[t]}$ Iones harbour on Christmas day laste, The fish of
the sea, the fo[wlls] of th[e] aire, the hills full of woodes, the varietie
of herbes and berries growinge there of there owne accord, the Climate,
the trade of fishinge and many other circumstances are most a[va]ylable
to drawe Inhabitantes to it, The soyle likewise is good, not rockie, in
most place[s] but very good mould, and deepe in some places without
stones, and in other pla[ces] with loose stones amonnge, there want[et]h
nothinge to make a flourishinge Country but cattle and the industry

[1] The West Indies.
[2] A ship built in the Low Countries.
[3] Purchas, *Pilgrimes*, XIX, 405, refers to Guy's visit to the island in 1608, which seems
to have been in preparation for settlement.

of men, without which our Count[ry] would be as bad as this; And seinge God hath ordeyned that the earth of it selfe should not be fruitfull without the sweate of mans browes; it is more to be marveiled at; y^t there is here that which it yeeldeth naturally, then that there is want of what wee haue. Adam havinge the whole earth to make choise of, could not find any place fruitfull without his labour and travell. Seinge all thinges cannot be done at one time, having considered what is most fitt to be set forward this nexte succeddinge yeare, what is my opinion I think good to propound, leaving the resolucion thereof to your good discretions, which is husbandrie, fishinge, and trade by husbandrie and fishinge, the Colonie wilbe soone able to supporte it selfe and by the fruits of the earth, and cattle vndertakers and tennents to take land of the Company wilbe in aboundance drawne hether; when they shall heare of our health, whereof by the grace of God I make no doubt, no more then if we were in England; for fishinge I thinke fitt that a ship of an hundred and fiftie tunns were sent hether, with only thirtie fishermen and foure Spilters,^{1} there are here already eight that are fishermen, and one spilter, and the rest here will serue for land men; boats shalbe made ready by vs now in the winter God willinge, here is a good beach and the fishinge neare, to be assured of a good place to fish and a beach, boates and stage may be worth more then one or tow hundreth poundes yearely for a shipp of that burthen, which the company may be assured of by the plantacion because they shalbe sure to be first here every yeare to take what stage they shall haue need of for there owne vse, There must be greate care had that the fishermen be good, for that is the ground of the voyage for trade, greate shippinge may be imployed betweene Rochall and this place, To bring salte and to returne laden with maste sparrs, and deales, three voyages may easily be made in an yeare, which salte maye be solde to the fishinge shipps before they come out of England, when there is any here in store; who to be assured of it, will gladly giue either fish or trayne for it at the end of the voyage, traine also may be bought of such shipps as goe to the straights or Spaine, but agreement must be made with them for it in England before they beginne there voyage, for then they doe dispose of it, if lead be sent hether in the sacke, for a smale matter it maybe sent hence to any parts of Spaine, or Italy, servinge so fitt for ballaste vnder the fishe If an expert ma[n] to make pitch and tarr were sent hether a doubl[e] commoditie would arise because by that meanes the woodes would be ridd the sooner, when a saw-mill is erected here

^{1} Men to split open the fish and prepare it for drying.

we maye serue the fishinge fl[ee]te w[ith] boords to make fishing boats whereof they bringe good store yearely from England I sawe so[me] of them in Italie, and tooke such particular notic[e the]reof, as I am in good hope with the workmen I haue here to sett vp one. The accoumpt of a glasse-house, I send you by which you maye perceave, that there is nothinge wantinge here to make it but worke men. At the end of the fishinge the next yeare, the number of such if the [c]ompanie as now are here, that will returne home willbe easily, and at better rates [s]upplied by spare men that are to be had out of the fishinge shipps; / A learned and godlie minister would be a greate comforte to vs all and a credit to the plantation. /

One *Master* Peter Coxe of Poole hath beene here coastinge this summer, who when he heard that I was to come and that a patent was obtained, was desirous to haue spoken with me, he hath take hom with him som mine which he found at an Iland called Belile, which, he is in greate hope will proue good; I doubt not but you may informe your selfe of the qualitie thereof; Hereafter at more leasure, I will make diligent search concerninge the mines, how the blommer man[1] came away from the shipp at minyott, I wrote *Master* Holworthy of, and doe expect one by the next shipp that cometh hether, if the yron mine here should not proue of good quantitie or qualitie yet the matter of yron is not to be despaired of; for by means of greate ships going with a fewe men, good may be done by yron mine brought out of England hether as I suppose consideringe that for the extraordinary chardge of the fraighte of the mine wood and all necessaries are to be had for nothinge, and that yron is now aboue fortie shillinges a tonne deerer then it was wont to be custome and imposte free, and for little or no fraighte, because it will serue for good ballaste vnder the fish, 800 tonne of mine will make 200 tonnes of barr yron which will not stand in aboue 400^{li} the fraighte after the rate of 10^s per tonne outwards and for the lading to be had here hence of trees, sparrs, and deales, I doubt not but that will make vp the rest if the fraighte be after the rate of the flemminge fraighte this voyage; – A note of such thinges I thinke fitt should be⋅ sent hether the next yeare I send inclosed./[2] – because all fishermen were vpon departure at our arrivall, and no house built nor any settled habitacion effected, I thought good to forebeare this yeare, and to reserue it for the next yeare, to giue solemne notice in an assemblie, of this our purpose of plantacion and the warrant and

---

[1] Bloomer man, i.e. a man skilled in the working of iron.
[2] The list has been lost.

auctoritie, wherevpon it is grownded, but privately so much was done as no man here was ignorant thereof, and that there is no intent to preiudice any fishermen./[1] When experience of the winter season is made, what is wantinge now in this my letter to giue your worshippes further satisfaction, I hope shalbe in some sort supplied; and in the meane time doe take my leaue, prayinge God to giue his blessinge to this our enterprise and to preserue your worshipps in safetie./

In Cupers Coue the sixte of October 1610

Your worshipps to command

Iohn Guy

[Endorsed:][2] severall very remarkable thinges in y^c new fFound land 14

2. 26 August 1611 AN INVENTORY OF THE PROVISIONS LEFT WITH THE SETTLERS AT CUPIDS COVE[3]

Vicesimo Sexto Die Augustii

Anno domini 1611

An Inventorie of what provision is Left at the English Coloni in Cupies Cove in the Newfound Lande[4]

Imprimis	26 buttes & pipes of bread also 4 dry fates of bread[5]
Item	14 pipe of beare/
Item	3 kinterkins[6] of butter/
Item	2 barrills of meale & one of oatemeal
Item	24 Cheeses
Item	1 barill & one kinterkin of aquavitie
Item	of graine 10 bushells of Wheate 10 of Ryee & 10 of barlye
Item	of beefe 3 hogsheades & 1 barell, 5 barells of Irishe beefe
Item	of porke 7 barrills & 1 kinterkin/
Item	6 sides of bacon

[1] The company's instructions to Guy, 26 May 1610, had required him to read both the charter and his own commission to the assembled fishermen to reassure them that their rights in the fishery would not be curtailed. Notebook of company records (Nottingham University, Middleton MSS, Mi X 1/1, ff. 12–14).

[2] Sir Percival Willoughby's papers on Newfoundland were endorsed and numbered by his grandson, the naturalist and fellow of the Royal Society, Francis Willoughby (1653–72).

[3] Nottingham University, Middleton MSS, Mi X 1/3.

[4] No figures are available on the number of settlers who wintered at Cupids in 1611–12, but there were probably no more than forty at the most.

[5] The capacity of some containers is known precisely; a pipe was the equivalent of two hogsheads or half a tun. A dryfat was a large vessel used for dry goods.

[6] A small barrel.

Item	3 barrell of Candells
Item	1 pipe of Canarie Wyne & 3 terces[1] of Rochell Wyne/
Item	1 puncheon[2] of viniger
Item	3 peces of ordinance/ minions[3]
Item	2 barrells of pouder
Item	30 Muskettes & Calivers[4] & 3 fowling peces
Item	12 bandileroes[5]
Item	12 Whipp sawes & 2 tenant sawes & fower hand sawes/
Item	3 brasse pottes 2 pannes 2 kittells & one posnett/[6]
Item	8 spades & 25 shovells 8 pickaxes and Mattockes/
Item	12 hathchets & 6 axes
Item	4 crowes of Iron
Item	tooles belonginge to the Cooper
Item	the tooles belonging to a smyth
Item	1 payre of blomers bellis[7]
Item	an Iron stove
Item	all the tooles belonginge to a sawier
Item	one still
Item	halfe a tunne of Iron/ & one C of steele
Item	one C of Leade
Item	all the Carpenters tooles accordinge to their notes/
Item	a Massones tooles accordinge to his note
Item	ii dredges/[8]
Item	one drume & one flagge & 2 C of mach
Item	bedes & boulsters fifteene
Item	ii crosbowes iii longe bowes with their arrowes/
Item	20 Rugges & 40 blankettes
Item	the Chest of lynen brought from England
Item	a kinterkin of pewter/
Item	60 shirts 16 capps 9 wastcoastes 12 Iackettes 5 payre of bretches & 5 paire of stockinges
Item	6 sythes
Item	50 payre of shooes & 3 paire of bootes
Item	one barrill of pitch
Item	an ould kedger[9] & 8 ould roades[10]

[1] Equal to one-third of a pipe, or forty-two gallons old-wine measure.
[2] A large cask. [3] A small kind of ordnance.
[4] Light muskets or harquebuses.
[5] Belts worn to help support a musket, with cases containing charge.
[6] A small, footed cooking pot.
[7] Bellows for the iron smithy. [8] Drag nets used for taking oysters.
[9] A small anchor or grapnel. [10] Rodes, or ropes, attached to a boat-anchor.

Item	13 netts & two saines[1]
Item	one coveringe of heare cloath & one of Canvace/
Item	one boult & halfe of Canvace
Item	23 boates sailes
Item	6 newe boates & one skiffe
Item	1 dozen of kipp nett irons[2] hookes, leades, lynes/
Item	2 payre of Cann hookes/[3]
Item	1 dozen of boates rothers/[4]
Item	1 dozen of stackkettes & 2 dozen of bread boxes/
Item	the shipps stage Cloath
Item	one dozen[li] of [sic]
Item	1 dozen randds[5] of trayne
Item	1 pestell & Morter/
Item	10 pipes & one *hogshead* of traine of the vineards[6] beinge not full/
Item	8 *hogsheades* sent in the W I[7] being the Companies parte/
Item	ij M of Wett fish
Item	10 tunnes of sault
Item	11 M of drye fish
Item	one great grindstone/
Item	6 pipes of traine in our stage
Item	paire of Iron anderons
Item	one bible & one booke of the generall practise of phisick/
Item	one boare, 1 sowe with 9 little piggs
Item	paire of tame pigeons/ & poultry
Item	6 goates
Item	1 black rabett/

[*Endorsed*:][8] The Inventorie of thinges remayning in Newfoundland 26 Aug: Anno 1611

21

---

[1] Large fishing nets.   [2] Tackle used in fishing.
[3] A contrivance for slinging a cask by the end of its staves, consisting of a rope or chain with a flat hook at either end.
[4] Rudders.   [5] Large casks.
[6] The ship the *Vineyard* which had been sent out to the island to fish for the company. Purchas, *Pilgrimes*, xix, 416.
[7] Perhaps an abbreviation for the name of a ship.
[8] By Francis Willoughby, F.R.S.

3. 1612 JOHN GUY'S JOURNAL OF A VOYAGE TO TRINITY BAY[1]

Discoverie made by John Guy in Newfoundland in anno 1612 in and about 48: degrees of Latitude towards the pole Articke:[2]

A Iournall of the voiadge of discoverie made in a barke builte in Newfoundland called the Indeavour, begunne the 7 of october 1612, & ended the 25th of November following: By John Guy of Bristow:[3]

The Iornall of our voiadge in the Indeavour begunne the 7 of October 1612.

October

7 This night by sayling & rowing we came to Harbor de Grace as farre in as the Pirates forte,[4] wheare the banke shippe roade,[5] wheare we remayned vntill the 17th day of the sayde moneth, & in the meane time did bring the banke shippe a shoare, land the salte vpon the higheste parte of the grownd thereaboutes, putting yt vp in a round heape, & burning of yt to preserve yt. Two anchors, & two old Iunkes[6] we lefte vpon the beache. The quantetie of salt was about fifteene tonnes.

17 We departed from Harbor de Grace, & that nighte came to Greene bay,[7] bothe the barke & the shalloppe. Theare weare in the barke fowerteene, viz.

1. Iohn Guy.
2. master Teage.
3. master Groote.[8]
4. George Whittington.[9]
5. Fraunces Tipton.
6. Edwarde Perrie.

---

[1] Lambeth Palace, MS 250, ff. 406–12v. Printed in Quinn, *New American world*, IV, 152–7.

[2] Written in a different hand from the journal itself.

[3] 'By John Guy of Bristow' written in a different hand from the journal.

[4] Peter Easton had made Harbour Grace his headquarters during the summer of 1612.

[5] A French ship from which Easton had seized the crew. Crout's journal, 1612–13 (Nottingham University, Middleton MSS, Mi X 1/66, f. 3). For details of the raid, see P.R.O., Privy Council Registers, PC 2/27, f. 41v; P.R.O., High Court of Admiralty, Examinations, Oyer and Terminer, HCA 1/4, f. 314; HCA 13/42, 19 Nov. 1612, Isebrande Dirrickson; High Court of Admiralty, Exemplifications, HCA 14/42, nos. 18, 47.

[6] Ropes or cables.

[7] Bay de Verde.

[8] Henry Crout, whose journal contains an account of this expedition and a great deal of information on the weather throughout the winter of 1612–13. Nottingham University, Middleton MSS, Mi X 1/66; printed in Quinn, *New American world*, IV, 157–78.

[9] Perhaps a relative of the Marmaduke Whittington who had died at Cupids on 15 February 1611. Purchas, *Pilgrimes*, XIX, 412.

7. Iames Holworthy.[1]
8. Iohn Crowder.
9. Iames Babacucke.
10. Georg Davies.[2]
11. Thomas Rowlie.[3]
12. George Lane.
13. George Vaughen.
14. Thomas Tayler.

And in the shallope five: viz.

1. George Wichalle.
2. Wm Hadden.[4]
3. Barthlemew Percevall.[5]
4. George Frewin.
5. Samuell Butler.

18 At two a clocke in the morning we put out of Greene bay, the wind North, we spent all that day in the barke to double the Grates[6] to goe into Trinitie bay, but could not, & soe late at nighte come backe to Greene bay againe. The shalloppe proceeded, & that nighte attayned vnto a harbour of the South side of Trinitie bay called Hartes content

19 We put out againe, the wind NW. a stiffe gale. We crossed Trinitie bay, & came to a roade vnder the land good for a...[tear in MS.] westerlie, & Northerlie windes, theare was harde by v[s ane] Iland, wheareby we tooke yt to be that which is called S. Catalinaes,[7] yt lyeth from Baccaleau NNW. Heere we roade without being able to goe

21 ashoare for want of a boate, vntill the 21th day, when at 4 of the clocke in the afternoone the wind came Northerlie, & soe we put

---

[1] Perhaps related to Richard Holworthy, a Bristol merchant and Newfoundland company member who was very active in the company's affairs.

[2] Davies, a cooper, died at Cupids on 27 January 1613. Crout's journal, 1612–13 (Nottingham University, Middleton MSS, Mi X 1/66, f. 11v).

[3] Son of Roger Rowley, a Shropshire gentleman and member of the Haberdashers company. By 1619 Rowley had succeeded Crout as Sir Percival Willoughby's principal agent in Newfoundland and had received, together with William Hannam also of Shropshire, half of Willoughby's land on the island. *DCB*, I; Cell, *English enterprise*, p. 76; indenture between Sir Percival Willoughby and Rowley and Hannam, 1618 (Nottingham University, Middleton MSS, Mi X 1/64).

[4] Or Hatton, one of the apprentices sent over by Willoughby in 1612. In April 1613 he and Robert Rossell wrote complaining of conditions at the colony and particularly of Guy's harshness. Hatton returned to England in August 1613. Nottingham University, Middleton MSS, Mi X 1/22, 24.

[5] Pearson, an employee on Willoughby's Nottinghamshire estate to which he returned in 1613, disillusioned with prospects for settlement. He wrote his own account of his adventures on the expedition in a letter to Willoughby, 2 April 1613 (*ibid.*, Mi X 1/21).

[6] Grates Point.

[7] Catalina Harbour; the island is perhaps Green Island.

to sea to get vp into Trinitie bay, & sayled all that nighte vntill midnighte with our mainesaile out, but after taken in vntill day. Our course was SW & SWBS moste commonlie, & sometimes S. & SBE to fetch the Souther side of the bay. When it was daylighte, we found our selves neerer the south side, then to the Northside, about two leagues farther vp in the bay then Hartes Content. By twelve of the 22 clocke the same day, we came to the Harbour[1] that the way overland from Avon[2] in the bay of Conception is marked vnto, wheare our shallope came happelie vnto vs from Hartes Content. This Harbour is [called] now by vs Mounteagle bay. Yt lyeth in S. & theare is ane Iland at the entrance, wheare we fownde good stoare of scurvie grasse. 24 Heere we stayed vntil the 24ᵗʰ day, & then both the barke & shalloppe proceeded partelie by sayling, & partelie by rowing vnto a harbour in the South bottome of Trinitie bay, which now is called by vs Savage Harbour.[3] Heere we fownd some savage housen, a holberte,[4] a wooden target, & small coffins[5] made of the barke of trees & a broad way leading from the seaside throughe the woodes.

26 The 26 day being about to departe heerehence, & under sayle, contrarie windes put vs in againe, & then I sent some to follow the said way to see how farre yt went, & wheather they could see any savages. Who within one houre returning, declared that they saw a great freshe water lake, wheather the said way did lead them, & two fires, one vpon ane Iland in the said lake & ane other vpon the side of the lake.[6] Whearevpon Iohn Guy, with fourteene more went to the said lake, wheare they had sight of the said fires, & of a canoa with two rowing in her in the said lake, and soe goeing through the woodes with what silence was possible, alongste the lake side at twilighte, they came within halfe a mile of the place of one of the said fires, wheare remayning two houres within nighte after they proceeded, & came to the said place, wheare they fownde noe savages, but three of theire housen, whearof two had bin latelie vsed, in one of the which the hearth was hot. The savages weare gone to the said Iland, wheather we could

---

[1] Hopeall?

[2] Probably modern Avondale.

[3] Probably Dildo Arm. Crout's journal mentions the presence of three islands in the harbour (Nottingham University, Middleton MSS, Mi X 1/66, f. 3v).

[4] A halberd. For a description and sketch of the spears used by the Beothuk for hunting, see Howley, *The Beothucks*, pp. 247-8 and sketch no. viii, facing p. 248. Crout's journal also mentions an arrow (Nottingham University, Middleton MSS, Mi X 1/66, f. 3v); and see Howley, *The Beothucks*, plates xx–xxii.   [5] Boxes.

[6] The presence of the lake and the island tends to confirm the identification of 'Savage Harbour' as Dildo Arm.

not goe for want of a boate. We fownd theare a copper kettle kepte
very brighte, a furre gowne, some seale skinnes, ane old sayle, & a
fishing reele. Order was taken that nothing should be diminished, &
because the savages should know that some had bin theare, every thing
was removed out of his place, & broughte into one of the cabines, and
laid orderlie one upon the other, & the kettle hanged over them,
whearin thear was put some bisket, & three or fower amber beades.[1]
This was done to beginne to winne them by fayre meanes. This time
of the yeare they live by hunting, for we fownd twelve stages hoofes
that weare latelie killed.[2] A little peece of fleshe was broughte away,
which was fownde to be a beaver cod,[3] which is foorthcoming to be
seene. Theire housen theare weare nothing but poules set in a rownde
forme, meeting all togeather alofte, which they cover with deere
skinnes.[4] They are about tenne foote broade, and in the middle they
make theire fire. One of them was covered with a sayle, which they
had gotten from some Christian. Soe all thinges in this manner lefte,
everyone returned by the moonelighte, goeing by the banke of the lake
vnto the entraunce of the made way, & a little before they came
theather they passed by a new savadge house almoste finished, which
was made in a square forme with a small roofe & soe came to the barke.

27 The nexte day we put foorth a flag of truce being a white flag.
The lake is about a mile from any parte of the harborough. Theare
issueth out of yt a very great brooke enough to drive three fordges
with the currant. Theare was seene at theire cabanes showes made of
Deere, & seale skinnes very artificiallie. They have two kind of oares,
one is about fower foote long of one peece of firre, the other is about
10 foote long made of two peeces, one being as long, big & rownd
as a halfe pike made of beeche wood, which by likelihood they made
of a biskaine oare,[5] th'other is the blade of the oare, which is let into
th'end of the long one slit, & whipped very stronglie. The shorte one
they use as a paddle, & thother as ane oare.

30 The 30 without any further business with the savadges, we
departed thence to the northerne side of Trinitie bay, and anchored all
that nighte vnder ane Iland.[6]

---

[1] Crout says that they took two or three children's shoes (Nottingham University,
Middleton MSS, Mi X 1/66, f. 4).

[2] The hooves of caribou which would have been saved to make glue.

[3] The inguinal sac of the beaver, from which *castoreum*, a substance used in European
medicine, was obtained.

[4] See Howley, *The Beothucks*, p. 245, and sketch vi.

[5] I.e. an oar used by Basque fishermen.   [6] Bull Island?

31 The 31th we rowed vnto ane harboure which now is called Alhallowes,[1] which hath adioyning vnto yt very high land from whence was seene a great bay which ranne into the land North. Yt was to the neereste place about 3 leagues over land SW. & some parte of yt did lie N.W. This muste needes be the bay of Placentia.

November

1 The barke & shalloppe put out of the said harborough to discoover bay within the head land which now is called the Elbow & being foorth, the shalloppe was sent before to see wheare theare was any harborough theare, & the barke returned to Alhallowes. Word was brought that theare was noe harborough, but a sandie banke for a league of a gray colour, & that a brooke came foorth apparantlie in one place, but that theare went soe great a sea as they could not get a shoare. They gave a good reporte of the likelihood of the place to yeeld good land. When they weare a league of theare was not fower fadome water.

3 The 3 day we departed from Alhallowes, & went Northwards towards a sound, which we weare in good hope woulde bring them to Placentia & theare in a harborough one the wester side of the sound we anchored. This lieth 7 leagues from Alhallowes North within a league of this harbour. In the waye from Alhallowes lieth ane other harbour, that hath before the entraunce a good space of two rockes. Theare our boate saw nine savage housen, vsed by them in their coasting: the sound heere is about two miles broad.

4 The 4th we put forward in the sound. The firste reach lieth NBW. westerlie one league, from thence NNW. halfe a league & from thence WNW. one league, wheare the sound did end. In that place was fownd eighte or nine savage housen in severall places, and a way cut into the woodes, which being prosequuted, yt was fownd to lead directlie to a harborough in the bay of Placentia distant onlie two miles W. which harbour in Placentia bay is now called Passage harbour. A river came vnto yt from the NNE.[2] they which went fownd theare fishe hookes a small cooper kettle, a fishing line & a lead, a target, a staffe & a French basket, but noe shew of housen. In two houres & a halfe twelue of the companie which went returned. Heere was fownd a new canoa

---

[1] Perhaps Great Mosquito Cove in Bull Arm, which is about five miles overland from Placentia Bay.

[2] Probably the bottom of Bull Arm looking towards Come by Chance in Placentia Bay. At this point the distance between Placentia and Trinity bays is about two miles. The 'river' would be Come by Chance brook.

ashoare, which now remayneth in the woodes at Pernecam,[1] by reason
of stormie wheather yt could not be broughte any further.

5   The fifte day Iohn Guy & tenne with him went from the barke
by land to the top of a very high hill, to take a full view of the bay
of Placentia, and all the contrey about. In their way they waded over
the river that runneth into Passage harborough, yt is five times greater
then any other river or brooke yet seane to the Southwardes: because
the foggienes of the weather hindred the prospecte they remayned
theare all nighte. About sunset yt cleered up from the SSW to the
Northwardes by the weste, & then the wester side of the bay of
Placentia was seene to lie W. WSW. & SWBW, & SW. About 10
leagues of theare was ane open into the maine sea, noe land appearing,
in which sound theare weare two small Ilandes in a righte line; SWBS
theare was land by which I thinke that all that lyeth betweene the said
open, & Cape St. Lawrence, which is the Cape one the wester side of
the bay of Placentia are Ilandes & that Passage harbour before spoaken
of is in the bottome of the bay of Placentia.

6   The 6 day they returned to the barke from the high hill, & about
two of the clocke in the afternoone, about two houres after the return,
theare was perceived a fire in the sownd a mile of, wheareupon all the
companie repayred aboorde, because yt could be noe other then the
doeing of savages. Presentlie two canoaes appeared, & one man alone
comming towardes vs with a flag in his hand of a wolfe skinne, shaking
yt, & making a lowde noice, which we tooke to be for a parlie,
whearevpon a white flag was put out & the barke & shallope rowed
towardes them: which the savages did not like of, & soe tooke them
to theire canoaes againe, & weare goeing away. Whearevpon the barke
whearyed onto them & flourished the flag of truce, & came to anker,
which pleased them, & then they stayed. Presentlie after the shalloppe
landed master Whittington with the flag of truce, who went towardes
them. Then they rowed into the shoare with one canoa, th'other
standing aloofe of, & landed two men, one of them having the white
skinne in his hand, & comming towardes master Whittington, the savage
made a loude speeche, & shaked the skinne, which was awnsweared
by master Whittington in like manner & as the savage drew neere he
threw downe the white skinne into the grownde. The like was done
by master Whittington. Wheareupon both the savages passed over a

[1] Perlican.

little water streame towardes master Whittington daunsing leaping, & singing, & comming togeather the foremoste of them, presented vnto him a chaine of leather full of small perwincle shelles, a spilting knife,[1] & a feather that stucke in his heare. The other gave him ane arrow without a head, & the former was requited with a linnen cap, & a hand towell, who put presentlie the linnen cap vpon his head, and to the other he gave a knife. And after hand in hand they all three did sing, & daunce. Vpon this one of our companie called Fraunces Tipton went a shoare, vnto whom one of the savages came running: & gave him a chaine such as is before spoaken of, who was gratefied by Fraunces Tipton with a knife, & a small peece of brasse. Then all fower togeather daunced, laughing, & makeing signes of ioy, & gladnes, sometimes strikeing the breastes of our companie & sometymes theyre owne. When signes was made vnto them that they should be willing to suffer two of our companie more to come one shoare, for two of theires more to be landed, & that bread, & drinke should be brought ashoare, they made likewise signes that they had in their canoaes meate also to eate. Vpon this the shalloppe rowed aboorde and broughte Iohn Guy, & master Teage a shoare, who presented them with a shirte, two table napkins & a hand towell, giving them bread, butter & reasons of the sun to eate, & beere, & aquavitae to drinke. And one of them blowing in the aquavitae bottle yt made a sound, which they fell all into a laughture at. After master Croote, & Iohn Crouder came ashoare, whom they went to salute giveing them shell chaines, who bestowed gloves vpon them. One of the savages that came laste ashoare came walking with his oare in his hand, & seemed to have some command over the reste, & behaved him selfe civillie. For when meate was offred him he drew of his mitten from his hand, before he would receive yt, & gave ane arrow for a present, without a head, who was requited with a dozen of pointes.[2] After they had all eaten, & drunke, one of them went to theire canoa, & broughte vs deeres fleshe dryed in the smoake, or wind, and drawing his knife from out of his necke he cut every man a peece, & yt savoured very well. At the firste meeting, when signes weare made of meate to eate one of the savadges presentlie came to the banke side, & pulled vp a roote, & gave yt to master Whittington. Which t'other savage perceiving to be durtie, tooke yt out of his hand, & went to the water to washe yt, & after devided yt among the fower. Yt tasted very well. He that came ashoare with the oare in his hand went, & tooke the white skinne, that they hayled us with, & gave yt

---

[1] A knife used for splitting fish.   [2] Nails or spikes.

to master Whittington, & presentlie after they did take our white flag with them in the Canoa, and made signes vnto vs that we should repaire to our barke, & soe they put of for yt was almoste nighte.

In the two canoaes theare weare eighte men, yf none weare women (for commonlie in every canoa theare is one woman). They are of a reasonable stature, of ane ordinarie middle sise; they goe bareheaded, wearing theire haire somewhat long, but rounded, they have noe beards. Behind they have a great locke of haire platted with feathers, like a hawke's lure with a feather in yt standing uprighte by the crowne of the head, & a small locke platted before. A shorte gowne or cassocke made of stag skinnes, the furre innermost that came downe to the middle of theire leg, with sleves to the middle of their arme, & a beaver skinne about theire necke, was all their apparell, save that one of them had showes & mittens, soe that all went bare legged, & moste barefoot.[1] They are full dyde of a blacke colour, the colour of their haire was diverse, some blacke, some browne, & some yellow, their faces something flat & broad, red with okir, as all theire apparell is, & the rest of their bodie. They are broad breasted, & bould, & stand very uprighte.

Theire canoaes are about 20 foote long, & 4 foote & a halfe broad in the middle alofte, & for their keele, & timbers they have thinne lighte peeces of dry firre rended, as yt weare lathes and in steede of boorde they vse the vtter birche barke which is thinne & hath many foldes, sowed togeather with a thread made of a small roote quartered, they will carrie fower persons well, & way not one hundred weight. They are made in forme of a new moone, stemme, & sterne alike & equallie distant from the greateste breadth. From the stemme & sterne theare riseth a yarde highe a lighte thinne staffe whyped about with small rootes, which they take hold by to bring the canoa ashoare. That serveth in steede of ropes and a harbour, for every place is to them a harboorugh, wheare they can goe ashoare them selves they take a land with them theire canoa, & will neaver put to sea but in a calme, or very fayre weather. In the middle the canoa is hygher a great deale then in the bow & quarter. They be all bearing from the keele to the porteles, not with any circular line but with a righte line. They had made a tilte[2] with a sayle, that they got from some Christian, & pitched a dozen poules in the grownd neere, one which weare hanged divers furres, & chaines made of shelles, which at that instant we fell not in

---

[1] Compare this description of Beothuk clothing with Whitbourne's assertion (below, p. 154), that they went naked.   [2] A tent.

the reckoning to what intent yt was done, but after yt came to our mindes as heereafter you shall perceive.[1]

7 The 7th day[2] we spent in washing, & in beginning a house to shelter vs when we should come theather heereafter, vpon a small Iland[3] of about five acres of grownd which is Ioyned to the maine with a small beache. For any bartering with the savages theare can not be a fitter place.

[8] Yt beganne to freeze, & theare was thinne Ice over the sound & because we heard nothing more of the savages we beganne to returne out of the sound, & comming to the place which the savages had made two dayes before the fire in, we fownd all thinges remayning theare, as yt was when we parted, viz. ane old boate sayle, three, or fower, shell chaines, about twelve furres of beavers moste, a foxe skinne, a saple skinne, a bird skinne, & ane old mitten set everye one vpon a severall poule, wheareby we remayned satisfied fullie that they weare broughte theather of purpose to barter with vs, & that they would stand to our curtesie to leave for yt what we should thinke good. Because we weare not furnished with fit things for to trucke, we tooke onlie, a beaver skinne, a saple skinne, & a bird skinne, leaving for them, a hatchet, a knife & fower needles threaded. Master Whittington had a paire of sezers which he lefte theare for a small beaver skinne, all the reste we lefte theare vntouched and came that nighte to the harbour that we weare in at our entring, which we call Flagstaffe Harbour,[4] because we fownd theare the flagstaffe throwen by the savages away. Thease savages by all likelihood weare animated to come vnto vs, by reason that we tooke nothing from them at Savage bay, & some of them may be of those which dwell theare. For in noe other place wheare we weare, could we perceive any tokens of any aboade of them at this point.

10 We departed from Flagstaffe harbour, & came that nighte to a harbour called Hartes content.

11, 12 The wind being NE, & the snow contynewing all day kepte vs in Hartes content.

13 The barke, & shalloppe departed from Hartes content. Before nighte the barke doubled the Grates,[5] & sayled betweene Baccaleau, & the maine into the Bay of Conception, and as they sayled they saw

---

[1] The Beothuk seem to have been more familiar with the fur trade than the English, presumably from contacts with the French.

[2] According to Crout the first snow of the winter fell on this day (Nottingham University, Middleton MSS, Mi X 1/66, f. 6).

[3] McKay Island?   [4] Hopeall?

[5] Grates Point.

above a dozen stages vpon the bare hilles neere Greene Bay.[1] After seaven houres turning in the bay, we boare roome with Greene bay to stay for the shalloppe, and at 11 of the clocke at nighte we anchored in the Eastermoste roade of Greene Bay.

14 We fownd by waying of one anchor, that the rockes had worne a sunder our hawser that we roade by, for the anchor, & twentie fadome of the hawser was lefte behind, for that & by reason of a sea which came into the roade out of the South, we soughte to recover th'other roade of Greene bay: which as we weare about to doe, the shalloppe came sayling out of Trinitie bay without the canoa, which they had towed from Truce sound vnto Old Pernecam, wheare foule weather forced them to land yt: & the sea was so wroughte as they could not come aboord vs.[2] We in the barke because we could not double the head of Greene Bay, stoode to the offing, and standing backe againe, perceiving that by reason of sagging in[3] with the smalnes of the winde we went to leewarde, we stoode out againe, & being foorth in the offing yt blew soe much wind at South as we weare forced to hull the moste part of that nighte.

15 This day when yt cleered vp, we saw land to the NW. of vs, which because we imagined that we had gone to the Northward by hulling,[4] we made accompte that yt had bin parte of the land one the Northside of Trinitie bay: this nighte also we weare forced to hull by reason of the fiercenes of the wind.

16 This day we saw the land againe, & still accompting yt to be betweene Bonaviste, & the Horselips we wroughte thereafter, sometimes goeing S. & SSW & SBE as the wind would permit vs, & sometimes NW to get neere the land.

17 Yt was a fog & we could not see above a mile from vs, vntill noone we went SSW. & then, being desirous to get neare the land to make yt to be sure wheare we weare we went NW. & weare within hearing of the rut of the shoare before we could see yt, and presentlie yt pleased god to send vs a cleere, the wind WNW & then we fownd our selves something to the Southward of Renoose. Then knowing that yt was the currant that carried vs the firste nighte that we hulled, to the Southwarde, and that the land which we saw alwayes was to the South of Cape S[t] Fraunces, yt was godes doeing that we went not to the South of Cape Razo.[5]

---

[1] Bay de Verde. [2] As Guy discovered later the shallop sank; see below, p. 87.
[3] Drifting off course. [4] Taking in all the sails and tying down the helm.
[5] Cape Race.

18 Being in the offing from Cape Broile, a SE. wind came & broughte vs to Torrebay, wheare we ancored at nighte.

19 We remayned heere expecting a fayre wind, & having noe boate with vs we made meanes by oares, & a hogshead to get some of our companie ashoare.

20 About 2 of the clocke in the morning the wind came to SE. wheareupon we departed from Torrebay, but before day the wind came to SW., & soe weare faire to recover Greene Bay againe in the roade which we lefte. This nighte was ane exceeding great storme, the wind WNW.

21 We put foorth of Greene Bay, choosing rather to continew turning in the bay, then to ride in such a roade, to the hazard of the losse of all our anchors.

22, 23 We got into the roade of great Belile, yt blowing a fierce gale of wind at W.N.W.

24 About Midnighte the 24th day the wind being SBE., we departed from Belile, but before we had proceeded as farre as the end of the said Iland, the wind came to the SW. & WSW., & blew soe much as we could beare noe sayle, but lay a hull vntill day, in doubte to be put out of the bay, & makeing accompte that we had great good hap, yf we could recover the roade from whence we came: and while we weare thus perplexed, the wind came to the North and broughte vs

25 in safetie god be praysed to Cupers Cove by tenne of the clocke in the forenoone the 25th day of this moneth of November, wheare we vnderstoode that the shalloppe which we lefte in Greene bay eleaven dayes agoe was caste away the morrow after, but all the men saved, who put the sayle, & theire apparell in safetie ashoare, & came homeward by land to Carbonera[1] in 8 dayes, having nothing to eate, but what they could find by the way, & from thence came in safetie home one sunday the 22th of this moneth.[2] Presentlie after the barke was arrived the wind was westerlie:/

---

[1] Carbonear.

[2] According to Crout the five men in the boat lost both their food and clothing. For three days they wandered in the area of Bay de Verde until they decided to follow the coastline home. They lived on roots and berries until they came to Carbonear where they found some fish left on one of the stages and a boat which they sailed to Cupids. Crout says they reached the colony on 23 November (Nottingham University, Middleton MSS, Mi X 1/66, f. 6v).

4. 10 April 1613 HENRY CROUT TO SIR PERCIVAL WILLOUGHBY[1]

in Cupers Cove the 10th of aprill 1613

Right Worshipp*full* my dewtie alwaies remembered: it may please you to vnderstand that yours the 24th of november I haue Re*ceived* by m*aste*r bollinge[2] the 29th of march by whom I Receaved some apparell for m*aste*r Thomas and some other small things as p*e*r this inclossed note shall apeare[3] for I Re*ceive*d not any letter for the receipt of it: vnderstanding ther was a young man came for aprentice and at barnstable he quitted them and caried certaine letters w*i*th him // ther fore I fear me ther wilbe somthing wanntting for the things weare taken out of the hampper by m*aste*r bollinge and put into his Chest because they wear all waitte at seaye: the Barke hauing verie Fowell weather and in some dannger as he said it was put into barnstable to newe Fitt his shipp: w*hi*ch cost him much money & m*aste*r governer told me he had Re*ceive*d a kind letter from you: I do insure you he doth respect m*aste*r Thomas verie much and I make no dowte god sending him well home you shall see a great alterration in him: I do not knowe yo*u*r mynd howe long you do determyne that he should stay but if he stay vntill the next year[4] he will wantt mor p*ro*vition of clothes and lynnen & we wear driven verie neer nowe against easter both for clothes and lynnen // before this came he had but one suett w*hi*ch was Forced to vse everie daie // and band*e*s he wants very much: he brought but 3 out of England and one old one // I do writt in regard I should be sorowe to see him wantt for such things knowing some hear will take notice of it thinking he is not respected of: and if it be yo*u*r pleasure he shall stay some butter and cheese may do him great pleasure the next wintter keeping it to him selfe // the pootte of Butter we brought the last year hath stood vs in great stead // this wintter hath bin verie hard ther hath died abowe 70 of our goates and many of our Pigg*e*s

---

[1] Nottingham University, Middleton MSS, Mi X 1/23, 59. Damaged. The letter is written on two large sheets of paper, each of which has been folded in two. The sheets had become separated by some time in the seventeenth century when Francis Willoughby endorsed and numbered each one. When the collection was numbered again in the 1950s, each sheet was given its own number.

[2] Master of the *Hope* of London, the first relief ship to reach the colony that spring. Crout's journal, 1612–13 (Nottingham University, Middleton MSS, Mi X 1/66, f. 16).

[3] The enclosure is now lost.

[4] Thomas Willoughby and Crout left Newfoundland in August 1613. Crout to Sir Percival Willoughby, August 1613 (Nottingham University, Middleton MSS, Mi X 1/24). In this letter Crout describes a journey to Trinity Bay which he had made in July 1613 to try to re-establish contact with the Beothuk.

and all our Cattell except one so Farr as we knowe except therbe any
living in the woodes: indeed yet [sic] was a great over sight in sending
over so many before such tyme as ther might haue bin better provition
made for them: to procure first to see wher corne will growe wherby
the may chance some strawe for they will looke for houssinge in the
wintter tyme: as I know the bese in other cold countrie // but ther
is no dowte by god help ground being once Ridd that in many places
yet will prove verie well I Iuge especially Rie // as this summer we
shall see the triall of wheat and Rie // for in our absence acoasting
ther was both sowen // and yet [sic] doth begine to apear vpp verie
fine[1] and I do insure you allso any kind of rootes will prove exceeding
well: as this year we had verie good cabbage and tornnaps growen:
but for the tornnops they are an exceeding good for the scarby[2] //
by triall yt hath recovered many of our sicke men: but we had eight
of [the] companie died[3] before any man had the experience of it which
roo[tes are] to be had all the winnter // and we had at one tyme some
6 weekes s[ince] more then halfe of our companie verie sicke and lame
in [this] desease: so rasing ther Rootes eatting them raw in very short
ty[me] yet did help them all // so they are excellent for that propose
and will serve for meat allso: they do eatt verie dilligate[4] [when] they
do [cook them?]

I hopp at master governer retorne from england to bring you a full
resolution of all bussines: and the estatt of the countrie for so Farr as
we haue coasted: which this Springe the govern[e]r was determyned
we should coast with our penice all round abowte the land: but his
going home hath disapointted all that busines except it be after his
retorne which wilbe somthing latte:[5] therfor you may not looke as
yet to haue a Full resolution and knowledgement of the countrie except
we might haue a boote to coast withall // which as yet sethince our
Comynge could procure none // but nowe I hoop to performe both

[1] By August Crout was reporting that the grain had grown well but, because it had
been sown too late, had failed to ripen. He recommended that in future seed be sown in
August rather than in October or November. *Ibid.*

[2] Scurvy.

[3] The dead were George Davies, cooper; Edward Garton, one of Willoughby's
apprentices; Edward Hartland, tailor, apprenticed to the company; John Toncks, a mason
receiving wages; a man whom Crout calls simply Willes and about whom he supplies no
details; Tobias, apprentice, from Ireland; Matthew Griggs, turner, receiving wages;
William·Wattes, carpenter, receiving wages. All died between 27 January and 11 March
1613. On 15 February Crout recorded that twenty to twenty-two colonists were sick.
Journal (Nottingham University, Middleton MSS, Mi X 1/66, ff. 11v, 12, 13, 13v, 14,
14v, 15).   [4] Delicate.

[5] Guy left for England in the *Hope* on 10 April 1613. Although Crout expected him
back by the end of the summer, he apparently did not return. Journal (Nottingham
University, Middleton MSS, Mi X 1/66, f. 16v); Cell, *English enterprise*, p. 71.

your & master Slany desire this sommer: therfore ther is no tyme
neglicted by me in performance of that bussynes // and to do anything
by land I could not // wanttinge verie much a compase diall to go
thorough the woodes // I wrott vnto your worship for one or 2 of
them // they are the necessaries thinges we want both for the land and
for a boote Therfore Sir I ame verie sorowe that your selfe and others
should haue that conceipt of me neglecting the tyme not in vewing
Then your lootes: which the lord knoweth my willing mynd if I might
haue had wherwithall to performed it [sic] rather then to haue stayed
at renoose in making of the fish and spoilling our clothes[1] // but I
knowe ther weare some I think scorned to torne a Fish which had good
wagges of the companie // and by ones nigligence I knowe ther is
many thinges lost of the companyes but I vnderstand yet [sic] is in vayne
to speak of the partie because he is much backed by good frinds:
therfore let every one bare his burden // for I perceave I ame hardlie
spoken of because I found fault withall for it did grive me to see how
thinges weare beazelled away at renoose even before my comynge away
in master bollinge:[2] Sir I ame not a litell sorowe that you and others
haue bin informed of great familaritie that I should haue with the pirates
and in carieng them many thinges: // I was ther but 2 tymes at
Ferriland which was bussines Touching our shipp which they had taken
awaye one of our shollaps // and allso to intreat with others For a
poore Frenchman which they had taken from renoose redy to departe
Loden with Fish and trayne // and they caried hir to Ferriland amongst
The rest of ther consarts // so comynge ther we found aboard eastone
divers masters of the Fishinge Shipps: so some of them I did know verie
well being of plymoth and darthmoth they being well accquanted with
him // I intreated them verie ernestlie to in treat Captaine eastone for
this Frenchman: being myselfe did not know him // so by great
intreatie he promised for ther sakes he should haue his ship againe and
all except tenn thousauntt Fishe for his provition wherof the Frenchman
was verie glad so he promised we should allso haue our shallopp againe
// but I learne after we weare gon never Regarding much his promise
For he and his companie Riffled the poor man of all and so gaue him
his shipp againe but not vittles nor seals[3] to Carie him home but was
Forced and his companie to haue help of some englishe men both for

[1] Crout and Thomas Willoughby had landed at Renewse and spent the summer of 1612
there.
[2] On 12 August 1612 Crout reported to Percival Willoughby that the colony's surgeon
had absconded from Renews with most of his supplies and that some of the apprentices
had stolen other things. Nottingham University, Middleton MSS, Mi X 1/1;.
[3] Sails.

vitell and sealls to carie him home [and e]astane vnderstanding that ther wear some rosting pigges at renoose we sent him 2 of 4 in regard he should not doe any other mischeefe as he did vnto all other men for vitell and monycion // besids we procured a note of his hand wher by any of his other shipps should not molest vs if we should haue meett with them goinge to cupers cove // as at our comynge ther we advertissed him howe all was passe vnto master governers and of the 2 pigges which he had a desire vnto: which Master governer liked well of for fear of other mischeffes he might do vs for as I did learne he had a mynd unto some of our goates cowes and great pigges which made vs to hasten them awaye the sooner in the barke // the second time I wentt ther I was with master boolling by his intreatie and master robartes only to see if we could procure for 3 men which rune away from master boolling with one of our bootes // but Comyng at Ferriland eastone beinge not ther could not gett our men againe and so retorned again as master boolling can informe you and master robartes allso but I learne they are not to be beleeued of some men: but if need be for to Iustifie my selfe at the tyme I was ther ther was some 6 or 8 masters // men of worth and suffiecency which I prayed them to intreat for me being they had some accquantance with him and myselffe not: nor none of his companie but 2 which I see at cupers cove before such tyme as I coasted for the beare // before that tyme I had never seen them so this is the effect and truth of the Familiratie [sic] I had with them // and allso of the thinges that I should carie them to which I leaue vnto your worshipp to consider of // so they made me drink with them: and that was all the kindness I Receiued from them or did expectt any other at ther handes.

Sir if it may so please you to give Creditt vnto my writtinge I do promise you of my Faith and salvation this is all the familiarities which I had with them // for if it had not bin for intreatie of others and for the good somthing did conserne our selues I had never come neer them // I do partly gather by whom thes infformations haue bin given of me // who hath allso wrongd me in sayinge as I learne that I should be one that should go aboute to betray him vnto the pirattes the lord doth know I had never such thought in my mynd: nowe I call to mynd master Spencir was ther in Companie when I was // who can Iustifie the truth // saying so well he might haue said so much of him but only fearing his Brothers displeasure, againe that my beinge hear was to litell porpose or small good vnto the companie // for to awnnswere that I Reffer my Selfe vnto the governer whom I hoop you shall

converse withall before his retorne from england // in the mayne time
not a litell grived in mynd of ther reportes without decer[t] or
deserving: wheras my hart and mynd was bent vnto this countrie and
allso incorraging others for dwelling hear which they can no way
mislike of it // but now & the[se] reports doth somthing dismay me
of hoopes to be had in [this] countrie being so soone crossed and
wronged which I [leaue] all to the tryer of the truth: not knowing as
yet [howe] to amend my selffe.

for my kinssman[1] I am verie sorowe that ther is allso disliking of
him but I ame sure so longe as he was able stand or go he wrought
very hard as barthellemew[2] can informe y[ou] // but ther is splynne
both against him and me I nowe perc[e]ave by that fellowe // I ame
sorowe as yet Falleth out that I ever I [sic] made your worshipp
accquanted with him or the Companye either ther hath not bin
contentment given by maynes of ther reportes I haue Received order
from master Treasurer[3] for a boote and men for to asist me in
Surveyinge of the country and your 2 loottes which last year could not
be performed by no maynes // The 7th of October[4] last we departed
from cupers cove with our penice to go acoastinge and that day at night
put into a harbour called havre de grace[5] stayinge ther some 3 daies
to vnlade some salt and bringing the French shipp ashoore which was
taken by Captaine eastone being some 15 tonnes of salte in hir but this
winitter all consumed with the waltter the 17th october we ankered
in green bay[6] which is part of your lotte of land the morning we wer
put into the seay: the 19th we ankered at Sainct Cattlins Iland[7] north
side of trinity The 22th in mountt eagell Baye[8] which was an exceedinge
good place in some places very good earth and excellent fine Cheerie
trees // 24th we ankered in Sollvagg baye:[9] so called because ther we
had the first sight of them // which is not abowe 2 days Iourney by
land from cupers cove: we had sight of them in a Fresh lake 2 mylls
from the watter side: but at night they go from the firme land and
dwell in a littell iland in the myddest of the lake the governer went
and some of the Company thinking to haue found them in ther housses
at night but they wear gone over unto the Iland: but found ashoore
in ther housses fyer and divers fours but the governer haue charge That

---

[1] Probably Richard Crout who wrote asking Percival Willoughby for employment in
Newfoundland or elsewhere in February 1612. *Ibid.*, Mi X 1/6.
[2] Bartholomew Pearson.   [3] John Slany.
[4] The account of the expedition follows closely that in Crout's journal and supplements
Guy's journal.
[5] Harbour Grace.   [6] Bay de Verde.
[7] Green Island?   [8] Hopeall?   [9] Dildo Arm.

no man should not touch any thing but found over ther fier a littel Brassen Kettel: in which our governer lefte some biskett points and beades finding some 12 deere feett which they had newly killed[1] ther housses allso covered with deere skins and so lefte them without doinge any other thing vnto them: in the night was seen a Canno go from the land vnto the iland with 2 men in hir The 30th we departed from this place coasting vnto the northside of Trinity in one place william hatten[2] had spied dirictly as he said some Irone stone neer the seay side but could not go ashoore the Sea went so loftie // but our governer did determyne to retorne Backe againe but after ward could not being the wintter did insue so Fast vppon us Butt the governer did mynd to retorne this spring into trynity againe: To have vewed every crooke and thinking allso to haue some parle agayne with the sollvagges // and afterwardes to haue gone all abowte to the north wards and so
adventures of ye new found land 1613 9[3] Round abowte all the land // but his going into england hath disapointed all 4th november wee ankered in truce sound which went very farr in: thinking sure yet [sic] had gone therowe into pleasaunce bay which wanttid but 2 mylls by land from one sid vnto the other

In this sound we Found a very fine Canno of the sollvages contrived in most skillfull manner which I thinke the governer doth mynd to send for england This day after dinner my selffe And others went into the country comyng ashoore we Found a great path made by the solvages which path we Followed which brought vs vnto a Faire river and much marshie ground being but 2 myells from the place that our penice was which river showeth to be great store of sammon by reassone the sea Cometh vp vnto it of pleasaunce Baye //: neer by that river we found some of the sollvagges housses // and ther they had lefte in a baskett many Fishing hookes and a brassen kittell and divers other triffling Things For they had made a great path waye which they be accoustomed to Carie ther Cannose that waye from one side vnto the other for they haue cutt the way and great trees aporpose for to pase The next daie after dinner we had sight of a Fier made by the sollvagges which was some 2 myells from vs by the watter side // so soone as we espied them & made to wardes them both with penice and Boott being of them 2 Cannose and 8 of them 4 in eache bootte: but as we did drawe neer them they Beinge ashoore made showes and signes with a Flagg of truce pointting vnto vs that we should come

---

[1] In his journal (Nottingham University, Middleton MSS, Mi X 1/66, f. 4), Crout mentions only three deer's feet; here he agrees with Guy.

[2] One of Willoughby's apprentices who rode in the shallop.

[3] In Francis Willoughby's hand.

vnto them crying with great voyces vnto vs // so we put out our Flagg
of truce to awnnswer thers: which did giue them great Content: so
the governor sending the boott ashoore: the bootte drawing neer the
shoore they began to be somethinge fearfull and gott againe into ther
Boottes: and weare rowinge away againe a great pace vntill we made
signes vnto them: then they retorned againe with ther Cannoose and
put one man ashoore with a wolffe skine in his hand in steed of a Flagg
of truce: so then the governer sent one ashoore after they sent another
ashore so did the governer allso // and so they made much sport
togeathers by the fier making signes and Tokins one to the other so
afterwardes the governer went ashoore and some 3 more caring [sic] with
him some biskitt and Butter and Beere: but they liked not very well
our Beere they did drinke very Littell of it but the aquavity did like
them well: they did giue vs Brassettes [sic] to hang abowte our neckes
and vnto the governer some 2 arrowes: ther Brasslettes weare of Littell
sheells[1] but they made accompte yet had bin a great present which they
gave vs: the governer gave them a verie good shirte // and they made
great signes for to haue our Flagg of truce which our governor
bestowed one them wherat they did verie much rejoice: allso he gaue
them other small triffells: as reassons and pointes: they gaue vs ech of
[vs] some of ther penycan[2] which had bin dried which it did eat [very]
well // before such tyme as we came ashoore they had h[anged] vp
divers sortes of fours uppon poolles by the watter sid[e] we made
accompt it had bin to drie them but v[nd]erstand Sethince they hanged
them vp as in afaire [sic] according vnto ther coustome for to sell them
// so night drawing neer they wear desir[ous] to depart from vs and
made showes allso we should [do the same] so presently as they departed
we went abord [our penice] they went away and lefte all ther skins
behind [them.] So the governer thinking they would haue retorned
againe the next daye but they come not: that whillst the day after the
governer with his company began to bild a house vppon an Iland being
it is in the Right Way as as [sic] they do trade to and froo // but the
second day ther came such a froost which did crayme all the bottome
of the soound over which vrged our Governer to hast awaye for feare
we should have bin Frossen in Coming Forth the sound by the place
wher we had parlle with them the governer seeing the skines still
hanging ther vppon the poolles / went ashoore with the bootte and
ther seeing all the skines Remayninge lefte a hattchett a kniffe sissers

---

[1] Guy calls them periwinkle shells. For a description of the wampum used by the
Beothuk, see Howley, *The Beothucks*, p. 241 and plate XXXV.   [2] Pemican.

and some other things and toke in the steed of that some 2 beavers skins a sabell and a bird skine and so lefte all the rest standing vpon the pooles: if it had not bin for fear to haue bin kept in with the Ice within 2 or 3 dayes without dowte we had come to haue spoken with them againe // so Farr as we could perceave it wear the very Same people which wear in the lak which the governer lefte in ther brassen kettell bread and pointes and amber beades for we Found the same boott saille which covered ther house wher we had parlle with them // they Finding at First to be so kindly dealte withall made them to followe vs along the coost we wanted small things to trook with them / so leaving all ther skins that wear resting vppon the poolls by the beach // they are people verie parsonable but only they do Reed all ther Faces with ockar and all ther skins // and they seemed to be verie Fatt / all goinge beare Footted except one which had showes of seills skine and had myttance vppon his hand // and in salutting would pull them of and kisse the tope of his Finger // all clothed with good Fours downne to the leags with a beaver skine abowte ther neckes but go allso bare leaged / they had more store of Fours in ther Bootes which they did not land // the governer hath written the discription of them in every manner which you shall see at large with Freequentting ther company but a litell tyme ther wilbe much good done by them: we did thinke to haue visitted them this winter by Land but being vpon the waye one dayes Iourney finding the snowe so deepe and snowing still retorned againe with much bad weather could not travell thorowe the woodes / but we made full accompt to haue visited them this sommer but the governer going home will nowe hinder it / I knowe of many small thinges which wilbe good to trock with them hearafter this // from some of your Lootte with a shalloppe a man may rowe vnto them in a daye as hearafter you shalbe farther infformed // Comyng backe out of Trynitie baye the 10th november at night we put into hartes Content // making accompt to gone [sic] the next day at the topp of the hills to haue taken vew of the country but the snowe Falling in such abundaunce that we could not sture anywher but only see the harbarr an excellent good plac for fishing for some 8 shipps // The 13th we came by the pointt of green wher [sic] is allso part of your Lotte which some tymes as I learne the solvages do come ther to huntt for deer // as we passed along [vn]der the Land with our penice even at the pointt we see some . . . deer[1] or more marshinge along one after another vpon the top of the hill

[1] Crout's journal refers to twelve or thirteen 'deer.' Nottingham University, Middleton MSS, Mi X 1/66, f. 6v.

That night we Ankered ther in a littell Cove thinking certainely the
next daie to have gone ashoore a huntting for some deer and to see
the country being it is hard allso by Backaloo : but our boote came not
to vs that night but put in at perlican and lefte ther our Cannoo so
by no maynes could we gett ashoore / 14th we wear put from thince
by Force of Fowlle weather and lefte one of our ankers behind vs even
as we wear putting into the sea our boote was come abowte The point
of the land which they wear willed to seeke for our Anker but could
not find it // so they going towards the shoore the sea being so Loftie
filled ther boott and drived ashoore against the rocks : they in great
daunger in saving of ther lives // but lost all ther clothes in a very
cold tyme and snowe weather / some five of them Barthellemewe was
one of them : lost an Irishe gownne and other things which afterwardes
I Furnished him with an old doblett and a paire of Breches stoking
being but Baer my selffe // for this Countrie doth vse very much hoose
and showes // hear is not provition left scarse of the companies to serve
the printices // therefore ther is nothing to be had nowe for Master
Thomas nor me // Sir after this mischaunce that they had cast awaye
the boott they wear put to great extreemitie For vitells // having not
anything to strike fier withall William hatton was allso with them //
they travelling some 9 or tenn daies vp and downne the woods and
open grounds and could not find ther waie // which before they gott
home wear like to be starved with hungar : all this tyme they wear in
travelling vppon your Loote of land vntill they came vnto Carbonnier
// but as Barthellemewe showeth me all thes partes as they passed too
and Froo was verie good open ground and verie good Long grasse in
yt Betwine that and perlican : for some 4 dayes they traversing betwine
green bay and perlican // for they had scarse any sight of the sune
nor any diall[2] so in the end ther owne reasone made them kept the
sea side at green bay they had sight of 4 or 5 companies of deer 4. 5
& 6 in a companie which came verie neer vnto them // they wantted
but a pece then they had killed divers allso they had sight of great of
[sic] partridg which was very straung above 100 in a companie hear
are great abundaunce all over in this Countrie // the deer would
followe after them : and gase at them : at green bay is very great store
of deer as I haue hard it by divers which haue killed some ther // allso
as they came alonge the coast they came wher were exceeding good
and faire burche trees and verie good earth and rivers in manie places
// which if good [sic] Lend me Life I wilbe resolved whollie this

---

[1] In Francis Willoughby's hand.
[2] A compass.

sommer // but abowte green bay much open ground and ther The deer doth hante // I do mynd to see it by Land allso if I could procure a diall // ther is allso in that quarter good store of beaver o[tt]er and Beavers nesses and many Foxes which partly nowe we knowe howe to take them // our men killed 3 faire beavers whills we wear acoasting in a Freshe lake watching when they go into ther ness & so to let out the watter and afterward killed them with staves and dogges but sure the solvages do shoutt them with arrowes.

Wheras you writ to indevour our selves for the killed [sic] of thes Beast in the wintter and sommer ther might be good store killed yf one would give attendaunce unto it and againe when the beast are killed by any of vs that we might haue the fours for your vse but we think in spending your shootte and powder it is reassone you Should haue the skins // which I do see a man shall never haue the Benefitt of that except any man do plante vpon his owne loote which then will put any in harte to kill some // as For example Barthellemewe watching this wintter some 3 nights for foxes killed one verie faire gray foxe the third night a verie fair black fox all blacke // which the governer Comandid to be brought into the steward rome we kept them 2 or 3 dayes without any demaunding thinking surely to haue sent them unto your worship we learne a black fox is worth verie much money // 20^{li} or more which you may be best in formed of in England. I knowe not wher the governer do mynd to deliver them to you or ells doth mind to put them to the Companies vse he doth carie all the skins home nowe with him but I pray let vs be resolved from you wher the skins we kill shalbe for your vse or the companys for it doth tak away the coragg of many and do not nowe care where they kill any or not because they can not haue the benefitt of them for ther frinds Master Thomas killid one allso when we weare acoasting // which it hath brought barthellemewe out of hart ever sethince not desiring to stay much longer hear except therbe plantation vpon your owne Loote he hath demanded leave of the governer at the Latter end of the year // I think the sending of malte and meall wilbe more waste in y^{tt} then in sending of Biskett and Beere from Bristowe // For as yet hear are not romes nor places Fitted for it: and sure for the health of men the provition from bristow is excellent good ther is this 8 of our people dead in the scurvie & some 22 more which wear sicke but god be thanked all were agayne recovered which nowe some do go home with the governer // by great chaunce ther was one first of our Companie did vse tornnopp routes which we had in the ground all this wintter vnder the snowe // which route hath sethince by Triall sufficient recovered them all to ther health but the other 8 wear dead before we had any triall of it in eatting of them rawe they wear so cribled most of them not able sture out of ther beades [sic] they haue a Farr sweetter taste then the english tornnope // Sir I pray excuse me because it is in some hast // desiring your worshipe not to think so hardly of me contrary vnto my good meayninge as the Lord doth knowe // that I should incorrie displeasure in seeking and preserving of thes things we had as you and master Slany shalbe infformed more of the truth hearafter // in the mayne tyme I besech your worshipe conceive but well of me as truth shall try all / so I end with my dayly prayers vnto the allmightie for you and my ladys longe Life and prosper health / for your sonne ther is no feere but you shall Receive great Comfort by him // but ther must be things sent some aquavity [the] aquavitie that we had last year stood vs in great sted

Your worships to Comand
Henry Crout

5. 1620 *A BRIEFE DISCOURSE OF THE NEW-FOUND-LAND*

A BRIEFE DISCOURSE of the New-found-land, *with the situation, temperature,* and commodities thereof, *inciting our Nation to goe* forward in that hope-*full plantation begunne.*
Scire tuum nihil est, nisi te scire hoc sciat alter.
EDINBURGH, Printed by *Andro Hart.* 1620.

TO THE RIGHT *WORSHIPFULL SIR* IOHN SCOTT *of Scots-Tarvet,* KNIGHT.[1] &c. SIR, you are like to haue none other accompt for the present than such as Marchant-Factors, after bad markets returne, that is, papers for payment, for liuers lines, The which though not so acceptable as more solide returnes, yet giues some satisfaction for the expenses of time questionable. I haue sent you a discourse of our Countrie penned at the request of friends, for the better satisfaction of our Nobilitie, vnpolished and rude, bearing the countries badge where it was hatched, onely clothed with plainnesse and trueth. I intreat your fauourable acceptation thereof, as your wonted clemencie hath

---

[1] Sir John Scott (1585–1670), lawyer and scholar, director of chancery of Scotland. Mason's only surviving letter from Newfoundland, written 30 August 1617, was addressed to him. Both men were friends of Sir William Alexander, a favourite of James I and holder of land in Nova Scotia and Newfoundland. *DNB*; National Library of Scotland, Advocates MSS, 17.1.19; Cell, *English enterprise,* pp. 75, 95.

beene to the Author, if you thinke it may doe good by incouraging any of your Countrie to the interprise, I am willing you publish it, other wise let it bee buried in silence as you shall thinke meetest, and esteeme mee still one of whome you haue power to dispose.

IOHN MASON.

To the Reader

For as much as there bee sundrie relations of the New-found-land and the commodities thereof, Some too much extolling it, some too much debasing it, preferring the temperature of the aire thereof before ours, the hopes of commodities there without paines and mineralles, as if they were apparent (which as I deny to bee a veritie, yet I affirme not to bee impossible) with other narrations dissenting from the trueth, the which although done out of a good affection, yet had they better beene vndone. I haue therefore (gentle Reader) hoping of thy fauourable construction, set downe in few and plaine tearmes out of that experience I haue gained in three yeares and seuenth [sic] monthes residence there,[1] the trueth, as thou shalt finde by proofe thereof, to the which I recommend thee and vs all to his Grace, that is able and will plant those that feare him in a better Kingdome. Farewell.

Thine and his Countries in part, not whollie his owne.

IOHN MASON.

A BRIEFE DISCOURSE of the Newfoundland with the *Situation, temperature, and commodities there*-of inciting our Nation to goe forward in *that hopefull plantation begunne.*

THE Countrie commonly knowne and called by the name of Newfoundland, albeit it is so much frequented and resorted yearely to, by thousands of our Nation and others, which haue scarcely so much as a superficiall knowledge thereof (onely so much as concerneth their fishings excepted) is an Iland or Ilands as some plats haue described it,[2] situate on the front of *America*, betwixt 46. and 52. degrees of Northerly

---

[1] Between 1616 and 1620.

[2] Maps of the mid-sixteenth century commonly represented Newfoundland as highly fragmented, some showing as many as ten separate islands. By the later part of the century many cartographers followed Mercator and Ortelius in showing four islands. The Hondius map of North America (*c.* 1590) and the Plancius map of Nova Francia (1592) depicted a single island. The first English map to do so was Edward Wright's world map, prepared for the second edition of Hakluyt's *Principal navigations* and engraved by Molyneux, which may have derived its representation of the island from Hondius. Cell, *English enterprise*, pp. 36–8.

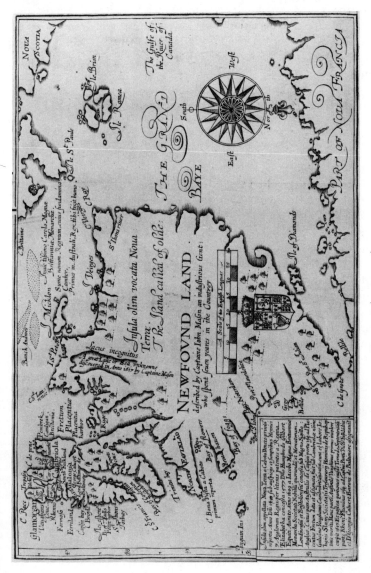

Fig. 3. John Mason's map

latitude,[1] of the bignes of *Ireland*. the Eastermost side thereof bounded with the Ocean extendeth it selfe nearest North and South: the variation allowed 100. Leagues, the South face deuided from the Iles of *Cap*. Bretone by the Gulfe of Sainct Lowrence a straigth of 27. Leagues ouer lyeth West. and by North northerly, and East and by South Southerly in length 77. Leagues, on the West part imbraced by the Grand-bay stretching it selfe Northeast and Southwest 75. Leagues. and on the North confined by the Norther arme of the Grand-bay which separateth it from the continent of *Noua Francia* making a fret of 7. Leagues wide, & is described by the Rhombe of W. and by North and E. and by S. 25. Leag. Almost of a Triangular forme sauing that many bays & Inlets making incroachment haue disfigured the face therof with Scars, eating into the land into 40 leagues space on the South part where we haue searched 30 as good Harbours as the world affords. The longitude thereof reackoned from the westermost part of the *Insula fortunata*[2] is 330 degrees, distant in the Line of West & by the South from our *Meridian* 45. degrees by common account which in the midle parallell of the difference the Latitude betwixt the lands end of *England* & the bodie of Newfoundland at 39. one halfe miles answerable to each degree in the same maketh 1764. miles or 588 Leagues. The aire subtle & wholesome, the Summer season pleasant conforme to the like latitude in Europe, sauing that ye woodie places in Iune & Iulie are somewhat pestered with small Flies bred of the rottenes of ruined woode & moysture like as in *Russia*. The Winter degenerating therfrom, being as cold & snowy as 60 degrees in Europe, & of the like temperature in December, Ian. Febr. March, as the northermest [*sic*] parts in *Scotland*. viz. The Hebrides and the Orcades[3] wherin I haue twise wintered,[4] or of the Coast betwixt *Hamburgh* & the mouth of the *Sownd* or *Nose* of *Norway*: yet more comfortable for the length of the day in Winter, which exceedeth theirs three hourse at the least. And albeit it be thus cold in the Winter season by accidentall meanes, contrarie to the naturall position thereof in the Spheare, yet it is tollerable, as by experience, so that there needs no Stoaues as in *Germanie*: Likewise fruitefull enough both of Sommer and Winter

---

[1] The extremities of the island are, to the south, Cape Pine (46° 37′) and, to the north, Cape Norman (51° 38′).   [2] The Canary Islands.

[3] The Orkneys.

[4] In 1610 Mason had been commissioned as commander of four vessels to assist in reclaiming the Hebrides from pirates. G. P. Insh, *Scottish colonial schemes, 1620–1686* (Glasgow, 1922), p. 34.

corne, an example for our confirmation thereof we haue in *Poland* one
of the greatest corne Countries of Europe & yet as cold and subject to
freizing as Newfoundland, as also our owne experience both in Wheate,
Rye, Barlie, Oates, and Pease, which haue growen and ripened there
as well and als [*sic*] timely as in *Yorkshire* in *England*. And for grouth
of Garden herbes of diuers sorts as Hysope, Time, Parsely, Clarie,[1]
Nepe,[2] french Mallowes,[3] Buglosse,[4] Collombines, Wormewood, &c.
There is at this present of 3. yeares old of my sowing, likewise
Rosemary, Fenell, Sweete marierim, Bassell, Purselyn,[5] Lettise, and
all other Herbes & Rootes: as torneps, Pasnepes, Caretts, and Radishes
we haue found to growe well there in the Sommer season. The common
wilde herbes of the Countrie are Angelica, Violets, Mints, Scabius,
Yarrow, Ferne, Salsaparilla, with diuers other sorts whereof I am
ignorant; But suppose would for variety and rariety compose another
Herball; of these kinds wee haue onely made vse of certain great green
leaues plentifully growing in the woods, and a great Roote growing
in fresh water ponds, both good against the Skiruye, and an other
prettie Roote with a blew stalke and leaues of the nature of a Skirret[6]
growing in a dry Beachy ground, good meate boyled: The Countrie
fruites wild, are cherries small, whole groaues of them Filberds good,
a small pleasant fruite, called a Peare, Damaske Roses single very sweet,
excellent Straberries, and Hartleberries[7] with aboundance of Rasberries,
and Gooseberries somewhat better than ours in *England*, all which
replanted would be much inlarged. There is also a kind of wild
Coranies,[8] wild Pease or Feetches in many places which we haue both
found good meat and medecine for the Skiruy; The Land of the North
parts most mountanye & woodye very thick of Firre trees, Spruce, Pine
Lereckhout,[9] Aspe,[10] Hasill, a kinde of stinking wood, the three formest
goodly Timber and most conuenient for Building. No Oakes, Ashe,
Beech, or Ellmes, haue we seene or heard of; the greatest parts of the
Plaines are marish[11] and boggs, yet apt to be drawen dry by means of
many fresh Lakes intermixt which paye tribute to the Sea; and on the
brinks of these Lakes, through which the water draines away from the

---

[1] A plant which must have reminded Mason of the wild or meadow clary (clear eye),
which was used in England as an eye-salve.
[2] Catnip.   [3] *Lavatera Olbia*.
[4] A name applied to several boraginaceous plants with rough, tongue-shaped leaves.
[5] A low succulent plant, *Portulaca oleracca*, used as a salad or pot-herb in seventeenth-
century cooking.
[6] An edible root, similar to a parsnip.   [7] Whortleberries or bilberries.
[8] Currants.   [9] Probably the larch pine, *Larix americana*.
[10] A tree of the poplar family.   [11] Marsh.

rootes of the Grasse, it florisheth, in the other parts of the Plaines where the water standeth and killeth the growth of the Grasse with his coldnesse it is rushie and seggy;[1] in some parts is barren, & mossie ground, but that that is firme and dry beareth good grasse. The Spring beginneth in the end of Aprill, & Haruest continueth while Nouember, I haue seene September and October much more pleasant than in *England*; the South part is not so mountanous nor so woodie, for being a little passed vp from the Sea coast the continent hath champion ground for 40. miles together in North and South extent of the like nature of the former, hauing pretty Groues and many fresh laks replenished with Eeles & Salmon-Troutes great, and in great plentie. The Beastes are Ellans,[2] Follow-deare [*sic*], Hares, Beares harmeles, Wolues, Foxes, Beauers, Catnaghenes excellent, Otteres, and a small beast like a Ferret whose excrement is Muske: And the Plantations haue prettie stoare of Swine and Goates. The Fowles are Eagles, Falcons, Tassills, Marlins, a great Owle much deformed, a lesser Owle, Bussards, Gripes,[3] Osprayes which diue for Fishes into the Water, Rauens, Crowes, wild Geese, Snipes, Teales, Twillockes,[4] excellent wilde Duckes of diuers sorts and aboundance, some whereof rare and not to be found in Europe, Their particulars too tedious to relate, all good meate, Partriches white in Winter, and gray in Summer, greater than ours, Butters,[5] blacke Birds with redd breastes, Phillidas,[6] Wrens, Swallowes, Iayes, with other small Birds, and 2. or 3. excellent kinds of Beach Birds very fat and sweet, & at the plantations[7] English Pigeons. The sea fowles, are Gulls white and gray, Penguins, Sea Pigeons, Ice Birds,[8] Bottle noses,[9] with other sortes strange in shape, yet all bowntifull to vs with their Egges as good as our Turkie or Hens, where with the Ilelands [*sic*] are well replenished. But of all, the most admirable is the Sea, so diuersified with seuerall sorts of Fishes abounding therein, the consideration whereof is readie to swallow vp and drowne my senses not being able to comprehend or expresse the riches thereof. For could one acre therof be inclosed with the Creatures therein in the moneths of Iune, Iulie, and August, it would exceed one thousand acres of the best Pasture with the stocke thereon which we

---

[1] I.e. covered with sedge.   [2] Elks.
[3] Vultures.   [4] Guillemots.
[5] Bitterns.
[6] Filladies, a small singing bird.
[7] As Mason makes clear (below, p. 99), there were two neighboring settlements when he was governor.
[8] Little auks or sea doves.
[9] A name applied to several of the dolphin family.

haue in *England*. May hath Herings on [*sic*] equall to 2. of ours, Lants[1] and Cods in good qua*n*tity. Iune hath Capline, a fish much resembling Smeltes in forme and eating, and such aboundance dry on Shoare as to lade Carts, in some partes pretty store of Salmond, and Cods so thicke by the shoare that we heardlie haue beene able to row a Boate through them, I haue killed of them with a Pike; Of these, three men to Sea in a Boate with some on Shoare to dresse and dry them in 30. dayes will kill commonlie betwixt 25. and thirty thousand, worth with the Oyle arising from them 100 or 120. pound. And the fish and Traine in one Harbour called Sainct Iohns is yearly in the Sommer worth 17, or 18. thousand pounds. Iulie, and so till Nouember, hath Macrill in aboundance; one thereof as great as two of ours, August hath great large Cods but not in such aboundance as the smaller, which continueth with some little decreasing till December; What should I speake of a kinde of Whales called Gibberts,[2] Dogfish, Porposes, Hering-Hogges,[3] Squides a rare kinde of fish, at his mouth squirting mattere forth like Inke, Flownders, Crabbes, Cunners,[4] Catfish, Millers,[5] thunnes &c.[6] Of al which there are innumberable in the Summer season; Likewise of Lobsters plentie, and this last yeare stoare of Smelts not hauing beene knowne there before. I haue also seene Tonnie fish in Newland; now of shell fish there is Scalupes, Musseles, Vrsenas, Hens, Periwinkles &c. Here we see the chiefe fishing with his great commoditie expressed, which falleth so fitly in the Summer season betwixt seed-time and Haruest that it cannot be any hinderance to either. I haue heard some countries commended for their two fowld Haruest, which heare thou hast, although in a different kinde, yet both as profitable, I (dare say) [*sic*] as theirs so much extolled, if the right course be taken; & well fareth, that country say I, which in one months time with reasonable paines, wil pay both landlords rent, seruants wages, and all Houshold charges. But peraduenture some squeaysie stomake will say, Fishing is a beastly trade & vnseeming a Gentleman, to whom I answere (*Bonus odor luti cum lucro*) & let them propund the Holanders to themselues for example whose Countrie is so much inriched by it; others say the Countrie is barren, but they are deceiued, for *Terra quae tegit se ipsam tegit Dominum*, and the great aboundance of Woodes and wilde Fruites which exceedingly florish there proue the contrary. And what thogh

---

[1] Or launce.
[2] Also known as finners, because of a large dorsal fin.
[3] Or grampus.   [4] Blue perch.
[5] A kind of ray.
[6] The distinction which Mason is making between 'thunne' and 'tonnie' fish is not clear.

the fertility of the soyle and temperature of the Climate be inferiour to *Virginia*, yet for foure maine Reasons to be laid downe it is to be parallelled to it, if not preferred before it, the which we will heere propound.

1 The first reason is the nearenes to our owne home, which naturally we are so much addicted vnto, being but the halfe of the way to *Virginia*, hauing a conuenient passage for three seasonable Monthes, March, Aprill, and May, which alwayes accomodate faire windes to passe thether, sometime in 14. or 20. dayes, seldome in thirtie dayes. Likewise the commodious returne in Iune, Iulie, August, September, October, and Nouember, sometimes in 12. 16. 20. and now and then in thirtie dayes.

2. The great intercourse of trade by our Nation these three-score years and vpwards, in no small numbers frequenting the New-found land, and daylie increasing, with the likelinesse thereof to continue, fish being a staple commoditie with vs, and so sellable in other countries yearlie imploying 3000. thousand [*sic*] Sea-men and breeding new daylie, also fraighting three hundreth Ships in that voyage, and releuing of 20000. people moe [*sic*] here in *England* (for most of these fishers are maried and haue a charge of Children, and liue by this meanes not being able to gaine halfe so much by another labour) furthermore the reuenew that groueth to the King by the customes of the *French*, *Spanish* and Straights goods imported, from the proceede of this fish trade suppose at the least to the value of ten thousand pounds yearely.

3 The conueniency of transporting plantors thether at the old rate, ten shillings the man, and twentie shillings to find him victual thether, likewise other commodities by shippes that goe sackes[1] at ten shilling per tunne out, and thirtie shillings home,[2] whereas *Virginia* and *Birmooda* fraightes, are fiue pound the man and three pound the tunne.

4 Fourthly and lastly, Securitie from foraine and domesticke enemies, there being but few Saluages in the north, and none in the south parts of the Countrie; by whom the planters as yet neuer suffered damage, against whom (if they should seeke to trouble vs,) a small fortification will serue being but few in number, and those onely Bow men. Also if any Warres should happen betwixt vs and other Nations, wee neede not feare rooting out. For the Yce is a Bulwarke all Aprill commonlie and after that during the whole Summer wee haue a garison of 9. or 10. 1000 of our owne Nation with many good and warlike

[1] Ships going to the fishery in ballast.
[2] The freight of a sack ship was usually reckoned by the month; see Cell, *English enterprise*, pp. 9–10.

Shippes, who of necessitie must defend the fishing season for their liuings sake, as they always formerlie haue done in the Warres with *Spaine*. And afterwards in the monthes of Haruest and Winter the winds are our friends and will hardlie suffer any to approach vs, the which if they should, the cold opposite to the nature of the Spainard [*sic*] will giue him but cold Intertainement; neither will the Plantours be altogether puffed vp with careless securitie, but fortifie in some measure knowing that *Non sunt securi qui dant sua Colla securi.*

Nowe hauing formerly layed downe the temperature of the Aire and disposition of the Weather in the Winter season to be cold and consequently different from other places of the same situation vnder the same Parallel in Europe, and by experience answerable to 59. or 60. degrees thereof. It will be expected that I should shew some reasons concerning the same which according to mine opinion (submitting my selfe to better Iudgements) I will set downe; It being a generall rule approued through *America* that any place vnder the same Parallel of another place in Europe is as cold as those places which are situate in 12. or 13. degrees to the North wards therof, and the same rule holdeth a like on either side of the Equinoctiall. For example, the straigths of *Magelan* in 54. to the South of the Equinoctiall, are more cold, snowie and boysterous than any part of Europe in 65. Likewise on this side the Line, the Country about the Riuer *Orenoaque*[1] and *Trinidade* in 9. or ten degrees is found as temperate as *Gualata*[2] vnder 23. degrees of more northerlie latitude in *Africa*. So likewise Sainct *Augustine* in *Florida* vnder 31. degrees is answerable to *Valadulid* in 42. degrees in *Spaine*, also the plantations vnder 37. degrees in *Virginia* are correspondent in the Winter to the temperature of *Deuenshire* or *Cornewell* vnder 50. degrees heare in *England,* and although their Summer bee some what hotter in regard of the nearenes of the Sunne, being then in *Cancer* within 15. degrees of their Zenith, the Radius therof then striking neare at a right Angle, causing a strange reflection, yet would it be much hotter if the Sun in his passage ouer the great *Oceane* 3000. miles broad vnder that Paralel, betwixt Europe & *America*, by the exhalation of the waterish vapours & much moisture thereout, into the middle region of the Aire, did not coole the same, which beinge made more grosse & thick with misty Clouds, his Beames cannot pearce through with their propre vigor and force, to heate the Earth; To this

---

[1] Orinoco,
[2] Walata, in the western Sudan; once the terminus of the trans-Saharan trade until superseded by Timbuktu.

cooling of the Sunnes heate helpeth also all those great fresh ponds and lakes so abounding in *America*. Fresh waters being more naturally cold than salt, and both colder than the Earth, of like qualitie also are the marish and Boggie groundes, the Lands not manured and therefore more naturally cold, the Country slenderly peopled, voide of Townes and Cities, whereof Europe is full; the smoake whereof and heate of fires much qualifieth the coldnesse of the Aire. Lastly the chiefest reason of the coldnesse in New-found-land in the Winter season is the Yce which beeing congealed into great firme Lands, euen from the North Pole, all alongst the Coast of *Gronland, Grenland*,[1] The North-west passage *Terra de laberador* & so towardes the Grand bay, all that tract hauing many Inlets and broken Lands apt as vnnaturall wombes to breede and bring foorth such Monsters, which being nursed in their ruder armes, till the Winter season past, are turnde foorth of doores in the Spring to shift for themselues, and being weary of their imprisonments in those angrie Climes with one accord as if they had agreed with winde and streame take Ferrie into New-found-land, which immuring vs in the months of Febru. & March,[2] both which are subject to northeast winds & blowing from this Yce causeth it very cold. The currant stil setting it southward as a Iaylor to bring it before the Iudge, neuer leaueth it till with the helpe of the outset of Sainct *Lawrence* Gulfe it be presented nearer the Sun to be broild by his scorching Beames and consumed. I cannot deny but in some Winters betwixt Christmas and March, Yce is bred in the Harbors and bayes of New-foundland, by reason of the calmenesse of the winds there incident, And the want of streames not causing motion in the Waters, and when it is so frozen, it is none otherwise then the Texsell or Inner Seas in Holand of 15. or 18. Inches thicknesse, and breakes and consumes in the Spring; all fresh Lakes frozen opens [*sic*] in the end of March or the beginning of Aprill, which brings with it many showers to wash away Snow, and bare the ground; and the midle of the Month many Ships arriue of the *English*, some *French*, and in the midest of May some Portingalls. All which as so many Reapers come to the Haruest, gathering in aboundance the wonderfull blessings of the Lord.

I might heare further discourse of our discoueries, conference with

---

[1] The distinction which Mason is making between 'Gronland' and 'Grenland', both common variants of Greenland, is not clear.

[2] Crout's journal records that the harbour at Cupids was frozen over for a few days at a time in the first three months of 1613 and once blocked by an iceberg. Nottingham University, Middleton MSS, Mi X 1/66, ff. 11v, 12v, 13, 15.

the Saluages by Master *Iohn Gye*, their maner of life: Likewise of the managinge our businesse in our plantations with the descriptions of their situations in 2. places 16. miles distant from other, on the northside the bay of conception;[1] of the manner charge and benefite of our fishings with the seuerall strange formes, and natures of Fishes, projects for making Yron, Salt, Pitch, Tarre, Tirpintine, Frank-Incense, Furres, Hope of trade with Saluages and such like, with many accidents and occurences in the time of my gouerment there, but these may suffice as *Verbum sapienti*; being of sufficient trueth to remoue errours of conceiuing the Countrie more pleasant by reason of his naturall sight in the Spheare, then it is indeede, also to convince and take away malicious and scandelous speeches of maligne persons, who out of enuy to GOD and good Actions (instructed by their father the Deuill) haue sought to despoile it of the dewe, and blamish the good name thereof. And lastlie to induce thee, gentle Reader, to the true consideration thereof as a thing of great consequence to our Nation not only at present, but like to bee much more beneficiall when the plantation there shall increase which God grant to his owne glorie and the good of our Common-Wealth.

FINIS.

---

[1] This is the only explicit reference we have to the existence of two areas of settlement in Conception Bay. The drying of fish demanded so much space that the first settlers may have felt the need to spread out as quickly as did their successors. The dispersed nature of the community was the despair of later government officials.

CHAPTER II

RICHARD WHITBOURNE, PROPAGANDIST

6. 14 February 1619/20   THE PRIVY COUNCIL CONSIDERS WHITBOURNE'S *DISCOURSE*[1]

Vpon a Proposicion made and a Booke this day delivered to the Boarde by Captaine Whitborne for a Plantacion in Newfoundland,[2] to the benifitt of the Fishing there and the good of his Maiesties Subiectes otherwise. It is ordered that the Earle of Arundell,[3] the Lord Carew,[4] the Lord Digbie[5] Master Treasurer,[6] and Master Comptroller of his Maiesties Houshold,[7] Master Secretary Naunton,[8] Master Secretary Caluert, and the Master of the Wardes[9] or any foure of them shall take aswell that Proposicion, and Booke as what is likewise offerred by Master Guy of Bristoll and others in that behalf,[10] into their serious consideracion, and vpon Conference with such persons as they shall thinke fitt to call before them, and due Informacion of the Condicion of that Country and the benifitt of a Plantacion there, to make Reporte to the Boarde of their opinions, and what course shalbe most requisite for establishing that Plantacion in case the same be found fitt to be entertayned, and proceeded in./

---

[1] P.R.O., PC 2/30, p. 425.

[2] The first edition of the *Discourse and discovery of New-found-land* which was published in 1620 by Felix Kyngston.

[3] Thomas Howard, second earl of Arundell (1585–1646); art collector; courtier; appointed to the privy council in 1616. *DNB*.

[4] George Carew, baron Carew of Clopton and earl of Totnes (1555–1629); soldier and statesman; became a privy councillor in 1616. *Ibid*.

[5] John Digby, first earl of Bristol (1580–1653); diplomatist and statesman; appointed to the privy council in 1616. *Ibid*.

[6] Sir Henry Montagu, viscount Mandeville, and first earl of Manchester (1563?–1642); statesman; in 1616 succeeded Sir Edward Coke as chief justice of the king's bench; appointed lord treasurer in 1620. *Ibid*.

[7] Henry Cary, viscount Falkland.

[8] Sir Robert Naunton (1563–1635); politician; secretary of state from January 1618 until January 1623. *DNB*.

[9] Lionel Cranfield, earl of Middlesex (1575–1645); financier; politician; appointed master of the court of wards in 1619 and privy councillor in 1620. *Ibid*.

[10] Guy's presentation has not survived.

7. 23 July 1620   THE PRIVY COUNCIL RECOMMENDS THE PUBLICATION OF WHITBOURNE'S *DISCOURSE*[1]

Whereas Captain Wytborne hauinge spent much tyme in Newfoundland hath set down in writinge divers observations and noates, touching the state and Condition of the Plantation; which hee desireth may bee published, for the fortherance and advansment of the said plantation; and to give incorragment to such as shall adventur therein. There llordships did give good approbation of his good indevor and purpasse. And ordered that according to his desire hee showld haue the printinge of that Booke; with this forther addition of favor that the Booke soe printed bee recommended to the Lord Archbishop of Canterburie[2] and the rest of the lord Bishops. To bee distributed to the severall parishes of the Kingdon [*sic*] for the Incoridgment of such as shalbee willinge to assist that Plantation ether in there persons or other wise./

8. *A DISCOURSE AND DISCOVERY OF NEW-FOUND-LAND*

A DISCOURSE AND DISCOVERY OF NEW-FOUND-LAND,[3] WITH many reasons to prooue how worthy and *beneficiall a Plantation may there be made, after a far* better manner than now it is.

TOGETHER WITH THE LAYING OPEN OF CERTAIN ENORMITIES and abuses committed by some that trade to that *Countrey, and the meanes laid downe for reformation thereof.*

Written by Captaine *Richard Whitbourne* of Exmouth, *in the* County *of* Deuon, *and published by Authority.*

As also, an Inuitation: and likewise certaine Letters sent from that Countrey; which are printed in the *latter part of this Booke.*[4] Imprinted at London by Felix Kingston. 1622.

---

[1] P.R.O., PC 2/30, p. 578.

[2] George Abbot (1562–1633); became archbishop of Canterbury and a privy councillor in 1611, having previously been bishop of London. *DNB.*

[3] Collated with the editions of 1620 (hereafter referred to as A), and 1623 (hereafter referred to as C). The edition of 1622 (hereafter referred to as B), was chosen as the master text because it, like C, contains a lengthy second part (the 'Invitation' and Winne letters, below, pp. 163–90, 195–206) not in A. All editions used are in the British Library; see *STC* for the variant issues of Whitbourne's books. In collating the texts, I have noted only variants in spelling and content that affect the sense.

[4] 'As...Booke' not in A.

SAMUEL, by Gods prouidence, Bishop of *Norwich*.[1] To all and singuler Archdeacons, Deanes, and other Officials, Parsons, Vicars, Curates, Churchwardens and all other Ecclesiasticall Officers and Ministers within my Diocese of *Norwich*,[2] and the seuerall Parishes thereof, Greeting.

Whereas letters haue beene addressed vnto me from the most Reuerend Father in God, the Lord Archbishop of *Canterbury*, his Grace, recommending, according vnto speciall directions, by him receiued from his Maiesty and the Lords of the Most Honourable Priuie Councell, the publication of a Discourse written by *Captaine Richard Whitbourne*, concerning *New-found-land*, and a Collection to be thereupon made in all the seuerall Parishes within this Kingdome of *England*: And that by my selfe and my Officers I would giue my best furtherance thereunto. Now, forasmuch as the publication of the said Discourse tends principally to the aduancement of his Maiesties Plantation already there begun, by inciting Aduenturers thereunto, as well for the propagation of the Gospell in that Countrey, as also for many great benefits that may be there gotten to all such as will be Aduenturers therein; and likewise for the generall good and inriching of the whole Kingdome, and not be any way burdensome, or hurtfull to any of his Maiesties subiects, as by the Discourse it self, herewith sent vnto you, doth more at large appeare; And for that his Maiesty and the Lords of the Councell haue so well approoued the said Captaines good endeuours herein, as to recommend him in an extraordinary manner; That towards his great trauels, charge, and expence of time, with seuerall Commissions, and otherwise in this businesse; and towards the Printing and free distributing his Bookes, and his seuerall great losses receiued at Sea by Pirats and otherwise, in aduenturing to further the said Plantation, and partly discouering the good which may come thereby vnto all his Maiesties subiects; The voluntary bounties of all his Maiesties subiects should be collected by his vse and behoofe, as by their Lordships Letters, and His Maiesties pleasure thereupon signified, which is Printed in the forepart of the Booke, doth appeare.

These are therfore to pray & require you my Brethren of the Ministry, in your seueral parish Churches & Chappels, thorowout my

---

[1] Samuel Harsnet (1561–1631); bishop of Chichester, 1609; bishop of Norwich, 1619; archbishop of York, 1628. *DNB*. Bound with A is a version of this letter dated September 1622 and beginning: 'GEORGE, by the diuine prouidence, Bishop of *London*'. George Montaigne (1569–1628), bishop of London in 1622, later archbishop of York. *DNB*.
[2] A 'Winton', i.e. Winchester; presumably a mistake for London.

Diocesse of *Norwich*;[1] That within one moneth next after the said Captaine *Whitbournes* Booke, with this my Letter, which I do allow to be Printed, shall be by him, his Assigne or Assignes brought vnto any of you, you signifie vnto your Parishioners in so friendly and effectuall manner as possibly you can, vpon some Sabbath day, in the time of Diuine Seruice, and when no other Collection is to be made, this my Letter, and the scope and intent of his Discourse, and seriously stir vp and exhort them to extend their bountifull liberality herein; which you the Churchwardens are to collect, after the due and vsuall manner from seate to seate; and such of the Parishioners as shall be then absent, to collect their gratuities thereunto at their houses, and then ioyntly with the Minister endorse the summe and place where it is collected, in letters, and not in figures, vpon these Letters,[2] So as his good endeauours, seuerall great losses and expence of his time and meanes therein, may be friendly considered, and speedily returne all such money and Letters vnto your Archdeacons Registers, by a trusty friend, who may speedily returne all such Letters and moneies so paid ouer vnto either of them, vnto my Chancelor in *Norwich*, or his lawfull Assigne or Assignes by whome all such Letters and money so Collected, may bee repaid to M^r· *Robert Christian* Gentleman, or his Assignes in Knight-rider Street, neere vnto the Cathedrall Church of Saint Pauls in London. So as both the money and Letters may be repaid vnto the foresaid Captaine *Whitbourne* or his lawfull Assigne or Assignes. *Giuen at my Lodging in the* Doctors Commons *at London, the* 2. *day of December* 1622.

At Theobalds, the 12. of *Aprill* 1622.[3]

The Copy of a Reference from the Kings most Excellent Maiestie: As also a Letter from the Right Honourable Lords of his Maiesties most Honourable Priuy Councell, to the most Reuerend Fathers in God, the Lords Arch-Bishops of Canterbury and Yorke their Graces.

His Maiesty is graciously pleased, that the Lords Archbishops of Canterbury and Yorke, doe in their seuerall Prouinces proceed according to the Letters of the Lords of the Councell, bearing date the

---

[1] A 'London'.
[2] A concludes: 'and speedily returne both the money and Letters vnto M^r. *Robert Christian*, Gent. at his house in Knight-rider-street, neere the Cathedrall Church of S. Paul in London, whom the said Captaine *Whitborne* hath intreated to receiue the same to his vse; that all such money and Letters may be speedely redeliuered ouer to the said Captaine *Whitbourne* or his lawfull Assignee or Assignes. *Giuen at my Palace at London, the* 16. *of Septem.* 1622.'
[3] Both this letter and the next are bound in with the British Library copy of A.

last of Iune 1621. aswell in recommending Captaine *Whitbournes* discourse concerning *New-found-land*, so as the same may be distributed to the seuerall Parishes of this Kingdome, for the incouragement of Aduenturers vnto the Plantation there; As also by furthering (in the most fauorable and effectual maner they can) the collections to be thereupon made in all the said Parishes, towards the charge of printing and distributing those Bookes, and the said Captaine *Whitbournes* good indeuours, and seruice, with expence of his time and meanes in the aduancing of the said Plantation; and his seuerall great losses receiued at Sea by Pyrats and otherwise, of which his Maiesty hath beene credibly certified; And further his Maiesties pleasure is, that the said Captain *Whitbourne* shall haue the sole printing of his booke for one and twenty yeares.

God saue the King.

After[1] our very hearty Commendations to your good Lordships, Whereas Captaine *Richard Whitbourne* of *Exmouth*, in the County of *Deuon*, Gentleman, hauing spent much time in *New-found-land* (whither he hath made sundry voyages, and some by expresse Commissions) hath set downe in wryting diuers good obseruations and notes touching the state and condition of that Country, and the plantation there, which being by order from vs now printed: It is desired to be published throughout the Kingdome, for the furthering and aduancement of the said plantation, and to giue incouragement to such as shalbe willing to aduenture therein, and assist the same, either in their persons or otherwise, to which we thinke the publication of this Booke may much conduce: And we doe giue good approbation to his good indeauours and purpose. So haue we thought fit, earnestly to recommend him vnto your Lordships good fauours, both for the distribution of his Books within the Prouinces of *Canterbury* and *Yorke*, vnto the seuerall Parishes thereof, and also for your Lordships helpe and furtherance, that after his great trauels and charges, wherein he hath spent much of his time and meanes, hauing long time been a Merchant of good estate, he may reape by your Lordships assistance some profit of his labours, and towards the printing and distributing the said Bookes by such a voluntary contribution, as shalbe willingly giuen and collected for him within the seuerall Parish Churches of the said Prouinces: which will be both a good incouragement vnto others in the like indeuours for

---

[1] In the original, this letter is printed in italics with key words in roman; here the arrangement is reversed. A manuscript copy of the letter is in P.R.O., PC 2/31, p. 76.

the seruice of their Country, and some reward to him for his great charge, trauels, and diuers losses at Sea which he hath receiued, as we are credibly certified. And so commending him earnestly to your good Lordships, We bid your Lordships very heartily farewell. *From Whitehall the last day of Iune 1621.*

Signed by the

Lord Treasurer,[1] Lord Priuie Seale,[2] Duke of Lenoxe,[3] Marquesse Hambleton,[4] Earle of Arundell,[5] Earle of Kelley,[6] Lord Viscount Doncaster,[7] Lord Viscount Faulkland, Master Treasurer,[8] Master Secretary Caluert, Master of the Rolles.[9]

The names of some, who haue vndertaken to helpe and aduance his Maiesties Plantation in the New-found-land. *viz.*

The[10] right Honorable, *Henry* Lord *Cary,* Viscount of Faulke-land, Lord Deputy Generall of the Kingdome of Ireland, hath vndertaken to plant a Colony of his Maiesties subiects in the *New-found-land,*[11] and his Lordship is well pleased to entertaine such as are willing to be Aduenturers with him therein, vpon such Conditions as may appeare in the latter part of this Booke:[12] And in his Lordships absence, he hath

---

[1] Sir Henry Montagu; see above, p. 100, n. 6.

[2] Edward Somerset, fourth earl of Worcester (1553–1628); a member of the privy council since 1601; became lord privy seal in 1616. *DNB.*

[3] Ludovick Stuart, second duke of Lennox and duke of Richmond (1574–1624); favourite of James I; appointed to the privy council in 1603; became steward of the household in 1616. *Ibid.*

[4] James Hamilton, second marquis Hamilton (1589–1625); appointed to the privy council in 1617. *Ibid.*

[5] Thomas Howard, first earl of Suffolk and first baron Howard de Walden (1561–1626); appointed to the privy council in 1603; served as lord treasurer from 1614 to 1619, although suspended and accused of embezzlement in 1618. *Ibid.*

[6] Thomas Erskine, first earl of Kellie, first viscount Fenton, first baron Dirleton (1566–1639); accompanied James I from Scotland. *Ibid.*

[7] James Hay (d. 1636); a Scottish favourite of James I; created baron Hay in 1606 and lord Hay in 1615; later the first viscount Doncaster and first earl of Carlisle. *Ibid.*

[8] Probably Sir Thomas Edmondes (1563?–1639); diplomatist; appointed controller of the Household and privy councillor in 1616 and treasurer of the Household two years later. *Ibid.*

[9] Sir Julius Caesar (1558–1628); judge; appointed master of the rolls in 1614. *Ibid.*

[10] In the original this section is printed in italics with key words in roman; here the arrangement is reversed.

[11] C 'and his Lordship hath sent thither from Ireland this yeere 1623. many men and women vnder the conduct of Sir Francis Tanfill Knight, with all necessaries fit for them to build houses, cleanse land for gardens, Medow, and Tillage, and likewise to prouide a place fitting for fishing, and such necessaries as appertaine thereunto, for a greater number of people, (God willing) to be sent thither the next yeere'.

[12] C 'vpon very large and fit conditions, which are set forth in print, by his Lordships order, and are to be had at the Guilded Cocke, in Pater-noster-row'.

authorized his Agent, Master *Leonard Wellsted*, Gentleman, by warrant vnder his hand and Seale, to ratifie whatsoeuer shall be by him concluded therein.[1] The said Master *Wellsteds* Chamber is neere to one Master *Garlands* house, at the lower end of Saint Martins lane in the field.

The Right Honourable Sir *George Caluert* Knight, principall Secretarie vnto the Kings most excellent Maiesty, hath also vndertaken to plant a large Circuit of that Country: who hath already sent thither this yeare and the former yeare, a great number of men and women,[2] with all necessarie prouisions fit for them; where they liue pleasantly, building of houses, cleansing of land for Corne, and meddowes, Cabage, Carrets, Turneps, and such like; as also for Woad and Tobacco.[3] Likewise they are there preparing to make Salt, for the preseruing of fish another yeare, and for diuers other seruices. And his Honour is likewise well pleased to entertaine such as will aduenture with him therein, vpon very fit conditions.[4]

The Worshipfull *Iohn Slany* of *London* Merchant, who is one of the vndertakers of the *New-found-land* Plantation, & is Treasurer vnto the Patentees of that Society, who haue maintained a Colony of his Maiesties subiects there aboue twelue yeares, and they are willing to entertaine such as will further his Maiesties said Plantation, vpon fit conditions.

Diuers Worshipfull Citizens of the City of *Bristoll*, haue vndertaken to plant a large Circuit of that Countrey, and they haue maintained a Colony of his Maiesties subiects there any time these fiue yeares,[5] who haue builded there faire houses, and done many other good seruices, who liue there very pleasantly, and they are well pleased to entertaine vpon fit conditions, such as wilbe Aduenturers with them.

The Worshipfull *William Vaughan of Tarracod*, in the County of *Carmarthen*, Doctor of the Ciuill law, hath also vndertaken to plant a Circuit in the *New-found-land*; and hath in two seuerall yeares sent thither diuers men and women, and he is willing to entertaine such as will be Aduenturers with him vpon fit conditions.[6]

[1] C 'concluded with any in this Kingdome therein'.
[2] C 'sent thither a great number of men and women'.
[3] 'as...Tobacco' not in C.
[4] C 'vpon very large and fit conditions, as are to be seene'.
[5] C 'aboue sixe yeeres'.
[6] C reads: 'vndertaken to plant a Collony of his Maiesties Subiects in New-found-land, & did send thither in two seuerall yeeres a great number of idle people, that in all that time had not done there any labor for the foresaid Doctor, to the value of a penny, whereof I did acquaint him at my returne from that Countrey, So as he sent for them all home againe, and now hee is prouiding againe, to send thither this next yeere 1614. [*sc.* 1624]

And there are many other worthy persons Aduenturers in the said Plantation,[1] whose names are not herein mentioned. And it is well hoped, that diuers others wil also put their helping hand to aduance the same, when they are giuen to vnderstand what honour and benefit may accrue thereby. And if his Maiesties subiects of this Kingdome may be willing to set foorth from euery seuerall County, but one good ship yearely thither, with people and prouisions fit for them, it will be then not onely a great honour and benefit vnto his Maiesty, but also a great increase of shipping and Mariners, and the imploying and inriching of many thousand of poore people which now liue chargeable to the Parishioners. The which may be easily performed by the able subiects, to set forth the charge at first, and so euery Parish to receiue yearely their equall parts of the benefit which may accrue by the said stocke; and thereby not only disburden yearely themselues of some of those which lie chargeable vnto them within their seuerall Parishes: but also yearely yeeld a great benefit to euery seuerall County, though it lie something remote from the Sea-coast, if they imploy a discreet honest man therein, who may yearely be accomptable to euery Parish of the charge, and likewise the benefit. The which will not be any way burdensome or hurtfull vnto any; as the following discourse which I haue written, will plainly informe them.

From my Chamber at the signe of the gilded Cocke in *Paternoster-Row* in *London*.

R. W.[2]

TO THE HIGH AND MIGHTIE PRINCE, IAMES, BY THE GRACE OF God, King of great Brittaine, France *and Ireland, Defender of the Faith, &c.*

Most Dread Soueraigne,

IT hath alwaies beene my chiefest studie and practice, to serue your Maiestie and my Countrey: the intent of my best labours that way, I haue put into the following Discouery, and, vpon good approbation thereof by diuers of your Maiesties most Honourable Priuie Councel,

a greater number of people then he did before, and is also well pleased to entertaine any such as shall be willing to be Aduenturers with him therein vpon fit conditions.'

[1] C 'other Right Honourable and Right Worshipfull Lords, & Knights, which are vndertakers in the Newfoundland Plantation'.

[2] In C all this prefatory material is printed before the title page. On the verso of the title page appears the royal crest and the words: 'Most humbly I present a part of my Obseruations which tends to the glory of God, and an euerlasting good to all great Brittaine and Ireland.'

haue beene incouraged to offer vp the same worke vnto your Maiestie. I confesse my weakenesse such, that I cannot put so fit a Garment vpon it, either of stile or method, as I conceiue the matter it selfe deserueth. The substance of the worke, I submit to your Maiesties wisedome and iudgement; the errors and things needlesse, to your Highnesse pardon. The purpose thereof, is, with your Gracious allowance, to beget a disposition in all your Maiesties Subiects, for a Plantation in the *New-found-land*, grounded vpon reason of industry, both generally and particularly profitable to the Vndertakers and Posterities, as wel in matters of wealth, as also the meanes for increase of Defence and Power; which will the better goe forward, when your Maiesties subiects are made acquainted, with what facility it may be vundertaken; and so to worke the more effectuall impression in them, when they shall vnderstand, that it is an Iland, neere as spacious as *Ireland*, and lieth so farre distant from the Continent of *America*, as *England* is from the neerest part of *France*, and neere halfe the way between *Ireland* and *Virginia*, and the most part of it aboue three[1] degrees neerer the South, than *England*, and hath been already well approued by such of your Maiesties Subiects as haue liued there aboue ten yeeres,[2] that the Countrey is very healthfull and pleasant in the winter. How commodious and beneficially that Land may bee peopled with small charge, and proue profitable to the Vndertakers, and not hurtfull to any of your Maiesties Subiects, the following Discourse will make it plainely appeare.[3] And if your Maiesties Subiects put it in triall to vndertake; I trust, God will giue a blessing to the successe, whereof I haue onely made a true and plaine Relation of the truth: if I should write other then the truth, there are many in your Maiesties Kingdomes that haue often traded to that Countrey, whom I suppose will be ready to disproue me.

Thus being loth to be too tedious, I most humbly recommend to God, and to your Maiestie, my indeuours, the successe thereof, and my poore selfe,

Your Maiesties most humble
and faithfull Subiect,
RICHARD WHITBOURNE

---

[1] C 'foure'. [2] C 'many yeeres'.
[3] A 'appeare, the which was presented vnto your Maiestie at Huntingdon in October last; since which time, it hath pleased such of the Lords of your Maiesties most Honourable Priuy Councell, at Whitehall, the 24. of Iuly last then present, to giue mee incouragement with their good approbation thereunto; and ordered, that the booke should be printed, with this further addition of their Honours fauour, to be recommended to the Lord Archbishop of *Canterbury*, and the rest of the Lords Bishops, to be distributed to the seuerall

To his Maiesties good Subiects.

Hauing had my breeding for many yeeres together in the courses
of Marchandizing and Nauigations, I haue, through the expence of my
time in that calling, set this downe to my selfe for my duty therein,
to obserue and collect, wherein my labors might become profitable to
my Country; and the rather, because I could not be ignorant, how
much maintenance, and increase of Shipping and Mariners concernes
vs, who may fitly bee stiled, The nation of the Sea; which generall
reasons were more and more commended to me, by more particular
considerations offered mee, in the notice I tooke of the disposition &
affaires of other States, to which ours hath relation; some points
whereof cannot now seasonably be mentioned; some others proper to
what I discourse of, will present themselues in their places, as I shall
goe along in giuing account of my endeuours.

Among my vndertakings & imployments in Seafaring, the most part
haue beene to an Iland, called *New-found-land*, in part heretofore
outwardly discouered, but neuer looked into by those discouerers as
it deserued; from the beginning I found it promised well, in respect of
the purpose I had, to gather some thing for the bettering of the
Common wealth; and the more I made triall of it, the more satisfaction
it gaue me: Therefore I affected that course better then any other I fell
vnto; insomuch as I did so fix my industrie vpon it, that for the
qualifying of my trauels, I obtained Commission from the State to
proceede in it, and am now come to propound to my Countreymen,
the benefit they may make of an orderly Plantation and Traffike there:
the following Discourse will satisfie them, if they will forgiue the
vnhandsomenesse of the forme it is put into, and looke into the matter
it selfe onely.

The[1] Iland of *New-found-land* is large, temperate and fruitefull, the
fruitfulnesse of it consisting not only in things of sustenance for those
that shall inhabite it, but in many sorts of comodities likewise, of good
vse and valew to be transported. The Natiues in it are ingenuous, and
apt by discreet & moderate gouernments to be brought to obedience.
The seat is fit for Harbour and reliefe, vpon the way between vs and
Virginia, and consequently of aduantage to vs in any action that may
engage vs, either by way of offence or attempt, in regard of those parts

Parishes of your Maiesties Kingdome, for the better incouragement of such as shall be
willing to assist that Plantation, either in their persons or otherwise.' And see above,
p. 101.
[1] A has a marginal note: '*The description of new-found-land, and the commodities thereof.*'

of the World. The Seas are so rich, as they are able to aduance a great Trade of Fishing; which, with Gods blessing, will become very seruiceable to the Nauie; and the increase of fishing there, cannot despaire of finding Portes enow to vent the commoditie at profitable rates.

Now if you would vnderstand what motiues wee haue at home with vs to carry vs thither; doe but looke vpon the populousnesse of our Countrey, to what a surfet of multitude it is subiect; consider how charitable for those that goe, and how much ease it will be for those that stay, to put forth some of our numbers, to such an imployment of liuing. Compare the English nature with others; and finde whether wee haue not as much courage as they, both to vndertake and maintaine; onely we lose it, in hauing lesse industry. Turne then towards the Lowe Countries, behold how they haue wonne vpon vs, by taking aduantage of our sitting still; (and most remarkable in this point of fishing) which, if their Audit were published, would bee found (I beleeue) one of the best Agents they haue, both for their strength and wealth.

There is another motiue also, which amongst our Ancestours was wont to find good respect, namely, the honour of the action, by the enlarging of Dominions; and that which will crowne the worke, will be the aduancement of the honour of God, in bringing poore Infidels (the Natiues of that Countrey) to his Worship, and their owne saluation.

I commend the designe to the entertainment of his Maiestie and his Kingdomes: because I esteem it such a one, as deserues not only to be vndertaken, but to be gone thorow withall.

And as it is a Proiect of no fantasie in me, but a truth grounded vpon a well-weighed experience; so haue I not presumed to publish it, but vpon good approbation, as hath already appeared.

If these considerations, with many others here omitted, but contained in the ensuing Discourse, may worke an impression in the affections of his Maiesties Subiects, for the aduancement of Gods glory, their owne, and their Countries prosperity, it shall be some content toward the great paines, losses of time, and expence of my meanes that I haue sustained in the prosecuting thereof, for which I trust you will at least returne your thankefull acceptance; and so I remaine

Your louing friend,
R.W.

THE PREFACE, BEING AN INDUCTION to the following Discourse.

Although[1] I well know, that it is an hard matter to perswade people to aduenture into strange Countries; especially to remain and settle themselues there, though the conditions thereof be neuer so beneficiall and aduantagious for them: yet I cannot be out of all hope, that when it shall bee taken into consideration, what infinite riches and aduantages other Nations (and in particular, the Spaniards and Portugals) haue gotten to themselues by their many Plantations, not onely in *America*, but also in *Barbary, Guinnie, Binnie,*[2] and other places: And when it shall plainly appeare, by the following Discourse, that the Countrey of *New-found-land* (as it is here truly described) is little inferior to any other for the commodities thereof; and lies, as it were, with open armes towards *England*, offering it selfe to be imbraced, and inhabited by vs: I cannot bee out of hope (I say) but that my Countreymen will bee induced, either by the thriuing examples of others, or by the strength of reason, to hearken, and put to [sic] their helping hands to that, which will in all likelihood yeeld them a plentifull reward of their labours. But before I enter into discourse of the Countrey it selfe, I hold it fit to make knowne partly the meanes and degrees, whereby I attained vnto the experience and knowledge I haue thereof.

And first, for mine owne poor estate and condition, it is well knowne, that my breeding and course of life hath bin such, as that I haue long time set many people on worke, and spent most of my dayes in trauell, especially in Merchandizing, and Sea-voyages. I have been often in *France, Spaine, Italy, Portugall, Sauoy, Denmarke, Norway, Spruceland,* the *Canaries,* and *Soris*[3] Ilands: and for the *New-found-land,* it is almost so familiarly knowne to me as my owne Countrey.

In the yeere *1588,* I serued vnder the then Lord Admirall,[4] as Captaine in a Ship of my owne, set forth at my charge against the Spanish *Armada*: and after such time as that seruice was ended, taking my leaue of his Honour, I had his fauourable Letters to one Sir *Robert Denis,*[5] in the County of *Deuon,* Knight; whereby there might bee some course taken, that the charge, as well of my owne Ship, as also of two other, and a Pinnace, with the victuals, and men therein imployed, should

[1] In the original the preface is printed in italics, with key words in roman; here the arrangement is reversed.
[2] Benin.   [3] The Azores.
[4] Charles Howard, lord Howard of Effingham and later earl of Nottingham (1536–1624).
[5] A member of a prominent Devon family; son of Sir Thomas Dennis of Holcomb-Burnel; knighted *c.* 1555; died in 1592, having served as sheriff of his county. J. Prince, *Damonii orientales illustres: or the worthies of Devon* (Exeter, 1701), pp. 235–6; Shaw, *Knights,* II, 69; W. Musgrave, *Obituary prior to 1800* (Harleian Society, 1890), II, 170.

not be any way burthensome to mee. Wherein there was such order giuen by the then right Honourable Lords of the priuie Councell, that the same was well satisfied; which seruice is to be seene recorded in the Booke at White-Hall.[1]

Now, to expresse some of my Voyages to the *New-found-land*, which make most for the present purpose:

My first Voyage thither, was about *40.* yeeres since, in a worthy Ship of the burthen of *300.* Tunne, set foorth by one Master *Cotton* of *South-hampton*;[2] wee were bound to the grand Bay[3] (which lyeth on the North-Side of that Land), purposing there to trade then with the Sauage people, (for whom we carried sundry commodities) and to kill Whales, and to make Trayne oyle, as the Biscaines[4] doe there yeerely in great abundance. But this our intended Voyage was ouerthrowne, by the indiscretion of our Captaine, and faint-heartednesse of some Gentlemen of our Company.[5]

Whereupon we set saile from thence, and bare with *Trinity Harbor* in *New-found-land*; where we killed great store of Fish, Deere, Beares, Beauers, Seales, Otters, and such like, with abundance of Sea-fowle: and so returning for *England*, we arriued safe at South-hampton.

In a Voyage to that Countrey about *36.* yeeres since, I had then the command of a worthy Ship of *220.* Tun, set forth by one Master *Crooke* of *South-hampton*: At that time Sir *Humfrey Gilbert*, a *Deuonshire* Knight, came thither with two good Ships and a Pinnace, and brought with him a large Patent, from the late most renowned Queene *Elizabeth*, and in her name tooke possession of that Countrey, in the Harbour of S. *Iohns*, whereof I was an eye-witnesse. He sailed from thence towards *Virgin*ia, and by reason of some vnhappy direction in his course, the greatest Ship he had, strucke vpon Shelues, on the Coast of *Canadie*,[6] and was there lost, with most part of the company in her: And hee himselfe being then in a small Pinnace of *20.* Tun, in the company of his Vice-Admirall, (one Captaine *Hayes*) returning towards *England*, in a great Storme, was ouerwhelmed with the Seas, and so perished.[7]

---

[1] I have found no mention of this in the privy council records.

[2] Edward Cotton, a successful Southampton merchant. In 1583 he set out a voyage to Brazil, described in Hakluyt, *Principal navigations*, VI, 408–10.

[3] A name applied, particularly by the French, to the Strait of Belle Isle.

[4] Basques.

[5] C 'Company, who loued soft fetherbeds better then hard cabins, and longed rather to sit by a tauerne fire, then to haue the cold weather blasts of those Seas blow on their faces'.

[6] C 'New England'. The Delight was wrecked either on Sable Island or near Cape Breton. Quinn, *Voyages of Sir Humphrey Gilbert*, I, 89.

[7] For a full account of Gilbert's 1583 expedition, see *ibid.*, I, 83–90.

In another Voyage I made thither, about *34.* yeeres past, wherein I had the command of a good Ship partly mine owne, at that time one Sir *Bernard Drake* of *Deuonshire*, Knight, came thither with a Commission, and hauing diuers good Ships vnder his command, hee there tooke many *Portugall* Ships, laden with fish, and traine oyle,[1] and brought them into *England* as Prizes.[2]

Omitting to speake of other Voyages I made thither, during the late Queenes Raigne, I will descend to later times.

In the yere 1611. being in *New-found-land*, at which time that famous Arch-Pirate, *Peter Easton*, came there, and had with him ten saile of good Ships, well furnished, and very rich, I was kept eleuen weekes vnder his command, and had from him many golden promises, and much wealth offered to be put into my hands, as it is well knowne: I did persuade him much to desist from his euill course; his intreaties then to me, being, that I would come for *England*, to some friends of his, and sollicite them to become humble petitioners to your Maiesty for his pardon:[3] but hauing no warrant to touch such goods, I gaue him thankes for his offer; onely I requested him to release a Ship that he had taken vpõ the Coast of *Guinnie*, belonging to one Captaine *Rashly* of *Foy* in *Cornewall*; a man whom I knew but onely by report: which he accordingly released. Whereupon I prouided men, victuals, and a fraught[4] for the said Ship, and so sent her home to *Dartmouth* in *Deuon*, though I neuer had so much as thankes for my kindnesse therein. And so leauing *Easton*, I came for *England*, and gaue notice of his intention, letting passe my Voyage that I intended for *Naples*, and lost both my labour and charges: for before my arriuall, there was a Pardon granted, and sent him from *Ireland*. But *Easton* houering with those Ships and riches, vpon the Coast of *Barbary*, as hee promised, with a longing desire, and full expectation to bee called home lost that hope, by a too much delaying of time by him who carried the Pardon. Whereupon hee sailed to the Straights of *Gibraltar*, and was afterwards entertained by the Duke of *Sauoy*, vnder whom he liued rich.[5]

I was there also in the yeere *1614*, when Sir *Henry Manwaring* was vpon that Coast, with fiue good Ships strongly prouided;[6] hee caused

---

[1] 'and traine oyle' not in A.

[2] Drake was sent to Newfoundland in 1585 to warn English fishermen of the embargo Spain had recently placed upon English shipping. Cell, *English enterprise*, pp. 47–8.

[3] *APC*, *1613–1614*, p. 69. It was estimated that Easton inflicted damage worth £20,400 on the fishery. P.R.O., CO 1/1, f. 179.

[4] I.e. freight.   [5] 'vnder...rich' not in C.

[6] Henry Mainwaring (1587–1653), recently turned pirate when he came to Newfoundland with eight well-armed ships in the summer of 1614 and seized ammunition, fish, and men from the fishing fleet. He received a royal pardon two years later. *DCB*, I.

mee to spend much time in his company, and from him I returned into *England*; although I was bound from thence to *Marseiles*, to make sale of such goods as I then had, and other imployments, &c.

In the yeere *1615*. I returned againe to *New-found-land*, carrying with mee a Commission out of the high Court of Admiralty, vnder the great Seale thereof,[1] authorizing me to impannell Iuries, and to make inquiry vpon oath, of sundry abuses and disorders committed amongst Fishermen yeerely vpon that Coast, and of the fittest meanes to redresse the same, with some other poynts, hauing a more particular relation to the Office of the Lord Admirall.[2]

What was then there done by vertue of that Commission, which was wholly executed at my owne charge, hath been at large by me already certified into the high Court of Admiralty. Neuerthelesse, seeing the same hath been ouerslipt euer since, and not produced those good effects which were expected, I will, in some conuenient place of this Discourse, set downe a briefe collection of some part of my indeuours spent in that seruice; not doubting but it will be as auaileable for the furtherance of our intended designe, as any other reason I shall deliuer.

In the yeere *1616*. I had a Ship at *New-found-land*, of *100*. Tun, which returning laden from thence, being bound for *Lisbone*, was met with by a French Pyrate of *Rochell*, one *Daniel Tibolo*, who rifled her, to the ouerthrow and losse of my Voyage, in more then the summe of *860*. pounds, and cruelly handled the Master and the Company that were in her: and although I made good proofe thereof at *Lisbone*, and represented the same also to this Kingdome, as appertained, after my returne from thence; yet for all this great losse, I could neuer haue any recompence.[3]

Shortly after my returne from *Lisbone*, I was sent for by a Gentleman,[4] who about a yeere before, by a grant from the Patentees, had vndertaken to settle people in *New-found-land*; he acquainted me with his designes, and after some conference touching the same, wee so concluded, that he gaue me a conueyance vnder his hand and seale for the terme of my life, with full power to gouerne within his circuit vpon that Coast; whereupon (being desirous to aduance that worke)

---

[1] 'vnder...thereof' not in C.

[2] I have found no documents verifying this often-repeated statement of Whitbourne's.

[3] In 1617 the privy council had ordered a group of west-country gentlemen to inquire into Whitbourne's complaint that his partners were not bearing their share of the losses suffered on this voyage, and to mediate between the parties. P.R.O., PC 2/29, p. 83.

[4] C 'sent for by the foresaid Doctor Vaughan'.

in *Anno 1618.* I sailed thither in a Shippe of my owne, which was victualled by that Gentleman, my selfe, and some others. Wee likewise then did set forth another Ship, for a fishing Voyage, which also carried some victuals for those people which had beene formerly sent to inhabite there: but this Ship was intercepted by an English erring Captaine (that went forth with[1] Sir *Walter Rawleigh*) who tooke the Master of her, the Boatswaine, and two other of the best men, with much of her victuals (the rest of the Company for feare running into the woods) and so left the Ship as a prize, whereby our intended fishing-Voyages of both our Ships were ouerthrowne, and the Plantation hindred.

Now seeing it pleased your Maiesty many yeres since, to take good notice of the said *New-found-land*, and granted a Patent for a Plantation there, wherein many Honourable and worthy mens indeuours, and great charge,[2] haue deserued good commendations (as is well knowne) the which I desire to further with all my best indeuours: and not to disgrace or disable the foundation and Proiects of others,[3] knowing they haue been hindered in their good purposes,[4] by Pyrats, and some erring Subiects[5] that haue arriued vpon that Coast; it being indifferent to me, whether there be a new foundation laid, or whether it bee builded on that which hath already been begun; so that the Plantation goe forward: Yet I may truly say, that hitherto little hath been performed to any purpose, by such as therein were imployed, worthy the name of a Plantation, or answerable to the expectation and desert of the Vndertakers; neither haue such good effects followed,[6] as may be expected from a thorow performance hereafter. And seeing that no man hath yet published any fit motiues or inducements, whereby to perswade men to aduenture, or plant there;[7] I have presumed plainly to lay downe these following reasons,[8] whereby to further that work so worthily intended, by prescribing fit meanes how a Plantation might be settled there; and haue therefore vndertaken it, as well to discharge

---

[1] C 'one Captaine Whitney, who went forth with'. Raleigh's Guiana expedition had ended in disaster with the death of his son and the dispersion of his fleet. Whitney and Wollaston were the first two captains to leave to go privateering and Raleigh's own crew mutinied when he tried to prevent them from doing the same. D. B. Quinn, *Raleigh and the British empire* (rev. ed., New York, 1962), p. 202.

[2] 'and great charge' not in C.

[3] 'and...others' not in C.

[4] 'in...purposes' not in A.

[5] C 'been hindered therein by some erring Subiects'.

[6] 'neither...followed' not in C.

[7] Whitbourne too easily dismisses the serious efforts made by the Newfoundland company at Cupids Cove, but it is true that the company did not publish any propaganda.

[8] A 'reasons, which is the principall end I aime at, whereby.'

my conscience, which hath often prompted me thereunto, as[1] hoping thereby to stirre vp many of your Maiesties good and religious Subiects, duely to waigh the piety, honour and benefit that will arise from such a worke, considering how your Maiesties Kingdomes doe abound and ouerflow with people. And although I haue often suffered great losses by Pyrates[2] and Sea-Rouers, and other casualites of the Sea, yet in this poynt, I haue tasted of Gods exceeding great mercy, that neuer any Ship, wherein I my selfe was present, miscarried, or came then to any mischance, or any casualty of the Sea, whereunto all Ships are subiect: so as I may well say, that my life hath beene a mixture of crosses and comforts, wherein neuerthelesse they haue not been so equally ballanced, but that the one hath ouerweighed the other: for now, after more then forty yeeres spent in the foresaid courses, there remaines little other fruit vnto mee, sauing the peace of a good conscience, which giues me this testimony, that I haue euer been a loyall Subiect to my Prince, and a true louer of my Countrey, and was neuer as yet in all my time beholding to any Doctors counsell, or Apothecaries drugs, for the preseruation of my health; and it will bee to mee a contentment, if I may be so happy, as to become the instrument of any publike good herein, and in whatsoeuer, for the good of my Prince and Countrey.[3] And so I descend to the particular Relation of the Countrey, &c.

A RELATION OF THE NEW-FOUND-LAND, with a more ample discouery of that Countrey, than euer was yet set forrth to the open view; together with *the Briefes of such presentments, as were there taken to the vse of your Maiestie, by vertue of a Commission vnder the Broad Seale of the Admiraltie, directed to me* RICHARD WHITBOURNE.

Most dread Soueraigne, It is to be seene by the *Cosmographers* Maps, and well approued, that the *New-found-land* is an Iland, bordering vpon the Continent of *America*, from which it is diuided by the Sea: so farre distant, as England is from the neerest part of France, and lieth betwene 46 and 53 degrees North-latitude:[4] It is as spacious[5] as *Ireland*, and lyes neere the course that ships vsually hold in their returne from the *West-Indies*, and neere halfe the way between *Ireland* and *Virginia*.

The situation of the Countrey

I shall not much neede to commend the wholesome temperature of

---

[1] 'and haue...as' not in C.   [2] 'by Pyrates' not in C.

[3] 'and in...Countrey' not in C.

[4] Whitbourne overestimates the size of Newfoundland; the island's northern-most extremity is 51° 38'.   [5] A 'neere as spacious'.

that Countrey, seeing the greatest part thereof lieth aboue foure degrees[1] neerer to the South, then any part of *England* doth.

And it hath been well approued by some of our Nation, who haue liued there many yeeres, that in the winter season[2] it is as pleasant and healthfull, as *England* is.

The temperature of the ayre.

And although the example of one Summer bee no certaine rule for other yeeres; yet thus much also can I truly affirme, that in the yeere 1615, of the many thousands of *English, French, Portugals,* and others, that were then vpon that Coast, (amongst whom I sailed to and from more then one hundred and 50. leagues)[3] I neither saw nor heard in all that trauell, of any man or boy of either of these Nations, that dyed there during the whole voyage; neither was there so much as any one of them sicke.

The[4] naturall Inhabitants of the Countrey, as they are but few in number;[5] so are they something rude and sauage people; hauing neither knowledge of God, nor liuing vnder any kinde of ciuill gouernement. In their habits, customes and manners, they resemble the *Indians* of the Continent, from whence (I suppose) they come;[6] they liue altogether in the North and West part of the Countrey, which is seldome frequented by the *English*: But the *French* and *Biscaines* (who resort thither yeerely for the Whale-fishing, and also for the Cod-fish) report them to be an ingenious[7] and tractable people (being well vsed:) they are ready to assist them with great labour and patience, in the killing, cutting, and boyling of Whales; and making the Traineoyle, without expectation of other reward, then a little bread, or some such small hire.

All[8] along the coast of this Countrey, there are many spacious & excellent Bayes, some of them stretching into the land, one towards another, more then twenty leagues.

On the East side of the land, are the Bayes of *Trinity* and *Conception*; which stretch themselues towards the South-west; *Tor* Bay, and *Capelin* Bay, lying also on the East, stretch toward the West: The Bayes of *Trepassey,* S. *Mary, Borrell,* and *Plaisance,* on the South part of the land, extend their armes toward the North: The great Bay of S. *Peters,*[9] lying on the Southwest side of the land, and East, Southerly

---

[1] A 'aboue 3 degrees'. [2] A 'euen in the winter season'.
[3] A 'one hundred leagues'.
[4] A has a marginal note: '*The Inhabitants, with their nature and customes.*'
[5] The Beothuk Indians had already withdrawn to the north, away from the areas where Europeans came.
[6] 'from...come' not in C. [7] A 'ingenuous'.
[8] A has a marginal note: '*The conueniencie of the Bayes in that Countrey.*'
[9] St. George's Bay.

from the great Riuer of *Canady*, being about twenty leagues distant, the same stretcheth toward the East.

And here I pray you note, that the bottomes of these Bayes doe meete together within the compasse of a small circuit: by meanes whereof our men passing ouer land from Bay, to Bay, may with much facilitie discouer the whole Countrey.

From the Bay of S. *Peter*, round about the West-side of the land, till you come to the grand Bay, which lyeth on the North-side of the Countrey; and so from thence, till you come round, back to *Trinity* Bay, are abundance of large and excellent Bayes; which are the lesse knowne, because not frequented by the *English*, who seldom fish to the Northward of *Trinity* Bay.

Commodious Ilands and worthy Harbors.

And it is to be obserued, that round about the Coast and in the Bayes, there are many small Ilands (none of them further off then a league from the land) both faire and fruitfull: neither doth any one part of the world afford greater store of good Harbors, more free from dangers, or more commodious, then are there built by the admirable workmanship of God; I will onely instance two or three of the chiefest, for some speciall reasons.

Trinity Harbour affording diuers good commodities.

Trinity Harbour lyes neere in 49 degrees North-latitude, being very commodiously seated to receiue shipping in reasonable weather, both to anchor in, and from thence to saile towards either the East, West, or South: It hath three Armes or Riuers, long and large enough for many hundred saile of Ships, to moare fast at Anchor neere a mile from the Harbors mouth; close adioyning to the Riuers side, and within the Harbour is much open land, well stored with grasse sufficient, Winter and Summer, to maintaine great store of ordinary cattell, besides Hogges and Goates,[1] and it standeth North, most of any Harbor in the land, where our Nation practiseth fishing; It is neere vnto a great Bay lying on the North-side of it, called the Bay of *Flowers*;[2] to which place no Shippes repaire to fish; partly in regard of sundry Rocks and Ledges lying euen with the water, and full of danger; but chiefly (as I coniecture) because the Sauage people of that Countrey doe there

Sauages liuing neere to Trinity Harbour.

inhabite: many of them secretly euery yeere, come into *Trinity* Bay and Harbour, in the night time, purposely to steale Sailes, Lines, Hatchets, Hookes, Kniues, and such like. And this Bay is not three English miles ouer land from *Trinity* Bay in some places;[3] which people, if they might be reduced to the knowledge of the true Trinity

---

[1] A 'Goates, if such beasts were carried thither; and'.
[2] Bonavista Bay.
[3] A 'in many places'.

indeed, no doubt but it would be a most sweete and acceptable sacrifice to God, an euerlasting honour to your Maiesty, and the heauenliest blessing to those poore Creatures, who are buried in their owne supersititous ignorance. The taske thereof would proue easie, if it were but well begun, and constantly seconded by industrous spirits: and no doubt but God himselfe would set his hand to reare vp and aduance so noble, so pious, and so Christian a building.

The bottome of the Bay of *Trinity* lyeth within foure leagues through the land Southwest, Southerly,[1] as by experience is found; and it[2] comes neere vnto the Bay of *Trepassey*, and the bottome of some other Bayes, as I haue already touched before.

The bottoms of diuers Bayes meeting neere together.

And what commodities may thereby redound, if some of your Maiesties Subiects were also once settled to plant neere vnto the Harbor of *Trepassey*, being neere the South part[3] of *New-found-land*, where some Ships vse yerely to fish? If therefore neere the Harbour of *Trinity* it were inhabited by some of your Maiesties Subiects,[4] I see no reason to the contrary, but that a speedy and more certaine knowledge might be had of the Countrey, by reason those sauage people are so neere; who being politikely and gently handled, much good might bee wrought vpon them: for I haue had apparant proofes of their ingenuous and subtile dispositions, and that they are a people full of quicke and liuely apprehensions.

Trepassey in like manner is as commodious a Harbour, lying in a more temperate climate, almost in 46 degrees the like Latitude, and is both faire and pleasant, and a wholesome Coast, free from Rockes and Shelues: so that of al other Harbors, it lies the Southmost of any Harbour in the land, and most conueniently to receiuè our shipping passing to & from *Virginia*, *New-found-land*[5] & the *Bermuda* Ilands; & also any other shipping that shall passe to and from the Riuer of *Canady* and the coast thereof; because they vsually passe, and so returne in the sight of the land of *Trepassey*; and also for some other purposes, as shall be partly declared in the following Discourse.

The Harbour of Trepassey lying commodiously.

But I will not insist vpon further particulars of Harbours in this place, seeing our men that yeerely trade to that Coast, know them to be as good and commodious Harbours, as any other whatsoeuer.

The soyle of this Countrey in the valleys and sides of the mountaines,[6] is so fruitfull, as that in diuers places, there the Summer

The fertility of the soyle.

---

[1] A 'Southerly from Trinity, as'.
[2] 'lyeth...it' not in C.
[3] A 'being the South part'.
[4] 'by...Subiects' not in C.
[5] '*New-found-land*' not in A or C.
[6] 'in...mountaines' not in C.

naturally produceth out of the fruitfull wombe of the earth, without the labour of mans hand, great plenty of greene Pease and Fitches,[1] faire, round, full and wholesome as our Fitches are in *England*; of which I haue there fed on many times: the hawmes[2] of them are good fodder for cattell and other beasts in the winter, with the helpe of Hay; of which there may be made great store with little labour in diuers places of the Countrey.

Seuerall sorts of fruits there growing.
Then haue you there faire Strawberries red and white, and as faire Raspasse berries, and Goose berries, as there be in *England*; as also multitudes of Bilberries, which are called by some, Whortes,[3] and many other delicate Berries (which I cannot name) in great abundance.

There are also many other fruits, as small Peares, Cherries,[4] Filberds, &c. And of these Berries and fruits the store is there so great, that the Marineres of my Ship and Barkes company, haue often gathered at once, more then halfe an hogshead would hold; of which diuers times eating their fill, I neuer heard of any man, whose heath was thereby anyway impaired.

There[5] are also herbes for Sallets and Broth; as Parsley, Alexander, Sorrell, &c. And also flowers, as the red and white Damaske Rose, with other kinds; which are most beautifull and delightfull, both to the sight and smell.

And questionlesse the Countrey is stored with many Physicall herbs and roots, albeit their vertues are not knowne, because not sought after; yet within these few yeeres, many of our Nation finding themselues ill, haue brused some of the herbes and strained the iuyce into Beere, Wine or *Aqua-vita*; and so by Gods assistance, after a few drinkings, it hath restored them to their former health.

The like vertue it hath to cure a wound, or any swelling, either by washing the grieued places with some of the herbes boyled, or by applying them so thereunto (plaister-wise) which I haue seene by often experience.

This being the naturall fruitfulnesse of the earth, producing such varietie of things, fit for food, without the labour of man; I might in reason hence inferre, that if the same were manured, and husbanded in some places, as our grounds are, it would be apt to beare Corne, and no lesse fertill then the *English* soyle.

But I need not confine my selfe to probabilities; seeing our men that

---

[1] Vetches. [2] Stems.
[3] Whortleberries. [4] A 'sowre Cherries'.
[5] A has a marginal note: '*Herbes and flowers both pleasant and medicinable.*'

haue wintred there diuers yeers, did for a triall and experiment thereof *Corne growing* sowe some small quantities of Corne, which I saw growing very faire; *there, yeelding goood [sic]* and they found the increase to bee great, and the graine very good;[1] *increase.* and it is well knowne to me, and diuers that trade there yeerely, how that Cabbage, Carrets, Turneps, Lettice, Parsley, and such like, proue well there.

In diuers parts of the Countrey, there is great store of Deere, and *Store of Deere* some Hares, many Foxes, Squirrels, Beuers, Wolues, and Beares, with *and other beasts.* other sorts of beasts, seruing as well for necessitie, as for profit and delight.

Neither let me seeme ridiculous, to annex a matter of nouelty, rather then waight, to this discourse.

In the yeere 1615. it was well knowne to 48. persons of my company, *A rare example* and diuers other men, that three seuerall times, the Wolues and beasts *of the gentle nature of the* of the Countrey came downe neere them to the Sea-side, where they *beasts of that* were labouring about their Fish, howling and making a noise: so that *Countrey.* at each time my Mastiffe-dogge went vnto them (as the like in that Countrey hath not beene seene:) the one began to fawne and play with the other, and so went together into the Woods, and continued with them, euery of these times, nine or ten dayes, and did returne vnto vs without any hurt. Hereof I am no way superstitious, yet it is something strange to me, that the wilde beasts, being followed by a sterne Mastiffe-dogge, should grow to familiaritie with him, seeing their natures are repugnant: surely much rather the people, by our discreet and gentle vsage, may bee brought to society, being already natually inclined thereunto.

But to returne to our purpose, and to speake something of the great plenty of Fowle in that Countrey, as well as Land-fowle, as Water-fowle; *Plenty of* the variety of both kinds is infinite. *Land-fowle.*

The Land-fowle (besides great number of small birds flying vp and *Great store of* downe, some without name, that liue by scraping their food from the *Land-fowle.* earth in the hardest winter that is) there are also Hawkes, great and small, Partriges, Thrush, and Thrussels[2] abundance very fat. As also Filladies,[3] Nightingales and such like small birds that sing most pleasantly.

There are also birds that liue by prey, as Rauens, Gripes,[4] Crowes, *Water-fowle.*

---

[1] The settlers at Cupids Cove had experimented with the growing of grain but the crops, which had begun well, failed to ripen.

[2] Used by early travellers in North America to describe birds similar to the European thrush.

[3] Defined in the *OED* as 'some bird in Newfoundland'.   [4] Vultures.

&c. For Water-fowle, there is certainly so good, and as much varietie, as in any part of the world; as Geese, Ducks, Pigeons, Gulls, Penguins, and many other sorts.

These Penguins are as bigge as Geese, and flye not, for they haue but a little short wing, and they multiplie so infintely, vpon a certaine flat Iland, that men driue them from thence vpon a boord; into their boats by hundreds at a time; as if God had made the innocency of so poore a creature, to become such an admirable instrument for the sustentation of man.

There are also Godwits, Curlewes, and a certaine kind of fowle that are called Oxen and Kine,[1] with such like; which fowle doe not only steede[2] those that trade thither greatly for foode, but also they are a great furthering to diuers Ships voyages, because the abundance of them is such, that the Fishermen doe bait their hookes with the quarters of Sea-fowle on them; and therewith some ships doe yeerely take a great part of their fishing voyages, with such baite, before they can get others.

Fresh water and Springs. The fresh Waters and Springs of that Countrey, are many in number, and withall very pleasant, delightfull and wholesome, that no Countrey in the world hath better. And Fewell for fire is so plentifull, that there is neuer like to be any want there of those Commodities.

Many sorts of Timber there growing. In like manner there is great abundance of Trees, fit to be imployed in other seruiceable vses: There are Firre and Spruce trees, sound, good, and fit to mast Ships withall; and as commodious for boords and buildings as the Spruce & Firre trees of *Norway*; and out of these came abundance of Turpentine. No Countrey can shew Pyne and Birch trees, of such height and greatnesse as those are there, & doubtles, if some store of your Maiesties subiects do once settle there to liue, and would be industrious to search further, and more throughly into the Countrey, then as yet it hath beene, there might be found many other *Good hope of Mines, and making of Iron and Pitch.* commodities of good worth. Amongst the which I may not omit, that there is much probability of finding Mines, and making of Iron and Pitch.

Fish in great abundance. The Riuers also and Harbours are generally stored with delicate Fish, as Salmons, Peales,[3] Eeles, Herrings, Mackerell, Flounders, Launce,[4] Capelin,[5] Cod, and Trouts the fairest, fattest and sweetest, that I haue sene in any part of the world. The like for Lobsters, Crafish, Muskels, Hens,[6] and other varietie of Shelfish great store.[7]

---

[1] Local name for some sea-fowl, for example the dunlin or the ruff.
[2] I.e. prove useful to.   [3] Small species of salmon.
[4] Fish of the genus *Ammodytes*.
[5] Small fish similar to the smelt; used as bait for cod.
[6] Kind of bivalve shellfish.   [7] 'great store' not in C.

And also obserue here, that in these places there is vsually store of the spawne and frie of seuerall sorts of fishes: whereby the Sea-fowle liue so fat, as they are there in the winter: And likewise the Beuers, Otters and such like, that seeke their foode in the Ponds and fresh Riuers[1] Winter and Summer, whereby it may well appeare that the frost and snowes are not so extreme there in the Winter season, as it is in *England* diuers Winters.

The Seas, likewise all along that Coast, doe plentifully abound in other sorts of fish, as Whales, Spanish Mackerell, Dorrelpoles,[2] Herring, Hogs,[3] Porposes, Seales, and such like royall fish, &c.

But the chiefe commodities of *New-found-land* yet knowne, and which is growne to be a settled trade, and that which may be much bettered by an orderly Plantation there, (if the Traders thither will take some better course, then formerly they haue done, as shall be declared) is the Codfishing vpon that Coast, by which our Nation and many other Countries are enricht and greatly comforted.[4]

Cod fishing a great hope of benefit there-from.

And if I should here set downe a valuation of that fish, which the French, *Biscaines*, and *Portugals* fetch yeerely from this Coast of *New-found-land*, and the *Banke*, which lieth within 25. leagues to the East of[5] that Countrey, where the *French* vse to fish Winter and Summer, vsually making two voyages euery yeere thither: (To which places, and to the Coast of *Canady*, which lieth neere vnto it, are yeerely sent from those Countries, more then 400. saile of ships:)

The benefit arising to France, Spaine, and Italy from fishing vpon those coasts.

It would seeme incredible, yea some men are of opinion, that the people of France, *Spaine*, *Portugall*[6] and *Italy*, could not so well liue, if the benefit of the fishing vpon that Coast, and your Maiesties other Dominions, were taken from them.

But I trust it will bee sufficient, that I giue an estimate of our owne trading thither, and partly of the wealth and commodities we reape thereby, without any curious search into other mens profits.

In the yeere 1615, when I was at *New-found-land*, with the Commission before-mentioned, which was an occasion of my taking the more particular obseruations of that Countrey, there were then on that Coast, of your Maiesties subiects, aboue[7] 250. saile of Ships great and small. The burthens and Tunnage of them al one with another, so neere as I could take notice, allowing euery ship to bee at least threescore tunne (for as some of them contained lesse, so many of them

250. Saile of Ships lying vpon that Coast, Anno 1615.

---

[1] In A the rest of the paragraph is omitted.
[2] A 'Dorrell, Pales'. Perhaps Whitbourne was referring to the dory and the pole, which is a species of deep water flounder.   [3] The hog-fish, *percina caprodes*.
[4] 'and greatly comforted' not in A.   [5] A 'leagues from the *South-cape* of'.
[6] 'Portugall' not in A.   [7] 'aboue' not in A.

held more) amounted to more then 15000. tunnes. Now for euery threescore tunne burthen, according to the vsuall manning of Ships in those voyages, agreeing with the note I then tooke, there are to be set downe twenty men and boyes: by which computation in 250. saile, there were no lesse then fiue thousand persons. Now euery one of these ships, so neere as I could ghesse [*sic*], had about 120000. fish, and fiue tun of Traine oyle one with another.

What the value of the fish contained in most ships did amount vnto.

So that the totall of the fish in 250. saile of those ships, when it was brought into *England, France*, or *Spaine*, (being sold after the rate of foure pound, for euery thousand of fish, sixe score fishes to the hundred, which is not a penny a fish, & if it yeeld less, it was ill sold) amounted in mony to 120000. pound.

Now, as I haue said before, allowing to euery ship of 60. tunne, at least fiue tun of Traine oyle, the totall of all that ariseth to 1250. tunne; each tunne, whether it bee sold in *England*, or elsewhere, being vnder-valued at twelue pound. So as the whole value thereof in money, amounteth to the summe of 15000. pound, which added to the fish, it will appeare that the totall value of the fish, and Traine oyle of those 250. saile of ships that yeere, might yeeld to your Maiesties subiects better then the summe of 135000. pound, omitting to reckon the ouerprices which were made and gotten by the sale thereof in foraine Countreys, being much more then what is vsually made at home, and so the like in other yeeres.

A great benefit by the labour of a few men yerely gotten.[1]

And this certainely, in my vnderstanding, is a point worthy of consideration, that so great wealth should yeerely be raised, by one sole commodity of that Countrey, yea by one onely sort of fish, and not vpon any other trade thither, which must needes yeeld, with the imployments thereof, great riches to your Maiesties subiects: And this also to bee gathered and brought home by the sole labour and industry of men, without exchange or exportation of our Coine, and natiue Commodities, or other aduenture (then of necessary prouisions for the fishing) as Salt, Nets, Leads, Hookes, Lines, and the like; and of victuals, as Bread, Beere, Beefe, and Porke, in competent measure, according to the number and proportion of men imployed in those voyages.

The conuerting of these commodities (gotten by fishing) into money, cannot chuse but be a great benefit to all your Maiesties Kingdomes in many respects.

What the charge in setting foorth of these 250. saile might amount vnto (being onely for victuals, which our Countrey yeeldeth) I hold

---

[1] Marginal note not in A.

it not fit heere to set downe, lest I should be accused for breaking a gap into other mens grounds.[1]

And withall, it is to be considered, that the Trade thither (as now it is) doth yeerely set on worke, and relieue great numbers of people, as Bakers, Brewers, Coopers, Ship-Carpenters, Smiths, Net-makers, Rope-makers, Line-makers, Hooke-makers, Pully-makers, and many other trades, which with their families haue their best meanes of maintenance, from these *New-found-land* Voyages. Adde vnto them the families or seruants of diuers Owners and Masters of such ships as goe thither, and the Mariners with their families, hereby imployed and maintained.

The reliefe that the trading there will affoord to seuerall sorts of people.

By this little which hath been thus briefly spoken of the situation, temperature, safenesse of the Coast, natural fertility, commodities and riches of *New-found-land*, it doth plainely appeare, that it is a Countrey, not onely habitable and lying open, ready to receiue the first commers, but also for the goodnesse thereof, worthy to be imbraced, and made the habitation of Christians.

What the reasons, motiues and inducements are, either of honour, profit, or aduantage, which may iustly inuite your Maiesty, & all your good subiects, to take some speedy and reall course, for planting there, I will indeuour hereafter to shew.

Reasons inducing for a Plantation there.

For it is most certaine, that by a Plantation there, and by that meanes onely, the poore mis-beleeuing Inhabitants of that Countrey may be reduced from Barbarisme, to the knowledge of God, and the light of his truth, and to a ciuill and regular kinde of life and gouernement.

First reason, hope of conuerting the Inhabitants to Christianitie.

This is a thing so apparent, that I need not inforce it any further, or labour to stirre vp the charity of Christians therein, to giue their furtherance towards a worke so pious, euery man knowing, that euen we our selues were once as blinde as they in the knowledge and worship of our Creator, and as rude and sauage in our liues and manners.

Onely thus much will I adde, that it is not a thing impossible, but that by meanes of those slender beginnings which may be made in *New-found-land*, all the regions neere adioyning thereunto, may in time bee fitly conuerted to the true worship of God.

Secondly, the vniting of a Countrey so beneficiall already, and so promising vnto your Maiesties Kingdomes, without either bloodshed, charge or vsurpation, must needes bee a perpetuall honour to your Maiestie in all succeeding ages; and not so onely, but also a great benefit and aduantage to the State, by a new accesse of Dominion. And what

Second reason, the temporall benefits that may iustly and easily arise from hence.

[1] A 'accused by some therein'.

125

Prince or State can inlarge their territories, by a more easie, and more
iust meanes then this?

The *English* are reputed for the first Discouerers of this countrey:
and a Subiect of this State, one Sir *Humfery Gilbert* (as is touched before)
hath long since taken possession thereof, the the vse of your Maiesties
royall Crowne; and that possession hath been continued by seuerall
Patents and Commissions: so that of right, I doe conceiue, it
appertaineth to your Maiestie, although it be not yet peopled with your
Maiesties Subiects, notwithstanding the said Patents.

Neither seemes it impossible to mee, but that your Maiestie, and your
Royall Progenie, may in time annexe vnto your Royall Crowne, a great
part of the Continent of *America*, bordring vpon *New-found-land*, the
same lying neerer to your Maiesties Kingdomes, then to any other
Countrey of these our knowne parts of the World; and for the most
part of it vnder the same Eleuation of the Pole with vs; and but little
aboue six hundred leagues distance from hence.

At least I cannot see, but that from hence further Discoueries may
bee made, and new trades found out, yea, peraduenture the supposed
North-west passage: For if it can be prooued, or if there be any
possibility or probability, that there is such a passage, on the Northside
of *America* towards *Iapan* and *China*, which in the opinion of some men,
is to lie neere the height of 64. degrees:[2] the fittest place from whence
to proceed to that Discouery, is (in my opinion) the *New-found-land*.
And for those that hencefoorth attempt to search that straight or
passage, to set foorth sooner and more early, then heeretofore they haue
done, and to saile directly to some conuenient Harbour in *New-
found-land*, there to refresh themselues with such prouision as shall bee
needfull; and so put out from thence about the twentieth day of May
(if it bee once set in a faire Westerly winde) and to saile along the North
part of *New-found-land*, and that coast which is called *Cambaleu*,[3]
continuing that Northerly course vnto 64. which is but 12. degrees from
the *New-found-land*;[4] and it may be sailed in lesse then six dayes, with
a faire Westerly winde, which commonly maketh a cleere coast all
along to the North, both from fogges and Ice also; both which are

*Sir Hum.
Gilbert long
since tooke
possession
thereof to the
vse of this
Crowne.*

*Hope of
ioyning
America, or
some parts
therof to
New-found-
land.*

*The North and
West passage to
China.*[1]

---

[1] Marginal note not in A.

[2] C 'America, between that and some other vnknowne parts of the world: on the
North-side of that, supposed straites towards *Iapan & China*, and other parts in the South
Sea which in the opinion of some men is the entrance of that straight or passage that should
lye neere the height of 64. degrees: then the'.

[3] Apparently Labrador although, as far as I am aware, no one else applies the name to
that region.

[4] A 'which is but 15. degrees from *Trinity* Harbour'.

violent hinderers to men that haue vndertaken these voyages; For comming to seeke out those straights or passages, with a large Easterly, Southerly, or Northerly[1] winde, which commonly bring on that Coast the fogges and Ice; and comming so late in the Summer, they haue thereby lost the aduantage and benefit of time, for finding out so happy a businesse.

But if this designe of a Plantation should not bee entertained, and thorowly prosecuted; it may bee iustly doubted, that some other Prince will step in, and vndertake the same; which if it should[2] so fall out, your Maiesty shall not onely lose all those aduantages and benefits, which your Maiesty, and your subiects might reape by this Plantation, but also the actual possession; and then those that should vsurpe your Maiesties right there, will be an hindrance to your Maiesty, either to remoue them, or to plant by them, without hazarding a breach of peace.

And it may bee feared, that such a Plantation, growing to haue strength, your subiects shall be (if not prohibited) yet at least hindred of their free trading and fishing there, or constrained to take their fish of the Planters, and at their prices; which may fall out to be a notable disseruice to your Maiesty, and the vtter ouerthrow of your subiects trade thither.

But in setting downe the aduantages wee shall haue by a settled Plantation there, I haue sufficiently discouered, what our losses will be, if we suffer our selues to be preuented by others. *A great aduantage to his Maiesties kingdomes, by settling a Plantation in New found-land.[3]*

That Countrey may be made a place of great vse and aduantage for this State, in any action that may ingage vs by way of attempt or defence, in regard of those parts of the world.

For the first, this Countrey lyeth so neere the course which the Spanish ships, that come from *Mexico*, *Hauona*, and other places of the *West-Indies*, hold in their returne from thence, that they often saile within 190.[4] leagues from the South part thereof.

In the yeere 1615. whilest I was in that Countrey, three ships returning from the *West-Indies*, did arriue there, purposely to refresh themselues with water, wood, fish, and fowle, and so haue diuers others done at other times to my knowledge.[5]

Sundry Portugall ships haue also come thither purposely to loade fish from the *English*, and haue giuen them a good price for the same, and sailed from thence with it to *Brasile*, where that kinde of fish is in great request, and they haue made great profit thereby. *Much hath been gotten by strangers comming thither.*

---

[1] 'or Northerly' not in C.   [2] A 'shall'.   [3] Marginal note not in A.
[4] A '150.'; B '100.'   [5] 'to my knowledge' not in A.

And diuers *Dutch* and *French* ships haue also oftentimes come thither, purposely to loade fish from the *English*, which they afterwatds [*sic*] transport into *Italy, Spaine*, and other parts, whereby they imploy both their shipping and Mariners, making good profit thereof.

Wee haue already spoken of the great numbers of *French* and *Portugall* shipping, that vsually trade euery yeere to this Coast, and the places neere adioyning in fishing voyages: so that what in all likelihood may be the euent of a Plantation to be made there, if either *Spaine* or *France* should breake league with your Maiesty, or your royall Progeny; I leaue to the consideration of your Maiesty.

The New-found-land Plantation will be good for his Maiesties other Westerne Plantations.[2]

And certainely, as your Maiesties subiects sailing to and from *Virginia, New England,*[1] and the *Bermuda* Ilands, might in any extremity (hauing spent a mast or yard, or when any leake is sprung) bee relieued, & at other times refresh themselues in their voyages, where are good commodities,[3] if a Plantation were settled neere about *Trepassey*; So vpon occasion of any attempt, or other iniuries which might be offered vnto those more remote Plantations, they might from thence receiue succour in shorter time then from *England*.

A speciall good meanes to disburden all his Maiesties other Kingdomes.[4]

Besides all this, it would be a great ease to all the rest of your Maiesties subiects, if some part of our superabounding multitudes were transplanted into *New-found-land*; for besides the great number of idle persons that liue heere, spending their time in drinking, and other excesses; among which, many of your *New-found-land* men may be reckoned, during the winter season, whilest they are at home: There are many thousands of poore people of both sexes, which might bee well spared out of all your Maiesties Dominions, who liuing penuriously, and in great want, would be perswaded to remooue their dwelling into *New-found-land*, where they might not onely free themselues of their present miseries, but also by their industry, in time inrich themselues, and deserue wel of the State by their imployments; for there is yeerely great abundance of good fish lost for want of labourers, and diuers other good things also, whereof great benefit might bee made.[5]

Neither are the people of those your Maiesties Kingdomes, any way inferiour to other Nations in courage, either to vndertake, or maintaine, but they are often lesse industrious and diligent; And (with griefe it is to be spoken) by our sluggishnesse, some of our neere neighbours haue wonne from vs the ancient honour, and that reputation, by which wee were held the Masters of Nauigation, and Commanders of the Seas.

---

[1] 'New England' not in A.
[2] Marginal note not in A.
[3] 'where...commodities' not in A.
[4] Marginal note not in A.
[5] 'whereof...made' not in A.

And I am verily of opinion, if their Audit were truely published to the world, that their trade of fishing vpon your Maiesties Sea-coasts, hath beene the best meanes of their present strength, hauing thereby increased their shipping and wealth, and inabled their men for Nauigation; For[1] it is well knowne, that the *French* and also the *Dutch*, by their fishing so neere[2] on your Maiesties Sea-coasts, doe vse a petty kind of picking away of infinite sums of mony yeerely from your Maiesties Kingdomes; not onely from North-Yarmouth, and other places thereby, all the time that the Herring fishing lasteth; but also at other places for Mackerell, Soles, Whitings, and other sorts of fish which they take, in sight of your Maiesties Kingdome,[3] and bring it heere to land daily, and sell it for ready money. Such daily gathering of coyne, may well bee remedied, if your Maiesties subiects would but forbeare to buy any fresh fish of other Nations, (which me thinkes they should) then Strangers should bee constrained to bring coyne into your Maiesties Kingdomes with their fish, to set poore people aworke to salt and preserue their Herrings, and other fish withall, when they bring it heere a-land; whereby some Customes and other duties will also grow to your Maiesty:[4] or otherwise they will leaue their daily fishing so neere your Maiesties Kingdomes (as now they doe) and then such fish will be the more plentifull for you Highnesse subiects to take, and thereby greatly incourage them to set forth and imploy many a poore man the more in fishing, then now there is; and it will then not onely preserue great sums of money yeerely from carrying away from your Maiesties Kingdomes, but also there will bee much more gotten, than now there is, and greater numbers of Mariners thereby yeerely increased,[5] to bee very seruiceable for the Nauy, when there may be cause.

Now that which is like to be the present benefit, and which (in my opinion) will weigh most toward the furtherance of this Plantation in *New-found-land* at first,[6] by reason of the many consequences therof, is the bettering of our Trade there, which will fall out exceeding beneficiall in diuers respects, if those who aduenture thither, will follow some better course then formerly they haue vsed: And in so doing, ships may then saile in much more safety thither, and returne yeerely

---

[1] C has a marginal note: '*A speciall thing worth the noting.*'
[2] 'so neere' not in A.
[3] C 'take, within two leagues of some parts of your Maiesties Kingdom'.
[4] 'to your Maiesty' not in A.
[5] A 'but also there will be more gotten, then now there is, and great number of mariners increased'.   [6] 'at first' not in A.

from thence much more richer then now they doe; For many disorderly courses are yeerly[1] committed by some traders and aduenturers thither, in setting forth to that Countrey, and practised by some of them when they arriue there. If these disorders were reformed, the great benefit expected will soone follow.

It is well knowne, that they which aduenture to *New-found-land* a fishing, begin to dresse and prouide their ships ready commonly in the moneths of December, Ianuary, and February, and are ready to set foorth at Sea in those voyages neere the end of February, being commonly the foulest time in the yeere. And thus they doe, striuing to be there first in a Harbour, to obtaine the name of Admirall that yeere;[2] and so, to haue the chiefest place to make their fish on, where they may doe it with the greatest ease, and haue the choyce of diuers other necessaries in the Harbors, which do them little stead: but the taking of them, wrongs many others of your Maiesties subiects, which arriue there after the first.

And thus by their hasting thither, oftentimes there comes not only danger to themselues, but also great mischiefe, and losse to many others which arriue there after the first; as it may by that which followes truly appeare.

For by the hasting foorth, as now they vse, they greatly indanger themselues, being many times beaten with rough and stormy windes; and oftentimes they are therby forced to returne backe with great losse both of mens liues and goods, as it is well knowne: So that to get the superiority to arriue there first into an Harbour, they will beare such an ouer-prest saile, and in so desperate a manner, as there are no true vnderstanding Sea-men that vse the like to any other part of the world, whereunto the Masters of diuers ships haue been often prouoked, not onely by their owne indiscretion; but also chiefly by the selfe-will ignorance of some careless Sailers of their Company;[3] For albeit when the fogges are thicke, and the nights darke, that sometimes they cannot discerne the length of three ships in the way before them, and the Ice often threatning much perill to them: yet on runnes the ship amaine, so fast as possibly shee may, when commonly most part of the company are fast asleep, euen with extreme hazard of their liues; Thus many

---

[1] 'yeerly' not in A.

[2] Both Edward Hayes, one of Sir Humphrey Gilbert's captains on the 1583 expedition, and John Guy, governor at Cupids Cove, referred to the custom of choosing 'admirals' in fishing harbours, but Hayes said that English merchants took turns at serving as admiral during the season. Hakluyt, *Principal navigations*, VIII, 51; P.R.O., CO 1/1, f. 125.

[3] 'whereunto...Company' not in A.

times both ships and men haue been suddenly cast away, in diuers *Dangers often* places,[2] to the vtter vndoing of many Aduenturers and families: So *happen by* had I my selue a ship lost, sailing to that Countrey, and diuers others *carelesnesse and* the like. *desperatenesse.*[1]

And also this vntimely setting foorth, consumeth a great quantity of victuals, that might bee saued to better purpose, and it forceth them to carry and recarry many more men in euery ship, euery voyage, then they neede, if they once take a fitter course in these voyages.

Then when they arriue there,[3] such stages & houses that the first arriuers into an Harbour find standing; wherein men set diuers necessaries, and also salt their fish, some men haue vsed to pul down, *Disorderly* or taken their pleasures of them; by which vnfit disorders of some first *courses.*[4] arriuers there yeerely, those which arriue after them, are sometimes 20. dayes and more to prouide boords and timber, to fit their boates for fishing; and other necessary roomes to salt and dry their fish on; whereby much time is lost, and victuals consumed to no good purpose; and thereby also another great inconuenience followeth, by reason[5] the voyages of the after-commers there, are often greatly hindred and prolonged, to the great hurt of your Maiesty, and many a good subiect: and the Mariners themselues which trade to that Country, and commit those great abuses, are thereby also much wronged, as they haue acknowledged in their presentments, by their disorderly behauiour there.[6]

Wherefore if such which henceforth aduenture to that Countrey, take some better course in that trade of fishing, then heretofore they haue vsed, they shall finde the greater safety of their aduentures, and much good the more thereby. For whereas heeretofore they haue vsed to make ready their ships to saile in those voyages, in such vnseasonable time of the yeere, whereby they often receiue such great hinderances and losses as aforesaid;[7] they need not then goe foorth in the said voyage, vntill the fiue and twentieth day of March, which is a fit time of the yeere to put to Sea from our Coast to that Countrey; the winter *Much time and* stormes beginning then to cease; And then any such ship which carries *victuals ill* in her thirty men in euery voyage, may well leaue six men there *spent.*[8] behinde them, or more, all the winter season, vntill the ships returne to them againe; And these six mens victuals will be saued, and serue

---

[1] Marginal note not in A.   [2] 'in diuers places' not in A.
[3] 'Then...there' not in A.   [4] Marginal note not in A.
[5] 'another...reason' not in A.
[6] A 'acknowledged by their owne disorderly behauiours'.
[7] A 'receiue great hinderances and losses'.   [8] Marginal note not in A.

to better vse, and thereby also likewise cut off that moneths setting forth in those voyages so soone in the yeere, as now men vse to doe, and then the victuals for that moneth, which is so vainly, and with such great danger consumed, may well maintaine those men, which are left in the Countrey all the winter season, till the ships returne to them againe, with a very small addition to it.

A good meanes to better mens voyages yeerely.[1] And if it may so please your Maiesty, that any subiect which will vndertake to settle people in the *New-found-land*, shall haue this priuiledge, that in case he leaue there a fifth person of such which hee carries thither in his fishing voyage to inhabit; whereby those men so left, might keepe a certaine place continually for theit [sic] fishing, and drying therof, whensoeuer their ship arriueth thither; then would all such which leaue people there, build strong houses, and[2] fitting necessary roomes for all purposes; and then in some of those necessary houses, or roomes, they may put their fish when it is dried;[3] which fish now standeth after such time it is dried, vntill it is shipped, which is commonly nigh three moneths of the yeere,[4] in great heapes packt vp vncouered; in all the heate and raine that falleth, whereby great abundance of good fish is there yeerely spoiled, and cast away for want of such necessary roomes: And for the want of such fit houses in that Country, some mens voyages (to my knowledge) haue beene greatly ouerthrowne; whereby diuers aduenturers haue receiued great losses:[5] and then a meane place to make fish on, will bee made much more commodious then the best place is now, that men so dangerously and desperately run for euery yeere; And thus euery mans fishing Pinnaces[6] may bee preserued in such perfect readinesse, against his ship shall yeerely arriue there againe; which Pinnaces are now often lost, and sometimes torne in pieces by the first arriuers there, very disorderly, and most shamefully.[7]

And if such Pinnaces, and such Stages and Houses may be there maintained and kept in such readinesse yeerely, it would bee the most pleasant, profitable, and commodious trade of fishing, and otherwise, vnto your Maiesties subiects, that is at this time in any part of the world.

For then euery ships company might yeerely fall to fishing, the very next or second day after their arriuall there; whereas now, it is aboue

[1] Marginal note not in A. [2] 'houses, and' not in A.
[3] For a description of the method used by the English in drying their fish, see Cell, *English enterprise*, p. 4.
[4] A 'commonly aboue two moneths, in'.
[5] 'whereby...losses' not in A.
[6] The small boats, manned by three to five men, used in the shore fishery.
[7] 'and most shamefully' not in A.

twenty dayes in euery voyage, vntill they are fitted for that purpose; and then such ships should not neede so soone to haste away from *England*, as now they vse to doe in these voyages, by one moneth at least;[1] mens liues might be then thereby much the better saued, lesse victuals wasted, and many dangers preuented. And so then euery ship in euery such voyage, may gaine quickly one hundred pound more then now they doe that vsually carry thither but twenty men,[2] by leauing of foure men there of twenty; And as the proportion (before named) holds for leauing sixe men in *New-found-land* of thirty, so the allowing of men to bee made proportionably from euery ship that trades there in fishing,[3] will soone raise many people to be settled there in euery Harbour where our Nation vseth to fish, and in other Harbours there also in little time.

Some ships by this course may then quickly gaine by fishing aboue two hundred pound,[4] and some three hundred pound and more, according to their greatnesse, more then they doe yeerely now; And those men so left, will at times manure land for corne, saw boords, and fit Timber to bee transported from thence, and search out for diuers other good[5] commodities in the Countrey, which as yet lye vndiscouered; and by such meanes the Land will bee in little time fitly peopled with diuers poore handy-crafts men, that may be so commodiously carried thither to liue with their wiues[7] and families: for women and youths may bee there well imployed to doe diuers fit seruices; which now the better sort of the Fisher-men are constrained to doe, for want of such other people there. *Great benefit to be gotten.[6]*

And that no man else should appropriate to himselfe any such certaine place, and commodity for his fishing voyage; except hee will in such manner settle a fifth part of his company there to liue: And then such Aduenturers thither will carefully prouide yeerely for such as they leaue thete [*sic*]; not onely for bread and victuals, but likewise for all necessary tooles, fit for any kind of husbandry; The charge thereof will yeerely repay it selfe, with the benefit of their labours that shall bee so left there, with great aduantage.

And for others which yeerely aduenture thither, and will not settle people there in such manner; they may hold on such[8] vnfit courses

---

[1] A 'twenty dayes vntill they are fitted: and then such ships should not neede so soone to haste away from England by one moneth at least'.
[2] A 'one hundred pound, that vsually carry in her but twenty men more then now they doe, by'.   [3] 'that...fishing' not in A.
[4] 'by fishing aboue' not in A.   [5] 'other good' not in A.
[6] Marginal note in A.
[7] In A the rest of the paragraph is omitted.   [8] C 'hold no such'.

in setting on to that Countrey, and take their places, as it falleth out, as formerly they haue done; wherein I am perswaded they will soone grow weary, when they shall see the great commodity and benefit that other men will gaine by settling of people there.

By this means will the burthens and numbers of your Maiesties subiects shipping bee greatly increased, and strengthned, and great numbers of Mariners yeerely augmented; and then our shipping may well trade thither two voyages in euery yeere, and more, whereas now they goe but once.

If you will know what victuals might bee saued by those sixe men of thirty so to bee left there, and so proportionably for greater numbers; this is the estimate.

The allowance of victuall to maintaine euery sixe men onely, to carry and recarry them outwards bound and homewards, is sixe hogsheads of beere, and 600. waight of bread, besides beefe and other prouision; which men, when they saile to and fro (as now they vse) doe little good, or any seruice at all, but pester the ship in which they are, with their bread, beere, water, wood, victuall, fish, chests, and diuers other trumperies, that euery such sixe men doe cumber the ship withall yeerely from thence: which men, when the voyage is made, may be accounted vnnecessary persons returning yerely from thence as now they vse to doe.[3]

But being left in the Countrey in such manner, as aforesaid; those parts of these ships that leaue those men there, that are so pestered now yeerely with such vnprofitable things, may be filled vp yeerely with good fish, and many beneficiall commodities, for the good of those Aduenturers that wil so settle people there to plant.

These men that may be so fitly left in the Countrey, will not onely bee free from the perils of the Sea, by not returning yeerely, as now they vse to doe, but will liue there very pleasantly; and (if they be industrious people) gaine twice as much in the absence of the ships that leaue them there, more then twelue men shall bee able to benefit their Masters, that are kept vpon most Farmes in *England* in a whole yeere.

For certainely I haue there already often seene, and knowne by experience, to my cost, that[5] the desired Plantation can neuer bee made beneficiall by such idle persons, as I found there the yeere 1618. when I was there with power, by vertue of a grant from the Patentees,[6] which

---

[1] Marginal note not in A. [2] Marginal note not in A.
[3] 'as...doe' not in A. [4] Marginal note not in A.
[5] A 'For certainly I haue already seene, and knowne by experience, that'.
[6] Vaughan and some unknown associates.

people had remained there a whole yeere, before I came neere, or knew any one of them; and in all which time they had not applied themselues[1] to any commendable thing; no not so much as to make themselues an house to lodge in, but lay most shamefully[2] in such cold and simple roomes all the winter, as the Fishermen had formerly built there for their necessary occasions, the yeere before those men arriued there.

Such persons are not fit to aduance your Maiesties most worthy intended worke there, but rather much disgrace[3] and hinder the same.

Therefore seeing those people that were so formerly sent to plant in the South part of the Countrey, to bee so vnfit for that seruice, as it is well knowne to many men,[4] I grew out of heart to behold such abuse to bee vsed by those that were so sent to plant.

Yet entring into consideration, how iniurious I should be to God, and (as I did conceiue in my conscience) trecherous to your Maiesty, and my Country, hauing once as it were laid hold on the plough, I should take it off and looke back; I did then incourage my retiring spirits: notwithstanding all my former wrongs then sustained by Pirats & such idle persons.[5] And although I found them that were so formerly sent to plant, so vnfit for that seruice; I did not onely consider of the fittest course whereby to aduance that worke, which was formerly so worthily intended; but also truly and plainely to write this Discouery, as now I haue, how commodiously and beneficially it may bee proceeded on; and so shipped some of them to returne home againe, and gaue others leaue to depart, all excepting sixe onely; to whom I gaue directions for building an house, and imploying themselues, otherwise then formerly they had done, vntill they heard from the Gentleman that sent them thither: And so they liued there pleasantly all the next winter.

Now hauing laid open a commodious and beneficiall course how that Land may be peopled, yet I suppose it may be questioned, that if a fifth man of some ships, or euery ship were so left in the Countrey; that it will rather lessen the number of Mariners, that may be ready heere at home to doe your Maiesty seruice, then to increase them: and so by misconceiuing therein, your Maiesties intended Plantation may be hindred.

To which I answere, that most ships which trade thither yeerely a

---

[1] A 'or knew any of them; and neuer applied themselues'.
[2] 'most shamefully' not in A.
[3] A 'your Maiesties intended worke, but rather disgrace'.
[4] 'to many men' not in A.   [5] 'by...persons' not in A.

fishing, doe commonly carry in them euery fifth person that was neuer
at Sea before, or such as haue but little vnderstanding in their
Compasse; neither knowledge of Sea-termes, or what to doe in a ship:
and those men are yeerely hired by the Owners, and Victuallers foorth
of ships in those voyages, and by the Master of the ship, and the better
sort of men for small wages, who haue the benefit of their shares;[1]
and they doe serue euen so fitly for some purposes in those *New-land*
voyages the first yeere, as some of those men doe that haue beene there
often: So that by carrying thither yeerely euery fifth man, such as were
neuer there before, there will be much aboue 1000. Sea-men increased
euery yeere by that trade; and they being left there the winter, will
at times kill Deere and other beasts, and also take store of fish to be
transported from thence,[2] and fowle for their prouision; and it will
harden them well to the Sea, and at other times they may imploy
themselues beneficially in Husbandry vpon the land, as seruants ought
to doe. So that whereas there goes now yeerely, as the trade is,
sometimes[3] aboue two hundred and fifty Saile of your Maiesties
subiects ships, with aboue fiue thousand men in them, and being yeerely
carried thither the fifth persons that was neuer at Sea before, there wil
bee by that course increased about fiue thousand Sea-men in euery fiue
yeeres; and whereas now there is trading thither aboue two hundred
and fifty Saile of ships in diuers yeeres,[4] there will be then in little time
(God blessing that trade) aboue foure hundred Saile of your Maiesties
subiects ships there imployed yeerely, which may bee an vnspeakable
greater increase of wealth, strength, and power vnto your Maiestie, and
all your Maiesties other Kingdomes,[5] than now it is.

And although it be well knowne, that the *New-found-land* yeeldeth
such great blessings from God, by the trade thither, as now it is,[6] to
maintaine Christians; yet many of our English Nation, who in great
fulnesse taste of them, doe there, as it were, most vnthankefully[7] tread
them vnder their feete; as may partly appeare by the following
Discourse. For it is most certaine that[8] our Nation, vpon their arriuall

---

[1] The practice in the Newfoundland trade was for the risk in a fishing voyage to be
shared among three parties: the ship's owner or owners, the victualler (who on occasion
was also the owner), and the master and crew. Each party received a third of the catch.
The crew's third was usually divided proportionately, according to each man's experience
and responsibility, and often a supplementary wage was also paid. See Cell, *English
enterprise*, pp. 14–18.

[2] 'to...thence' not in A.   [3] 'sometimes' not in A.

[4] 'in diuers yeeres' not in A.

[5] A 'there imployed; which may be a greater increase of wealth, strength and power
to your Maiestie and Kingdomes'.   [6] 'by...is' not in A.

[7] 'most vnthankefully' not in A.   [8] 'it...that' not in A.

yeerely to that Countrey, doe cut downe many of the best trees they can finde, to build their stages and roomes withall, for their then necessary occasions; hewing, rinding, and destroying many others, that grow within a mile of the Sea, where they vse to fish.

The rindes of these trees serue to couer their Stages,[1] and necessary roomes, with turfes on them; so that in few yeeres, I feere, that most of the good timber trees neere the Sea-side, where men vse to fish, will bee either felled, spoiled or burned: yet at our peoples departure from such Roomes and Stages, they will suffer but little thereof to stand, whereby to doe any man seruice the yeere ensuing.

These are such great abuses, which are most lamentable to bee suffered, and therefore it is great pitty[2] that it is not redressed: for no Nation else doth the like; neither doe the Sauage people, after such time as our Countrey-men come from thence, either hurt or burne any thing of theirs, that they leaue behinde them; so that those trees, and that timber might be conuerted to many seruiceable vses, for the good of your Maiesty, and your Highnesse Subiects, if reformation thereof were had.[3]

Now I thinke good to make knowne partly what abuses bee also offered to the Harbours and Rodes in *New-found-land*, that are so beautifull, & so excellent, ordained by God, for ships to ride safe in at anchor, as there are not better in any part of the world; yet for all this beauty of theirs, and the commodity that wee receiue by them; these disorders diuers men of our Nation[4] doe there commit, *viz.*

All ships, for euery voyage they make there, take in many exceeding great stones, therewith to presse their dry fish in their ships, which worke being done, they cast many of these stones into the Harbours where they ride at Anchor, which are to be seene lying in great heapes in some places, within three fadome of water, to the great indangering of ships and cables; to the perill also both of mens liues, and their goods, and likely in time to choake vp or spoile many excellent Harbors in that Countrey, if prouision be not by your Maiesties high authority made to the contrary.

All these former abuses are confessed by diuers Masters of English ships, in the briefe of the presentments, that follow in the latter part[5]

---

[1] Wooden jetties extending into the sea. The cod was thrown up onto the stages from small fishing boats, and there it was cleaned and readied for drying.

[2] A 'These are things lamentable to be suffered, and great pitty'; C 'These are such great abuses, which are most lamentable and shamefull to be suffered, and therefore great pity'.

[3] In A the paragraph concludes 'your Maiestie and your subiects.'

[4] 'of our Nation' not in A.   [5] 'the latter part' not in C.

of this booke, as may appeare,[1] the which being made knowne to the subiects that aduenture thither, I am confident (in my opinion) that they should all most humbly[2] desire your Maiesty, that there may bee some better gouernment established there, than now it is:[3] and that such which plant there, may not abuse or hinder any such which[4] yeerely come thither a fishing, whereby they should haue any iust cause to complaine the one against the other, as now they doe.

And because my desire is, that not onely Merchants, or such as liue neere the Sea-side, but also all others that shall giue their furtherance to this Plantation, either by aduenturing their moneys, or sending men thither (because it is to be vndertaken by men of good ability) in such manner, as diuers[5] wealthy men doe in other Countreys, ioyning their purses to further any such good worke: I thinke it fit to shew how such persons may aduenture to that Country, though they dwell farre from the Sea-coast; and others likewise that dwell neere, may doe it with little trouble, but onely by a trusty seruant, to giue account yeerely of his disbursings, and likewise of his receits; which (I trust) will bee very beneficiall to all such as will aduenture therein. Yet I suppose that[6] some, who dwell farre from the Sea-coast, may say, they are so farre off, that they should be but little the better for a Plantation to bee made in *New-found-land*, and so may hold it a needlesse thing for them to know how beneficiall that Countrey hath long time beene to these your Maiesties Kingdomes; and how it may in little time be worth double to your Maiesties subiects, in respect of what now it is, euen in the onely trade of fishing, besides the good that may come by other trades and commodities to be had from thence.[7]

To such therefore that should so obiect, that those that liue farre from the Sea, whether Gentlemen or others; and are not experienced in affaires of this nature, cannot so conueniently aduenture thither: I answere, that none of your Maiesties Subiects dwell further then 100. miles from the Sea-side, which is no great iourney; By the same reason, that Commodities brought from Forraine parts, and landed on your Maiesties Sea-coasts,[8] and Hauen-townes, are dispersed thorow all

<hr>

[1] A 'All these abuses are confessed in the brief of the presentments, that follow in the latter part of this booke, the '. See below pp. 159–61 for the further evidence to which Whitbourne refers.   [2] 'most humbly' not in A.

[3] In 1611 John Guy had issued regulations forbidding the annual fishermen from committing the abuses that Whitbourne here describes, but nine years later the New-foundland company was still complaining of the fishermen's destructive behaviour. P.R.O., CO 1/1, f. 125; *APC, 1619–1621*, p. 158.

[4] 'plant...which' not in A.   [5] A 'the'.

[6] 'Yet...that' not in A.

[7] A 'come by other commodities.'   [8] A 'on our Sea-coasts'.

places of your Maiesties Kingdomes, and so vented (our men liuing thus in any of these places) may with as little difficulty aduenture to the *New-found-land*, and also[1] into other Countries; For as we haue the example of diuers, both Gentlemen and others of *Italy*, *Spaine*, *Germany*, *Sauoy*, the Low Countreys, and other places that come yeerely, some of them more then 200. miles to the City of *Siuill*, purposely to saile from thence to the West-Indies, and these doe yeerely returne rich; So it may be also well vnderstood by the following Discourse, how commodiously there may be sent many people from any part of your Maiesties Kingdomes to bee there imployed, that haue but small meanes to liue, and bee very beneficiall to themselues, and all those which shall be so imployed there.[2]

The first thing therefore that I will aduise any subiect that is but little acquainted with sea-affaires, and such as shalbe willing to aduenture in the desired Plantation, is, to acquaint himselfe with an approued vnderstanding man in Sea-affaires, and also with a secoud [sic];[3] and then with both their opinions and his owne iudgement, he may set forward therein, with greater[4] hope of the better successe; for to my knowledge, diuers worthy Gentlemen that haue aduentured to the Seas; partly through their own conceit, seeming to know that which they did not, haue also oftentimes bin animated on by some turbulent spirits that haue outrun themselues, and so brought men in such mindes, that on the coast of *Guinnie* there, they might gather vp gold along the Sea-shore, washed vp with the Sea in great abundance; and likewise if they would aduenture to the *West-Indies*, there they should load their ships with Gold-oare, and draw it aboord their ships with Wheele-barrowes, and then share it by the pound; and such like proiects.

Thus, by such meanes, diuers worthy Gentlemen haue runne so farre at Sea, in some such vnfit voyages, by ill directions, that they haue quickly brought land to water, and neuer knew how to shape a course to recouer vnto their land againe; God send all those that will henceforth aduenture to the Seas in any Plantation or otherwise,[5] good Pilots, and it will be the greater hope of good successe to follow.[6]

Now for those that will put their hands to the furthering of your Maiesties Plantation in *New-found-land*,[7] my opinion is, they are best either to buy a Ship of 100. Tun, and a Pinnace of 40. Tun, or neere

---

[1] 'to...also' not in A.   [2] A 'themselues, & will imploy thẽ there'.
[3] A and C 'second'.   [4] A 'great'.
[5] 'or otherwise' not in A.   [6] 'to follow' not in A.
[7] A 'furthering of a Plantation in *New-found-land*, my'; C 'furthering of your Maiesties Plantation, my'.

such burthens, or else to hire the like Ship to serue for the passing of people, victuals, and prouisions, in the Spring of the yeere, fit for such a purpose, and for the returning of such fish, and other commodities from thence, as those men so sent and imployed, may procure with their labours; and those Ships and men so sent, may bee so fitted and prouided with Salt, Nets, Hookes, Lines, and such like prouisions, as those Ships and men are, which yeerely saile thither a fishing.

The best course of the two, as I conceiue, is for any such, to buy a Ship and a Pinnace to serue for that purpose, and then the Pinnace may bee sent thither before the bigger Ship, wherby to settle and begin to such a conuenient place for habitation, as God shall direct them; whither the greater ship may repaire: and they may imploy themselues all the time that there is good to be done in fishing, in that trade onely, and betweene the saile of the Shoales of fish, they may build houses, and prouide[1] other necessary things in perfect readinesse to be transported into *Spaine, Portugall,* and other places beyond the Seas; much cheaper then the Hollanders doe, seeing it is to be had there easily with mans labour only: And therefore more commodiously from thence for vs, from those parts, then the Hollanders are able to serue them, as now they doe, who buy such commodities with their money in *Spruce-land, Norway,* and other places, and yet thereby gaine much, and increase a number of Shipping and Mariners, and set them a worke continually in such trade.[2]

Now hauing shewed how men may vndertake to further this Plantation, by prouiding ships for the fishing trade, as is formerly expressed: I suppose that some worthy men, that may be zealous and willing to further so pious, honourable, and beneficiall a worke, may bee vnwilling to trouble themselues with the fishing trade, and yet very willing to further the said Plantation, after some other course [3] that may be lesse troublesome to them, which they may very well performe in this manner:

They may hire a ship with men, and victualled to saile from any part of your Maiesties Kingdomes, to the *New-found-land,* to carry people, victuals, beasts, and other prouisions in such competent number, as may bee fit to passe in such a ship, as any one shall so hire; and hauing landed such people and prouisions there to plant, the said ship may there reloade fish from the fishermen; (and if any will plant

---

[1] 'prouide' not in A.   [2] 'in such trade' not in A.
[3] A 'other manner that'.

in that manner) they are to bargaine for their fish heere in *England*, with such as doe set forth ships in the fishing trade, which fish may be bought beforehand of them, to be deliuered there at eight shillings the hundred waight, or neere that price, and to pay for the same within 40. dayes, more or lesse, after such times heere in *England*, that there comes from thence the sight of any Bills of Exchange, from those that receiue the fish there in that maner; and the ship so hired, being there loaden, may saile from thence vnto *France*,[1] *Portugall*, *Spaine*, or any other Port within the straights of *Gibraltar*;[2] I suppose the fraight of euery Tun of fish so to be transported there, will bee neere four pound the Tun, twenty hundred waight to the Tun; which fraight and hire for the ship, men and victuals, in all that time, it may be agreed to bee paid there where the fish is sold; so that for the hire of the ship, men and victuals, there will be no occasion to disburse any money, before the ship safely arriue to either of the places aforesaid, where, by Gods assistance, any one shall so intend to make sales; and there the ship so hired may bee set free; and then what more soeuer the fish may yeeld, may bee to discharge the buying of the fish in the *New-found-land*, and what profit may accrew ouer and aboue the fraight and hire of the ship, men, and victuals being discharged, will redound to the good of any man that will aduenture so to plant, and hire his ship in that manner; and such course may any sufficient man take euery yeere to further the said Plantation, wheresoeuer he dwell in any of your Maiesties Kingdomes,[3] and so haue one ship to make three voyages there in a yeere, that shall but land people and prouisions for them, and presently reloade such Fish, Masts, Deale-boords, Beames, Timber for buildings, and other commodities, such as those people which hee had formerly sent, should haue prouided in readinesse; with which commodities, if hee returne to *Spaine* or *Portugall*, it will yeeld ready money: and if hee returne with it to the City of *London* and Port of *Bristoll*, or any other place within your Maiesties Kingdomes, it will also not onely yeeld ready money, but it will be a means to imploy many the more of your Maiesties Subiects and shipping therein; so that the *Hollanders* and other Nations should not bring so much of such commodities into your Maiesties Kingdomes as they do now yeerely,

---

[1] 'France' not in A.

[2] '*Gibraltar*; and vnto *Marsellis* or *Naples*'. Whitbourne is here describing a very common arrangement in the trade whereby contracts for the sale of fish were made before a ship left England. In some cases the cargo to be received in exchange was also prearranged. See below, p. 144 and Cell, *English enterprise*, pp. 18–21.

[3] 'wheresoeuer...Kingdomes' not in A.

and carry away much coyne for the same, as it may be well vnderstood.[1]

And withall it is to be considered, that whereas now there are yeerely at *New-found-land* of your Maiesties Subiects ships in the fishing trade, at least 15000. Tun burthen of shipping, as is already expressed, and that these ships yeerely carry thither, neere halfe their lading of salt, to saue their fish withall, which cannot be lesse then 7000. Tun, the which salt, whether it be bought in *Spaine*, *Portugall* or *France* at a cheape rate, it cannot cost lesse then seuen thousand pounds, which is but twenty shillings the Tunne, adding the fraight thereunto for bringing it from those parts, it cannot stand in lesse then twenty shillings a Tunne more, which is seuen thousand pounds more; so that the salt may stand those that trade thither, as the trade is now, yeerely,[2] with the waste and transportation of it thither, much[3] aboue foureteene thousand pounds; of which summe, there is much[4] aboue seuen thousand pounds yeerely bestowed in other Countries, which I should gladly shew some fit meanes that it may bee henceforth saued and brought into your Maiesties Kingdomes in Coyne, or some other good commodities.

The which may be very fitly, commodiously, and beneficially done, if those which yeerely aduenture thither, will settle people there in such order as aforesaid, in euery Harbor where they vse to fish, and prouide pannes in euery such Harbor to boyle salt to preserue their fish withall; the which may bee performed there very cheape; so in that maner one panne will make twenty bushels of good salt in euery four and twenty houres for that purpose; onely with mans labour and the salt water; and not as some doe vse, to make salt vpon salt; and there it wil be vndertaken to be made with the wood-fire (which may be there had with little labour) without Charcole or Sea-coles; and that salt so made there, shall not stand in foure pence[5] the bushell, to those that will prouide to make it there in that manner: and now salt stands those that aduenture there, neuer lesse than twenty pence a bushell,[6] and sometimes three shillings the bushell and aboue.

And it is well approued by all those that yeerely fish for Ling, Cod,

---

[1] 'as...vnderstood' not in A. In response to considerable agitation against Dutch participation in the carrying trade in fish and other goods, a bill was proposed in 1621 that would have barred aliens from the carrying trade. When it failed to pass, royal proclamations were issued in the two following years imposing restraints on the activities of foreign merchants. R. G. Lounsbury, *The British fishery at Newfoundland, 1634–1763* (New Haven, 1934), p. 29; *CSP Dom., Add., 1580–1625*, pp. 661–2.

[2] 'yeerely' not in A.

[3] 'much' not in A.

[4] 'much' not in A.

[5] A 'threepence'.

[6] In A the paragraph ends here.

and Herrings vpon all your Maiesties Sea-coasts, that salt orderly boyled in such manner, doth much better preserue fish, and keepe it more delighfuller in taste, and better for mans body, then that fish which is preserued with any other kinde of salt; And I am well assured, that such fish as is salted with the finest white salt, will sell farre better in Siuill, and other places of *Spaine* and *Italy*, where I haue beene often,[1] then that which is preserued with any other kind of muddy salt; and thus by taking such a fit course for making thereof in *New-found-land*, it will not onely saue a great deale of coyne yeerely in your Maiesties Kingdomes, but also imploy,[2] and greatly inrich your Maiesties Subiects thereby.

There is no question to bee made, but that those ships which may bee so procured to carry people thither, will yeerely returne from thence deepe loaden with good fish to diuers places beyond the Seas, and make good profit with the imployments thereof, (if fit prouision be made to take fish withall as it ought to be: for euery man, the better hee doth prouide himselfe for that purpose, shall reape the greater benefit thereby at the first) and not bee able to returne from thence, Deale-bords, Masts, and such like, vntill such time as shipping be builded much greater, and fitter for that seruice then now they are.

The trade to the *New-found-land* being thus followed, as it may well be, your Maiesties Subiects may then haue there yeerely, aboue 400. saile of good ships from all your Maiesties other Kingdomes, which will be alwayes in readinesse[3] to bee called home from thence, without imbarment of any forraine Prince, vpon lesse then foureteene dayes warning, if the winde serue, with aboue eight or ten thousand of[4] lusty, strong and seruiceable Sea-men in them, vpon any occasion of seruice, when some other ships and Mariners that are then abroad in voyages, to the *East*, or *West-Indies*, and diuers other places, will not be so speedily called home; neither (when they come) so lustie and strong, as those which vse to the *New-found-land* are, if your Maiesty and Kingdomes haue at any time[5] neuer so great need of their seruice.

Which being considered, must needs bee also a great terror to any forraine Prince that shall proffer to quarrell with your Maiestie, when he shall consider that your Maiesty may so speedily be furnished with so many seruiceable ships of your subiects, and so many Saylors, and that but from that onely place of trading.

---

[1] 'where...often' not in A.   [2] 'but also imploy' not in A.
[3] 'ships from your Maiesties Kingdomes ready to'.
[4] A 'aboue eyght thousand of'.   [5] 'at any time' not in A.

So, againe it is to bee considered, that yeerely from the *New-found-land*, as the trade is now, the Subiects bring from thence to the value much aboue the summe of 135000 pounds: what the benefit and imployment therof, and the imployments of ships and Mariners are thereby, may be well considered; and that trade carrieth not away any coyne out of the Land, as some others doe; neither any other commodities: and therefore it may be well vnderstood what a great benefit shall arise to all your Maiesties Kingdomes, if the trade be once orderly settled and increased as aforesaid; and then your Maiesties Subiects ships will be much bigger builded for that trade, and better furnished with good Ordnance, fit for any defence; & likewise then Ordnance will not bee so much sold into other Countreys (as there hath beene great abundance in my time) which Ordnance so sold (I feare) if occasion should bee offered, may shoot their bullets at our owne bosomes, as it is already too much seene.

And whereas my opinion is, that it is better to buy ships for that trade, then to take them to hire (as some doe) which yeerely send ships thither, to loade either fish or Trayne oyle, and transport it into *France*, *Spaine*, and other places; is, because that those which hire ships for that purpose, are[1] bound by conditions vnder hand and Seale, which wee call Charter parties; wherein it is expressed, in how many dayes the owners of the ships are to make them ready, and how many dayes they must stay there, to attend the Marchant, and such like conditions: And although the place where they ariue, be neuer so much ouerlaid with the like commodity that they bring; yet there must they discharge and also relade, according to the conditions in the Charter partie;[2] though such Commodities, which they are to relade, bee there much dearer, then at some other place not farre from it; which hath beene a great losse to many Marchants; yea, diuers cauils haue risen thereby between them that haue taken and letten Ships in that manner.[3]

Therefore I hold, that the buying of Ships to follow that seruice, is the best & profitablest course that may be taken therein; for then they may send them to *New-found-land*, or where they thinke good at all times of the yeere, and to any place, or so many places as may please God to direct them, to make their sales and imployments; and likewise to vent the same, where they may be best aduised.

[1] A 'Trayne and transport it into *France*, *Spaine*, and other places; those which hire ships, are'.　　　　[2] 'according...party' not in A.

[3] Certainly there were drawbacks to such contracts; on the other hand, the charter party gave the owner or charterer very precise control over the conduct of the voyage. See Cell, *English enterprise*, pp. 18–21.

Such as will vndertake to send people to that land, as aforesaid, I *A speciall* would also aduise them to acquaint themselues with a fit man to be *thing.*[1] Master in each Ship, that vnderstands the order of a fishing voyage to that Countrey; and hee will procure fit Fisher-men, to goe with him for that purpose,[2] and likewise acquaint them with euery particular thing that is fit for such a voyage.

And withall it is to bee obserued, that for euery such seruant that any Master will send thither to plant, and liue there all the yeere, he is to haue a single share allowed vnto euery man alike of such fish as is taken, whilest they labour together in the Summer time with the ships company with whom they are, though afterwards they stay in the land, and follow some other seruice for their Masters, whiles the ships are imployed abroad in venting their commodities, and vntill they returne to them againe, to the *New-found-land*; which single share of fish so taken, may well defray all the charge and hire that any man shall haue of his Master, who doth stay there all the winter, with good aduantage.

Note also I pray', that any ship which shall be so imployed to fish *A great charge* only, as now men vse to doe, if she be 100. Tun, doth commonly carry *to be fitly* in her 36. men and boyes; and that ship will saile well to the *saued.*[3] *New-found-land*, and from thence to the *Straites* of *Gibraltar*, or any other part of Christendome, with 20. of the former 36. men: so that 16. of the said company may very well remaine there, till the said ships returne to them againe, and doe good seruice to your Maiesty and themselues, but most of all to those who shall send so great a number thither to liue all the yeere; whereas now these 16. men lye still in the ship at great charge euery voyage, much pestering the ships with their persons, victuals, chests, and diuers vnprofitable things to no good purpose, as is touched before; which places in the ship may be filled with good fish and other profitable things, if those 16. men were left behinde in the Countrey, where they may be well imployed, which is almost the one halfe part of such a ships company.

By this it may plainely bee vnderstood, that the victuall which those 16. men spend sayling thither, and returning homeward, and a moneths victuall at least, for all those 36. men, will yeerely be saued to maintaine them there all the winter season, with the helpe of very little victuals to it: and also it wil be a great good ease to the Common-wealth, to

---

[1] Marginal note not in A.
[2] Usually the master was responsible for hiring the crew and for working out arrangements concerning their pay. See Cell, *English enterprise*, pp. 15–18.
[3] Marginal note not in A.

leaue so many there all the Winter; and after this rate proportionably from diuers ships, great companies may commodiously and beneficially be raised to remaine there in little time, from such as will voluntarily and willingly entertaine their certaine places to make their fish on, and plant: for the most part of those men, who may so well and beneficially remaine there to plant, may be, some handicraftsmen with their wiues, and some such other people as your Maiesties Kingdomes may very well spare, doing good to themselues, their masters and Common-wealth, learning experience, and to bee fit for diuers and other seruices.[1]

Mariners to be increased.

I am also confident in my opinion,[2] that if *New-found-land* may be thus planted, our Shipping and Mariners will be so greatly[3] increased, that we may hereafter furnish *France*, *Spaine*, *Portugall*, and other Countries, with such kind of fish as those Seas doe yeeld; and so by this meanes the whole fishing trade on that coast, may be drawne into the hands of your Maiesties subiects only; and whether then I or no, it will be most worthy, and better for your Maiesties Kingdomes in generall, let each man iudge.[4]

No Nation to bee forbidden fishing.

I doe not intend that other Nations should bee prohibited the free priuiledge of fishing, which for many yeeres they haue inioyed there with vs; or that wee should assume it vnto our selues by strong hand, or constraine those that come thither, to take their fish of vs, and at our prices: but this is my only meaning: That whereas at this present, the French, Biscaines, and Portugals send yeerely to that Countrey many hundred[5] saile of ships, as I haue already declared, our men by sayling thither with fewer persons, and in lesse danger in euery ship then now we doe, by multiplying their voyages, & spending lesse time and victuals in the same, and by carrying more and better fish in euery ship then now they vse to doe, may be able not onely to furnish *France*, *Spaine*, and *Italy*, with those commodities, but also to sell farre better cheape, then any of these nations can possibly fetch the same from thence with their owne shipping and labours. And which of these nations will then aduenture thither, let any man iudge,[6] when hee knowes that his returne will be a certaine losse.

Furres of diuers sorts.

Moreouer, our men wintring there, might take of the beasts of the Countrey yeelding Furres, when they are in season, and in their

---

[1] A 'fit for seruice.
[2] A 'opinion (wherein I submit my selfe to deeper iudgements), that'.
[3] 'greatly' not in A.
[4] A 'and whether then, it will be better for your Maiesties Kingdomes, let each man iudge.'
[5] 'hundred' not in A.   [6] 'let...iudge' not in A.

perfection; So that in processe of time, they may also settle a traffike with the Sauages for their Furres of Beuer, Martons, Seale, Otters, and what else is of worth amongst them.

Shipping also (the walls and Bulwarkes of your Maiesties Kingdomes) will bee heereby not onely maintained; but also greatly increased, both in number and burthen, which would bee a great aduantage to your Maiesty, and a notable defence and addition of strength vnto your Maiesties Kingdomes vpon all occasions.[1]

Shipping maintained.

Many more poore Artificers and others will bee then in great numbers heereby set a-worke, what now there are; and by the increase and bettering of this Trade, a very[2] great augmentation of your Maiesties Reuenues in your Customes must of necessity follow.

Artificers set on worke.

And certainely, if this trade and Plantation were once settled in such manner, it would prooue, as I conceiue, to bee[3] more commodious and beneficiall then any other Plantation your Maiesty hath elsewhere in those Western parts of the world;[4] for, as I haue said, it bringeth in great wealth by mens labours, and carrieth away nothing but a little victuals, which would be consumed by so many idle persons in lesse then halfe the time, which haue no imployments, and yet the Kingdomes receiue no benefit by such Drones neither.

Wealth brought in, none carried away.

Much more might be said to the purpose: but I desire not to inuent, or inlarge matters beyond my obseruations; yet thus much also may I truely say, that the fishing trade onely[5] on the coast of *New-found-land*, is a sure and good trade to great Brittaine, and therefore deserues to bee cherished; for trading thither and returning from thence, wee little feare the Turkes bondage and circumcision, nor any outlandish Inquisition, nor the Imbarments[6] of any Prince, nor such contagious heates, as those finde that trade neere the Line, neither the danger and hurt of Art-wormes,[7] where-with ships that trade to most parts Southward, are sometimes much spoiled; nor many other hazards and inconueniences, to which some of our other tradings are subiect.

Fishing on the coast of New-found-land, great security to great Brittaine.

And as this Plantation will bee in all respects so beneficiall, as any of those your Maiestie holds abroad elsewhere: so may the same bee effectually proceeded on in much more safety, and with a great deale lesse charge.

For first of all, touching the transportation of men, victuals and other necessaries from hence into *New-found-land*, it wil be by the cheapest

Transporting of men, victuals,

---

¹ 'vpon all occasions' not in A.
³ 'as...bee' not in A.
⁵ 'trade onely' not in A.
⁶ I.e. embargoes. A 'Imbarkements'.

² 'very' not in A.
⁴ 'in...world' not in A.

⁷ Wood worms.

and other
necessaries from
hence at an
easie rate.
and easiest way that can be possibly be; for there will be no occasion to hire any ships expresly for that voyage, as is vsually done to other of your Maiesties Plantations, from whence hauing vnloden, ships doe returne sometimes with few commodities.

But those ships that goe there yeerely empty to the *New-found-land*, onely to loade fish and Trayne oyle, and so to depart from thence, cannot be lesse in number some yeres[1] then 40. saile: Therefore whatsoeuer shall be thought fit and necessary to be transported from hence, towards the furtherance and setting forward of that Plantation, may be, not only by the Fisher-men, but also[2] by those Ships and Barkes carried thither, which loade fish and oyle[3] with a very little charge, and without trouble or hinderance to their voyages; and for the prouiding and furnishing of the Plantation with victuals and prouisions for their liuelihood, the chiefe want at the beginning will be Corne, (the Countrey it selfe yeelding plenty of beasts, fowle, fish, and fruits, as was before spoken of:) yea, much good fish is there yeerely cast away, which might be made good food for the Planters, if it were preserued. And if need be, ships may saile from thence in fiue dayes with a faire
Ilands
abounding with
great store of
beasts for
prouision of
victuals.
wind, to the Ilands of *Flowers*, & *Azores*, which Ilands abound in Wheate, Beeues, Sheepe, Goates, Hogs, Hens, Potatoes, Muske-millions,[4] Onyons, and many other fruites which they may haue there at cheape rates; and if that should faile, our Countrymen that stay there, may bee supplied with as little inconuenience and preiudice, as to any other Plantations, vntill the Countrey shall be by their paines and industry made fit to beare Corne.

For the settling of people there, I haue sufficiently declared, it being that they, who shall either alone or with their family voluntarily goe thither, haue good conditions, both for allowing them land, and other conuenient priuiledges.
Imployment for
all in the
absence of our
men.[5]
For the imployment of men in the absence of the shipping, it will be very beneficiall in many respects; so that although thousands of your Maiesties people should at once goe thither, and so yeerely,[6] yet there would be present imployment for them all: no man shall neede to liue idely for want of worke.
The quicke
returne of our
people, a
comfort to their
Countrey men.
And as *New-found-land* is neerer to vs by more then 300.[7] leagues then *Virginia*; and farre from any of the Plantations of the King of Spaine, which peraduenture might make this businesse the more

[1] 'some yeres' not in A.
[2] 'not...also' not in A.
[3] 'which...oyle' not in A.
[4] Musk melons.
[5] Marginal note not in C.
[6] 'and so yeerely' not in A.
[7] A '400.'.

difficult; so those of this Plantation will haue a great comfort and encouragement abone [sic][1] all others, in that they shall not be left desolate in a remote Country, to shift for themselues, as some haue bin,[2] but that after fiue moneths past, they shall againe see great numbers of their countrey men, and also of other Nations,[3] and haue their company the rest of the yeere.

Neither are there in that part of the Countrey any Sauages, to oppose and resist our mens planting, as it falls out in many other places; Those that are there, liue in the North and West parts of the Countrey (as hath beene said) where our Nation trades not; But on the East and South side of the Land, where the English doe fish, and which is the fittest place for a Plantation, there is not the least signe or appearance, that euer there was any habitation of the Sauages, or that they euer came into those parts, to the Southward of Trinity Bay; of which I could also giue some reasons, if it were not a thing needlesse to trouble this discourse withall.

No Sauages in that part where our Nation trades.

And as they shall stand in no feare to receiue hurt from the Sauages, so may they be easily secured against the iniury of Pyrates, who sometimes come thither, and not onely take from the fishermen, victuals and other prouision and munition, and haue thereby strengthened themselues, but also haue carried away from them many seruiceable mariners into *Barbary* and other parts, and thereby made many a poore widdow and fatherlesse childe;[4] and it is to be feared, that those men so carried from the *New-found-land*, who seeing their estates and their families so ouerthrowne, may be prouoked to animate the Turkes men of warre, to saile thither to take the spoyle of our Nation, and others that are yeerely a fishing on that Coast (which God defend) whereby to hinder that Trade, or the desired Plantation.

Security from Pyrates, and the Sauages.

The which inconuenience that is so to be feared, may be easily preuented by maintaining two good ships of warre, of 200. tunne apiece, and two Pinnaces of 40. tunne apiece well prouided, to bee there maintained all the Summer time, and that the Commanders of them may haue power, that if any great force of the Turkes, or any others should at any time come thither, whereby to disturbe your Maiesties

---

[1] A and C 'aboue'.
[2] Perhaps a reference to Sir Walter Raleigh's 'lost' colonists.
[3] 'and...Nations' not in A.
[4] In 1612 the pirate Peter Easton had taken ships, men and supplies from the fishing fleets at the Avalon peninsula. He had intended to seize as many as a thousand men and use them in his attack on the treasure fleet coming from Spanish America. Nottingham University, Middleton MSS, Mi X 1/12; Purchas, *Pilgrimes*, XIX, 417; P.R.O., CO 1/1, f. 179.

Subiects in their trade of fishing, or attempt to hinder the Plantation; that then to raise a greater force from the Fishermen and Planters to defend any such attempt.

An easie contribution for maintenance of their security from Pyrates.

The charge of which ships & Pinnaces of warre, so to bee yeerely maintained there for that seruice, may be easily and commendably defraied, with your Maisties allowance therein, if euery Ship and Vessell of your Maiesties subiects, fishing on that Coast, will voluntarily contribute thereunto the value of a good daies[1] fishing in the whole voyage, which will bee abundatly [sic] recompenced vnto them, in regard that they may then fish continually and securely many a daies fishing the more in euery voyage, which now oftentimes they dare not doe;[2] And then these two Ships of warre, and two Pinnaces so to be maintained, by such a small contribution to be paid for their seruice at *New-found-land* in dry fish, they will so scoure the Seas euery yeere going forth thitherward bound, and likewise in their returne, that no Pirate of any Nation durst come neere the Southerne parts of your Maiesties Kingdomes; neither to lie in waight in the course sailing to and from the New-found-land, for those that trade thither, as yeerely heretofore they haue done, and ouerthrowne many a mans voyage.[3]

Hollanders attended with men of warre.

For which course, wee haue the example of our neighbours the Hollanders, who generally in all their trades, but most specially in their fishing vpon your Maiesties Sea-coasts, are attended with men of warre, which are defrayed by a certaine contribution from those men, in whose defence they are imployed. And by this meanes the Marchants and Traders of Holland, receiue farre greater assurance and benefit, then if euery Marchants shippe should set themselues forth in warlike manner in their owne defence. For besides the security they haue, and sauing the charge which such prouisions would require, they haue also much the more roome in their Marchants ships for their Commodities.

Many seruiceable men and Mariners bred thus.

And these ships thus sent to guard their Fleets, which are called Wafters,[4] doe continually breede many fit[5] seruiceable Sea-men, not only Mariners, but also good souldiers, and fit Commanders, that are well experienced how to command in Ships vpon all occasions; for

---

[1] A 'halfe a good daies'.

[2] In 1620 the Newfoundland company had suggested that each ship contribute 500 fish, perhaps a fiftieth part of one boat's catch, towards the cost of maintaining a warship at the fishery. P.R.O., PC 2/30, f. 453. Sir George Calvert made a similar suggestion, see below, p. 280.

[3] For example in 1611 seventeen ships on their way from Newfoundland to the Mediterranean were attacked by pirates; five years later seven ships bound for Italy were seized. P.R.O., High Court of Admiralty, Oyer and Terminer Examinations, HCA 1/47, ff. 261–1v.; *CSP Dom.*, 1611–18, p. 426.

[4] I.e. armed vessels acting as convoys.   [5] 'fit' not in A.

without such fit Commanders in good Ships, there is but small hope
of good seruice to be performed by them; and if the *New-found-land*
men may be thus guarded with two such Ships, and two Pinnaces, it
would not only in little time breed many a Gentleman and others in
them to bee well experienced how to command in ships, vpon any
occasion of seruice, but also it will make your Maiesties subiects Ships
that trade thither, so strong, that they neede not feare the greatest force,
that any Prince should at any time send thither to disturbe or hinder
them, neither in returning from thence vpon any occasion to doe your
Maiestie seruice.

If after all this, I should be demanded by those which know not the
Countrey, what other places in the Land are also fit to be peopled at
first, so well as the Harbors of *Trepassey*, and *Trinity* (of which I haue
already spoken) whereby those which will aduenture thither, may not
be doubtfull to plant in other Harbors, although I haue first expressed
them for some speciall reasons, as it may be well vnderstood, the one
of them lying North-most, where our Nation vseth to fish neere the
Sauages, and the other lying in the South-most part of the Land, and
neere vnto the passages of diuers ships that saile yeerely to and from
other places of the world, as is already plainely shewed; yet there are
many other excellent good Harbors where our nation vseth to fish,
lying betweene them both, which are very good for ships to moore
fast at anchor, and easily to be defended from enemies, that shall at any
time attempt to molest such as shall plant in them: and better for fishing,
then either of the foresaid two Harbors are, of which I will particularly
expresse some of their names.

First,[1] the Harbor of Saint *Iohns*: *Foriland*: *Formosa*: *Agafort*:[2] Harbor
de Grace: *Renouze*: and diuers other good Harbors, *Bayes* and *Rodes*,
where there is good fishing, and are fit places for ships to ride in at
anchor[3] the Summer time: and as it is already shewed, that the
bottomes of diuers Bayes, that are expressed to be in this South part
of the Land, doe euen meete together, within the compasse of a small
circuit, neere vnto the Bay of *Pleasance*;[4] So likewise not far from
Trepassey, which lyeth six leagues to the West, from the South cape
of the Land, which is called Cape *Derasse*,[5] and six leagues to the
North-ward of the said Cape, lyeth the Harbor of *Renouze*, which is

---

[1] A has a marginal note: '*Good Harbors, Bayes and Rodes for Ships and Fishing.*'
[2] I.e. Ferryland, Fermeuse, Aquafort.
[3] 'at anchor' not in A.
[4] A 'Bay of Trepassey'; C 'do come something neere together; So'.
[5] I.e. Cape Race.

a place easily to be defended, there being at a low ebbe not 18. foot
water fine sand: yet in danger to be spoiled by the stones and ballast
that are throwne into the same, which are to be seene in great heaps
when the water is cleare, as commonly it is in a faire Sun-shining day,
right vnder the ships, where they ride at anchor.[1] These stones and
ballast, so throwne into the Harbors by Christians, is very dishonourable
to our Nation[2] (if there bee not some better course taken therein) it
is to be sorrowed, that the offenders are not seuerely punished.

Close adioyning to the Harbour of Renouze, are aboue 300.[3] Acres
of good land, that is cleere without Woods or Rocks, and lieth
commodiously to be ouerflowne[4] with fresh Riuers in the Summer
time, with very little labour, as I haue well obserued: and within a mile
further off from the said Harbours, lye many thousand[5] acres more of
very good open land, that are able to receiue and relieue many hundreds
of Cattell, and fit, with little labour, to be manured for Tillage.[6]

There are yeerely neere vnto the said Harbor of Renouze, great store
of Deere seene; and sometimes diuers of them haue been taken. There
is a man yet liuing, that was once at *New-found-land* in a ship with me;
and he in one voyage did there, neere vnto the Harbour of Renouze,
kill 18. very large and fat Deere, as it is well knowne, yet he went with
his Peece but seldome for that purpose, & would then haue killed many
more, if he might haue been spared from other labour to attend

thereon: whereby it may be well vnderstood, that there is great store
of Deeres flesh in that Countrey, and no want of good fish, good fowle,
good fresh water, and store of wood, &c. By which commodities people
may well liue there very pleasantly.[7]

From the said Harbour of Renouze, it is not aboue twelue[8] miles
ouer land to the Harbor of Trepassey, and not farre from thence to
the bottome of Trinity bay, and within three leagues vnto the Harbour
of Renouze, are three very good Harbours, where our Nation vseth
to fish, which lie to the Northward of it.

Now whereas there haue been some doubt and[9] reports made of
great cold in that Countrey, by people that haue traded thither, who
(I suppose) neuer saw any other Countrey, but onely that, and their
owne natiue soyle; and such when they haue returned from thence one

---

[1] 'right...anchor' not in A.   [2] 'is...Nation' not in A.
[3] A '200.'.   [4] 'or...ouerflowne' not in C.
[5] A 'hundred'.
[6] C 'Tillage: and so in other places of that Countrey the like'.
[7] 'By...pleasantly' not in A.   [8] A 'ten'.
[9] 'some doubt and' not in A.   [10] Marginal note not in A or C.

voyage, though they neuer vnderstood, or felt the nature and temperature of other Clymates, neither consider the goodnesse of *New-found-land*, as it is now partly made knowne, haue giuen a great deal worse report of that Countrey, then in reason they should; and if such were but a little acquainted, or would vnderstand of the great cold that is at times in *Muscouia, Sweidon, Norway, Spruce-land, Poland, Denmarke* and other Easterne and Northerne parts of the World, where the people liue well and grow rich; such ill reporters of *New-found-land* would speake better of that Countrey, and[1] alter their opinions; And[2] although the Ice is so great in those other parts of the World in the Winter season, commonly aboue foure[3] moneths together, that neither Ship nor Boat can passe in all that time, from one place to another, but lye still fast frozen, yet in that season, where Ships vse to saile the Summer time from one place to another, Carts and Coaches doe passe vpon the Ice,[4] and the people in all those North parts of the World, liue there rich and exceeding well.

Ships also in *Holland* and in those neere places, in some Winters doe lie there fast frozen a long time together: and likewise it hath beene in some Winters so hard frozen in the Riuer of *Thames*, aboue *London-bridge* neere the Court, that the tenderest faire Ladies and Gentlewomen that are in any part of the world, who haue beheld it, and great numbers of people, haue there sported on the Ice many dayes together, and haue felt it much[6] colder there, then men doe that liue in *New-found-land*.

The cold is not so great there as it is in England.[5]

Now if such men, when they come from thence, that haue but little experience of the colde in other Countries; neither take due obseruation of the colde that is sometime in *England*, would listen to men that haue traded in the Summer time to *Greeneland*, for the killing of Whales, and making of that Traine oyle (which is a good trade found out) and consider well of the abundance of great Ilands of Ice, that those Ships and men are there troubled withall at times, they would thereby bee perswaded to speake but little of the colde in *New-found-land*: yet praised be God, seldome any of those Ships and men that trade to *Greeneland*, haue taken any hurt thereby.

Wherefore I desire to satisfie any that shall bee willing to further this Plantation, and cleare those reports and doubts that are feared by

---

[1] 'speake...and' not in A.
[2] C 'opinions, and peraduenture be ashamed of their ignorance therein; And'.
[3] A 'other parts the Winter season, commonly foure'.
[4] In A the paragraph ends here.
[5] Marginal note not in A.   [6] 'much' not in A.

People liue there with little apparell.[1] some people of the cold there; and also to let them know, that the Sauage people of the Countrey that liue in the North parts,[2] endure it so well, that they liue there naked Winter and Summer. And also my selfe, that haue beene there often, and diuers others of our Nation,[3] that haue traded there, endure the greatest colde we haue met withall there at any time, in our faces, neckes, and eares, as well as any Gentlewomen in *England* doe the colde in their naked bosomes, neckes and faces in the Winter time, when they goe so vncouered; and therefore I doe conceiue, that it is but a little needlesse charie nicenesse vsed by some that trade there, that complaine any thing of the cold in that Countrey, by keeping themselues too warme: which cold (I suppose) some that haue bin there, may feele the more, if they haue beene much accustomed to drinke Tobacco [*sic*], stronge Ale, double Beere, or haue beene accustomed to sit by a Tauerne fire, or touched with the French disease, such peraduenture may, when they come to a little cold, wheresoeuer they bee, feele it the more extremely then otherwise they would.

Furthermore they may be also more fully satisfied of the cold in that Countrey by a Gentleman, one Master *Iohn Guy*, late Maior of the City of Bristoll, that liued there two yeeres together, and diuers others also of sort & qualitie, many yeeres so pleasantly, and healthfull with their wiues and families, as if they had liued in England.[4]

And whereas there come some yeeres vpon that Coast great Ilands of Ice, which are congealed in the North, farre from thence, as it may be well vnderstood, and that the Coast of *New-found-land* lieth in longitude from the South Cape thereof to the graund Bay, which is the North-most part of the Countrie, North, North-East, and South, South-west, aboue fiue degrees; and that from thence, any ship being off from that Coast twelue Leagues, and sailing North, North-East, may *The Ice there is congealed in the North.*[6] run on, till they come to the North-ward of 70.[5] degrees, and no land to hinder him, neither from thence any land found, in that altitude, directly East vnto Greeneland, where the trade is for killing of Whales, which is much[7] aboue 400. leagues distance from that Course.

Therefore it may bee well conceiued, as it hath bin approued by diuers men that haue attempted to seeke out some new Discoueries,

---

[1] Marginal note not in A or C.   [2] 'that...parts' not in A.
[3] A 'my selfe, and most our Nation, and others'.
[4] There had been women at the Cupids Cove settlement at least since 1612 and the first English child had been born there in March 1613. Bristol Record Office, MS Calendar 07831; Nottingham University, Middleton MSS, Mi X 1/66, f. 16.
[5] C '60.'.
[6] Marginal note not in A or C.   [7] 'much' not in A.

in those North parts of the world, that there is alwaies abundance of great Ilands of Ice, which the current setting very strongly from thence, by reason of some Strait and passage[1] that the Sea hath from those large Seas that lie on the North side of Tartaria, and those other vnknowne parts of the World,[2] and sets towards the Coast of *New-found-land*, with the said Current and North winds, & do there in little time dissolue, and thereby they make the ayre and water some thing the colder there. Those Ilands of Ice are not dangerous vnto Ships being once descried, as by their whitenes they may in a dark night when men looke out for them; for they will driue along so fast with the wind, as I haue often prooued, that if a Ship bee vnder the Lee of an Iland of Ice, and there strike downe his sayles, the Ice will driue faster with the winde, then the ship will driue before it, so that a ship may turne from it when there is cause.

Ilands of Ice there speedily melt.[1]

Thus hauing shewed (as I conceiue) the reasons that such Ilands of Ice are seene some yeeres on the Coast of *New-found-land*; I will also shew my opinion partly, why there are such Fogs there also sometimes.

It is well knowne vnto all those that haue seene the Country and obserued it, how the Land is ouergrowne with Woods and Bushes that haue growne, and so rotted into the ground againe (in my opinion euersince the floud) the rottennes therof hath so couered the earth, and Rocks in diuers places of the Countrey in great thicknes, and by reason thereof, the open land and woods doe a long time in the Summer contain a great moisture vnder the same, so that a man may obserue, when the heate of the yeere comes on, a kind of Fogge arising continually from it.

The cause of the Fogges.[4]

Therefore, in my opinion, which I submit to deeper Iudgements, if those vnnecessary bushes, and such vnseruiceable woods were in some places burned, so as the hot beames of the Sunne might pearce into the earth and stones there, so speedily as it doth in some other countreys, that lye vnder the same eleuation of the Pole, it would then there make such a reflection of heate, that it would much lessen these Fogs, and also make the countrey much the hotter Winter and Summer, and thereby the earth will bud forth her blossoms and fruites more timely in the yeere, then now it doth,[6] and so bring the Land more familiar to vs, and fitter for Tillage, and for Beasts, and also for Land-fowle,

How to abate the Fogs, and to make the Countrey better.[5]

---

[1] C 'some Strait passage'.   [2] 'and...world' not in C.
[3] Marginal note not in C.   [4] Marginal note not in C.
[5] Marginal note not in C.
[6] A suggestion that Whitbourne did recognise the problem of the island's short growing season which, elsewhere in the *Discourse*, he ignores.

then now it is; and thereby those Ilands of Ice that come on that coast
at any time, will the sooner dissolue, which do speedily melt, when
they come neere the South part of that Land, &c.

Also, it may be obiected by some, that the countrey is rockie, and
mountainous, and so ouergrowne with trees & bushes, in such a
Wildernes, that it will be an endles trouble to bring it to good
perfection: and such like obiections are often vsed, as if they would
haue[1] such a Land cleansed to them without labour. Yet my hope is,
when any such shall reade ouer this Discourse, and consider well of
the particular motiues herein expressed, whereby a Plantation there
should bee imbraced, they will be well satisfied therein, and I suppose,
forbeare to say it is such a rockie, and cold countrey as is vnfit to be
planted,[2] thereby to bee vnited vnto your Maiesties Royall Crowne.

I haue been seuerall times in *Norway*, where the Countrey is in most
places more rockie, and mountainous then the *New-found-land*, and lies
aboue six degrees more to the North, and yet very beneficiall to the
King of *Denmarke*, where many of his Maiesties Subiects liue rich and[3]
pleasantly; but the *New-found-land* is much more pleasant to liue in.

I haue often seene the Coast of *Biskay* and *Portugall* all along the
Sea-Coast, how rocky, barren and mountainous these countreys be in
most places, although they lie in a pleasant and temperate Climate; if
such which should dispraise the *New-found-land*, had seene it, and
trauailed in those parts[4] as I haue, they would not onely like well, and
be in loue to further the desired Plantation, but also admire how the
people in those other Countries doe liue by their good industrie, and

Rocks and
Mountaines
good for Seeds,
Roots and
Vines.

seeke out little places amongst the Rocks, and in the sides of Hils and
Mountaines, to set and sow their seedes for Rootes, Cabage, Onions,
and such like, whereby they receiue great comforts: for all alongst those
parts on the Sea-coast, their best meanes of liuing is by fishing, and
other trades by Sea. The like benefit may all such haue, that will plant
at *New-found-land*, and much better in many other things, as is already
sufficiently touched.

Likewise it is well knowne to all those that haue trauailed from thence
all along the Coast of *Spaine*, euen to *Granada*, how barren and rockie
those parts of *Spaine* are also in most places; and yet the people by
their good industry, plant many of their Vines and other fruits, on the
sides of some steepe Hils amongst the Rocks, where men are faine in

---

[1] C 'often vsed, by some that are backward to good works, which would haue'.
[2] In A the paragraph ends here.
[3] 'rich and' not in A.   [4] 'and...parts' not in A.

diuers places, euen to creepe on their hands and knees to prune the said Vines, and gather the Grapes of them, to make their strong wines, and sweete Raysins withall, which wee so much delight to taste. In those toothsome, and delightfull Commodities, our Marchants bestow much money, which the *New-found-land* trade and Commodities had from thence, will be able in little time, if it be peopled as aforesaid, to supply all your Maiesties Kingdomes withall, with the sales of such commodities had from thence, to be imployed therein,[1] and some other good commodities also.

Likewise from *Granada* to *Carthagena, Allegant,*[2] *Denia,* and from thence euen to the Citie of *Valencia,* which is a large circuit, the most parts all along, as I haue trauelled,[3] are very barren, rockie and mountainous; that very few Cattell, Sheepe, Goats, or any other beasts are able to liue there; and yet doe the people in those parts vse great industry, to plant their Vines and other fruits, whereby they seeke out their best meanes they haue to liue: and likewise also in diuers other places neere the *Mediterranean* Sea, from thence to *Bassalonia, Marsellis, Sauoy,* and *Genoway,* and in diuers other places in *Italy,* these Countries are very Rocky and Mountainous, as I haue well obserued:[4] & yet those places doe abound with many other rich blessings, by meanes of the peoples good industrie there; and so by reason thereof, the people in all those parts from the Coast of *Biskay,* vnto *Italy;* & also the most parts of *France, Gascoyne, Brittaine, Normandy* and *Picardy,* are by the *New-found-land* fish and trade to that Countrey[5] greatly relieued: which fish is in all those parts in great request, & steeds[6] them greatly, and doth sell very well there most commonly, and so likewise in *England* great abundance thereof is spent; which being well considered, I know no reason to the contrary, but that the Subiects of all your Maiesties Kingdomes should be most willing to further that Plantation, and shew their good industry to cleanse Land there for Corne & Woade, and plant diuers kindes of fruits, which questionless will also proue so well there as in *England;* and[7] then will it be to all your Maiesties other[8] Kingdomes such a nurcery to get wealth, and to increase and maintaine Shipping, and beget seruiceable Sea-men, as great *Brittaine* had neuer the like,[9] nor any other Christian Prince in the World.

With these good blessings which are before recited, being followed

---

[1] In A the paragraph ends here.
[2] Alicante.
[3] A 'trauelled by land, are'.
[4] 'as...obserued' not in A.
[5] 'and...Countrey' not in A.
[6] I.e. proves useful to.
[7] A 'proue very well there; and'.
[8] 'other' not in A.
[9] In A the paragraph ends here.

by industrious spirits, there is a great hope of a plentifull haruest vnto your Maiestie & Kingdomes thereby; God send good Seedsmen and Planters to set it forward, as I trust in God it will haue, seeing it hath already had many right Honourable and worthy Fathers to commend it.

And although that sithence I presumed to write this Discourse, I haue bin often vpon diuers occasions[1] dishartned from proceeding herein; Yet, when I did remember *Columbus* his good indeuours, that first & patient Discouerer of the *West Indies*, whom, if God had not hartened him on with a worthy mind, & a bosom armed for all the stormes of crosse fortunes, he had neuer finished that Honourable attempt for finding such an happie businesse out: the which Discouery of his, hath euer since filled the Spanish cofers with gold and siluer, and made that Nation Lords of the greatest riches vnder the Sunne: and although that attempt of his, was held at first impossible to come vnto any good effect, and *Columbus* laught at by some: yet euer sithence, by his attempt, I may say, that *Spaine* hath had from thence to helpe furnish other Christian Kingdomes with gold, siluer and diuers other great riches; and also now to that countrey so discouered, those commodities that great *Brittaine* may yeerely well spare, and other Countries also, are the better vented: and so likewise, may the *New-found-land* and the parts of *America*, neere thereunto, proue also beneficiall for diuers trades in little time,[2] vnto all your Maiesties other Kingdomes.[3]

These good motiues considered, what great good comes vnto Christian Kingdomes, by Forraine Plantations, and what infinite wealth is yeerely brought from the *West Indies* into *Spaine*, as I haue there often[4] seene landed; doe put mee in great hope, that if there bee an orderly Plantation settled in *New-found-land*, the trade to that Countrey by your Maiesties Subiects, and other places thereby, may yeerely be so beneficiall to your Maiestie and your Highnesse other Kingdomes, as the *West Indies* are now yeerely worth to the King of *Spaine*.

Now hauing thus commended the Countrey of *New-found-land*, in my opinion, it ought not to bee one of the least motiues, whereby to further this Plantation, the setting of some better order and gouernement amongst the Fishermen, and all other of our Nation that yeerely trade there, then now there is; so that there may be a reformation of such abuses as are there yeerely committed; wherein it is well knowne, that I haue already vsed my best endeuors, when in the yeere 1615. at which

[1] 'vpon diuers occasions' not in A.
[2] In A the paragraph ends here.
[3] C 'Kingdomes, if it be followed as it should bee.   [4] 'often' not in A.

time I had a Commission with me for the purpose vnder the broad
Seale of the Admiralty, and did then therewith set forth, to follow that
seruice from the Port of Exceter, in the County of Deuon, on the 11.
day of May 1615, in a Barke victualled and manned at my owne
expence of time and charge,[1] and I did then arriue at the Coast of
New-found-land, in the Bay of Trinity; vpon Trinitie Sunday, being
the 4. of Iune, and anchored the same day in the said Harbour of
Trinity; and there, in the name of the holy and indiuiduall Trinity, *The first*
began, to the vse of your most Sacred Maiestie, by vertue of that *Inquest that*
Commission, to send forth a Precept, to call the Masters of those *impanelled in*
English ships, that were then riding at Anchor, and also the Masters *New-found-*
of some other English ships that were neere thereunto, and so began *land.[2]*
to hold the first Court of Admiralty in your Maiesties name, that euer
was (as I beleeue) holden in that Countrey, to the vse of any Christian
Prince, and proceeded therein according to course of Law, as the tenor
of my Commission did warrant mee therein; and also in other Harbors
of the said Coast I did the like; Part of which abuses there committed,
I haue already touched: so likewise I will briefly insert a part of the
seuerall presentments of such iniuries,[3] that were then deliuered vnto
me, as aforesaid, vnder the hands and seales of those 170. Masters of
English Ships, to the vse of your Maiesty: which presentments were,
vpon my returne from the said voyage, deliuered by me into your
Maiesties high Court of the Admiralty, and then by those Masters of
ships there impannelled, such abuses as follow, they did acknowledge,
and order, that henceforth with your Maiesties allowance might be
redressed, &c.

1. First, they did all acknowledge, that there is but little difference *The first*
of daies obserued amongst the Fishermen; some men presuming to goe *Article there by*
to Sea, and to fish with hooke and line, vpon the Sabbath day, as vsually *presentment.[4]*
as vpon the weeke dayes.

2. Secondly, that diuers of our Nation doe take into their ships very
great stones, to presse their dry fish withall; which worke being done,
they cast those stones into the Harbors where their ships vse to ride
at anchor; which will vtterly spoile the Roades and Harbors in that
Countrey, and bee to the indangering of Ships and Cables, yea and
mens liues also, if it be not reformed in time.

3. There are many men yeerely, who vnlawfully conuey away other
mens fishing boates, from the Harbour and place where they were left

[1] A 'manned with 11. men and boyes at my own charge'.
[2] Marginal note not in A.
[3] C 'Iuries'.   [4] Marginal note not in A.

the yeere before in that Countrey; and some cut out the markes of them; and some others rippe and carry away the pieces of them, to the great preiudice and hindrance of the voyages of such ships that depend on such fishing boates, and also to the true Owners of such boates.

4. There are some men, who arriuing there first into a Harbour, doe rippe and pull downe Stages, that were left standing for the splitting and salting of fish the yeere before; and other Stages some men haue set on fire: which is a great hindrance to the voyages of such men as are not there with the first in the Harbour, for that they must then spend 20. dayes time and more,[1] for preparing new Stages, and fitting new Pinnaces, and other necessary things, in euery voyage before they be settled to fish.

5. There are also some, who arriuing first in Harbor, take away other mens Salt that they had left there the yeere before, and also rip and spoile the Fats[2] wherein they make their Traine oyle, and some teare downe Flakes,[3] whereon men yeerely dry their fish, to the great hurt and hindrance of many other that come after them.

6. Some men likewise steale away the bait out of other mens Nets by night, and also out of their fishing boates by their ships side, whereby their fishing, from whom it is so taken, is ouerthrowne for the next day.

7. They did acknowledge, that some men take vp more roome then they neede, or is fitting to dry their fish on, whereby other mens voyages are oftentimes greatly hindered.

8. They also found, that diuers of your Maiesties subiects haue come to that Coast, in fishing voyages in ships not appertaining to any of your Maiesties subiects, which they conceiued worthy of punishment, and reformation.

9. They did acknowledge, that some men rip, and take away Timber and Rayles from Stages, and other necessary roomes, that are fastened with nailes, Spike or Trey naile;[4] and some men take away the Rindes & Turfe wherwith diuers necessary roomes are fitly couered for seruiceable vses, and likewise take away Stakes that are fastened in the ground with Rayles on them, whereupon men vse to dry their fish; and that some set the standing Woods in the Countrey on fire, which haue in little time burned many thousand acres; and that there are some

---

[1] 'and more' not in A. [2] I.e. dryfats or large casks.
[3] Erections of branches laid over a wooden frame, on which the fish was spread to dry in the air and sun.
[4] Spike nails: large strong nailes with small heads. Trey or tree nails: wooden pegs.

which yeerely take away other mens Trayne oyle there by night; which they conceiued worthy of reformation.

10. They found, that diuers idle persons, which were hired for those voyages, when they come thither, notwithstanding that they were still in health, would not worke, and were so lazy and idle, that their worke was to little purpose: which was worthy of punishment.

11. Against all these great abuses, and diuers others committed in the said *New-found-land* (which[1] they did set downe in their seuerall presentments, as by them it may at large appeare, they did all condescend, and order from that time thenceforth, that no subiect to your Maiesty should commit any more such abuses in that Countrey: which may bee very wel remedied, seeing they tend to the aduancement of the Trade, and quietnes amongst the Fishermen, and to the glory of God, the honour and good of your Maiesty, and the generall benefit of the Common-wealth.

12. They did further present to the vse of the Lord Admirall of *England*, two small Boates, Anchors, and a small Grapple, that were found in the Sea vpon that Coast, which were there prized to bee worth two shilling sixepence apiece, amounting to seuen shillings sixepence.

Now hauing laid open how commodious and beneficiall it will bee *Briefe notes.*[2] to your Maiestie and Kingdomes, to settle a Plantation in the *New-found-land*, and also made knowne some vnfit courses that are yeerly vsed by some Fisher-men that aduenture there: and likewise shewed a part of some great wrongs that haue beene committed there by Pirats and some[3] erring subiects; and also touched a little, that there haue not beene such fit courses taken by some of those that haue beene imployed to that Countrey in the Plantation already there begunne, as they should haue done, by reason whereof it is to bee feared, that some of those Honourable, and other right Worshipfull persons that vndertake the same, and that haue beene at some great charge therein, seeing their good indeuours and charge take no better successe, they may waxe cold and weary in disbursing more thereunto, and so by their remissenesse the Plantation might bee giuen ouer, and the Countrey left to the spoile and vsurpation of some other Prince that may vndertake the same, and then reape the haruest of your Maiesties Subiects labours, that shall then trade to that Countrey, &c. And therefore shewing how it may be prouided for by your Maiesty, and all those wrongs henceforth remedied; he that is in fault may speake

---

[1] Brackets not closed.　　　　　　[2] Marginal note not in A.
[3] 'Pirats and some' not in C.

for himself.[1] Now I suppose, that some, who may finde themselues a little touched heerein, may not onely enuy mee, for laying open that which I haue; whereby to preuent such further dangers and inconuenciencies in that Countrey, and to further such a worthy worke: and therefore I may bee vniustly taxed, as many worthy men haue beene, for well doing: For although I haue by Pyrats, and other crosses receiued great losses, yet doe I acknowledge my selfe much bound to God my Creator, who hath preserued mee from many dangers in my time, and always (praised be God)[2] safely to return with my ship, goods and men[3] wherein I was; I doe also most humbly giue God[4] the praise, that I am now so happily ariued with this my plaine and true Discouery, vnto the view of your most Sacred Maiestie, and the right Honourable Lords of your Maiesties most Honourable Priuie Councell, and my Countrey, whereby to shew what in all likelihood the effect of a Plantation will there produce; vsing also many arguments, motiues and inducements to perswade a generall willingnesse thereunto.

And these excellent benefits distribute themselues, betweene your Maiesty and your Subiects: your Highnesse part will bee the Honour of the Action; the access of Territory, increase of strength and power, aduantage against other Princes, augmentation of Reuenew, and ease of your Maiesties Kingdomes, &c. The Subiects part will be the bettering and securing of their Trade; inriching of themselues; reliefe of other Trades; and a meanes of further Discoueries.

Good for all.[5]

But these two haue a relation and dependencie the one on the other, that neither can subsist without the other; I will not therefore diuide your Maiestie from your Subiects; your Highnesse prosperity being their happinesse; and their wealth, your Maiesties riches.

The first thing which is to bee hoped for, and which hath euer beene your Maiesties principall care, is the propagation of the Christian Faith: and by that meanes onely, the poore vnbeleeuing Inhabitants of that Countrey may bee brought to the knowledge of God, and a ciuill kind of gouernement: and it is not a thing impossible, but that from those slender beginnings which may bee made in *New-found-land*, all the Regions adioyning (which betweene this place, and the Countries actually possessed by the King of Spaine, and to the North of *New-found-land*, are so spacious as all Europe) may be conuerted to the true worship of God.

Infidels brought to the knowledge of God.[6]

---

[1] 'he...himselfe' not in A or C.
[3] 'goods and men' not in A.
[5] Marginal note not in A.

[2] 'always...God)' not in A.
[4] C 'giue his Maiesty the'.
[6] Marginal note not in A.

The next is, the vniting of a Countrey so beneficiall already, and *The inlarging* so promising vnto your Maiesties Crowne, without bloodshed, charge, *of your Maiesties* or vsurpation, which must needs bee a perpetuall Honour to your *Dominions.*[1] Maiesty, in all succeeding ages; neither will it bee an Honour onely to your Highnesse, but a benefit to the State, by a new accesse of Dominion; And what Prince can inlarge his Territories by a more easie and more iust meanes then this, seeing that of right it appertaineth vnto your Maiesty, and therefore deserues to be imbraced?

Now if it may so please your most excellent Maiesty, not onely to lend your eare to a Proiect of this nature, but also to approue the matter proiected; and vouchsafe the furtherance therein, the which, out of my soules deuotion, and zealous affection to doe seruice to your Maiesty and your Kingdomes, I tender on my knees; most humbly beseeching your Highnesse, both to accept of my honest and zealous intent, as also to pardon my boldnesse and presumption therein; for it is, and so hath euer beene my resolution, rather to beare the burthen of pouerty, then iustly to deserue, or giue cause of reproach; and to subiect all the dayes of my life, and the manifold dangers thereof, thereby to approue my selfe a profitable member, both to your Maiestie, and to my Countrey that gaue me my first breath; for which onely cause I haue aduentured to publish this my simple and plaine Discourse, whereunto my very conscience hath a long time, and still doth not forbeare to sollicite me.

The prosecution and perfection of the worke, I leaue to the pleasure of God, and your Maiesties happy directions; in the discourse and discouery whereof, if I haue either beene tedious, or any other way offensiue, it is to bee imputed to my want of learning: and so, though perhaps I doe not satisfie some mens curiosities, yet I hope I haue sufficiently informed their iudgements; and beseech God to incline their affections to the furtherance of so pious, and so profitable a businesse, as this appeareth to be.

And so I rest, and euer will remaine a faithfull and loyall Subiect to your Maiesty, an hearty and true louer of my Countrey, and a zealous well-wisher to this intended Plantation.

Richard Whitbourne.[2]

THE SECOND MOTIVE AND INDUCEment, as[3] a louing inuitation to all his Maiesties Subiects; shewing the particular charge for *victualing forth*

---

[1] Marginal note not in A.
[2] Edition A does not contain the second part of the *Discourse*, included in B and C, but does have the Conclusion, see below, pp. 195–206.
[3] C 'INDUCEMENT ADDED TO my former Discourse, as'.

a Ship of 100. *Tuns burthen, with* 40. *persons, for the aduancing of his Maiesties most hopefull* Plantation *in the* New-found-land;[1] and likewise what yerely benefit may accrue thereby vnto such as shall bee Aduenturers therein;[2] as also some other grants which will bee granted vnto euery such Aduenturer.

Gentle Reader,[3] I haue in my former Discourse something like vnto a Harbinger, chalked out the way for a Plantation in the *New-found-land*, whereby it may prooue to bee a worke both profitable and necessary for his Maiesties Kingdomes in generall. But because the affections and resolutions of men, doe sometimes freeze, instead of heating; and most decline, when to the eye of the world they seeme most to aduance: I haue therefore aduentured to fortifie and assist my former Discourse, with this second, by vnfolding other reasons to make it more apparant, that to settle an orderly Plantation in that Countrey, it beares diuers great perswasions with it, yea such as haue all the grounds, and runnes on all the feet of good probabilities, as Religion, Honour, Empire, and profit, the which may bee performed[4] with small charge, and to haue yeerly good benefit with great facility. Therefore I purpose now more plainly[5] to acquaint all such vndertakers of that Plantation, what particular profit may redound to themselues and posterities, and what honour, through their industry, will accrue thereby vnto all his Maiesties other Kingdomes. Beare therefore, I beseech you, with my rough stile, and plaine meaning, in which I striue rather to shew truth in her owne brightnesse, then to heape applause, or glory to my selfe. To crowne that Country of *New-found-land* with due praises, it may (by the approbation and fauour of his Maiesty) be iustly stiled a sister-land to this great Iland of *Brittania, Ireland, Virginia,* the *Summer Ilands, New-England,* and *Noua Scotia.* And that shee may claime her selfe this bold and honourable title, the world, I thinke, will be on her side, especially, because from her owne mouth doth shew what infinite and vnspeakable benefit for many yeeres together, the negotiation of our Kingdome with her, hath brought to all our people, not onely by the increase and maintaining of Mariners and shipping, but also by the inriching of many a Subiect; and so consequently, by relieuing of many thousands of families, which else had liued in miserable wants, for lacke of honest imployments, our English hauing more then fourescore yeeres

---

[1] C '*New-found-land,* which is now worthily vndertaken: and'.

[2] In C the paragraph ends here.

[3] In the original the preface to the reader is printed in italics, with key words in roman; here the arrangement is reversed.

[4] C 'well performed'.　　　　　　　　　[5] 'more plainly' not in C.

together, made thriuing and profitable Voyages to that Countrey, the
possession whereof began in our late Soueraigne of happy memory,
Queene *Elizabeth*, and so continues more strongly now in his Maiesty,
without the claime, interest and authority[1] of any other Prince. This
proper and commodious situation of the place, together with the
correspondency of benefits, which not onely great Brittaine, but also
other Countries may, and doe receiue[2] from the same, filles mee more
with an ardent desire so to haue her called (*Sister-land*.) And worthily
may that Royalty bee bestowed vpon her: for as great *Brittaine* hath
euer beene a cherishing Nurse and Mother to other forren sonnes and
daughters, feeding them with the milke of her plenty, and fatting them
at her brests, when they haue beene euen starued at their owne. Euen
so hath this worthy Sister-land, from time to time, giuen free and
liberall entertainment to all that desire her blessings, and chiefly (aboue
all other Nations) to the English. What receiue we from the hands of
our owne Countrey, which in most bountious manner wee haue not
had, or may haue at hers? Nay, what can the world yeeld to the
sustentation of man, which is not in her to bee gotten? Desire you
wholesome ayre? (the very food of life) It is there. Shall any Land
powre[3] in abundant heapes of nourishments and necessaries before you?
There you haue them. What Seas so abounding with fish? What shores
so replenished with fresh and sweet waters? The[4] wants of other
Kingdomes are not felt heere; and those prouisions which many other
Countries want, are from thence supplyed.[5] How much is *Spaine, France
Portugall, Italy*, and other places beholding to this noble part of the
world for fish, and other commodities (it is to bee admired) let the
Dutch report: what sweetnesse they haue suckt from thence by trade
thither, in buying of fish, and other commodities from our Nation:
and (albeit all the rest should be dumbe) the voyces of them are as
Trumpets lowd enough to make *England* fal more & more in loue with
such a Sister-land. I am loth to weary thee (good Reader) in acquainting
thee thus to those famous, faire and profitable Riuers, and likewise to
those delightfull, large and inestimable Woods, and also with those
fruitfull and inticing Hills, and delightfull Vallies; there to hawke and
hunt, where there is neither sauage people, nor rauenous beasts to hinder
their[6] sports. They are such, that in so small a piece of paper as now
my loue salutes thee with, I cannot fully set them downe as they

[1] 'interest and authority' not in C.   [2] C 'yeerely receiue'.
[3] Pour.
[4] C 'waters? Sure, not other part of the world hath better. The'.
[5] C 'yeerely supplied'.   [6] C 'your'.

165

deserue. And therefore I doe intreat thee with iudgement, with patience, and with a true desire for the benefit of thy dread Soueraigne and Countrey, to reade ouer this Discourse, which (I trust) may incourage thee to further so hopefull a Plantation as it appeareth to be; and also, I trust, giue thee ample satisfaction, and iust cause to answer opposers; if any out of ignorance, or any other sinister respect, shall seeke to hinder so honourable and worthy designes. So wishing thee all happinesse, I rest

Euer thine for my Countries good,
RICHARD WHITBOURNE.

A Loving Invitation to all his Maiesties Subiects.[1]

Now for the better incouragement of Aduenturers vnto the said Plantation and Trade to that Countrey, I haue acquainted you in the forepart of my Discourse, that the right Honourable Lord Deputy Generall for the Kingdome of Ireland, hath vndertaken to plant a Colonie of his Maiesties Subiects in that Countrey; and his Lordship is well pleased to entertaine such as will aduenture with him to further the same, vpon very fit conditions: and that such as will aduenture thither in person, and continue there fiue yeeres as seruants to his Lordship; and those which shall bee Aduenturers with him in the said Plantation, shall not onely haue fit yeerely wages, with all necessary prouisions; but also at the end of his fiue yeeres seruice, shall haue to him and his Assignes in fee for euer, a hundred Acres of such land and woods as that Countrey affordeth, vpon such fit conditions as are expressed in a small Treatise which I haue written, and dedicated vnto his Lordship; which is to be had at the signe of the gilded Cocke in Paternoster-rowe, in *London*.[2] And whosoeuer will aduenture therein a hundred pound, shall not onely haue two thousand Acres of such woods and land measured out to him in fee for euer vpon fit conditions, but also haue some outher priuiledges, and conuenient places to salt and dry fish on, for so many people as any such Aduenturer shall at any time imploy there, and such as will be Aduenturers with him; and hee shall also haue the yeerely benefit, which may accrew by his foresaid summe of a hundred pound to be so aduentured. The which said summe, and any other greater or lesser summes, which are to bee so disbursed, are to raise a greater summe, to bee as a stocke for the setting

---

[1] There are substantial differences in this section between the two editions. Consequently the 'Loving invitation' from edition C is printed below, pp. 168–72, in square brackets.
[2] *The discourse containing a loving invitation* of 1622; see below, pp. 207–20.

foorth of shipping, men, and prouision, necessary for the aduancement of the said intended Plantation, and imploying of people in the fishing trade, and other labors, as the time may serue for the general good of all such as shall so aduenture therein.[1] So it may be plainely vnderstood, that the said Lord Deputy will not take the benefit of any such summe as may be so aduentured with him therein: but that euery such Aduenturer shall yeerely haue also the benefit of his owne aduentured summe, as the said Lord Deputy and other Aduenturers are to haue rateably.

Also the right Honourable Sir *George Caluert* Knight, Principall Secretary to the Kings most Excellent Maiestie, hath vndertaken to plant a Colony of his Maiesties Subiects in that Country, and hath already most worthily sent thither in these last two yeeres, a great number of men and women, with all necessaries fit for their liuelyhood, and they are there building of houses, clensing of land, and making of salt; whereof they haue already sent home a good quantity of the said salt so already made, which hath beene there well approoued to bee so good for the salting, and fit preseruing of such kind of fish as is taken on that coast; and likewise for any other kinde of victuals, as any other salt whatsoeuer.

By which tryall therein, it is very likely that the making of salt there, may in little time, not onely be a great benefit vnto all those which shall aduenture thither; but also by meanes thereof, great summes of money will be yeerely preserued in all his Maiesties Kingdomes, which are now bestowed in *France, Spaine,* and *Portugall,* for salt, by his Maiesties Subiects, and transported for the *New-found-land* voyages; and those people which are already there imployed, haue done many other good seruices, as it may appeare by those letters which are Printed in the latter part of this Booke, which doth giue good incouragement vnto the foresaid right Honourable Secretary, that his worthy vndertakings and proceedings in the said Plantation doe prosper so well; and his Honour is also well pleased to entertaine such as shall be willing to bee Aduenturers with him therein, vpon very fit conditions, which are to bee seene set foorth in Print, at the signe of the gilded Cocke in Pater-noster-row, in *London.*

There are diuers others which are formerly mentioned, that haue vndertaken to plant seuerall Colonies in that Country, which haue already sent thither great store of people, and they intend to send

---

[1] For a fuller description of the terms under which adventures would receive land in Falkland's colony, see below, pp. 214–16.

yeerely more there. So that there is great hope the said Plantation will prosper well.

Now my hope is, that for the better aduancemēt of the said Plantation, the great benefit which is very likely to be gotten yeerely thereby, will incourage some to affect that, which Religion, charity, or the common good cannot: for my selfe haue no other purpose, by thus laying open the benefits and necessary consequences, which may be gotten by the imbracing of such a Sister-land vnto his Maiesties other Kingdomes.

But for the honour and benefit which may accrew thereby vnto my dread Soueraigne, and for the generall good of all his Maiesties Subiects; and not to perswade any men to aduenture thither, but for honour and profit; nor are these perswasions to draw children from their parents to goe thither, neither men for their wiues, nor any seruants from their masters; but onely such industrious people, as with free consent will goe, or may be spared from such Cities and Parishes, that will but apparrell some of their fatherlesse children, of fourteene or fifteene yeeres of age, and some such yong married people, as haue but small meanes to set themselues forth; who by their good industry may liue there pleasantly, and grow rich in little time.

[A Loving Invitation to all His Maiesties Subiects.[1]

MY honored Countrymen, Worshipfull, Yeoman and al others: It is a custom at our great English entertainemes & Feasts, to prefer the best and daintiest dishes to the second course, as wel to please the pallate for relish, as the stomake for disgesture: such is now this my Inuitation, being as it were a second messe to my former Discourse; not only thereby to incourage the Honourable and worthy Subiect to better their [*sic*] estates: but also to harten the industrious, that haue but small meanes, and liue in want, seldom filling their bellies with good food, or couering their bodies with good clothes. All which foresaid benefits, food, apparell, and other pleasures are to bee had in *New-found-land*, either by aduenturing with your purses, or by going thither in person, and therfore I haue, for the better satisfying and animating of Aduenturers thither, and to establish those good trades, which may be yeerely made to that Countrey, added these following aduertisements, to fortifie and second my former discourse; which, praised bee God, hath not only receiued good approbation from his Maiestie, but also

---

[1] Extract from edition C.

from the Right Honorable Lords of the priuie Councell; and likewise so farre preuailed with the cleerenesse and solidity of some of their Honours wisedomes, and iudgements, as that they rely much on the naturall truth, and plainnesse of my reasons which I haue deliuered for the aduancement of his Maiesties aforesaid most hopefull Plantation, as that out of their good affection, and noble dispositions, they haue already vndertaken to plant seuerall Colonies in that Countrey.

This consideration hath (according to my bounden duty) moued me to be as careful as possibly I might, therby to aduance that worke, which long since was most worthily intended, as formerly appeares: I haue therefore thought good to annex vnto my former discourse, these second motiues & reasons following, which I haue gained by my often aduenturing to that countrie, and other parts of the world, by such obseruations and notice as principally I tooke, for the inlarging of Gods Church; Secondly, the Honour and benefit which may accrue thereby vnto my dread Soueraigne, and his Highnesse Royall Progeny: and thirdly, for the generall good of all his Maiesties Subiects.

Now my hope is, that whosoeuer shall be pleased to reade that my former Discourse, with my ensuing motiues, will not so slight the same, or take occasion, without cause, to dislike them: for although they are plaine, yet I affirmatiuely auerre, they are true, and as I haue delited in the latitude of matter, and not in the altitude of words, so haue I written it out of mine owne certaine knowledge and experience, and not out of any borrowed speculations, hauing in many yeeres, often played the practike part in that Country, as wel as the Theorike: and thereby know how to reduce my former contemplation into action, as it shall appeare, whensoeuer it may please his Maiestie, or the State to command me.

And seeing the foresaid Plantation is so worthily respected, and lately vndertaken, as it is well knowne, with great zeale and iudgement: So I no way doubt, but they will bee the meanes to settle it with renowne and profit, and be the more circumspect therein, by reason of other mens errors in businesse of the like nature, so to prouide and forecast the euents which may follow, wherby their good purposes therein may not be hindred, like expert Pilots, who by the Discouery of rockes & shelues, know how to auoid them, and by the sight of other mens ship-wrackes, know the more perfectly how to eschew the like danger, and preserue their owne.

And as those worthy men formerly mentioned, haue vndertaken to erect and found a Plantation in that countrey, so are they willing to entertaine all such as shall be desirous to aduenture with either of them therein, to further their said designes with their purses, or with their persons and purses, vpon fit and large conditions, as it may appeare, to any that shall inquire of those foresaid Vndertakers: and as for such conditions, as the foresaid right Honourable Lord Deputy Generall for the Kingdome of *Ireland* will grant vnto any, which shall be willing to aduenture with his Lordship, to further his designes in the *New-found-land*, I presume vpon my certaine knowledge, to signifie herein the effectuall points thereof, which are more at large to be seene set forth in print, and to be had at the signe of the Golden Cock in Pater-noster-row in London, which will plainly informe any that will aduenture with him one hundred pounds, shall not only haue the yeerely benefit therof to his owne vse and behoofe, what is thereby gotten in the fishing trade, and on the Plantation; but also haue two thousand acres of such land and woods there measured out to him, with fit prerogatiue of the one halfe of a Harbour, or Rode where ships vse to ride at ankor, for making of their fishing voyages, thereunto adioyning, in fee for euer: to dispose thereof, how and to whom he list; paying vnto his Lordship and his heires twenty pence yeerely, as a rent for the said land, woods and prerogatiue, and so maintaine a fit number of people vpon the same, and any such Aduenturer shall haue in fee likewise, a conuenient place to build a stage and other necessary roomes to salt fish on, and for a dwelling house, with a sufficient circuit of ground thereunto adioyning, to dry fish on, and for some other purposes, as shall be fit for such a company, as are easily imployed to that Countrey, in a ship of 100. Tunnes burden, neere vnto the harbors of *Formosa* and *Renouze*; where his Lordships Colony is at first to be settled, and fortified; So as any such vndertaker do within such a conuenient time, as hee shall bee thereunto inioyned by his Lease, settle and inhabite there, neere vnto the place where the Colony shall be settled, eight persons at least, and so many more as any such shall thinke good to take the charge, and likewise the benefit of their labors to his own particular vse, paying for the said space of ground for Stage roome, House, drying of fish and other purposes, but 20. shillings yeerely, and to haue timber there to build with, vpon the same; and wood to burne in the said house, so much as any such vndertaker will haue for the fetching of it from the woods.

And whosoeuer will aduenture with him therein 200. pounds, shall haue double so much in all respects, as he shall haue which aduentures 100. pound: and whosoeuer shall be pleased to aduenture with his

Lordship, any greater or lesser some, shall haue proportionably in all respects, according to the rate, and equality of his aduenture.

And likewise such as are willing to goe and liue in that Countrey, that haue meanes of themselues, or from their friends, to set themselues forth with apparell and things necessary for one whole yeere at first, and shall serue there fiue yeeres, as seruants vse to doe; shall haue, not only a large and sufficient sum of wages paid him yeerely, as hee shall bee agreed withall; but also haue at the end of his fiue yeeres seruice, one hundred acres of land and woods to build and plant on, within the circuit of *New-found-land*, not farre from the Colony, where now at first it is settled, in fee for euer, to dispose of, as any such shall thinke good; paying for the same at the Sealing of his Lease, (as a fine for his admittance,) at his income therunto, Ten shillings, and euer after but a penny of rent by the yere, to his Lordship, and his heires.

Thus euery such Aduenturer shall not onely haue a great quantitie of Land, Woods, and other priuiledges there vpon fit conditions; but also the yeerely benefit of such a summe, as any one shall so aduenture, and likewise an equall part of all such benefit, as may bee gotten by such people as shall bee hired to serue there, as aforesaid, to liue there, as well of their owne industry in the Fishing Trade, as otherwise; so as euery such Aduenturer is likewise to beare an equall part of the charge, according to such Iust accounts as will be taken of euery particular thing by his Lordships Treasurer, or Committies, which are appointed for the more orderly proceeding in the said *New-found-land* Plantation.

Likewise the right Honourable, *Sir George Caluert*, Knight, principal Secretary of State to his Maiestie, hath already sent thither within these three yeeres a great number of people, where they liue very pleasantly doing many good seruices; besides the making of salt, whereof they haue sent home to his Honour a quantity, which hath beene there well approued to be so good for salting of fish, and other victuals, as any other salt; and those men commend well the Countrey, as it may appeare, by some of their letters, sent from thence, which are inserted in the end of this booke; by which letters, they do also not only well approue, what I haue written of that Country; but also gaue his Honor, and al those which are already Aduenturers with him, good incouragement, that the Country is so commodious, and their aduenturing thither so prosperous, as that there is dayly a greater hope then euer there was, that the said Plantation will, by Gods fauour, take excellent successe if more such worthy persons bestow their assistance either in purse or otherwise: and his Honour is also well pleased to entertaine any such therein, as will repaire vnto him, vpon fit and conuenient conditions.

Thus it may be well vnderstood, that both their Honourable vndertakings in the said most hopefull Plantation are for the publike good, and that my purpose by my former Discourse, and these second motiues, is not only for such Aduenturers to gaine honour and benefit to themselues and posterities, but also in charity to many, and for a generall good to all; for I dare constantly affirme, that what I haue written concerning that countrey, and the trades there already knowne is (vpon my life) true: why then should not many other persons, such as God hath blessed with the wealth of this world, gladly vndertake so worthy a worke, and aduenture some part of that wealth, to aduance a businesse so noble, & to send thither such as shall well like, not onely to see a Country, where people are seldome pinched with want, and where they liue fat and as healthy, as in any other part of the world, the Countrey being full of Hawkes, Partriges, Thrushes, and other Fowles, hunting Deere, and other beasts, with delicate Fruits which are there in great aboundance; But likewise to doe, and obserue what possibly they may, to find out some other good things in that spacious Iland, which as yet lye vndiscouered; as Mines, Minerals, Wood, Berries for diers and such like, for the generall good of all his Maiesties other Kingdomes?

Now I trust, that many other worthy and Industrious persons, when they shall vnderstand of these noble conditions, how requisite and necessary the *New-found-land* Plantation wil be vnto all his Maiesties other Kingdoms, they will I doubt not, but make a good construction of these my endeauours, whereby to further the same, by perusing those reasons and perswasions which I haue deliuered, which are not to draw any young men and young women from their parents, to goe thither, as diuers such are already willing so to doe, neither men from their wiues, nor seruants from their Masters, (as there are a great number of such doe also seeke to be imployed,) but onely such industrious and willing people, as of themselues, or may by their friends helpe, haue fit meanes to set themselues foorth orderly, and that others with their friends consent will goe, and may be spared from such Cities, and parishes, as will set forth some of them orderly, to plant there, be they either youths of foureteene or fifteene yeeres of age, and some such yong married people as haue but small meanes of themselues to doe it, who by their good Industrie may liue there pleasantly, and grow rich in little time.]

And if any man desire to bee further satisfied of that Countrey, then my Discourse shall informe them, they may inquire of any vnderstanding man, as hath spent some part of his time in that Countrey, and thereby also[1] consider wherein any such can giue sufficient reasons to confute or contradict what I haue written thereof, that haue thus freely thrown my selfe with my mite, into the treasury of my countries good. And so I descend vnto the charge of what I formerly promised.

The Charge as followeth.

	li.	s.	d.
In primis, eleuen thousand waight of Bisket bread, bought at xv. shillings the hundred waight	082	10	0
Twenty sixe Tunne of Beere and Sider, at 53. shillings 4. pence the Tunne	069	06	8
Two Hogs-heads of very good English Beefe	010	00	0
Two Hogs-heads of Irish Beefe	005	00	0
Ten fat Hogs salted, Caske and Salt	010	10	0
Thirty bushels of Pease, at	006	00	0
Two Firkins of Butter	003	00	0
Two hundred waight of Cheese	002	10	0
One bushell of Mustard-seed	000	06	0
One Hogs-head of Vineger	001	05	0
Wood to dresse meate withall	001	00	0
One great Copper Kettle	002	00	0
Two small Kettles	002	00	0
Two Frying pans	000	03	4
Platters, Ladles, and Cans for Beere	001	00	0
A paire of Bellowes for the Cooke	000	02	0
Locks for the bread Roomes	000	02	6
Tap, Boriers, and Funnels	000	02	0
One hundred waight of Candles	002	10	0
One hundred and thirty quarters of Salt, at 2.s. the bushell, 15. gallons to the bushell, is 16. shillings the quarter	104	00	0
Mats and dynnage to lye vnder the Salt	002	10	0
Salt Shouels[2]	000	10	0

[1] 'thereby also' not in C.
[2] In C this and the preceding item are combined and valued at £3.10s. Because of this error Whitbourne's total of £420 1s. 4d. is ten shillings too little in C.

173

More for repairing of 8. fishing Boats,			
500. foot of Elme boords, of an			
inch in thicknesse, at 8.s. the hundred[1]	002	00	0
Two thousand nayles for the said boats and Stages, at			
13.s. 4.d. the thousand	001	06	8
Foure thousand nayles, at 6.s. 8.d. the thousand	001	06	8
Two thousand nayles, at 5.d. the hundred	000	08	0
Fiue hundred waight of Pitch	002	00	0
A barrell of Tarre[2]	000	10	0
Two hundred waight[3] of blacke Ocome	001	00	0
Thrummes for Pitch mabs[4]	000	01	6
Bolles,[5] Buckets, and Funnels	001	00	0
Two brazen Crocks	002	00	0
Canuase to make boate sailes, and small ropes fitting			
for them; at 25.s. for each saile	012	10	0
Ten Boates, Anchors, Ropes	010	00	0
Twelue doozen of fishing lines	006	00	0
Twenty 4. doozen of fishing hooks	002	00	0
Squid hooks and Squid line	000	05	0
For Pots and liuer Mands[6]	000	18	0
Iron workes for ten fishing Boats	002	00	0
Ten keipnet[7] Irons	000	10	0
Twine to make keipnets, &c	000	06	0
Ten good Nets, at 26.s. a Net	013	00	0
Two Saines,[8] a greater and a lesse	012	00	0
Two hundred waight of Lead	001	00	0
Small Ropes for the Saines	001	00	0
Dry-Fats for the Nets and Saines	000	06	0
Flaskets, and bread boxes	000	15	0
Twine for store	000	05	0
For so much Hair-cloth as may cost	010	00	0
Three Tun of Vineger[9] Caske, for water	001	06	8
Two barrels of Otemeale	001	06	0
One doozen of Deale boords	000	10	0

---

[1] In C this item reads: '500. foot of Elme boords, at 8 s. the 100.'
[2] In C this item and the preceding one are combined: 'For Stonepitch and Tarre 002
10 0'.   [3] 'waight' not in C.
[4] Short pieces of coarse yarn, used for mops (mabs).   [5] Bowls.
[6] Baskets.
[7] Hook and net used in fishing.
[8] Seine. A fishing net which hangs vertically in the water.
[9] 'Vineger' not in C. Cask used to acetify wine.

One hundred waight of Spikes	002	05	0
Heading and splitting Kniues	001	05	0
Two good Axes, 4 hand Hatchets, foure short Wood hookes, two drawing Irons, and two Adizes	000	16	0
Three yards of good woollen Cloth	000	10	0
Eight yards of good Canuase	000	10	0
A grinding stone or two	000	06	0
An Iron pitch-pot and hookes	000	06	0
One thousand fiue hundred of dry fish, to spend thitherward	006	00	0
One Hogs-head of *Aqua vitae*	004	00	0
Two thousand of good Orlop[1] nailes	002	05	0
Foure arme Sawes, 4. hand Sawes, 4. Thwart Sawes, three Augers, 2. Crowes of Iron, and 2. Sledges, foure Iron Shouels, two Pickaxes, Foure Mattocks, and foure Cloe Hammers[2]	005	00	0
More for some other small necessaries	003		4
The totall summe of which particulars} is,	420	1	4

All which former prouisions, the Master of the Ship, or the Purser are to be accoûtable vnto the Aduenturers in euery voyage, what is spent thereof, and what is left of the same, with those which shall continue there to plant; of which number, if but ten persons remaine there, they may well haue reserued for them of the former victuals and prouisions, these particulars following, *viz.*

Fiue hundred waight of the Bisket bread, fiue hogs-heads of beere, or sider, halfe a hogs-head of beefe, foure whole sides of bacon, 4. bushels of pease, halfe a firkin of butter, halfe a hundred waight of cheeses, a pecke of mustard-seede, a barrell of vineger, twelue pound waight of candles, two pecks of oatmeale, halfe a hogs-head of *aqua vitae*, two copper kettles, one brasse crock, one frying pan, a grinding stone, and all the axes, hatchets, wood-hooks, augers, sawes, crowes of iron, sledges, hammers, mattocks, pickaxes, shoouels, drawing irons, splitting kniues, haire-cloth, pynnaces sailes, pynnaces anchor-ropes, a sayne, some nets; and keepe all the eight fishing boats, and the iron works appertaining to them, in perfect readinesse there, from yeere to yeere; and many of the other small necessaries, when the fishing voyage is made, as pikes, nayles, and such like, which may serue to helpe build

---

[1] I.e. nails to be used for the orlop, or deck.
[2] After the first item, the number of tools is not stipulated in C.

houses, cleanse land, and such like seruices fitly for the Inhabitants to labour withall in the winter time, whiles the Ships are wanting from them.

Now to make an estimate what fish all the 40. persons fit for such a voyage, may well take, and keepe eight fishing boats all the summer time there at Sea, with three good fishermen in euery of the said boats; you shall vnderstand, that so many men doe vsually kill aboue twenty fiue thousand fish for euery boat,[1] which may amount vnto two hundred thousand, sixe score fishes to euery hundred: and diuers Ships being so well prouided as aforesaid, haue yeerely taken[2] there, aboue thirty fiue thousand, for euery boate: so as they not onely load their Ship, but also haue sold great[3] quantities, besides their loadings yeerely to Merchants; and if such Ships which are so well manned for that purpose, cannot make saile of such fish as they take ouer and aboue their loading; then they vsually giue ouer taking of any more fish in diuers yeeres, when there is great abundance easily to be taken, because there are not any Marchants to buy it, nor no fit houses to lay vp the same in safety for another yere.

Now to make[4] an estimate but of twenty fiue thousand of fish, for euery of the eight boates, it will at that rate amount vnto two hundred thousand; which may be a fit quantity to fill and load a Ship of an hundred Tun burthen, if the fish bee not very small; if it be large, a Ship of that burthen will not loade so much, besides the water, wood, victuall, and other prouisions, fit for so many men as shall saile in the said Ship from thence, to make sale and imployments of the said fish; which, as I conceiue, will bee a fit course so to doe, and thereby great charge, and some aduenture will be saued in carrying the same directly to a market, in regard what it would be, if it should bee returned home into *England*, and then afterwards relade the same againe and send it to a market.

Wherein my opinion is, that the said Ship, hauing her voyage at *New-found-land*, should saile from thence directly to *Marseiles* or *Talloon*,[5] which places lying within the Straits of *Gibraltar* in the French Kings dominions, where the customes vpon Fish are but little, and the Kentall lesse then ninety English pounds waight; and the price of such Fish there I haue not knowne, to be sold for lesse at any time, then

---

[1] C 'boat, though they are but bad fishermen, which'.
[2] C 'aforesaid, and hauing good fishermen, doe yeerely take'.
[3] C 'their ships, but also haue sold in some yeeres great'.
[4] C 'And therefore will I make'.   [5] Toulon.

twelue shillings of currant English payment for euery Kentall, and commonly a farre greater price; and there speedy sales are vsually made of such Fish, and good returnes had: and if any man will returne his money from thence, hee may haue sure bills of exchange, for payment thereof heere in London, vpon sight of any such bills.

The foresaid two hundred thousand of Fish, loading the said ship, it will then make at Marseiles aboue two and twenty hundred Kentalls of that waight; which being sold but at twelue shillings the Kentall, amounts to thirteene hundred and twenty pounds sterling, and is —— 1320. pounds.

A Ship of that burthen to serue the voyage, being hired by the moneth, when she is there vnloaded, may be then there paid for her hire, and so discharged; or being hired for a longer time, may returne from thence vnto some other place in Spaine, to bee reloaded home with some Marchandize, which may be well performed, and the said Ship returne in fit time to saile againe vnto *New-found-land* the yeere following, with lesse charge then the first yeere; and then greater hope of benefit it will bee to the Aduenturers then the first yeere, when people are there before-hand, and all things in fit readinesse against their comming.

There may well be of the foresaid two hundred thousand of Fish, twelue Tun of Traine Oyle, or a greater quantity, the which being sold and deliuered in *New-found-land* at ten pounds the Tunne, as commonly it is the price there, it will amount to the summe of sixe score pounds, and is —— 120. pounds.

And also there may be well made ouer and aboue the foresaid quantity of two hundred thousand dry fish, ten thousand of large greene fish;[1] which being sold in *New-found-land* but at fiue pounds the thousand, it will amount to the summe of fifty pounds; I say, 50. l. which greene fish being brought into England, it may yeeld aboue ten pounds the thousand; and the twelue Tunne of Traine oyle, being likewise brought home, is vsually sold at some places in this Kingdome, for aboue eighteene pounds the Tunne, and sometimes at twenty; which ouerprices of the said Oyle and greene fish, I doe heere omit to summe the same, what it may be more.

Now if the foresaid two hundred thousand of fish may be sold at Marseiles, at sixteene shillings the Kentall, as often such fish is, and much

---

[1] I.e. fish preserved simply in salt, instead of being dried slowly by a mixture of salt and sun. The continental fishermen on the Bank usually took their fish home green (or wet), but the method required too much salt to be common among the English.

dearer; the two thousand two hundred Kentals, will then amount to the summe of seuenteene hundred and threescore pounds. —— 1760. pounds.

And it is very likely, that the foresaid eight fishing boates being well manned, and stay[1] [sic] continually fishing in the Countrey, vntill the 15. day of October,[2] as they may well, they may then take aboue thirty fiue thousand of fish for euery boate, as diuers yeeres many men haue done in much lesse time: which will then amount to fourescore thousand more then the former two hundred thousand.

The which fourescore thousand so gotten ouer and aboue the Ships loading, may bee otherwise disposed of at *New-found-land*; be it more or lesse, it may yeeld there foure pounds the thousand, allowing to that price all the Traine oyle and greene Fish which may come thereof: so that there may be well gotten ouer and aboue the Ships loading, foure-score thousand of Fish, and much more; the which at foure pounds the thousand will amount to the summe of ——0320.li.s.d

Adding thereunto the former summe of ——1320—00.—0.
And also for the aforesaid Oyle ——0120—00.0.
And also for the tenne thousand greene Fish ——0050—00.0.
And also for the ouer-price at Marseiles, being sold at sixteene shillings the Kentall, it will be some ——0440.—0.—0.
Totall Summe ——2250.—0.—0.—0.

Of which summe, bee it more or lesse, whatsoeuer is gotten in the voyage; if victuals, Salt, and the other former prouisions, bee prouided at reasonable cheape prices: Then the Master and Company haue a third part thereof, allowing some small matter from the same, towards the victualling; and there is another third part likewise to bee allowed towards the Ships trauell and charge, deducting some thing likewise thereof towards the Master of the Ship, for taking the charge, and for some other of the better sort of men, which they vsually haue ouer and aboue their shares of the former third: and the other third remaines vnto the Victuallers forth of the Ship.

So that the voyage amounting as aforesaid, to the summe of two thousand, two hundred & fifty pounds: A third will bee the summe of seuen hundred and fifty pounds for the victualling part; from which deducting the former charge of 420.li.—01.s.—04.d. which is to bee for the victualling forth of a Ship with forty persons; there may remaine

---

[1] C 'staying'. [2] C '28. day of September'.

to the Aduenturers for the bearing the Aduenture, and all Charges discharged, the summe of 331.li–11.s. And in some yeeres, when salt, bread and beere is deare bought; the victualling part is allowed the one moity or halfe part of what is gotten in the voyage, and the Company and Ship the other halfe part.

Now omitting to write of any greater price, which may bee gotten vpon the sales of the two hundred thousand of fish at *Marseiles*, or the benefit which may be made vpon the returnes of the money for the same from thence, or what may be gotten by the imployments of the foresaid summe, at the place where the sales are made.

Likewise what may be more gotten vpon the traine Oyle and green Fish, if it bee not sold in *New-found-land*, but brought home, and sold here at the best hand:

And if a ship bee hired by the moneth to performe this voyage, wich may be ended in lesse then nine moneths, the ship to be free at *Marseiles*, when the fish is vnloaden there; and being hired at forty pound a moneth or much cheaper; it may then bee esteemed what may bee fitly gotten by hiring of a ship in that manner, if the fish and traine Oyle amount vnto the prices, as it is valued: if it yeeld more, then the greater benefit will come by hiring of a ship; if lesse, after the rate accordingly.

And if Pans bee prouided for the making of Salt in the *New-found-land*, as fitly and cheaply it may be, then will the charge in setting forth of any ship by the Aduenturers, be much lesse, and the benefit much the greater.

Now whereas there are but twenty foure men of the forty nominated to fish; the other are to labour the fish at land, (of which sixteene) seuen are to bee skilfull headders, and splitters of fish; two boyes to lay the fish on a table, and three to salt the fish, which labour, three women may fitly do; three men may fetch a-land salt, and tend to wash fish, and and [sic] dry the same; which may bee two house Carpenters and a Mason, the other may bee a woman, which makes vp sixteene to be left a-land, who may be fit to prouide meate, and to wash and dry fish so well as men, and for other labours also.

And those persons which remaine there, should be hired by the yeere, whose yeerely wages will not be aboue 8. or 9. pounds a couple one with the other, and apparell themselues; which apparell the aduenturers are to prouide, and those which are thus hired, to allow for the same againe out of their yeerely wages. The which yeerely wages, for euery couple of those which should continue there, will be borne yeerely on that part of the fish and oyle, which may come to the Companies part,

179

as aforesaid, if the businesse be orderly carried; So that the victuals of those persons which should remaine there to plant, from the 20. day of March, vnto the 20. day of Nouember; and their whole yeeres pay should euery yeere be, as it were charged and raised out of the Companies third part, from yeere to yeere;

Neither should the aduenturers bee any other way charged for them, but onely for some fit quantity of Meale, Mault, Beefe, Porke, Butter, Cheese, *Aqua vitae*, and some other fit things to serue them in winter, vntill the Ships returne to them againe, in the beginning of euery Summer; and then they are to bee againe as of the Ships company.

In which time of winter, their labours vpon the land, in building of houses, sawing of boords, squaring of timber, manuring of land, and doing other seruices, may wel defray the said charge, with good benefit ouer and aboue the same.

And then the second yeere, euery of those persons, which so shall remaine there, may haue their equall shares with the Fishermen, which may well pay their wages and charge that the Aduenturers should bee at for them, with a greater[1] benefit then in the first yeere.

This is the order and course which I haue long time had an opinion and considered of, whereby to aduance his Maiesties good purpose for the said Plantation,[2] so that an orderly and beneficiall Plantation in the *New-found-land*, is to bee at first proceeded on, and not by carriage of beasts thither to till the Land, before such time as prouisions bee made for them to liue in Winter, which will require some time to fit Meddowes at first for hay, and fit houses for them.

A Ship of a hundred Tun burthen, being thus imployed, may also well carry in her the first yeere for increase, Hogs, Goates, and Poultry, which will not be chargeable, nor pester much roome in the Ship, and they will prooue and increase exceeding well there, as I haue often prooued, and bee at very little or[3] no charge in keeping of them there: And after the first yeere, the said Ship sailing thither with a lesse number of people, prouision being made there in readinesse, she may carry in her great store of Beasts, and prouision for them.

And for the better proceeding in this Plantation, it will be good for such Aduenturers as shall imploy a Ship of 100. Tun, with 40. persons, to hire two small Barkes, neere the burthen of 30. Tun apiece by the moneth, to be victualled and manned by them, which should serue as in a fishing voyage, with ten persons in each Barke, and they should

---

[1] C 'with farre greater'.   [2] 'for...Plantation' not in C.
[3] 'very little or' not in C.

haue in euery of them, all prouisions fit to keepe two Fsher [sic][1] boates at Sea, either of them all the Summer, and then those Barkes may also well carry some beasts for increase; and they should depart hence before the Ship of a hundred Tun burthen, for some speciall seruices to prouide against the greater Ship ariues, and then the Ship[2] of a hundred Tun, with 40. persons, need not depart out of England, before it bee towards the end of March; which Barkes, if either of them bee there timely in the yeere, it may bee, in many respects, worth much more, for the good of the fishing voyage, and the said Plantation, then their hire by the moneth will amount vnto, as for many reasons which I can deliuer.

And then taking that course, there may bee some sales made before-hand of a hundred thousand of fish, or a greater quantity to some Merchants, to be deliuered in *New-found-land*, and to receiue money for the same here in London, vpon Bills of Exchange. All which, by Gods assistance, may bee well performed, and the bigger Ship also, well loden, to saile from thence to some good market, to make sales of the same.

And then one of those Barkes may load all such traine oyle as may be gotten in the voyage, and returne with the same, where it may be thought best to make sale therof: And the other Barke may then load all such greene fish as may be made, and return home to England, or elsewhere to dispose thereof.

Thus it may bee all well performed, and store of fish left for the prouision of those which are to stay in the Countrey to inhabit: and also for the hogs and water-fowle to feed on in the Winter when there is cause.

Now whether it may be best to buy a Ship of 100. Tun burthen, or bigger, to serue for the said voyage, or to hire such a one by the moneth, for that purpose;[3] I leaue it to the consideration of the Aduenturers themselues.

Thus it may well be vnderstood, that the said Plantation will bee for the generall good of all his Maiesties Subiects, and not hurtfull to any: And it will bee also a most speciall benefit, and good for all those which yeerely trade there in fishing, what now it is, though they settle no people there to plant, whereby to keepe and maintaine their certaine places, there to salt and dry their fish on; by reason that those which shall inhabit there, will, vpon request, and some small gratuity, preserue

---

[1] C 'Fisher'.   [2] C 'Shippes'.
[3] 'for that purpose' not in C.

their fishing Boats yeerely[1] from spoyling, so as they may haue them and their Stages, and all commodious and necessary rommes so pleasantly, and in such perfect readinesse, yeerely against their comming thither, which will vndoubtedly be worth vnto them in their fishing voyages, many thousands of pounds more yeerely then now it is, as it cannot bee denyed by any that knowes the manner and order of those voyages.

Now whereas I haue formerly made but an estimate what number of Fish forty persons being there so imployed, doe vsually take, and so all others may doe the like, and orderly make the same in the Summer time, when they haue set saile from England, in that voyage neere the end of March, and returned home from thence neere the twentieth day of September, such as haue in the same Summer, after they haue arriued there, felled and brought all their Timber, with great labour and paines out of the Woods, and spent aboue twenty dayes about the same, and in building of their Stages, and other large necessary roomes there, to split, salt and dry their fish in, and also in building and repairing their fishing Boates, which hath beene more labour and paines to them in doing thereof, then all the taking and making of such a great quantity of fish as aforesaid hath been vnto them;[2] so that it may be well conceiued, what an vnspeakable charge, labour, and time is now yeerely so spent[3] by disorderly courses therein, which may bee well saued yeerely, and imployed to much better purpose in that Countrey, if order bee taken so, as those Stages and fishing Boates may be there from yeere to yeere fitly preserued, and thereby will bee not onely a greater benefit yeerely more gotten then now there is, vnto all his Maiesties Kingdomes, but also many great perils at Sea, in sailing thitherwards bound in such vnseasonable times of the yeere, and in such desperate manner as some men vse to doe, preuented; and also there will be yeerely a greater abundance of fish the more taken, by continuing there a longer time to fish, then as now men vse to doe.

And whereas I haue before giuen but an estimate what such a quantity of fish so taken may yeeld, being a part thereof disposed away at *New-found-land*, and the greater quantity thereof transported from thence vnto *Marseiles*, and there sold as aforesaid: It may, as I suppose, dis-hearten some men from aduenturing, to further the said Plantation in that kind, because it is wel knowne, that in returning from *New-found-land* vnto *Marseiles*, or to any other places within the Straits

---

[1] C 'Boats & stages yeerely'.
[2] C 'vnto such a number of men as aforesaid'.   [3] C 'ill spent'.

of *Gibraltar*, to make Sales and imployments of such a quantity of fish, that the course by Sea in sailing thither, and returning from thence, is something long; and the perils that may happen in that course by Pyrats, and the Turkish Rouers, are very dangerous: Therefore I haue presumed more at large, to adde vnto my former Discourse this further incouragement and instruction, to any which may be willing to aduenture with any of the aforesaid Vndertakers.

That if any such Aduenturers will returne from thence with their Fish into Spaine, or Portugall, the dangers of the Sea are much lesse, and the course much shorter, then they are in sailing to *Marseiles*,[1] and the price of such Fish is commonly sold there at a price,[2] and better returnes are to be had from Spaine, and Portugall, then from *Marseiles*.[3]

And whosoeuer should returne from *New-found-land* with their Fish vnto any Port of the Coast of Biskay, which is very neere vnto vs, they shall most commonly finde a greater price for it there, then sometimes those doe that saile with it vnto *Marseiles*, Spaine, or Portugall.[4]

And whosoeuer so aduenturing shall returne from *New-found-land* with his Fish vnto any of these Cities in France; as namely, Naunce, Burdeaux, Rochell, Bayon, Roane,[5] or to diuers other places within that Kingdome, which is euen heere at our owne homes: That kind of Fish is in all these parts of France in so great request, and yeerely selles there at so great a price, and so good payment for it there, as it is sold either in *Marseiles*, Spaine, Portugall, or the Coast of Biskay; and very good imployments are there to bee made, which will yeeld good profit, being brought into England, Scotland or Ireland.

Hauing thus plainly expressed with what facility the *New-found-land* Plantation may bee orderly proceeded on, I haue thought good also to relate how such Aduenturers to that Countrey may yeerly make much greater benefit of trade, in returning from thence, then I haue as yet written, or that any man which I haue heard of, that hath as yet put in practice such a fit course,[6] leauing it to those that will make triall thereof, as their owne iudgements shall aduize them.

---

[1] This was probably true, although the Barbary pirates were venturing into the Atlantic with increasing frequency in the 1620's. For example, in 1625 twenty-seven English ships would be captured before they could reach the Straits of Gibraltar. *CSP Col., 1574–1660*, p. 75.

[2] C 'at a very good price'.

[3] C '*Marseiles* in some yeeres'.

[4] C 'Portugall: for in some yeres a hundred English waight of such fish is sold there for aboue 80. Royals of plate which is 40. shillings.'

[5] Rouen.

[6] C 'practice, or spake of, leaing [*sic*]'.

It is well knowne, that from the *New-found-land*,[1] vnto a place called the Banke, which lyeth East from thence towards England, 25. leagues in the like altitude: which Banke is a sand, and in most places twelue leagues broad; and in length North-east, and Southwest, about 100. leagues; on which Banke there is no lesse then 20. fadome of water at any place, and there doe fish yeerely aboue 100. saile of French Ships, Winter and Summer, some of them making two voyages there in a yeere, and another voyage to some other place also in the same yeere, and spend much time of the same yere at their owne homes likewise.

I haue often (sailing towards the *New-found-land*) met with some French Ships comming from thence, deepe loden with Fish, in the first of Aprill, who haue taken the same there, in Ianuary, February, & March, which are the sharpest moneths in the yere for storms and cruell weather.

To which Banke may our Nation, such as will aduenture therein, and doe great good in fishing, saile from the *New-found-land* in the latter part of the Summer, when the Fish begins to draw from that Coast, as commonly it doth when the Winter comes on; I meane, such shipping as are to be imployed by whomsoeuer may vndertake to plant there, and likewise any other Ships that saile thither a fishing, as now they vse to doe, who hauing disposed away such fish and traine oyle as they take there in the Summer time vnto Merchants, as vsually euery yeere some such as aduenture thither haue done, they may then (Salt being made there, as it may be fitly and cheaply) take in thereof a fit quantity, and fresh-water, wood, fresh fowles great store,[2] and other victuall, and likewise a sufficient quantity of Herrings, Mackerell, Capeling, and Lawnce, to bait their hookes withall, for taking of fish on the said Bank; because such bait the Frenchmen are not able to haue, that saile purposely to fish there, but are constrained to bait their hookes with a part of the same Codfish which they take there, wherewith they load their Ships.

The which fish so yeerely taken there, is much larger, thicker, and sweeter, then the same kind of fishes are, that are taken on the Coast of *New-found-land*, or those parts neere thereunto. Whereby it may be well vnderstood to be much more necessary and beneficiall, for such as will saile there to fish, to carry such kind of bait as aforesaid, with them, to put on the hooks; & then they shal the more speedily load their Ships then the Frenchmen may possibly doe, who haue there no such bait to put on their hookes[3] to fish withall, neither any other fresh

---

[1] C '*New-found-land*, homeward bound vnto'.
[2] 'great store' not in C.
[3] 'to...hookes' not in C.

victuall of flesh kinde, wood, or fresh-water to dresse their meat withall, but only such as they carry with thẽ from France.

Whereby it may be wel conceiued, that the fishing which the Frenchmen haue there on the same Banke, is a very profitable trade vnto them; seeing they not onely saile thither of purpose to fish in the hardest time of Winter, which is aboue 650. leagues distance from the neerest part of Faance [sic];[1] and in all which time to liue vpon the Sea in such a cold place, with but little wood, wherewith to make somtimes a good fire to dresse their meate, and to sit by to warme themselues.

All which hardnesse of liuing so on the said Banke,[2] in that manner, the gaine which they make by the said fishing trade, doth make them greatly to delight therein: whereby it may be well vnderstood, to be a farre better trade for such as fish the Summer time at *New-found-land*, and doe prouide for that purpose; they may there reload their Ships againe with good fish, in twenty dayes and lesse, comming thither so well prouided as aforesaid: and so they may then merrily at times sit by a good fire, when they haue laboured hard all day; whereby they will bee the better able to take more fish there in a day, then so many Frenchmen shall bee able to take in two dayes, and with a greater pleasure therein.

And thus may any performe the said voyage homeward bound from *New-found-land*, and[3] in fit order, and bee at no charge about trimming of any Ship, which shall serue in such a voyage, but onely as is used euery yeere for the *New-found-land* voyage onely, and with a very small addition of Bread and Beere to be allowed more thereunto.

Neither need the Masters and Sailors of any Ships that will vndertake the said voyage, prepare themselues with any other apparell or necessary prouisions, then they yeerely vse to doe for the *New-found-land* voyage onely.

Which voyage, so to bee performed from the *New-found-land*[4] to the said Banke, I am of opinion diuers men will gladly vndertake, when those Plantations, now lately intended in that countrey, are orderly settled; which is likely to proue very profitable, for any that will prepare themselues for that purpose, seeing it will bee vnto such as a double voyage of benefit, and all vnder one charge.

And whosoeuer will so imploy Ships, they may saile with their loading so gotten there, vnto France, Portugall, or Spaine, where that

[1] C 'France'.
[2] C 'liuing so there, in'.
[3] 'from *New-found-land*, and' not in C.
[4] C 'from thence to'.

185

kinde of fish doth vsually sell at a great price; and returne loaden from thence (by Gods assistance) yeerely against Christmas, with some Salt,[1] Oyle, Wine, Fruit, and some Royalls of Plate, or French Crownes, and so make foure voyages in three quarters of a yeere, and all vnder one setting forth from *England, Scotland* or *Ireland*.

And then, such as shall be imploied in that voyage, may afterwards spend the time at their homes merrily, vntill it be towards Aprill in euery yeere, which is timely enough to set forth againe in the said voyages.

And if any Ship so imploied, doe returne from thence directly home to England, that kinde of Fish will sell so well here, and is so good as any powdered Codde which is taken in the North Seas, or vpon the Coast of England or Ireland.

Thus briefely and plainely, but not curiously, I haue runne thorow my intended taske of my second motiues and reasons, which leads to the aduancement of his Maiesties most hopeful Plantation in the *New-found-land*; not that my resolution is any way to insinuate with the capacity, either of the highest, or meaner sort of people, thereby to inuite them to the setting forth of this great and happy enterprize, further then the solidity of the truth, and well grounded probabilities shall direct and leade them; but rather to informe their iudgements of the naturall state, condition, benefits, and trades to that Countrey, which promiseth so many hopes; and these hopes so much assurance of a most flourishing and succesfull issue, that indeede, to vse but few words for all, we neede much desire to know such a Sister land as the *New-found-land* is, and to loue it as we should.

But as the smallest terrestriall action cannot possibly prosper, without Gods diuine assistance, to perfect and finish it: so this great worke, so pious and noble of it selfe, as tending to the propagation of so many Christian soules to God, will (by his eternall prouidence and great mercy) be both furthered and blessed in the attempt, preseruation, and establishing thereof.

As for myself, who out of mine own experience, and the integrity of my thoughts, am confident, that the end will crowne the beginning of this most hopefull Plantation, I shall euer like a true-hearted Englishman, & his Maiesties most humble and faithfull Subiect, religiously desire and wish to see it in a faire forwardnes & good proceeding: yet howsoeuer, as vertue is subiect and incident to be crossed, and maligned by the followers of vice; and that we sometimes

[1] 'Salt' not in C.

see many excellent and noble proiects strangled or made abortiue in their births: Euen so this great worke may (perhaps) be either blasted by nipping whirlewindes at home, or decay and die, through some fatall and disastrous misfortune, in the miscarrying or vnskilfulnesse of such as may seeke, and so be imployed in the managing and conducting thereof, as many worthy attempts haue beene, by taking such vnfit agents and proceedings.[1]

And if it should so happen by any such mis-leading therein (which God defend) in either of those worthy Vndertakers[2] good purposes, or whomsoeuer, hauing already, or shalbe at any time thereunto well affected; let the fault then, gentle Reader, be imputed where it ought to be, and not vnto the illnesse of the Climate, which hath beene so well improued:[3] neither to the Countrey, which is well knowne to be so fruitfull, as hath beene before related: neither vnto those peaceable Seas there, which are very seldome tempestuous with any boisterous stormes, and doe so plentifully abound with such great variety of seuerall sorts of Fish, and multitude of Sea-fowles as hath beene likewise expressed; Neither let me, gentle Reader, that haue thus freely throwne my selfe with my mite into the treasury of my Countries good, be mis-censured for any thing which I haue written in this discourse, which hath been so worthily and well approued:

For now my desire is, for the auoiding of any mis-leadings therein, & for the better proceedings and good successe thereof, that those people which are to be imployed thither, at first should be diligent people and industrious to labour, and subiect to be directed by such as well vnderstand, how to imploy euery seuerall person there at all times, not only in the fishing trade when that time serues; which indeede is the only instrument and sinewe (as I conceaue) that is best like at the first to giue comfort, and hold life vnto so great and worthy a worke; and therefore requisite to be followed, in such manner as it may giue comfort vnto all such as shall be willing to aduenture therein; for as there is a speciall care taken euery where in time of haruest, to be industrious and carefull, as well to reape and gather the sheaues from the fields into some places of safety in the Summer time, as there is to till the land, and sow the seede in the Winter season; So is there

---

[1] C 'proceedings, which is a most speciall thing to be carefully looked vnto.'

[2] I.e. Calvert and Falkland. It seems probable that when Whitbourne published the 1622 edition, he hoped for employment with either Falkland or Calvert. By 1623 he was connected with Falkland as the additional detail on Falkland's colony in C confirms, see above, pp. 170–1.

[3] C 'so well proued to be so healthfull as any other part of the world'.

also a speciall regard to be had, that a prouident course be taken with all such, which are to be imployed to that Countrey, that they should be either skilfull or industrious to doe such things as shall be fitting when time serues, or to bee directed by those that are well experienced therein; and then vndoubtedly it will giue great comfort vnto all such as are or shall be pleased to be vndertakers thereof, because that in Summer time, when those great shoales of the Cod-fish draw to that coast to spawne, and take their fills on multitudes of smaller fishes, which they follow there, close to the cliffes and sands; commonly aboue thirty dayes together, before they hale off from the shore againe, and in such manner, they come three seuerall Shoales of the Cod-fishes in the Summer time: The one of them followes on the Herrings: the other followes the Capling, which is a fish like the Smelt: And the third followes the Squid, which is a fish something like the Cuddell.[1]

And at those times there vsually go many boates forth a fishing from that coast, onely with but three men in each boat; And those three being fit Fishermen, will daily take at those times aboue 1200. of those Codfishes, six score to the hundred, and euery of those fishes with the Oyle which comes of them, being valued but at a penny for euery such fish, which is a cheape rate, it will amount to bee worth six pound starling, being splitted, salted, and dried, as the same ought to bee; wherein there is good industry, experience, and much iudgement to be vsed; otherwise, such fish cannot be taken and fitly preserued, as it ought to bee, whereby to defray the charge, and bring profit withall to the Aduenturers, as I much desire that all such may haue: so that it may be well vnderstood, it is good angling with the hooke and line there, when a single man may take in that imployment aboue forty shillings worth of fish day by day; for I haue often seene there, that those who haue bin most industrious in taking and well handling of such fish, haue certainely beene most willing, fittest and readiest to build, and doe any other good seruice there, at such times whilest the fish failes; when some others that are vnskilfull in the one, will stand idely, and talk with their hands in their Gloues or Pockets, and doe but little to any purpose in the other; like vnto those that come on the Stage to act their part in a Comedy, but performe it not in any respect sufficiently; so that they are not onely scoffed and hist at; by the beholders but also those which are at the charge, and chiefe Actors thereof, receiue some disgrace and wrong thereby; euen so I haue often

[1] I.e. cuttle, belonging to the genus *sepia*.

knowne there some proper men of person, which haue not beene well acquainted with those affaires; yet haue had some other good parts in them, and would speake well when they haue come from thence, yet neuer did they performe any thing there worthy of any great commendations.

Thus, gentle Reader, I haue endeuoured with much trauaile, expence, and losse of time, to make it plainely appeare, that it will be honourable and beneficiall vnto all those that shall be willing to aduance[1] the said Plantation; although I expect to receiue but small benefit thereby to my selfe,[2] or for my great expence, and losse of time herein; yet[3] I shal euer giue God the praise, if al others which shalbe yet willing to aduenture therein may,[4] and I shall, among many great losses, and discontents which I haue had, I trust in God, beare this one content[5] to my graue, that I haue euer bin a true louing Subiect to my Prince & Countrey; & in the sollicitation by this my discourse, and otherwise, I haue dealt truly with his Maiesty, carefully and vprightly with all those which shall be willing to assist the said Plantation.

Now if any which shal not be willing, or it may be is not able to performe a part, for the perfecting of this great & most hopeful worke, should dislike that I haue thus laid open a gap for al his Maiesties Subiects into those grounds, which some men do seeme to challenge and appropriate, as it were, vnto themselues, and so would not haue all others of his Maiesties Subiects made acquainted with the trade and benefit, which is there like to bee obtained: they may therein (as I conceiue in charity) be compared to be something like vnto *Esops* dog, which could eate no Hay, neither would he suffer the hungry Asse to feede thereon. Yet my hope is, that such may well vnderstand by what I haue written, that my true desire is, to shew vnto any of them, that by the said Plantation and trading to that Countrey, being so well followed, as it may orderly be, that all his Maiesties Kingdomes, which now are beholding vnto other countries for some necessary commodities, might not only be furnished with the like from thence, but also in taking of such fish, as those Seas do yeeld at an easier rate then now we vse to haue them: whereby we may serue *France*, *Spain*, *Portugall*, *Italy*, and other places, much cheaper with that sort of fish,

---

[1] C 'to helpe aduance'.　　[2] C 'my selfe in acquainting you herewith, or'.
[3] C 'yet howsoeuer it bee, I'.　　[4] C 'may make profit thereby, and'.
[5] C 'this good cõtent'.

then any of these other nations shalbe able to fetch the same from thence, and thereby to haue and retaine all the trade of that countrey, vnto his Maiesties Subiects hands only: & that whereas there sail in some yeers to yᵉ country aboue 250. saile of Ships from England only, with aboue 5000. English men in them, by whose labours, there is yeerely gottẽ into this Kingdom, aboue the sum of 135000 li. and also therby many families set on worke and relieued: then it may be well vnderstood, what a great benefit and strength it will be, when there shal saile thither 500. saile of ships, & aboue 10000. seruiceable Subiects in them, which will be able to gaine, with the help of such numbers of other men, women & children, as may yeerly be so commodiously carried thither in few yeeres, when the Subiects are made acquainted with such an orderly course, as may be taken for the aduancement of the said Plantation.

Whereby there may be thus yeerely gotten, not only much wealth, but also great strength against such time, as any Prince should breake league with his Maiestie, that then to haue in such readines 500. saile of his Subiects Ships, so ready to come from thence, with more then 10000. seruiceable sea-men in them, in lesse time then 15. dayes warning, if the wind serue, which is so short a time, as Saylers may be prest in some part of this Kingdome, and be able to come from thence vnto his Maiesties Nauy Royall at Chattam, vpon any occasion of seruice.

The like strength by Sea, there is not any other Prince in the world able to call home vnto him in so short a time of his owne subiects, from any one place of trading, if he haue neuer so great occasion.

Thus, God blessing the said Trade and Plantation, it will be, not only a great augmentation to his Maiestie in his reuenues and customes, but also a generall good vnto all his Highnesse Kingdomes and Subiects, both in inriching of aduenturers in particular, & also in strengthening the wall of defence, which God hath set about our natiue nest, *Great Brittaine*, namely, Nauigation, which must needs be much cherished and furnished by this Seminary of Fishers, imployed in such Colonies, and out of that shoale, will be alwaies in readines and of ability to be translated higher, from fishing vessels, into fighting Ships Royall; and so are always vsefull for peace or warre, merchandize or defence, as the occasions of our estate and welfare shall require.

R.W.

A Conclusion[1] *to the former Discourse*, containing a particular description and relation[2] of somthing omitted, touching the Natiues of that Countrey: As also of a strange Creature seene there; and likewise the reason why I haue not set forth a Map of the *New-found-land* in this Booke.

Gentle Reader:

When[3] you haue perused my former Discourse and Discoueries contained therin, and such good approbation, as it[4] hath receiued, which giues me euen an assurance, it wil also receiue good acceptance frō all his Maiesties well affected[5] Subiects; when it shall be presented vnto you, and if it do so appeare vnto me,[6] I shall be the better incouraged to set forth, what I haue taken motiues [*sic*] of,[7] in my trauels to that Countrey, concerning the seuerall depths of the water, and diuersities of the ground in euery seuerall depth that hath come in the Tallo,[8] on the end of the Leade, when it hath been cast into the Sea, which I conceiue to bee necessary for those that shall henceforth trade thither, because as yet, no man, to my knowledge, hath vndertaken so to doe: and whensoeuer[9] it may please his Maiesty, or the State shall seeme good to command me, I shall be ready with my life and meanes to make a perfect discouery and description of the seuerall Head-lands, Bayes, Harbours, and Roads, for Ships to anchor; as also the Ilands, Rockes and Shelues round about the *New-found-land*; which as yet no

---

[1] The conclusion to A is similar to that in B and C; however, it begins differently: 'A conclusion to the Reader, containing a particular Description, and relation of some things omitted in the former Discourse.

Gentle Reader, seeing my former Discouery receiued such good approbation and allowance before it was printed, it puts me in some hope, it will also receiue good acceptance from all his Maiesties well-affected Subiects, now that it is published; the which when I shall vnderstand, by their thankfull acceptance, I shall be incouraged the more willingly, to set forth what I haue obserued touching the Altitude of some head-lands of that Coast, on the East side of the *New-found-land*, and also the Deepes, and seuerall soundings, that I haue taken notice of in my trauels to that Countrey; which I conceiue to be necessary for those that shall henceforth trade thither; which as yet no man, to my knowledge, hath vndertaken; and also be ready with my life and meanes whatsoeuer I haue, or may haue in this World, to discouer other Bayes and Harbours round about that land, which are yet vndiscouered, whereby to finde out some other new Trades with the Natiues of the Countrey; for they haue great store of red Oaker'; see below, p. 193.

[2] C '*former Discourse*, with a Relation'.

[3] This section (to p. 195 below) is in italics with key words in roman; here the arrangement is reversed.

[4] C 'When you haue perused such most worthy approbation as my former Discouery and Inuitation hath receiued'.

[5] 'well affected' not in C.   [6] 'vnto me' not in C.

[7] C 'taken notice of'.

[8] The lump of tallow, cupped in the lead, which indicated the nature of the bottom when soundings were taken.

[9] C 'hath vndertaken: and whatsoeuer it'.

man hath done: neither are there (I suppose) but few men liuing[1] of his Maiesties Subiects, that did at any time saile round about the Land, betweene the Continent of *America* and that, whereby to set forth a true Map of that Countrey, which as yet there is not, but imaginarily, because such as haue vsually trauelled there, haue alwayes made their Voyages in the Harbours and Roads on the East, and Southmost parts of that land, but neuer on the West and North parts thereof;[2] and so by such an imployment, (which may be well performed with a very small charge)[3] there is no doubt, but that some other good discoueries of trade may bee made in some other parts of that Countrey, and also with the natiues there; not only with those which liue in the North and Westmost parts of the *New-found-land*,[4] but also with those which border in the maine Continent of *America*, neere thereunto. For it is wellknowne, that they are a very ingenious and subtill kinde of people (as it hath often appeared in diuers things) so likewise are they tractable, as hath beene well approoued,[5] when they haue been gently and politickly dealt withall: also they are a people that will seeke to reuenge any wrongs done vnto them, or their Woolues, as hath often appeared. For they[6] marke their Woolues in the Eares with seuerall markes, as is vsed here in *England* on Sheepe, and other beasts, which hath been likewise well approued: for the Woolues in those parts are not so violent and deuouring[7] as Woolues are in other Countries. For no man that I euer heard of, could say, that any Woolfe, Leopard, Beare, or any other beasts did euer set vpon any man or boy in the *New-found-land*, although diuers times some men haue been by themselues in the Woods,[8] when they haue suddenly come neere vnto them, and those Beasts haue presently vpon sight of any Christian, speedily runne from them. Neither are there any Snakes, Toads, Serpents, or any other venemous Wormes, that euer were knowne to hurt any man in that Countrey, but onely a very little nimble Fly, (the least of all other Flies) which is called a Muskeito; those Flies seeme to haue a great power and authority vpon all loytering and idle people that come to the

---

[1] 'liuing' not in C.

[2] Despite a brief flurry of interest in the west coast and the gulf of St Lawrence in the 1590s, the English had not generally been active on the west coast. In 1616 and 1617 John Mason, then governor at Cupids Cove, had spent the summers exploring the south coast and may have reached St George's bay. But his map, first published in Vaughan's *Cambrensium Caroleia* (1625), was more accurate and had a richer nomenclature for the familiar west coast. See above, p. 91, and Cell, *English enterprise*, pp. 36–8, 48–51, 73–4.

[3] '(which...charge)' not in C.

[4] C 'of the land, but'.   [5] 'as...approoued' not in C.

[6] C 'Woolues: for in the North parts of that country they'.

[7] 'and deuouring' not in C.   [8] C 'Woods and sleeping, when'.

New-found-land: for they haue this property, that when they finde any such lying lazily, or sleeping in the Woods, they will presently bee more nimble to seize on them, then any Sargeant will bee to arrest a man for debt: Neither will they leaue stinging or sucking out the blood of such sluggards, vntill, like a Beadle, they bring him to his Master, where he should labour: in which time of loytering, those Flies will so brand such idle persons in their faces that they may be knowne from others, as the Turkes doe their slaues.

Now it[1] may be well vnderstood, there is great hope that those parts of the world will yeeld seuerall commodities of exceeding worth, whereon diuers good imployments may bee made for[2] great numbers of his Maiesties Subiects.[3] For it is well knowne, that the Natiues of those parts haue[4] great store of red[5] Okar, wherewith they vse to colour their bodies, Bowes, Arrowes and Cannowes, in a painting manner; which Cannowes are their Boats, that they vse to goe to Sea in, which are built in shape like the Wherries on the Riuer of Thames, with small timbers, no thicker nor broader then hoopes; and in stead of boards, they vse the barkes of[6] Birch trees, which they sew very artificially and close together, and then ouerlay the seames with Turpentime, as Pitch is vsed on the seames of Ships, and Boats:[7] And in like manner they vse to sew the barkes of Spruise and Firre[8] trees, round and deepe in proportion, like a Brasse Kettle, to boyle their meat in, as-it-hath been well approoued by diuers men; but most especially to my certaine knowledge, by three Mariners of a Ship of Tapson,[9] in the Country of *Deuon*; which Ship[10], riding there at Anchor neere by mee, at the Harbour called *Hearts-ease*, on the North side of *Trinity Bay*,[11] and being robbed in the night, by the Sauages, of their apparell, and diuers other prouisions, did the next day seeke after them, and happened to come suddenly where they had set vp three Tents, and were feasting, hauing three such Cannowes by thẽ, and three Pots made of such rinds of trees, standing each of them on three stones, boyling, with twelue Fowles in each of them, euery Fowle as big as a Widgeon, and some so big as a Ducke: they had also many such Pots so sewed, and fashioned like

---

[1] C 'Now by what I haue written, it'.   [2] C 'made to set a-worke great'.
[3] C 'poore Subiects'.
[4] From this point the conclusions to the three editions have only minor variations.
[5] C 'of exceeding good red'.
[6] A 'Arrowes and Cannowes withall, which Cannowes are built in shape, like the Wherries on the Riuer of Thames; but that they are much longer, made with the rinds of'.   [7] 'as...Boats' not in A.
[8] 'and Firre' not in A.   [9] Probably Topsham.
[10] A 'meate in, which hath been well proued by three Mariners of a Shippe'.
[11] 'at the Harbour...Trinity Bay' not in A.

leather Buckets, that are vsed for quenching of fire, and those were full of the yolkes of Egges, that they had taken and[1] boyled hard, and so dryed small as it had been powder-Sugar,[2] which the Sauages vsed in their Broth, as Sugar is often vsed in some meates. They had great store of the skins of Deere, Beauers, Beares, Seales, Otters, and diuers other fine skins, which were excellent[3] well dressed; as also great store of seuerall sorts of flesh dryed, and by shooting off a Musket towards them, they all ran away naked, without any apparell, but onely some of them had[4] their hats on their heads, which were made of Seale skinnes, in fashions like our hats, sewed handsomely, with narrow bands about them, set round with fine white shels. All their three Cannowes, their flesh, skins, yolkes of Egges, Targets, Bowes and Arrows, and much fine Okar, and diuers other things they tooke and brought away, and shared it among those[5] that tooke it; and they brought to mee the best Cannow, Bowes and Arrowes, and diuers of their skins, and many other artificiall[6] things worth the noting, which may seeme much to inuite vs to indeauour to finde out some other good[7] trades with them.[8]

Now also I will not omit to relate some thing of a strange Creature, which I first saw there in the yeere *1610.* in a morning early, as I was standing by the Riuer side,[9] in the Harbour of Saint *Iohns,* which very swiftly came swimming towards mee, looking cheerfully on my face,[10] as it had been a woman: by the face, eyes, nose, mouth, chin, eares, necke, and forehead, it seemed to bee so beautifull, and in those parts so well proportioned, hauing round about the head many blue streakes, resembling haire,[11] but certainly it was no haire, yet I beheld it long, and another of my company also yet liuing, that was not then farre from mee, saw the same comming so swiftly towards me: at which I stepped backe; for it was come within the length of a long Pike, supposing it would haue sprung aland to mee, because I had often seene huge Whales to spring a great height aboue the water, as diuers other great Fishes doe; and so might this strange Creature doe to mee, if I had stood still where I was, as I verily beleeue it had such a purpose. But when it saw that I went from it, it did thereupon diue a little vnder

---

[1] 'taken and' not in C.   [2] 'as...powder-Sugar' not in A.
[3] 'excellent' not in A.   [4] 'some...had' not in A.
[5] A 'those three'.   [6] 'artificiall' not in A.
[7] 'good' not in A.
[8] C 'with them, which God grant may be speedily put in practice.'
[9] A 'water side'.   [10] 'On my face' not in A.
[11] A 'round about vpon the head, all blew strakes, resembling hayre, downe to the Necke (but'.

the water, and swam towards the place where a little before I landed, and it did often looke backe towards mee; wherby[1] I beheld the shoulders & back down to the middle, to be so square, white and smooth as the backe of a man; and from the middle to the hinder part, it was poynting in proportion something like a broad hooked Arrow: how it was in[2] the forepart from the necke and shoulders, I could not well discerne; but it came shortly after, to a Boat in the same Harbour (wherein one *William Hawkridge* then my seruant was,) that hath been since a Captaine in a Ship to the *East Indies*, and is lately there so imployed againe;[3] and the same Creature did put both his[4] hands vpon the side of the Boat, and did striue much to come in to him, and diuers then in the same Boat; whereat they were afraid, and one of them strucke it a full blow on the head, whereby it fell off from them: and afterwards it came to two other Boates in the said Harbour, where they lay by the shore: the men in them, for feare fled to land and beheld it.[5] This (I suppose) was a Marmaid, or Mareman.[6] Now because diuers haue writ much of Maremaids, I haue presumed to relate what is most certaine, of such a strange Creature that was thus then seene at *New-found-land*, whether were a Maremaid or no, I leaue it for others to iudge:[7] And so referre you to the perusall of the Copies of those Letters following, which haue been lately sent from the *New-found-land*, which I doubt not but they[8] will also giue you some satisfactions[9] of what I haue written of that Countrey, whereby to bring you the more in loue to the imbracing of a Plantation in that Countrey, which may be well stiled a Sister-Land;[10] which God grant to blesse and prosper, &c.

R. W.

A Letter[11] from Captaine *Edward Wynne, Gouernour of the Colony at* Ferryland, *within the* Prouince of Aualon, in Newfound-land, vnto the

---

[1] A 'long Pike. Which when this strange Creature saw, that I went from it, it presently thereupon diued a little vnder water, and did swim towards the place where before I landed; whereby'.

[2] A 'proportioned in'.

[3] A 'againe by Sir *Thomas Smith*, in the like voyage; and'. Sir Thomas Smith (1558?–1625), merchant; governor of the East India company and treasurer of the Virginia company. *DNB*.

[4] C 'its'.   [5] 'and beheld it' not in A.

[6] 'or Mareman' not in A.

[7] In A the conclusion ends thus 'or no, I know not; I leaue it for others to iudge, &c. R.W.'   [8] 'I...they' not in C.

[9] C 'good satisfaction',   [10] 'in...Sister-Land' not in C.

[11] Neither this letter nor those that follow is included in A. C 'The Coppy of a letter from'.

Right Honourable Sir GEORGE CALVERT Knight, his Maiesties Principall Secretary. Iuly 1622.[1]

May it please your Honour:

Vpon the 17. day of May, I receiued here. your Letters of the 19. of February from the hands of *Robert Stoning.* Vpon the 26. of the same, a ship of Master *Iennins*, with your people and prouision, arriued here in safety: and from the hands of Captaine *Powell* I receiued then your Honours Letters of the 14. of March. And vpon the last of Iune Master *Iames* came hither, from Renouze, and the Salt-maker Master *Iohn Hickson*; from whose hands I receiued two Letters more: that by Master *Iames* being of the 4. of May, and the other by *Hickson* of the 10. of the same.

All these being receiued by me, with an humble and a most thankefull hand, first, vnto God for your Honors health, and next, to your Honour for your continuall fauour towards me, beseeching the same Almighty God, long and long to continue your health, to the aduancement of his glory, both here, at home and else-where: I most humbly pray you to build vpon my dutifull care and diligence, in the setting forwards and following of your Honours businesse, euen to your best aduantage, and aduancement of the worke, and also that I shall bee a dutifull obseruer of your pleasure and commandement.

And so with the like humility, I doe present your Honour with the good tydings of all our healths, safety and good successe in our proceedings (Gods holy Name be praisd for it.) It followeth now (as my duty requireth) that I render vnto your Honour a due account of what hath beene done by vs here this yeere, and of all things else, which appertaines vnto me to doe.

This was the last letter sent into England the yeere before, 1621.[2] Therefore it may please your Honour, that as soone as I had deliuered my last Letters of the 5. of September, I immediately addressed my selfe onely to our businesse: Notwithstanding our diligent labour & extraordinary paines-taking, it was Alhallontide before our first range of building was fitted for an habitable being. The which being 44. foot of length, and 15. foot of bredth, containing a hall 18. foot long, an entry of 6. foot, and a cellar of 20. foot in length, and of the height, betweene the ground floore and that ouer head about 8. foote, being deuided aboue, that thorowout into foure chambers, and foure foot high to the roofe or a halfe storie. The roofe ouer the hall, I couered with Deale boords, and the rest with such thatch as I found growing

---

[1] C 'Iuly 1622. *who ariued there with his Company in Iuly 1621.*'
[2] Marginal note not in C.

here about the Harbour, as sedge, flagges and rushes, a farre better couering then boords, both for warmth and titenesse. When I had finished the same with onely one Chimney of stone-worke in the hall, I went forward with our kitchin, of length 18. foot, 12. foot of breadth, and 8. foot high to the eues, and walled vp with stone-worke, with a large Chimney in the same. Ouer the kitchin I fitted another Chamber. All which with a staire-case and conuenient passages, both into the Kitchin and the roome ouer it, were all finished by Christmas eue. This is all the building with a hen-house,[1] that we haue beene able to accomplish before Christmas.

Many things else were done by vs in the *interim*, as the getting home of timber trees, firewood, the raising vp of a face of defence to the water-side ward, with the earth that we digged both for celler and Kitchin roome, (which we found a very laborious worke) also the sowing of some wheat for a triall, and many other businesses besides.

After Christmas, we imployed our selues in the woods, especially in hard weather, whence wee got home as many boord-stocks, as affoorded vs aboue two hundred boords, and aboue two hundred timber trees besides. We got home as much or[2] as many trees, as serued vs to palizado into the Plantation about foure Acres of ground, for the keeping off of both man and beast, with post and rayle seuen foote high, sharpened in the toppe, the trees being pitched vpright and fastened with spikes and nayles.

We got also together as much fire wood, as will serue vs yet these two moneths. Wee also fitted much garden ground for feede, I meane Barley, Oates, Pease, and Beanes.

For addition of building, we haue at this present a Parlor of foureteene foote besides the chimney, and twelue foot broad, of conuenient height, and a lodging Chamber ouer it; to each a Chimney of stone-worke with Staires and a Staire-case, besides a tenement of two roomes, or a storie and a halfe, which serues for a Store-house till wee are otherwise prouided. The Forge hath been finished this fiue weekes: the Salt-worke is now almost ready. Notwithstanding this great taske for so few hands, wee haue both Wheat, Barley, Oates, Pease and Beanes about the quantity of two Acres. Of Garden roome about halfe an Acre: the corne, though late sowne, is now in earing: the Beanes and the goodliest Pease that I euer saw, haue flourished in their bloomes this twenty dayes. Wee haue a plentifull kitchin garden of Lettice, Raddish, Carrets,

They were but twelue men all the last Winter vntill the new supply came in the Spring following.[3]

---

[1] 'with a hen-house' not in C.   [2] 'as much or' not in C.
[3] Marginal note not in C.

Coleworts,[1] Turneps and many other things, We haue also at this present, a flourishing medow of at least three Acres, with many hay-cocks of exceeding good hay, and hope to fit a great deale more against another yeere. In the beginning of the last Winter, we sunke a well, of sixteen foote deepe in the ground, the which affords vs water in a sufficient measure. The timber that wee haue got home first and last, is aboue fiue hundred trees of good timber. There haue beene aboue three hundred boords, besides the former, sawed since the arriuall of Captaine *Powell*. We haue also broken much ground for a Brewhouse roome and other Tenements. We haue a Wharfe in good forwardnesse towards the Low water-marke. So that our indeuour that way affords a double benefit, the one of ridding and preparing the way to a further worke, the other of winning so much voyd or waste ground, to so necessary a purpose as to enlarge this little roome, whereon (with your Honours leaue and liking) I hope to fortifie: so that within the same, for the comfort of neighbour-hood, another row of building may be so pitched, that the whole may be made a prettie streete.

For the Countrey and Climate: It is better, and not so cold as England hitherto. My comfort is, that the Lord is with your Honour, and your designes: for wee haue prospered to the admiration of all the beholders in what is done. And thus with my humble dutie remembred, I rest,

Your Honours most humble and faithfull seruant,
EDWARD WYNNE.

Ferryland 28. Iuly 1622.

Postscr.

The ships with the rest of our prouision arriued here this morning: and what is omitted by me, shall by Gods helpe shortly be performed. Your Honour hath greater hopes here, then heretofore I haue beene able to discerne. All things succeede beyond my expectation.

Another Letter[2] to Master Secretary Caluert, *from Captaine* Daniel Powell, *who conducted the new supply of men, that went for the Plantation, the last Spring, dated at* Ferryland 28. *Iuly* 1622.

Right Honourable:

May it please your Honour to vnderstand, that on the 18. of Aprill, my selfe, and all the company, whose names I sent you in the List,

---

[1] General name for any plant of the cabbage kind.
[2] C 'The Contents of a Letter to'.

by my last from Plymouth tooke shipping there, & on the 26. of May (Gods holy Name be euer praised for it)[1] wee all arriued safe and in good health in New-found-land. Our[2] iourney proued so long by reason of the contrary windes[3] we continually had. For at the last three weekes together, wee were forced to trauerse the Seas to and againe, and got not forward to the Westward in all that time one hundred leagues.

The accidents which happened in our ouerbound passage were these: The first weeke after our being at Sea, three of our Ewe-Goats by reason of their extreme leanenesse when they were bought and brought aboord, died, so that now we haue but onely one Ewe-Goate and a Buck-Goate left: the other Buck dying likewise within few dayes after our Landing.

On the 16. of May, the furnace in our ship tooke fire, and as God would haue it, burst forth in the day time; otherwise it had endangered both ship and vs.

On the 26. as aforesaid, early in the morning we descryed land in New-found-land, a little to the Northward of the Bay of Bulls, and before night came to anchor in Capeling Bay within one league of *Ferryland*. The next morning our ship came about to Ferryland Harbour, and there landed all our people, where wee found the Gouernour and all his company in good health, as we[4] all continue in the same, praised be God for it.

The Coast and Harbours which we[5] sailed by, are so bold and good, as I assure my selfe[6] there can bee no better in the world:[7] but the Woods along the Coasts, are so spoyled by the Fishermen, that it is great pitty to behold them, and without redresse, vndoubtedly wil be the ruine of this good Land: For they wastfully barke, fell, and leaue more Wood behinde them to rot, then they vse about their Stages, although they imploy a world of Wood vpon them: and by these their abuses doe so cumber the Woods euery where neere the shore, that it is not possible for any man to go a mile in a long houre.

The Land whereon our Gouernour hath planted, is so good and commodious, that for the quantity, I thinke[8] there is no better in many parts of England. His house which is strong and well contriued, standeth

---

[1] 'Gods...it' not in C.   [2] C 'their'.
[3] C 'of much contrary winds.' The rest of this paragraph and all of the next two are omitted in C, which takes up again: 'where he [*sic*] found the Gouernor'.
[4] C 'they'.   [5] C 'he'.
[6] C 'he doth assure himselfe'.
[7] The remainder of the paragraph is omitted in C.
[8] C 'he thinkes'.

very warme, at the foot of an easie ascending hill, on the South-east, and defended with a hill, standing on the furtherside of the Hauen on the North-west: The Beach on the North and South sides of the Land locke it, and the Seas on both sides are so neere and indifferent to it, that one may shoot a Bird-bolt into either Sea.[1] No cold can offend it, although it bee accounted the coldest Harbour in the Land, and the Seas doe make the Land behind it to the South-East, being neere 1000. Acres of good ground for hay, feeding of Cattell, and plenty of Wood, almost an Iland, safe to keepe any thing from rauenous beasts.

Aquafort some two or three myles from Ferryland.[3]

I haue, since my comming, beene a little abroad, and finde[2] much good ground for Medow, Pasture, and arable, about *Aquafort*, as well neere vnto the head of the Harbour, as all the way betweene that and *Ferryland*. The neerenesse of the place, and the spaciousnesse of those grounds aforesaid,[4] will giue comfort and helpe to the present Plantation, and quickly ease your Honours charge,[5] if a Plantation bee there this next Spring settled. If therefore it will please your Honour to let me be furnished against that time, but with thirteene men, and giue mee leaue to settle my selfe there, I make no doubt (God blessing my indeuours) but to giue your Honour, and the rest of the Vndertakers such content, that you shall haue good incouragement to proceed further therein. So for this time being loth to trouble your Honour any further, vntill the returne of *Master Wicot*, I humbly take my leaue, and euer rest ready to doe your Honour all possible seruice to the vttermost of my power,

Ferryland 28.

Iuly 1622.

Your Honours humbly at command,

Daniel Powel.

Another Letter[6] *to Master Secretary* Caluert, *from Captaine* Wynne, *of the* 17. *of August,* 1622.

May it please your Honour;

Vpon the 17. day of May, your Honours Letters of the 19. of

[1] 'on the South-east...either Sea' not in C.

[2] C 'he hath since his arriuall there, bin abroad, and findes'.

[3] Marginal note omitted in C.

[4] 'about Aquafort...grounds aforesaid' not in C.

[5] In C the letter concludes: 'charge, and doth desire to bee furnished with thirteene men, and to giue him leaue to settle himself nere vnto the harbor of Agafort: he makes not doubt (God blessing his indeuours) but to giue Master Secretary, and the rest of the Vndertakers such content, that they shall haue good incouragement to proceed further therin. So he humbly takes leaue, and I [*sic*] will euer rest ready to doe Master Secretary all possible seruice to the vtmost of his power. *Your Honours humbly at command,* Daniel Powell.'

[6] C '*The Coppy* of another Letter'.

February, I receiued here from the hands of *Robert Stoning, &c.* And so forward as in his former Letter of the 28. of Iuly, relating the manner and proportion of their building.

We haue Wheat, Barley, Oates and Beanes both eared and codded,[1] and though the late sowing and setting of them might occasion the contrary, yet it ripens now so fast, that it carries the likelihood of an approching haruest.

We haue also a plentifull Kitchin-Garden of many things, and so ranke, that I haue not seene the like in England. Our Beanes are exceeding good: our Pease shall goe without compare; for they are in some places as high as a man of an extraordinary stature: Raddish as big as mine arme: Lettice, Cale or Cabbedge, Turneps, Carrets, and all the rest is of like goodnesse. We haue a Medow of about three Acres; it flourished lately with many cockes of good hay, and now it is made vp for a Winter feeding. Wee hope to bee well fitted with many Acres of Medow against another yeere: of Pasture land, we haue already to serue at least three hundred heads of Cattell: and to all this, if it please God, a good quantity of seed-ground shall be fitted, and such buildings as we shall be able to accomplish.

Now in the next place it may please your Honour to vnderstand; That touching this Countrey, the Summer time heere is so faire, so warme, and of so good a temperature, that it produceth many herbes and plants very wholesome, medicinable and delectable, many fruit trees of sundry kinds, many sorts of Berries wholesome to eate, and in measure most abundant; in so much as many sorts of birds and beasts are relieued with them in time of Winter, and whereof with further experience I trust to finde some for the turne of Dyers.

Our high leuels of Land are adorned with Woods, both faire and seemely to behold, and greene all Winter. Within Land there are Plaines innumerable, many of them containing many thousand Acres, very pleasant to see to, and well furnished with Ponds, Brookes and Riuers, very plentifull of sundry sorts of fish, besides store of Deere, and other beasts that yeeld both food and furre. Touching the soyle, I finde it in many places, of goodnesse farre beyond my expectation: the earth as good as can be: the grasse both fat and vnctious; and if there were store of Cattell to feed it vp, and with good ordering, it would become a most stedfast nourishment: whereof the large breed of Cattell to our Northerne Plantation,[2] haue lately giuen proofes sufficient, though

---

[1] I.e. the beans had produced pods.
[2] Perhaps the settlement at Cupids Cove.

since, they haue been most shamefully destroyed. The ayre heere is very healthfull, the water both cleere and wholsome, and the Winter short and tolerable, continuing onely in Ianuary, February, and part of March; the day in Winter longer then in *England*; the nights both silent and comfortable, producing nothing that can be said, either horrid or hideous. Neither was it so cold heere the last Winter as in *England* the yeere before. I remember but three seuerall dayes of hard weather indeed, and they not extreme neither; for I haue knowne greater frosts, and farre greater snowes in our own Countrey.

At the *Bristow* Plantation, there is as goodly Rye now growing, as can be in any part of *England*: they are also well furnished with Swine, and a large breed of Goats, fairer by farre, then those that were sent ouer at the first.

The stones, kernels and seeds that *Stoning* brought mee, were put into the ground presently after his arriual, the which are already of a pretty growth, though late set; for they came to my hands but vpon the 17. of May.

The Vines that came from *Plimmouth*, doe prosper very well: nay, it is to be assured, that any thing that growes in *England*, will grow and prosper very well here: whereby it plainely appeares vnto your Honour, what manner of Countrey the same is. Therefore it may please you to giue credit vnto no man that shall seeme to vrge the contrary. And for my part, seeing that by the prouidence of God and your Honours meere fauour towards me, this imployment is falne to my lot, I trust that neither Gods grace in me, nor the experience that I haue gained by the trauels of my youth, will suffer me to wrong your Honour. Farre be it from mee to goe about to betray you and my Countrey, as others haue done that haue beene imployed in the like trust. I trust also, that what I haue vndertaken either by word or writing, will bee found the Characters of a true and zealous minde, wholy deuoted vnto your Honours seruice, the good of my poore distressed Countrimen, and to the aduancement of Gods glory.

It may please your Honour to vnderstand, that our Salt-maker hath performed his part with a great deale of sufficiency, by whom I haue sent your Honour a barrell of the best Salt that euer my eues beheld, who with better settling doth vndertake to better this, which hee hath made already. I shall humbly also desire you to remember my last yeeres suit, that our delicate Harbours and Woods may not be altogether destroyed. For there haue been rinded this yeere not so few as 50000. trees, and they heaue out ballast into the Harbors, though I looke on.

It may likewise please your Honour to giue expresse order; First, that such as be sent hither hereafter, may be such men as shall be of good strength:[1] whereof wee stand in need of sixe Masons, four Carpenters, two or three good Quarry men, a Slator or two, a Lyme-burner, and Lymestones, a good quantity of hard Laths, a couple of strong maids, that (besides other worke) can both brew and bake, and to furnish vs with wheels, hempe, & flaxe, and a conuenient number of West-country labourers to fit the ground for the Plough.

Secondly, that no more boyes and girles be sent hither, I meane, vpon your Honours charge, nor any other persons which haue not beene brought vp to labour: for they are vnfit for these affaires.

Thirdly, your Honour of necessity must send some Gunnes and a Gunner with his necessaries: for the place and time doe require it. It is a durable Chattel; they will command the Harbour, and secure all.

Wee stand also in need of another brewing Copper, some Clapboords, more Iron and steele, brick, some Lime, and Tiles for a beginning, whilest the Slate-quarry is in fitting.

A compleat Magazine of all things will be necessary with victuals, linnen, woollen for apparell and bedding, with better couerleds, shooes of wet leather, Irish-stockins, coorse knit-hose, coorse ticks, good flocks[2] in caske, and in stead of cloth, coorse mingled kersies,[3] and no canuase suits, nor any ready made: But otherwise it may please your Honour to send Taylors, such as will helpe to gard the place, and doe other things. The like of other Trades-men, and all to be furnished out of the Magazine, vpon account.

I went to *Formouse* and *Renouze*, vpon the fourth of this moneth, to buy salt for your Honour against the next yeere, because it is so deare in *England*, & that which is now bought for the next yeeres fishing, amounts to the number of 186. hogs-heads.

It may please your Honour, that another Iron mill, and two Bridewell mils may be sent hither, and then our bread-corne may be sent vnground: and if at any time it should happen to take wet, it may be dryed againe.

We want a doozen of leather buckets, a Glazier, some glew, rats-bane, two fowling peeces of sixe foote in the barrell, and one of seuen foote, with a mould to cast shot of seuerall sizes for fowling.

The last yeere I shewed your Honour of much courtesie receiued

---

[1] C 'men as shall bee thought fit, and may be such men as shall be of good strength'.
[2] Material of wool or cotton used for quilting garments and for stuffing beds and mattresses.
[3] Coarse narrow cloth, usually ribbed.

from sundry Masters: many this yeere haue done the like, though some likes not our flourishing beginning and prosperity. Howsoeuer, I haue proceeded with a great deale of care and respect vnto your Honours commandements, to vse them with all humanity. I hope you will be pleased to send vs the Plough next yeere, and Gunnes; for the time requires it. And so I conclude, resting

Your Honours most humble, thankefull and faithfull seruant,

Ferryland 17.   EDWARD WYNNE.
    August. 1622.

The names of all those that stay with me this yeere.

Captaine Powell.	*Henry Doke,* Boats-master.
Nicholas Hoskins.	*William Sharpus,* Tailor.
Robert Stoning.	*Eliz. Sharpus,* his wife.
Roger Fleshman, Chirurgion.	*John Bayly.*
Henry Dring, Husbandman.	*Anne Bayly,* his wife.
Owen Euans.	Widdow *Bayly.*
Mary Russell,	*Ioseph Parscer.*
Sibell Dee, maide.	*Robert Row,* Fisherman.
Elizabeth Kerne. } Girles.	*Philip Iane,* Cooper.
Ione Iackson. }	*William Bond.* } Boats-masters,
Thomas Wilson. } Smithes.	*Peter Wotton.* }
Iohn Prater. }	*Ellis Hinckson.* }
Iames Beuell, Stone-layer.	*Digory Fleshman.* } Boyes.
Beniamin Hacker, Quarry-man.	*Richard Higgins.* }
Nich. Hinckson. }	In all 32.
Robert Bennet. } Carpenters.	
William Hatch. }	

I looke for a Mason, and one more out of the Bay of *Conception.*

A Copy of a Letter from N. H.[1] *a Gentleman liuing at* Ferryland *in* New-found-land, *to a worthy friend* W. P. *of the* 18. *of August,* 1622.

SIR,

My humble seruice remembred; accounting my selfe bound vnto you in a double bond, namely, loue, and duty: I could not bee vnmindfull to shew the same vnto you in these rude lines, thereby to acquaint you with our health, the temperature of our Countrey, and the commodities and blessings therein. And first, for the first:

---

[1] Probably Nicholas Hoskins, whose name is included in the list of settlers above.

Concerning our health, there is not any man amongst our company, that hath beene sicke scarcely one day since he came, but hath been able to follow his worke. The Climate differs but little from *England*, and I my selfe felt lesse cold heere this Winter, then I did in *England* the Winter before, by much. The ayre is sweeter: for I neuer smelt any euill sauour in the Countrey, nor saw any venemous creature to hurt me.[1] Gods blessings vpon this Land are manifold: As for Wood and Water, it passeth *England*: the one most sweet in growing and burning, the other most pleasant to taste, and good to drinke. For in the Whitson-holidayes (I taking with me Master *Stoning*) did coast some ten miles into the Countrey Westward from our Plantation, to make some discouery of the Countrey, and to kill a Deere; and being some 5. miles into the Land, where wee lodged that night in a Wood,[2] wee found much Champion ground, and good leuels of one, two, three, or foure hundred Acres together, and at the foot of each Mountaine and small hill, wee alwayes met with a faire fresh Riuer, or a sweet brooke of running water, whereof we freely dranke, and it did quench my thirst as well as any Beere, and much refresh vs both, and neuer offended our stomackes at all. Wee trauelled three dayes, but found no Deere saue their footings, which came to passe by meanes of a great fire that had burned the Woods a little before, ten miles compasse. It began between *Formouse* and *Aquafort*: it burned a weeke, and then was quenched by a great raine.

I know not who, or what he was that gaue fire to it, but I thinke he was a seruant hired by the diuell to doe that wicked deed, who (I doe not doubt) will pay him for his worke. In the night, the Wooluse being neere, did something affright vs with their howlings, but did not hurt vs: for wee had dogs, fire and sword to welcome them. As for the Beares, although there be many, they beare vs no ill will, I thinke, for I haue eaten my part of two or three, and taken no hurt by them. Foxes heere are many, and as subtill as a Fox, yet haue we coozened many of them of their rich coates, which our worthy Gouernour keepes carefully, as also of Cattagena's and Otters, whose couerings wee preserue as fitting presents for greater persons. The Fowles and Birds of the Land are Partriges, Curlues, Fillidayes, Black-birds, Bulfinches, Larks, Sparrowes, and such like. Those of the Sea, are Goose, Ducks of foure sorts, Capderace, Teale, Snipes, Penguyns, Murres,[3] Hounds,[4]

---

[1] 'to hurt me' not in C.   [2] 'in a Wood' not in C.
[3] A name applied to several species of guillemots.
[4] The long-tailed duck, *Harelda glacialis*, whose gabble resembles the cry of a pack of hounds.

Sanderlins,[1] Redshankes[2] and others; all very fat, sweet and wholesome. The Fowles of prey, are Tercels,[3] Gos-hawkes, Falcons, Laners,[4] Sparhawkes,[5] Gripes,[6] Ospreis, Owles great and small, Rauens, Gulls, Pitterils,[7] and some others; and of most of these sorts I haue killed many. As for the plenty of Codfish, it is well knowne vnto you. Salmons, Eeles, Mackarell, Herrings, Lance, Caplin, Dogfish, Hollibuts, Flowkes, Lobsters, Crabs and Muskles: All, and more then all these are here in great plenty, very good and sweet meat. The wilde fruit and Berries, are small Peares, Cherries, Nuts, Resberries, Strawberries, Barberries, Dewberries, Hurtleberries, with other, all good to eate. Many faire Flowers I haue seene heere, which I cannot name, although I had learned *Gerrards* Herball by heart. But wilde Roses are heere both red and damaske, as fragrant and faire as in *England*. All our Corne and seeds haue prospered well, and are already growne almost to perfect maturity. What shall I say? To say that I know not, I dare not. Thus much I know, as an eye-witnesse, and much more good the Countrey doth promise to shew me: the which, when I see you, my heart shall command my tongue to certifie you. Our Gouernours Letters (I doubt not) will bring you newes at large: I wrote but this in haste, to satisfie my selfe, and shew my duty, desiring you to looke thorow it, as thorow a prospectiue glasse, wherein you may discerne a farre off, what I haue seene neere hand, and see that your poore well-wishing friend is aliue, and in good health at *Ferryland*, who in the lowest step of duty takes his leaue, with prayers for your preseruation, and will euer remaine,

Your seruant to bee commanded,

Ferryland, 18.   N. H.
August. 1622.

---

[1] Sanderlings; small wading birds.
[2] A wading bird.
[3] Male hawks.
[4] Lanners, i.e. falcons.
[5] Sparrowhawks.
[6] Vultures.
[7] Pittells; birds of prey.

CHAPTER III

LORD FALKLAND'S COLONY

9. RICHARD WHITBOURNE'S 'INVITATION'[1]

The Southmost part of your Circuit in that Land, which is now called by the name of South-Fawlkland,[2] lyeth neere in forty sixe degrees and a halfe of Northerly latitude, beginning on the East side of that Iland at a certaine harbour called Renowse:[3] And from thence West vnto a certaine Bay in that Iland, called by the name of Pleasaunce:[4] And from the foresaid harbour of Renowse towards the North, so farre as halfe the way betweene another certaine Harbour there, called Agafort, and another Harbour called Formosa: And from thence towards the West, so far as the foresaid Bay of Pleasaunce: And so from the said West line towards South, vnto the abouesaid West line, which commeth there from the aforesaid Harbour of Renowze: And all that which is inclusiuely within the said Circuit.

From the said Harbour of Renowze, vnto the middle way betweene the said Agafort and Formosa: it is in breadth South and North, aboue 6. English miles: And in length no lesse then 50. East and West.[5]

Formosa is a Harbour fit for any Ship, of what burthen soeuer, there to ride well at Anchor, and stretcheth towards the West from the entrance thereof, neere foure miles; into which Harbour there yeerely comes aboue 20. saile of English Ships, which haue commodious places to salt and dry fish on: and also diuers Portugall Ships; It is a Harbour that with small charge may be well defended, so as no Pirats might come in there, but by leaue. The Land on the North side of the said Harbour, neere a mile in length by the Harbours side, is fit for drying of fish, and other purposes; the rest of the North side of the said Harbour, to the innermost part thereof, by the Harbours side, is something rocky, where grow store of Firre and Spruise trees, and other

---

[1] Extract from Richard Whitbourne, *A discourse containing a loving invitation both honourable and profitable to all such as shall be adventurers, in the New-found-land* (Felix Kyngston, 1622), sig. B 2v–D 3v.

[2] Among Sir Henry Salusbury's papers is a summary of this description of Falkland's holdings. N.L.W., 5390.

[3] The latitude of Renews is 46° 56′ N.   [4] Placentia.

[5] It is closer to sixty miles from Renews to Placentia Bay, although the land is bisected by St Mary's Bay.

Fig. 4. Henry Cary, viscount Falkland

fruits. There are diuers commodious places on the South side of the said Harbour, for salting and drying of fish, and building of houses, and many more such conuenient places may very fitly be made there, when people begin to inhabite that place. For the fertility of the soyle, in diuers places betwene Formosa and Renowze, I thinke it to be so

208

good as any other Land in all that Countrey, not onely for the pleasantnesse of the Climate it lyes in; but also for the goodnesse, commodious and leuell lying of many hundred acres in large valleyes of good deepe earth, open and cleane, without rocks and trees, which (questionlesse) is fit for Wheat, Rye, Barley, and other graine: As also for Flax, Hempe, Woad, Tobacco,[1] and many other purposes. How the goodnesse of that Circuit is towards the West, from the innermost parts of these two harbours, I cannot directly write of; more then fiue miles. The which Land further into the Countrey, as I did often obserue it, standing on the hils, it seemed to me, so far as I could descry, to be very pleasant, and promise well. There are large ponds, and a faire, broad, and long riuer of deepe fresh waters vpon the hils, betweene the said two harbours; wherein are store of good Trowts taken some times; And the Firre and Spruise trees growing round about the said Ponds and Riuer fresh and greene, Winter and Summer, with such flagrant shewes, as no trees in such a Clymate can make a more delightfull sight of greennesse, then those doe there; whereon the Thrush, Thrussels, Nightingales, and other birds doe often sit and sing so pleasantly, as if they were neuer pincht with cold, or want of food, as such birds are in England diuers winters.

Betweene the harbours of Formosa and Renowze, it is three English miles, where wayes may be commodiously and easily made both for man and beast, to trauell from one of the said harbours to the other: And in my opinion (which I submit to better censures) the fittest place within that Circuit, first to settle a Colony, is neere vnto the harbour of Renowze, which lyeth fiue degrees more towards the South, then the City of London; which is no lesse then 280. English miles: It is a very pleasant place for that purpose, hauing seuerall large valleyes, which are more then three hundred acres of good open land, deepe earth, cleane without rockes and trees, lying vnder the hils on the Northside of them very commodiously; which are fit to bee imployed (with little labour) for corne, meddowes, pasture, or whatsoeuer. And there are seuerall brookes of fresh water which fall into the said harbour, where comes yeerely great store of good Salmons, Salmon-peales, Trowts, and other fish, of which kinds there are taken great store.

Looke into the woods, and open lands neere vnto Renowze; there comes often great store of Deere, and other beasts, which are fit for profit and delight: As also in and neere thereunto infinite numbers of

---

[1] This is the only time that Whitbourne suggests that tobacco might be grown in Newfoundland.

land-fowle, and sea-fowle: and in Summer time, there are abundance of fruites, as there are not better of such kinds else-where: As also herbes, and pleasant flowers which grow there naturally very plentifully. And diuers Fishermen haue carried thither seeds, and sowed them in conuenient places; whereby they haue often had good Cabbage, Lettice, Beetes, Carrets, and such like, very faire and good: and for Turneps, I neuer saw better then there, both for greatnesse, rellish, and goodnesse; I esteeme them to be equall with any Potato roots which are growing else-where. There is also store of Spruise, Firre, Pine, and Birch trees fit for many seruiceable purposes: And many long rushes which are fit to couer houses withall, as the reed of wheat or rye, wherewith diuers mens houses of good ability are couered: And I am also of opinion, vpon some proofe which I made, that there are lime stones, which is a speciall necessary to begin a Plantation withall.

There come yeerely to that harbour of Renowze aboue twenty saile of English Ships, to fish, besides other Nations, and there are commodious places for them all to salt and dry fish on; and much better, in time, may those places bee made for that purpose: And there come also into those two harbours, Ships and Barkes yeerely from England, and other places, to load fish, and traine oyle, from the Fishermen: In which Ships great store of people and prouisions; as also beasts may be cheaply carryed thither.

There is a small Iland of stones and Beach, at the innermost part of the harbour of Renowze, whereon a ship of sixty tunne burden may well labour to make his fishing voyage on; which is neere the circuit of two acres of ground, and it doth ebbe and flow in and out by both sides of the said Iland, sixe foot of water vpright euery tide, and that tide runnes halfe a mile aboue the said Iland, where it is very deepe water, and of a good breadth: Diuers Ships doe yeerely salt, and dry their fish, aboue the said Iland on both sides of that Riuer; although there is not water for any Boate to passe in or out by the said Iland at euery low water, for the space of more then an houre. And there may be commodiously a Bridge made on either side, in lesse then halfe a day, fit to passe at al times, both for man & beast, from one side of the harbour to the other, vpon any occasion, which is a greater commodity, for that purpose, then any other harbour in that land, which I know that hath the like. And from thence to the harbours mouth, a peece of Ordnance will shoote a Bullet leuell; and so the like aboue, to euery place where men vse to salt and dry fish: so that if a fortification be made in that Iland, where the fresh Riuers are so pleasant, it will not only offend any enemie, from comming into that harbour; but also defend such Ships and men which come yeerely there a fishing, or to trade.

And if any enemies should at any time come thither by land from any other place, to pretend hurt to any man there; he cannot be at any place on either side of the said harbour, where men vse to labour about their fish; but that a peece of Ordnance, being placed on that Iland, will shoote a Bullet to any such; so that by such a fortification, euery man which comes there, may in more security reape the benefit of their labours, then some men haue done in that Countrey in former times. And then there may fitly be some shelters builded, whereby to succour such Beasts as are carried thither at the first, so as no deuouring beast of that Countrey may spoile them by night: and in the day time, they may feede in the pleasant valleys, and vpon the hils, euen close by the said Iland, on both sides of the said harbour, where a peece of Ordnance will shoote a Bullet vnto them if there be cause.

There vsually come euery yeere in the fishing trade, vnto the harbours of Formosa, and Renowze, aboue eight hundred English men; which men may, to assist one another vpon any occasion, come together in lesse time then two houres warning, either by Sea or Land. And there is yeerely all the Summer time, great fishing neere vnto both the said harbours mouthes, where men may, when they thinke good, stand vpon the land, and call vnto the Fishermen to come into the said harbors vnto them; which is also such a good commoditie for securitie, as few harbours in that land haue the like.

In both which harbours, there is store of Lobsters, Crabbes, Muscles, and other Shell-fish; And aboue the foresaid Iland, it is the most commodious place for Geese, Ducks, and other Water-fowle, winter and summer, as there is not the like in any other harbour on the East side of that Land, to the Southward of the Bay of Conception; whereof those men, which I left there all the winter season, in *Anno* 1618, made good proofe, and so likewise the winter before that time, and sithence.

THus hauing expressed a part of the commodiousnesse of the Land and Sea, neere vnto the harbours of Formosa and Renowze; I will also relate a part of the commodiousnesse, and great hope of good, which may come vnto such as will be Aduenturers with your Lordship, in your other circuit of Lands in that Countrey, now called by the name of *Trinity Land*, which beginneth at the middle way of the entrance into the Bay of Trinity in 48. degrees, and two terces of Northerly latitude;[1] and from thence towards the West, vnto the inmost part of the said Trinity Bay, and from the inmost part of Trinity Bay, vnto the bounds of the Sea, on the West side of that Land.[2] And from the foresaid latitude, at the entrance into the said Trinity Bay, directly from thence towards the North, so farre as the Northmost part of a certaine small Iland, lying neere the latitude of 51. degrees, called by the name of *Penguin Iland*;[3] And from thence to the Westermost part of the *New-found-land*, in that latitude; And from that latitude on the West side of the sayd *Trinity Land*, so farre to the South, as the foresaid West line, which commeth from the inmost part of the foresaide Trinity Bay; And all the Lands, Harbours, Bayes, Roades, Ilands, and whatsoeuer, which is inclusiuely within the said circuit.

The Cape *Bona vista*, is the head land on the North side of the entrance into Trinity Bay, and there is a reasonable good harbour, where Ships doe yeerely vse to fish, called the harbour of *Bona vista*, and diuers small Ilands are neere thereunto; where yeerely breed great aboundance of diuers sorts of Sea-fowles, of which birds and their egges, men may take so many of them as they list; And from the harbour of *Bona vista*, vnto a little harbour called S. *Catalina*, on the North side of Trinity Bay, where fisher Boates doe often harbour, vpon some occasions; it is neere sixe leagues West South west in, towards the said Bay; And from thence vnto a Roade for Ships, called *English Harbour*, towards the North-west, it is two leagues, where some yeeres 6. or 7. saile of good Ships haue made their fishing voyages; And from thence to the North-west, halfe a league, lieth a harbour, called *Salmon Coue*, where some yeeres 10. saile of good Ships haue made their voyages; And from thence to the West a league, lieth a good Roade, called *Robin Hoods Bay*, where some yeeres 6. good Ships haue made their voyages; From thence vnto the West, halfe a league, lye the best harbours in that Land, called by the name of *Trinity Harbour*, where some yeeres, aboue 20. saile of good Ships haue made their fishing voyages; And from Trinity harbour towards the West two leagues, lieth the harbour of *Bonauenter*, where some yeeres 5. or 6. good Ships make their voyages; And from thence to the West neere two leagues, lyeth a Riuer or Inlet nauigable, fit for any ship to saile in, stretching towards the North, which I may well call the Riuer of *Bonauenter*, because it is supposed to runne into the Bay of Flowers, which lyeth on the North

---

[1] I.e. 48° 41′ N. [2] I.e. Placentia Bay.
[3] Probably Groais Island, which lies just to the south of the 51st parallel.

side of Trinity harbour; At the entrance of of [*sic*] which Riuer, some yeeres, diuers Ships haue rid there at anchor, to make their voyages; And from thence West 4. leagues, lieth a harbour called *Hartsease*, where diuers good Ships haue made their voyages; And betweene the foresaid Riuer of *Bonauenter*, and the said harbour of Hartsease; there is a very good harbour, stretching towards the North, aboue 6. leagues, called *Hayleford Hauen*, where Ships doe not vse to fish, by reason there are no conuenient places to dry their fish on, neere the entrance into the said harbour. And aboue the said harbour of Hartsease, to the Westermost part of Trinitie Bay, it is no lesse then twelue leagues; And there is also good fishing farre into the Bay, within the said harbour of Hartsease, as by good proofe hath beene often made.

Betweene the said harbour of Hartsease, and the foresaid English harbour, there are many delightfull and fruitfull Ilands, none of them aboue a mile from the Land; And the Bay of Trinitie is in breadth, at the neerest place, which is right ouer against the harbour of Hartsease, aboue 5. leagues; And those that fish on the South side of the said Bay, doe yeerely send their Boates to the North side, for baite to take their fish withall; because such baite is there in great aboundance; And on those foresayd Ilands, there yeerely breed innumerable store of Geese, Ducks, Gulls, and other Sea-fowle, to which places the natiues of the Countrey doe often come from the North, and fetch those Fowles and their egges as they haue beene often seene so to doe.

There haue diuers yeeres been aboue sixty saile of good Ships fishing in the foresaid Trinity harbour, and those foresaid Bayes, Roades, and harbours, and they haue all made as great thriuing voyages there, as any other Ships haue made at any other place in that Countrey; all that North side of Trinity Bay lyeth pleasantly against the South, being neere in the latitude of 49. degrees, by which it may be well conceiued, the Climate of it selfe should be very pleasant, considering that the City of London is more then three degrees to the North, then that place, which is no lesse then 180. English miles; and there is all such fruits in great abundance, as are formerly recited in my discouery of that Countrey and all such sorts of fish of what kind soeuer, so plentifull, as in any other part to the Southward on that Coast; and the Firre, Spruise, Pine, and Birch trees are there much greater, and longer, and the Countrey fuller of woods, then it is to the Southward; and if some people doe once begin to inhabite there, questionlesse, there is great hope in doing much good, not onely in fishing, and manuring of land, but also in sawing boords, and squaring of Timber, fit to be transported from thence into other Countries; as also for making of Iron, Salt, Sope, Pitch and Tarre; whereby good profit may be gotten; considering what commodities in all Europe do more decay then wood, whereof there is no likelihood (in the opinion of man) euer to be any want thereof in that Countrey. So that it may be well conceiued, it is a good neighbor Countrey to lay hold on, seeing it may be possessed so fitly.

Thus according to my certaine knowledge, I haue partly shewed how your seuerall Circuits lye in that Countrey; and partly the great hope whereby it may incourage diuers worthy men to become suiters vnto your Honour, to bee Aduenturers to further the same, when they shall also bee made acquainted with such bountifull conditions, as you will be pleased to grant vnto euery such Aduenturer.

Which conditions, are as it hath pleased your Lordship something to acquaint me withall, That any who will aduenture 100. pounds to settle a Colony neere vnto the foresaid harbour of Renowze, and towards the setting forth of such shipping thither yeerely in the fishing trade, as it may please you; and such as shall aduenture therein to thinke good, wherby to aduance the said Plantation, and also to defray the charge in setting forth such shipping with good profit.

So that such shipping so imployed, shall carry people yeerely, and prouisions, for all such as shall continue there, and such beasts, and all other necessaries as may be thought fit, and not to hire any other Ship for that purpose onely: And that any Aduenturer shall not onely haue his equall part, proportionably of the benefit which may be yeerly gotten there, by the fishing; but also such part of the benefit as may be gotten by the labours and industry of those which shall yeerely bee sent to remaine there, as seruants to you and the Aduenturers, who are to prouide for them.

And also any such shall likewise haue (which aduentures 100. pounds to be imployed as aforesaid) the one halfe part and prerogatiue of one of the foresaid Harbours, Bay, or Road on the Northside of Trinity Bay, and the circuit of two thousand acres of such land and woods as is next adioyning thereunto, in fee for euer to be holden of your Lordship, by the rent of a penny by the yeere for euery such hundred acres of land and woods, which is twenty pence by the yeere for two thousand acres.

And also he shall haue in fee for euer, to him and his assignes, a conuenient place to build a Stage, and necessary roomes to salt fish on, and to build a dwelling house, and other conuenient houses, neere vnto the harbours of Formosa and Renowze, with a sufficient circuit of ground to dry fish on, and for some other purposes, fit for a ship of fourescore Tun burthen.

So that any such vndertaker doe within a fit time limited, settle and maintaine there to inhabite eight persons at least; and so many more as he shall think good; and take the benefit of their labours to his owne particular account, which may bee worth yeerly a great profit to any such Aduenturer, and to pay for the same as a rent by the yere 10.s. And for default of not continuing there yeerely, after a fit time limited, eight persons; or for non payment of the foresaid rents of ten shillings by the yeere; and the abouesaid rent of twenty pence by the yeere: then any such vndertaker shall forfeit his right, title and interest in all such land and woods; and likewise in the said place for salting and drying of fish (but not the benefit of such a summe as he shall so aduenture.) And if any such aduenturer, or any of his seruants or assignes, shall at any time finde within your said lands there, any mines of gold, siluer, or what metall soeuer, hee shall yeeld vnto your Lordship or assignes an indifferent part thereof.

And whosoeuer will aduenture 200. pounds, may not onely haue a whole Harbour, Bay, or Road to himselfe in fee for euer, and foure thousand acres of land, and woods thereunto adioyning on the North side of Trinity Bay; but also a conuenient place, and ground to build Stages and houses, and for drying of fish fit for a Ships fishing voyage of 160. tunne burthen, neere vnto the harbors of Formosa and Renowze; so that any such Vndertaker, or his assignes doe, within such a conuenient time as shall bee set downe in his grant, maintaine there sixteene persons, as his seruants or tenants, and to pay double so much rent by the yeere, as whosoeuer aduentures but 100. pounds as aforesaid: And likewise he shall receiue double so much of the benefit and good, which may come by the aduenture of any such summe, in setting forth of such shipping as are to be imployed as aforesaid: and also the like by the labours of those which shall be imployed in the intended Plantation.

And whosoeuer shall aduenture lesse then 100. li. be it 80. li. 60. li. 50. li. 30. li. or 20. li. shall haue lesse proportionably in euery respect, what hee shall haue that aduentures 100 pounds: And whosoeuer shall aduenture 200. pounds or a greater sum, or but 100. pounds or a lesse summe, should disburse the one moity or halfe part thereof his first yeere, whereby to make prouisions for the fishing voyage, and shipping to bee in perfect readinesse in fit time.

And any man which shall thus aduenture 200. pounds or a greater or lesse summe, hee should bring in the other halfe part of such a summe as he doth promise, and subscribe to aduenture the second yeere at conuenient time, wherby to make fit prouisions in readinesse of all necessaries, as shall be then thought fitting for the yeere following, and then by Gods assistance, there is great hope of gaine to bee made, and good proceedings in the said Plantation.

Some of those which will be Aduenturers in this manner, may bee as Committees, to giue their best opinions, what they should conceiue to be most fitting in euery respect; whereby there may bee the more orderly proceedings therein, and whatsoeuer any 4, 5, 6, or a more number of them may think fit: one, or more of them may at conuenient times acquaint your Honour withall, whereby it may the more speedily bee put in action, and you so little troubled withall, from your other waighty occasions as possible may bee: And so one of the said Committees to be as Treasurer, who may keepe the bookes of accounts, of whatsoeuer may be so aduentured, and likewise to bee receiued, which will giue a good content to euery Aduenturer.

And as concerning the manner how Ships and men should bee imployed in this intended Plantation, I shall as followeth acquaint you; whereby there may be hired some industrious men, which are most pliable for the fishing voyage, agreed withall in time to saile in such shipping, and with such men some others may goe to be as Seruants in the voyage, which may be Tradesmen, and their wiues; who will labour fitly in the fishing, whiles it lasteth, and afterwards continue there to plant.

It is to be vnderstood, that a Ship which vsually carrieth there in an ordinary fishing voyage 30. men and boyes, and returnes yeerely with them, should not, that is thus imployed, carry aboue 34. men, women and some Youths of 13. or 14. yeeres of age, whose victuall and wages, for more then three quarters of the yeere, will be euen defrayed vpon the ordinary charge of the fishing voyage; for any such Ship may well be sailed thither, and home againe, with lesse then twenty men; So that those other fourteene may be accounted vnprofitable passengers to be carryed, and so recarryed from thence as vsually is done. .

And therefore it is requisite, that such as shall remaine there to inhabite, should bee agreed withall in time, whereby to prepare themselues for that purpose, and not to seeke after such in haste; for then should you not onely haue those which are not so fit as I doe wish, for that purpose; but also they will be much more dearer (as I haue often proued what they will be) if they be taken when they proffer their seruice.

And he that is either a fit house-Carpenter, Mason, Smith, Brickmaker, Lime-burner, Turner, Tyler, Husbandman, Gardener, or what trade soeuer, and will carry his wife with him, should be so agreed withall at first; so that notwithstanding their trades, they should help to fish, and labour diligently about the same, when time serues for all building of houses, which is a thing will fitly bee done at all times, very commodiously, with little labour and lesse charge, when the fish faileth.

And if any Aduenturer will send thither a kinsman, friend, or seruant, to be imployed in the said Plantation, which will take paines, hee may haue a fit hire allowed him by the yeere, as the Treasurer, and one, or more of the Aduenturers may thinke fit: And any such so imployed may see such lands and woods allotted out for his said Master or friend, and yeerely certifie him from thence what fit proceedings there are in said Plantation.

And also any that shall serue their 5. yeeres industriously, may not only be well paid, as hee shall be agreed withall, but you will then also giue him 100. acres of land and woods in the South part of that Countrey in fee for euer to him, his heires and assignes, if he will continue there to liue, or any other man for him; which is to be holden of your Honour, paying at the sealing of his Deed, 8. shillings, and euer after but a penny rent by the yeere for the said hundred acres: which will be a good incouragement to such as will go there to liue; and be also a fit meanes to people the Countrey, with such as may be well spared from all his Maiesties Kingdomes. And thus in time they may finde out diuers good commodities there, which as yet lye vndiscouered, whereof there is great hope in some speciall thing, which I omit to write of.[1]

By this it may be partly vnderstood, what great hope of good there may come vnto his Maiesty, and all his Maiesties Kingdomes, by settling people to inhabite there, seeing it is a Countrey already so well approoued, to be so healthy and warme in winter as England, and yeelds yeerly, as the trade is now in fishing onely aboue 150000. li. into this Kingdome, besides the great maintenance and increase of shipping, and Mariners; and the relieuing of many families, the which trade onely

[1] This kind of hint, presumably of mineral wealth, is somewhat out of character.

may well, in little time, be worth double so much yeerely to his Maiesties subiects, then now it is, besides the great hope of gaine which is there to be gotten otherwaies.

In the yeere of our Lord God 1615. being there with a Commission directed vnto me out of his Maiesties high Court of Admiralty, for the reformation of abuses, and settling of fit orders amongst such as yerely trade to that Countrey, wherein I did spend much time, and was at great charge; and then sailing from harbour to harbour; I found the masters of English Ships then there, willing to haue such abuses reformed, and thereunto aboue 170. of them being impanelled in seuerall inquests for that seruice, they did deliuer vnto me their seuerall presentments vnder their hands & seales, to the vse of the Kings Maiesty; which were the first Iuries that euer were impanelled there, to the vse of any Christian Prince; In which presentments are contained diuers orders, which vpon my returne from thence, I did present into the high Court of Admiraltie; in which seruice I tooke notice there was on that Coast aboue 250. saile of Ships great and small of our Nation, with aboue 6000. Subiects in them.

Now if it may please his Maiestie, and that but 200. of such Ships which yeerely saile thither a Fishing, will leaue there in the end of the yeere, when their voyages are made, but foure persons from euery of them, there to inhabite with fit prouision for them, vntill the next Summer that the said Owners Ships repaire thither againe, and take the benefit of their labour in that time: then after that proportion there will be aboue 800. persons fitly and cheapely left there, and maintained the first yeere: and so euery yeere some people so left, both men and women, will not onely bee a great case to this Kingdome, but also saue a great charge in carrying thither, and in returning yeerely from thence so many persons, and they will be also worth vnto such Aduenturers, as will so leaue them there, in diuers labours, whiles the Ships are wanting from thence, a great benefit, and also the greater security vnto euery such Ship and company, that haue people so left in the Countrey, to prouide against their comming; whereby they need not then saile thitherward bound so timely in the yere, and in such casuall and so desperate a manner, as yeerely now they vse to doe. And if such a beneficiall course be taken for peopling of that Land, how may there be a fitter Plantation settled there, or elsewhere, let any man iudge; and so fit to be vnited vnto his Maiesties other Kingdomes, without charge, bloodshed, or vsurpation. Any man that will thus aduenture, shall not only haue a great quantity of land there to him & his heires, with many other priuiledges, vpon fit conditions; but also he shall haue the yeerely benefit of such a summe as he shall so disburse, for the setting foorth of any such shipping, and the labours of such as shall be so imployed; so that your Lordship intends not to haue the benefit of any such summe, as shal be thus aduentured therein by any other man, but only your equall part, of such a great summe as you pretend, by Gods assistance, to aduenture therein likewise.

Then who will not be willing to imploy a part of his estate, or to goe himselfe, or send a friend to inhabite that Countrey, though he haue but small meanes; or but onely his merit to aduance his fortune, there to tread and plant that Land, he shall so purchase by his good indeuours, if hee haue the taste of vertue and magnanimity? What to such a mind can be more pleasant, then building a foundation for his posteritie, so to bee gotten without preiudice to any, if hee haue any zeale in Religion? What can he doe lesse hurtfull to any, or more agreeable to God, then to seeke to conuert the poore Sauages (which liue in the North part of that Country) to know their Creator and Redeemer? What so truely suites with honour and honestie, as by informing the ignorant, and reforming things vniust, teaching vertue, and gaine to our natiue mother Country, another Kingdome, neere as spacious as Ireland to attend her, where there may bee found imployments for those that how liue idlely? Which is so far from wronging any, as to cause posterity to remember them, and remembering them, euer to honour that remembrance with prayse.

Then who would liue at home idely, that may bee there imployed, or thinke himselfe worthy to liue, only to eate, drink, and sleepe, and so die; hauing consumed that carelesly, his friends got worthily, or by vsing that talent miserably, which may thus maintaine vertue honestly?

Now my hope is, that gaine will make some to affect that, which Religion, charity, and the common good cannot: I hauing for my owne part no other purpose herein, but for the generall good of all his Maiesties Subiects, and not any desire to perswade any man to aduenture thither, but for honour and profit: neither is my purpose by these perswasions, to draw children from their parents, men from their wiues, nor seruants from their masters; but onely such as with a free consent will goe, or may bee spared from such Cities and Parishes, that will but apparell some of their fatherlesse children of fourteene or fifteene yeeres of age; and some such yong married people, as haue but small meanes, to set themselues forth; who by their good industry, may liue there pleasantly, and grow rich in little time; And if any man, which shall be willing to aduenture thither, desire to be further satisfied, they may reade my discouery of that Countrey, & what defect is found in either, they shall find supplied in me to further their good desire therin, that haue thus freely thrown my self, with my mite, into the treasury of my Countrys good, which I esteeme worth much more then *Columbus* could certainly giue the Spaniards at his first enterprise of any such certainties of great wealth, by his designes in the West Indies, as since hath bin there found: and although I cannot now at first promise to haue such Mines of gold in *New-found-land*, yet let vs in that Plantation something imitate our neere neighbors the Hollanders, whose wealth and strength gotten in few yeeres only by fishing, are good testimonies, wherby they haue in little time gotten their wealth & strength; and if the Plantation at *New-found-land*, be orderly proceeded on, the trades thither, & at other of his Maiesties Westerne Plantations, would questionlesse in time afford yeerly a greater quantity of gold and siluer into all his Maiesties Kingdomes, then all the Mines of the West Indies doe now yeerely yeeld to the King of *Spaine*, and with lesse hazard, & more certainty & felicity. And thus I descend to the charge of victualling forth a Ship of 100. Tun, with 40. persons, to bee imployed for the more orderly proceeding in the said Plantation.[1]

10. 24 Dec. 1622   RICHARD WHITBOURNE TO LORD FALKLAND[2]

Right honourable and my very good Lord; My private occasions beinge such and so vrgent at this present, as I hope your Lordship wilbe pleased to have me excused, and to spare my attendance vppon your Lordship for a season in Ireland; yet in the meane tyme, I have thought it my bounden duty, to offer some matters, vnto your Lordships wisdome to be considered of, and then to be imparted, as your Lordship shall see cause vnto such Lords, Knightes, & other gentlemen of that kingdome, as shall freely and voluntarily offer themselves with their purses to the furtherance of soe honourable a designe of your honor, as is the plantacion of New-found-land.

That there is a certaine and assured benefitt to arrise vnto those who shall adventure therein, I have already, and I hope sufficiently declared in that poore labour of mine, which I have of late vnder your Lordships

---

[1] Whitbourne then reprints the list which is also in the *Discourse and discovery*; below, pp. 173–5.   [2] B.L., Sloane MS 3827, ff. 15–18.

proteccion published to the veiw and censure of the world, vnto which I must referr all those, who are desirous to be informed and satisfied herein;[1] But this I have thought good to informe your honour, that the season is now to farr past, for any retorne of proffitt to be made this yeare, only it is fitt and necessary, that your Lordship presently fall in hand to make provision of a fitt & convenient vessell of somme 40 or 50 Tunn to be in a readdynes fitted with men, both to carry her to and fro, against Aprill next at the furthest; whereby to begin the plantacion there in somme fitt order against an other yeare;/

To this end and purpose it is most necessary that your honor should move all such as purpose in deede to adventure in that worke with their purses, forthwith to subscribe their names, vnto your Lordship and what ever the some bee, that they shall thinke fitt to promise, that they at the tyme of their subscripcion put into his hands, which your Lordship and they shall appoynt to be the Common Treasurer for this purpose; one third part thereof forthwith paid, without which thinges necessary may be so vnprovided against Aprill next, as they are at this present; and thereby all hope of the second yeares proffitt cut off, as is already lost of this; as also that they vndertake & assume vnto your Lordship to paye in an other third part in September next to make provision for the yeare followinge, which must be made to the full; both for men, and all other thinges necessary for that plantacion; And for the last third part to be paide in March followinge to beare the chardge of the Sommer and winter followinge, which shall by the grace and blessinge of God; bringe in the chardge with good proffitt, of all that shalbe from this tyme till then chardged vppon this plantacion;

For the Shipp it selfe to be hired, now for this yeare I conceave that your Lordship shall most easily provide her heere in London, and at the easiest rate, if they whom your honor shall imploy therein, vnderstand himselfe [sic] well and the matter which hee goes about; and for the carriadge of her to and fro; choice must be made of the most sufficient Fishermen; that maye be heere had; such as have beene vsed to those partes, and beene acquainted with the manner of Fishinge there, without which, they which shall goe to remayne there, will not be able to make fitt provision for themselves for the Winter followinge:/

They that are so carryed thither this Springe from England, cannot be lesse in nomber then 12; of which nomber there should be two house Carpenters, one Brickmaker, which also maye have skill to laye them,

---

[1] *A discourse containing a loving invitation*, see above, pp. 207–20.

one stone Mason, one Tyle maker, one Smith, one Husbandman, one Gardiner with his seedes, one Shipwright, which maye be able to build, and to guide a boat at Sea, for the vse of Fishinge, who maye well provide a dozen of good Fishinge Boates, in readynes against an other yeare, as I shalbe readdy to advise him, one Seaman which maye guide the rest, from Harbour to Harbour; one Lime Burner, for the Shipp may be fittly ballasted with lime stone vnder the provisions so cheape as ballast; which will easily be had in the west partes of this kingdome, one Cooper which wilbe very necessary for many special purposes/

And for such a greater nomber of people, as are not to be provided heere, maye be shipt from Ireland; As touchinge the providinge of such a shipp heere, and of those which are to remaine in the Country, there are divers things necessary, which wilbe better, and att easier rates provided heere then in Ireland, as beere, biskett bread, and all manufactures whatsoever necessary for that plantacion; Corne, beeffe, butter, porke and some other provisions, wilbe I suppose, at more easy rates provided there then heere;/

The shipp beinge thus provided heere; I thinke shee were best to be sent from this vnto Galloway; which is not passinge some two dayes Iorney, and a halfe from Dublin; and is almost halfe the waye from hence to New found land, besides, that place affordes, beeff, porke, and all other provisions for the Sea better, and in greater plenty, then any other part of that Country can doe, Whereas if the Shippe should come at Dublin, going and comminge they shall neede so many change of windes, as maye give a greate staye & hinderance to the iourney this yeares:/

And from Galloway, to South Falkland in New found land, at Renouze, where I thinke best for your Lordship first to settle your Colony, It maye be a very short passage, and then will such a fitt master and Company, as shall saile in the said Shipp thither, and wheresoever, doe many good services, whiles they are in that Country, for the setlinge of those that shall inhabite there, and for takinge of Fish for them to live by there all the winter;

There is also something more, which I shall make bould to offer vnto your Lordships consideracion, which is this, to fraight a Shipp for this voyage to New-found-land, and to have her retorne from thence empty, will prove a greate and vnfitt chardge to your Lordship and the Adventurers; For the ease therefore of this chardge; It wilbe fitt that some course be taken to have her Laden there with fish, and to saile directly from thence vnto a Markett with the same, whereby vppon the retorne, the whole fraight wilbe dischadged [sic], and happely some proffitt accrue over and above vnto your Lordship and the Adventurers, as in my booke it will informe any therein/.

And for the better effectinge hereof, I have thought good to advertise your Lordship, that master Secretary Calvertes shipp, which is to sett forward in February next, and to spend the next Sommer in Fishinge there, is likely, God blessinge her proceedinges, to take a farr greater quantity of Fish, more then she wilbe able to carrye awaye from thence, with such a greate nomber of people; as his honour will have there; which people, as are now in the Country have there already above 150 quarters of Salt at a very cheape hand, part of which fish so taken may serve to loade your Lordships shippe, that maye be hired as aforesaid. And it wilbe an easy matter, as I thinke for your Lordship to finde a merchaunt for that fraight of Fish in Gallowaye or some other part of Ireland, if your Lordship and the Adventurers with yo^u, will not run the hazard of a markett for it your selves;/–

Only if your honor wilbe pleased to be informed, that master Secretary must be agreed withall for such a quantity of Fish before the settinge forward of his shipp, to furnish your Lordships shipp of her loadinge in New found land, at a certaine price, which fish as I conceave, if it may be bargained for; within ix^s the English hundred waight of good and marchauntable fish, and to paye for the same vppon sight of Bills of Exchange from thence, vnto master Secretary, when the fish is receaved there; heere in England vppon reasonable tyme after;[1] And so may your Lordships Shipp be fittly loaden there, and retorne to a markett with it vnto Bourdax in Fraunce, or where it may be thought best, and with the imploymentes thereof she may retorne loaden with wynes or other merchaundice vnto Dublin, Galloway, or any other place in Ireland, where your Lordship and the Aduenturers shall thinke good;/

And if any marchaunt in Ireland will take the Fish at the price as it maye be bought of master Secretary Calvert, or whomsoever in Newfoundland, and make payment thereof; he maye send a Servant of his in the shipp that maye be thus hired; who maye be his Factour, and take accompt of this fish, and to make sales and imploymentes thereof at Bordax or any other place in France, or the coast of Biskay;/

And any such marchaunte so bargaininge for the fish, and havinge

---

[1] Whitbourne was describing a very common practice among English merchants. While possibly the fish bought under such a contract might cost a little more, the merchant was assured of a full cargo and avoided having his ship sail home half-empty.

the Shipp so to be hired to loade the same, and passe with it to a markett as aforesaid and returne into Ireland, and there dischardge of such merchaundice, as she shalbe reloaden with all; I thinke it fit in my opynion, he should allow for every Tunn fraight of fish, Twenty hundred waight to the Tunn, at least iiij^{li} and x^s for every Tun, which wilbe, but iij^{li} a Tuns fraight from Newfound land to Bordax, and from Bordax to Dublin or Gallowaye, but xxx^s if any marchaunt allow but iiij^{li} x^s for every tunns fraight; which may very neere dischardge; not only the hire of the shipp; for the whole voyage, but also for eight mens wages, and their victualls that maye saile to and fro all the said voyage from hence, vntill then, that the shipp & men be dischardged in Ireland; And vntill that tyme, there will not be, any greate cause to chardge your Lordship, neither the Adventurers with your honor in the plantacion, about any matter for rigginge, and providinge the shipp, or those men that shall saile in her to and fro:/

And if your Lordship shall thinke good of these direccions, such a smale shippe provisions and men, as maye be provided heere, and be ready to sett saile from hence towards Ireland in Aprill next, to receave in such other people and provisions, as to your good Lordship and the Adventurers maye seeme good; And at somme other tyme, shippinge men and provision, may be sett forth from thence to advaunce your Lordships intended great worke; In the meane tyme; I maye be readdy heere to doe my best whereby to further your Lordships good purpose there, or wheresoever else your Lordship shalbe pleased to commaund me/

Now by such preparacions, as maye be made this next Sommer, by those which shalbe so sent, maye well provide in fitt readines to entertaine such Shippinge, men and provision as shalbe thought good to be sent the next yeare vnto them/

Then there may be great proffitt made to your Lordship and all the Adventurers therein, and all chardges of this first yeare, and the Second fittly dischardged, And withall the building of howses, clensinge of land and many other services maye be orderly performed with greate pleasure; and little paynes;/

. To my certaine knowledge your Lordship hath within your Circuite of South Falkland, not only the Commodiousnes of a Couple of good Harbours, but also many hundred acres of so good open land, cleere without Rockes, or trees, and the Land very fatt, and deepe soyle of earth, such as I thinke noe part of Virginea, New England, or Nova Scotia hath better, and is fitt to entertaine, above 500 bease [sic] the

Second yeare, if winter provision for haye, and Litter be provided for them in readynes, before such bease be sent thither, which provisions maye be well performed close adioyninge to the Harbour of Renouze with little labour;/

And as touchinge your Lordships Circuite, on the North side of Trinity Baye, there are a greate nomber of very good Harbours, much good land, many fruitfull Ilands, greate store of deare, and other beastes; land Foule, & water Foule, greate aboundance of Spruise, Firr, Pine, and Birch trees, fitter for mastes Bourds, and buildinge, then such as are in South Falkland, and the fishing in Sommer tyme so good there, as elsewhere; the fresh Rivers are so sweete and pleasaunt, and so well stored with Salmons Trouttes as also divers sortes of shell fish there, as not in any part of that Country better, and lyeth in a temperate Climate; The savage natives of that Country, live on the North side of it, with whom there is greate probabilities much good maye be done;/–

And for better satisfaccion to any Lord, knight, gentleman or marchaunt of Ireland that shalbe willinge to be an Adventurer, and desires to know vppon what condicions, your Lordship will at lardge informe such therein;/

I vnderstand by master Secretary, and also by master Welstide that your Lordship desires to have, an other mapp of the Newfoundland, wherein his honour and your Lordships Agent, willed mee to give direccions; which I have taken care of, and it cannot be finished, vntill it be shortly vppon Twelveth daye next,[1] which wilbe I trust accordinge to your Lordships good likinge; And some other thinges at my comminge into Ireland, I shalbe ready to give vnto your Lordship, my best opinion, whereby to further your Lordships good purpose in the said plantacion;

Thus my honorable good Lord, I have presumed bould, to putt your honor in minde, of some speciall matters, which as I conceave maye tend; and turne to the advauncement, and furtherance of your honourable intendment for that plantacion; humbly cravinge perdon for this, and all other my boldnes, and desiringe to be reputed; such as I shall ever live and die/

London this 24th of December 1622

Your Lordships humble and faithful Servant
Ric: whitbourne[2]

---

[1] 6 January 1623.
[2] The signature is in a different hand from the rest of the letter.

[*Addressed*:] To the right honourable my very singular good Lord the Lord Viscount of Falkland; honourable deputy generall of the Realme of Ireland; att the kinges maiesties Castle of Dublin these with speed.

[*Endorsed*:] Captaine Whitbourne December 24° Received 30 ejusdem

11. 8 Jan. 1622/3   LEONARD WELSTEAD TO LORD FALKLAND[1]

my verie good Lorde

I acquaynted your Lordship by my laste of the 31th of 10ber wha[t] monies had beene Receaved, & payd by me for your Lordships vse, & Sollicyted Sir Ph[ilip] Carye[2] to doe the like, whoe had prevented your desire in that particular, if th'accommptes betweene himselfe & master Williams (concerninge your affayres) had bene drawn to theire period, your Creditors continue their daylie supplications for monyes, whose necessities I[3] cannot relieue without your further supplie[4] which I daylie expect,[5] the Summes Receaved being wholye disbursed with some overplus, Concerninge the plate by your Lordships appoynctment to be deliuered vnto mistris Spykard,[6] parte whereof beinge sould by ward the Goldsmyth; and that which remayneth your Armes taken out, It is therefore Sir P[hilip] C[aryes] opynion that a vallewe of gold in specie, coresponsive vnto the intended plate wilbe better accepted & more vsefull, whose opynion I had followed, if your Lordships pleasure had bene soe signifyed, but haue respected the performance of either vntil I Receaue your Lordships resolution which I humbly beseeche maye retorne speedily in all, Concerninge the Newfownd Land[7] affayre I sent you by the last pacquett Capten Whitbornes directions & bookes & sythence by Conference with master Bawle a gentleman of the privy Chamber touchinge the intended plantacion there by your lordship & master S[ecretary] Calvert, fownd him very desirous to vnderstand both the discouery and present estate thereof wherevpon I gaue him one of Capten Whitbornes bookes & referred him to him for Amplyer satisfaction wherewith I acquainted the Capten. Maister Bawles Ambition tendinge to be either a gouerner there or in the next place of Eminency[8] which to obteyne he would adventure both his person

---

[1] B.L., Add. MS 11033, ff. 18–19v; damaged.
[2] Third son of Sir Edward Cary and brother to Falkland; member of parliament for Woodstock between 1614 and 1625; died 1631. Wood, *Alumni Oxonienses*, I, 247.
[3] 'whose...I' underlined.
[4] (relieue...supplie' underlined.
[5] 'I...expect' underlined.
[6] 'vnto...Spykard' underlined.
[7] 'the...Land' underlined.
[8] 'or...Eminency' underlined.

and the best parte of his estate.¹ Other gentlemen there be of his quallity with desire to be adventurers some in person others estate, they desiringe to vnderstand your Lordships Condicions which you shall² please to propound & send hither by the next retorne that a preparation be made to sett forward with the first of the next Springe / Soe Cravinge your Lordships pardon in all doe humbly take leave & allwayes remayne

[St] martins Lane
8: Ia[nuary] 1622

> your Lordships faythfull servaunt to be Commaunded
> Le[onard] Welstede³

[Addressed:] To the right honourable my verie good Lord the Lord Deputye of his maiesties Kingdome of Ireland theise: att Dublyn Castle

[Endorsed:] Welsteed of the 8ᵗʰ of Ianuary 1622. Received 13° ejusdem de Mistris Speckards Plate Master Baule and Nuewfound Land. / to send Monny. Answered.

12. *A SHORT DISCOURSE OF THE NEW-FOUND-LAND*

A SHORT DISCOURSE OF THE *NEW-FOUND-LAND*: CONTAYNIG [sic] DIVERSE REASONS and inducements, for the planting of that *Countrey*. *Published for the satisfaction of all such as shall be willing to be Adventurers in the said Plantation.*
DUBLIN, Printed by the Societie of Stationers. M.DC.XXIII.

TO THE RIGHT HONOURABLE HENRY LO: CARY, Viscount of *Falkland*, Lo: Deputie generall of IRELAND, and one of his Majesties most honourable privie Councell in the Realme of *England*.

MY LORD:

I⁴ present unto the view of your judicious censure, this short Discourse, or rather, an abstract of a Discourse, intended only as a satisfaction unto such, as may be willing to joyne with your Lordship, in so noble a designe as is the plantation of the *Newfound-land*: wherein it is not to be doubted, but that many will follow your Lordships stepps

---

¹ 'estate' underlined.   ² 'you shall' underlined.
³ Nothing is known of Welstead, except that a Roger Welsted who matriculated at Merton College, Oxford, in 1636 was described as the son of Leonard Welstead, gentleman of Harfield, Middlesex. Wood, *Alumni Oxonienses*, IV, 1597.
⁴ The dedication is printed in italics with key words in roman; here the arrangement is reversed.

in so honourable a Worke, especially in this Kingdome, where the name of a *Plantation* is so farre from being a stranger, as it hath beene the originall cause from whence very many have derived their happinesse. I cannot denie, but that the weake handling of this discourse, better beseemes the poore demonstration of my zeale to your Lordships service, then any possibility to comprehend the worthinesse of the action, within the compasse of a bare relation. Such as it is, I could easily set downe, having the same before, as it were, made to my hands, by such as have been eye-witnesses of whatsoever is here related:[1] so that I may fitly answer with *Aristophans*, to one that demanded, whether the Comedy, by him promised, were performed; It is made (quoth he) and wants nothing but the putting in verse. As it was delivered to me, so I recommend it to your Lordships protection, and surcease any further writing, least I might wish that the saying were verified to me, *Tibi silentiũ laus.*

Your Lordships humble servant,

T. C.[2]

A DISCOURSE OF THE NEW-FOUND-LAND.

There are five things, which seeme as it were with one consent to render the plantation of *Newfoundland* happie and prosperous; which will evidently appeare upon examination of the proposition ensuing. *viz.* That the action is Honourable, Lawfull, Profitable, Easie and Necesssarie.

The Honour of the action   The Honour of the action is double: for first, it tends to the honour of God in propagating of Religion; so as by this meanes that countrey which hitherto hath onely served as a den for wilde beasts, shal not only be repleat with Christian inhabitants, but the Savages who live in the adjoining continent of *America* (amongst whom not so much as the name of Christ hath ever beene yet heard) may in time be reduced to Civilitie and Religion. Secondly, it tends to the honour of his Majestie, and that by the addition of Territory, and encrease of Dominion, for as much as by the only plantation of *Newfoundland*, an Iland every way as bigge and spacious as *Ireland*, may without bloudshed or usurpation, be brought to bow under the waight of his royal Scepter.

---

[1] The author evidently had a copy of Whitbourne's *Discourse and discovery* and he relied heavily upon it, as is noted below.

[2] For the possible identity of T. C., see above, p. 39. Of about the right age would have been Thomas Cary, a grandson of lord Hunsdon who was first cousin to Falkland's father. *Visitation of Hertfordshire, 1572 and 1634*, ed. W. C. Metcalfe (Harleian Society, 1886), p. 135.

The Lawfulness of the cause, will be made plaine by this: in as much *The* as it cannot be proved, that any part of that country, comprehended *Lawfulnesse of* within his Majesties grant, hath ever yet beene inhabited either by *the action.* Christian or Infidell; so as by this plantation wee shall be so farre from wronging any Prince or State, or diseising any man of his inheritance, as wee shall performe a worke no doubt acceptable to God, in making true use of that which from all eternitie was created for the benefite of mankinde.

2 His Majesties undoubted right to this countrey, is next to be considered: for first of all, it was discovered by *Sebastian Cabot*, in the name and at the proper charges of *Henry* the seventh King of *England*, in the yeare 1596. [*sic*] which is about 127. yeares since,[1] and immediately upon the discoverie of the Indies by *Christopherus Columbus.*

3 This discovery was strengthened by the actuall possession which Sir *Humfrey Gilbert* Knight tooke thereof, in the yeare 1583. in the name and to the use of Queene *Elizabeth* of famous memory. for a perpetuall witnesse whereof, hee erected on the shoare a Pillar, whereupon the royal Atmes [*sic*] of *England* were supported.[2]

4 Which possession of his, hath since received perfection by severall plantations, made thither from *England* by vertue of his Majesties Letter Patt. as the London plantation, which hath beene setled there this xij. yeares:[3] the Bristoll plantation, this v. yeares; and the plantation of the right honourable Sir *George Calvert* Knight, (principall Secretarie to his Majestie) for this ij. yeares last past.

The Profite which may arise by this plantation, is first of all *The Profite* communicated to the king by augmentation of his customs & revenues: *which may* to the State, by encrease of Ships & Mariners; to the Kingdome of *plantation.* *Ireland* (from whence this plantation is to be undertaken) in generall, and to each private Adventurer thereof in particular.

The generall profite which may accrue hereby to *Ireland*, is as *The generall* followeth. First, it will open a way, whereby the commodities of this *profit.* Kingdome may be vented, as Beefe, Porke, Butter, Cheese, Aqua-vitae, and all sorts of victualls; as also Ruggs,[4] Frises,[5] linnen cloth, &c. Next

---

[1] The practice of attributing John Cabot's 1497 voyage to his son, Sebastian, and of dating it 1496 began with the publication of the first volume of Giovanni Battista Ramusio's *Delle navigationi et viaggi* in 1550. John Cabot and his three sons had received a patent from Henry VII in 1496, but no expedition was made in that year. The older Cabot subsequently received a pension from the king. J. A. Williamson, ed., *The voyages of the Cabots and the English discovery of North America* (London, 1929), pp. 25–7, 33, 74–6, 232–3.

[2] For a description of the ceremony, see Hakluyt, *Principal navigations*, VIII, 54.

[3] Thirteen years before, in 1610.

[4] Rough woollen material; a kind of coarse frieze.

[5] Coarse woollen cloth, with a nap usually on one side.

of all, it will establish manufactures, by setting people on worke in building of ships, making of Netts, Ropes, Lines, Hookes, Sailes and Pullies. Besides, it will relieve a great number of other trades, as Brewers, Bakers, Coopers, Carpenters, Smithes, and the like; wherein *Ireland* being defective, it is to bee imagined that, for the hope of gaine, great numbers of them will daily be transported from *England*, to the singular profite & commoditie of this kingdome. Lastly, there can no reason be given to the contrary, why the forraine vent of the *Newfoundland* fish, being so acceptable in *France*, *Spaine* and *Italy*, may not yearely returne great quantities of mony.

The particular profite.

The particular profite, which may arise at the first, by this trade, to each private Adventurer, proceedeth chiefly from the excellent fishing upon that coast; which is a thing so universally knowne, as the fame thereof hath long since beene spred through all the parts of Christendome: witnesses hereof may be the French, Biskaners and Portingalls, who yearly send thither, and to the parts adjoyning, for that only trade of fishing, more then 400. sayle of Ships: of the English there are yearely at the least 250. saile of Ships great & small, which by computation cannot take lesse fish then will amount in money to 120000. li. being sold in *England* after the rate of 4. li. the 1000. (which is not one penny a fish). Besides, the Treyne Oyle, which (being under-valued at 12. li. the tunne in *England*) amounteth to the summe of 15000. li. omitting to reckon the over-prices, which are made by the sale thereof, in forraine parts.[1]

Neyther is the trade of fishing a thing in it selfe contemptible, seeing it is well knowne to be the chiefest trade, and principall goldmine of the united Provinces of the Low-countries, and the only meanes whereby they have not onely supported themselves against their powerfull adversaries, but in the middest of their warres they have growne to such excessive wealth and power, as their strong and bewtifull townes, their plenty of gold and silver, their multitude of ships & mariners, may sufficiently witnesse, to the admiration of the whole world.[2]

Another commoditie may be had there, which may prove in time wonderfull beneficiall to the Adventurers; and that is the making of Salt: for whereas there is yearely carried thither, by the English alone, to the value of 7000. li. worth of Salt, not reckoning the fraight, which will arise to 7000. li. more: and whereas it stands those that carrie it

---

[1] See above, pp. 123–4.
[2] This paragraph is strongly reminiscent of a passage in John Smith's *Description of New England* (1616); see *Works*, I, 194.

thither now, at the least xx. d. the bushell, it may be made in *Newfoundland* (Pannes being erected for the same purpose) under the value of iij. d. the bushell. which may easily be performed, in regard that one Panne will make above 20. Bushels of good Salt in every 24. houres, onely with one mans labour; the salt water & fire-wood excepted, which may be there had with little paines and no charge.[1]

The profite which may come by the land plantation, is questionlesse very great, if the skinnes and furres of the wilde Beasts onely, which are there found in great quantity, were duely valued. As for example; Deere, Bevers, Marterns, blacke Foxe, Seales, Otters, Ounces or Leopards, Buffles, Lusarnes[2] and Sables: of which skinnes there have in one yeare beene brought into *France* (from those Westerne parts)[3] not so few as 25000. It appeares by an Act of Parliament made 2 *Ed.* 6. that the Trade out of *England* to *Newfoundland,* was commonly frequented in those dayes:[4] which being neere 80. yeres since, its to be marvailed, that by the negligence of our men, the countrey, in all this time, hath beene no better searched. Yet upon such slender relations as the Fishermen make after their yearely voyages thither, it may certainly be concluded, that there is nothing which our East and Northerly countries of *Europe* yeeld, but the like also may be had from thence as plentifully by time & industry, namely, Ropes, Pitch, Tarre, Soape-ashes, Deale-boords, Masts for Shipps, Hydes, Furres, Flaxe, Hempe, Corne, and many more.

The facilitie and Easinesse of this plantation, may bee made apparant divers wayes: first, in regard of the neerenesse in situation, it being not above twelve or fourteene dayes sayle from the West of *Ireland*: in relation to which, it is the next countrey unto it of any part of AMERICA, and neere halfe the way betweene *Ireland* and *Virginia*.

Secondly, in regard of the healthfulnesse and temperature of the ayre; it lying betweene the degrees of 46. and 53. Northerly Latitude.[5] A clyme approved, both by reason and experience, to bee farre more agreeable to our constitutions, then countries lying neerer the Sunne, and consequently abounding with excessive heate. As for the opinion, conceived by diverse Marriners, of the extremitie of colde in that countrey, because sometimes they finde it so when the Isles of Ice passe alongst the shoare: it may bee answered, That the Ice found there in

The profite by the land commodities

Ann. Dom. 1584. [sic]

The Easinesse of this plantation.

---

[1] See above, p. 142.   [2] Lynxes.
[3] I.e. the St. Lawrence.
[4] An act of 1548 classed the Newfoundland fishery with the old-established fisheries of Iceland and Ireland.
[5] He uses Whitbourne's latitudes; see above, p. 116.

the Spring of the yeare, is not originally of that clymate, but rather comes from the more Northerly parts of the world, driven by the Northerly windes, neere that coast; where (within a verie short time) it is consumed by the warmth of the countrey. For the proofe whereof, the Letters written from thence the seventeenth of August last 1622. from Captaine WYNE, Governour of Master Secretarie CALVERTS plantation, may bee alledged, whose verie wordes are these: *Neyther was it so colde here the last Winter as in* ENGLAND *the yeare before. I remember but three severall dayes of hard weather indeede, and they not extreame neyther: for I have knowne greater Frosts, and farre greater Snows in our owne countrey.*[1]

A third inducement for the easie planting of this countrey, is the commoditie of shipping, which yearely goe thither out of *England*, in a manner emptie, to the number of two hundred and fiftie sayle; whereby the provisions for the plantation may not onely be carried at an easie rate, but the planters, everie five moneths, much comforted with the sight of a great number of their countreymen.

Fourthly, omitting to speake of the securitie this plantation hath from the invasion of the Savages, there being never anie seene in those parts, nor without two or three hundred miles off [sic] the intended plantation. Likewise letting passe the securitie of this Trade from the imbargement of forraine Princes, it is necessarie that something be spoken of the commodities which the countrey yeelds for the use and behoofe of man.

The Woods of the countrey are Firre trees, able to mast anie Shippe, Pines and Cypresse trees, all yeelding Gumme and Turpentine: There are also Oakes, Ceders, Hathornes, Birch-trees, Alder, Willow, Filberds, Cherrie-trees, Peare-trees, Mulberry-trees, &c. Roses as common as Brambles; Straw-berries, Goose-berries, and Raspis as common as grasse. There is much open ground, producing excellent grasse; whereof the large breede of cattell, in the Northerne plantation there, hath given proofe sufficient.[2] The countrey is replenisht with manie goodly Springs, Rivers, and Lakes, and those very delightfull and wholsome. There are great store of Hawkes, Partridges, Pheasants, Thrushes, Black-birds, Canary birds, Nightingales, &c. There are also infinite numbers of Geese, Duckes, Pigeons, Gulls, Penguins, Godwits, Curlewes, Swanns, &c. The Rivers and Harbours are stored with Salmonds, Peales, Eeles, Herring, Mackarell, Flounders, Cod, Trouts,

---

[1] Quoted from the letter printed in full above, pp. 200–4.
[2] See above, p. 201.

Lobsters, Cre-fish,[1] Oysters and Muskles:[2] in the later of which, there have beene found above fortie Pearles in one Muskle, and generally all have some. There is a certaine report of a Portugall that found one Pearle worth three hundred Ducats.

Such English Seedes as are transplanted there prosper aswell, and better, then in *England*, as Beanes exceeding good, Pease as high as a man of extraordinarie stature, Raddish, Cabbedge, Turneps, Carretts, and all the rest of the like goodnesse. At the *Bristow* plantation there was as goodly corne the last Summer as can be in anie part of *England*. They are also well furnished with Swine, and a large breed of Goates, fairer by farre then those that were sent over at first. The Vines which were sent thither, doe prosper very well, whereby it is to be assured that anie thing that growes in *England*, will thrive and flourish there exceedingly.[3]

Lastly, the present and speedie return of commoditie the first yeare by the fishing onely, is a matter of no small consequence for the easie support and upholding of this plantation: which will the more plainly bee made manifest, if the manie advantages and commodities, which the Planters have over them who onely come to fish, and returne againe, be righly [*sic*] and truely considered.

For first,[4] they who both fish and plant, neede carrie no more men then they doe which goe to fish onely. For example: a Shippe or Barque which usualy doth carrie thither foure and thirtie men, doth not make use of above twentie of them for sayling of the same Shippe; so that the other foureteene serve for nothing but building of stages, barrelling and salting of fish, and other the like land imployments: insomuch that both in going thither and returning back, they are but needlesse and unprofitable feeders. Now these being left there, the charge of transporting and feeding them is not onely saved; but the ship (which before was cumbred with them and their provisions) is, by this meanes, become more capable of any maner of fraight.

Next, they (who plant aswell as fish) endanger not their shippes, in setting out too early in the yeare, nor consume so much victualls; as they that goe onely to fish, doe, for no other end, but that thereby they may get the better choyse of harbours and stages.

Thirdly, they shall have their stages, houses, and boats kept safely

---

[1] Crayfish.
[2] His list of Newfoundland's resources is very similar to Whitbourne's; see above, pp. 121–2.
[3] See above, pp. 201–2.
[4] Each of the five points that follows is taken from Whitbourne; see above, pp. 131–4.

in their absence; whereas those who goe for nothing but to fish, are at least twentie days in building of new stages: likewise their Boats are oftentimes split, and most yeares many a hundred pounds worth of fish spoyled meerely for want of houses and convenient places to put it in.

Fourthly, the Planters, by fishing in those times the ships are absent, may continually provide their lading against their comming; whereby they may, with ease, make three voyages in one Summer: whereas they who fish onely, make but one.

Lastly, they may make Salt there (as hath beene said before) under three pence the bushell; whereas it stands them in, who bring it thither, at the least twentie pence the bushell.

The Necessitie of this plantation.

Now concerning the Necessitie of this imployment, and the like, there are two principall inducements: the one whereof, is the decay of Trade; the other, the over-aboundance of people. The decay of Trade is so apparent, and the remedies thereof so hopelesse, considering the warres thoroughout Christendome; as these times doe fitly seeme to paralell the dayes of king EDWARD the sixt, wherein such difficultie was then found in everie place for the venting of the English cloathes, as by an order of State it was decreed that Shippes should bee sent forth under the conduct of Sir *Hugh Willoughby* and *Richard Chancellor*, for the discoverie of new countries, lying towards the Northeast, whereby the commodities of *England* might that way bee dispersed: which designe succeeded so happily, that although Sir *Hugh Willoughby* lost his life in the action, yet *Richard Chancellor* proceeded so fortunately and prosperously on his voyage, that in the end he discovered a passage by Sea unto the vast dominions of the Emperour of *Russia*, which for that time supplied the former defect of trade, by venting great quantities of English wares, namely Cloath, Tinne, and Leade, into those countries. This trade being now in a maner decayed and lost, may with as great reason and probabilitie, bee renued by new discoveries made towards the North-west. For, omitting that the Savages (which inhabite upon the firme land of AMERICA) when they come to have but a taste of civilitie, will make wonderfull account of our garments and apparell, as well for the diversitie of the colours, wherein they are exceedingly delighted, as for the necessitie of covering, especially in those Northerly Regions; yet in another respect it may bee effected, and that is by the discoverie of the North-west passage (whereof there is great hope) leading into *China*, *Iapan*, and other rich countries of the East.

Which passage, as it hath beene often attempted by the English

Nation, yet never with such encouragement of successe as of late yeares; so the countrey of *Newfoundland*, lying in lesse then sixe dayes saile from the entrance into the said passage,[1] may serve as a singular instrument for the accomplishing of so glorious an enterprise, which (according to the opinion of *Babtista Ramusius*, and other learned men) hath hitherto beene reserved for some renowmed [*sic*] Prince, or worthie man, whereby hee might make himselfe rich, and the world happie.[2]

Moreover, the people in these parts being encreased to such excessive numbers, as the land seemes alreadie to groane under the multitude of the inhabitants; the disburthening of them at home, and the multiplying of them abroade, were, without all question, a worke of great desert, and worthie the undertaking: for as much as by this meanes so manie reall and royal effects may be produced, that is to say, the Christian Religion propagated, his Majesties Dominions enlarged, his Customes and Revenues augmented, numbers of people relieved, the private Adventurers enriched, the commodities of the Kingdome vented, and great wealth in a short time returned.

FINIS.

Conditions propounded by the right honourable the Lord Viscount *Falkland*, Lo: Deputie generall of the Kingdome of IRELAND; to all such as wil joine with him for the plantation of a Colonie in the South-East parts of *Newfoundland*.

Whosoever[3] doth adventure one hundred pounds, towards the charges of this next yeares voyage, and deliver the same unto Sir SAMUEL SMITH of the Citie of *Dublin* Knight,[4] Treasurer for the said Plantation, or to the Treasurer for the time being, before the first of November next ensuing the date hereof, shall not onely have his equal part proportionably of the benefite which may be yearely be gotten there by the Fishing; but also such part of the benefite as may be gotten by the labours and industry of those which shall yearely be sent to remaine there, as Servants to the Adventurers, under the command of Sir FRANCIS TANFIELD knight, Governour of the Colony, and of

---

[1] Either Hudson or Davis Strait. There had been a series of north-west passage voyages in the second decade of the seventeenth century, beginning with Henry Hudson's expedition of 1610.

[2] In his section dealing with voyages in search of a north-west passage, Hakluyt quotes from the preface to the third volume of Ramusio, *Delle navigationi et viaggi*, in which he says: 'But it seemeth that God doth yet still reserve this great enterprise for some great prince to discover this voyage of Cathaia.' *Principal navigations*, VII, 150.

[3] In the original this section is printed in italics with key words in roman; here the arrangement is reversed.   [4] See above, p. 43.

such as shall be joyned with him, as assistants, for the well ordring of the intended plantation.

Also everie such Adventurer as aforesaid, shall likewise have the one halfe part and prerogative of one Harbour, Bay or Roade, lying on the North side of *Trinitie Bay*, and the circuit of two thousand acres of such Landes and Woods as are next adioyning thereunto, to be holden in Fee for ever, by the yearely rent of one penny the yeare for every such hundred acres.

Also he shall have in Fee for ever, a convenient place to build a Stage and necessarie roomes to salt Fish on, and to build a dwelling house, and other convenient houses, neere unto the Harbours of *Formosa* and *Renowse*, with a sufficient circuit of ground to dry Fish on, and for some other purposes, fit for a ship of fourescore tunns burthen.

Upon condition, that every such Vndertaker doe, within three yeares after the date of his Graunt, maintaine upon the said Land, to his owne use and benefite, eight persons at the least: paying as yearely rent for the same, the summe of ten shillings.

And whosoever shall adventure two hundred pounds, shall have a whole Harbour or Roade to himselfe in Fee, and foure thousand acres of Land, lying on the North side of Trinity Harbour, and ground to build Stages and Houses upon, neere the Harbours of *Formosa* and *Renowse*, fit for a Shippes voyage of one hundred and sixtie Tunnes burthen:

Upon condition, to pay double the rent, and to maintaine as many people more upon his Land, as hee is tyed too, which adventures but one hundred pounds.

And whosoever shall adventure more then one hundred pounds, or lesse, be it fourescore, threescore, fiftie, thirtie, twentie or ten pounds, shall have more or lesse proportionably in every respect, what hee shall have that adventures two hundred pounds.

Also any Labourer or Artificer, that is willing to adventure his person in this action, shall not onely receive good wages by the yeare, such as he shall be agreed withall for at his sending thither, and have liberty to return upon halfe a yeares warning, given by him to the Governour in *Newfound-land*; but likewise have (if hee continue there five yeares) to him and his heyres in Fee, over and above his said yearely wages, one hundred acres of Land, in the South part of that Countrey, if hee will continue there to live, or any other for him, paying but one penny rent by the yeare for the said hundred acres.[1]

---

[1] The italics end here.

If anie man (that wil be an Adventurer, eyther in person or purse) desire to bee more fully informed, touching anie thing herein contained, let him bee pleased to repaire unto Sir *Samuel Smiths* house, in the Citie of Dublin aforesaid, and there he shall receive such further satisfaction, as hee or anie other, in reason can require.

FINIS.

13. 27 Feb. 1625/6   RICHARD WHITBOURNE TO LORD FALKLAND[1]

Right honorable Lord. My most humble & bounden dutie in all respectes is & shall be every most trulie remembred vnto your good Lordshipp in what I may by Gods assistaunce &c.—

This daie I received your Lordships Letter dated the 10th of September last, which was before I came from Dublin, and withall a Letter from master Chaloner[2] bearing date the 26th daie of December last, Soe as I feare your Lordship maie take some offence against mee in not returning answeare to your Lordships foresaid Letter vntill now. I did expect to haue heard from your Lordship at Christide last as master Iohn Veale[3] sent mee worde from Kilbigam I should, and therevppon I made staie of some fitt fishermen for your Lordships service to be sent to Dublin, and because I heard never a word from your Lordship nor any other therein, I caused those men to dispose themselves otherwise; I deliuered your Lordships Letter directed to the right reuerent Lord Bishopp of Exeter,[4] and his Lordship was most glad to heare soe from your Lordship, and your right noble Ladie and of all your Lordships right Honourable Sonnes & daughters,[5] as I did more at large acquaint his Lordship withall; and his Lordship did them most worthile Commend of both your sonnes whome he knew well to haue many good partes in them, & did alsoe wish to haue the Companie of your Lordships second sonne[6] to liue here in this Countrey with him, wherevnto I

---

[1] B.L., Sloane MS 3827, ff. 67–8v.

[2] A servant of Falkland's, whom he seems to have used as a courier. *CSP Ire., 1625–1632*, pp. 12, 104.

[3] Veale, or Veel, was Falkland's secretary and a relative of secretary of state, Edward Nicholas. He may have been the John Veale who matriculated from Trinity college, Cambridge, in 1612. *Ibid.*, pp. 218, 420; J. and J. A. Venn, *Alumni Cantabrigienses*, pt. 1, vol. IV (London, 1927), p. 297.

[4] Valentine Cary (d. 1626), a connection of the Carys, lords Hunsdon; educated at Cambridge; became bishop of Exeter in 1621. Fuller, *Worthies*, II, 546; Le Neve, *Fasti*, p. 83.

[5] By his wife, Elizabeth, Falkland had five sons and six daughters.

[6] Lawrence, or Lorenzo, Cary (1613–1642).

answeared that I would signifie soe much vnto your Lordship, There
haue bene a great nomber died with the plague in the Cittie of Exeter
this yeare, & as yet not altogether ceased; and before my Lord Bishopp
removed from thence, one of his servantes died therein, wherevppon
his Lordship removed to a house 7 myles from it, and there with his
familie soe leived as none should come nere him, fearing the worst,
In which tyme his Lordship procured manie hundred poundes, & sent
for the reliefe of the Inhabitauntes of the said Cittie, such summes as
the like hath not bene knowne by an Bishopp of this Kingdom within
his Diocesse; and by reason of the saide infection; The worshipfull your
Lordships kinsman William Cary Esquire[1] removed from Exeter 40
miles from thence; and Sir Fraunces Fulford[2] setled himselfe to his
house in Dorsettshire; Soe as I sent your Lordships Letter vnto him by a
friende, and deliuered your Lordships for master William Carie to my
Lord Bishopp, and his Lordship was well pleased to deliver the same
with his owne hand and conferred with him concerning the Contentes
of both your Lordships Letters; presentlie vppon such conference with
my Lord Bishopp, there came news partely what ill successe his Maiestie
Fleete had, that went to the Coaste of Spaine,[3] which I believe your
Lordship hath bene at large informed of. Which late voyage hath much
daunted many men that before bare good affections to plantations, and
the Newfoundland voyages, that will not now be perswaded vnto
neither of them. / What my Lord Bishopp, and those foresaid worthy
Gentlemen will doe in adventering this yeare to the Newfoundland with
your Lordship theie being Parliament men,[4] I know not; As for the
Letter your Lordship wrote to one Iohn Streate of Dartmouth, he tooke
it very thankfullie, he being long tyme a great adventurer to the
Newfoundland, the last yeare he had 7 or 8 Shippes there for his owne
accompt, and now afraide to sett any one Shipp there, and divers men
are soe doubtfull to adventure there, that it is not like there will be
manie English Shipps there this yeare, & those that doe are like to be
in some danger. /[5] And wheras it hath pleased your Lordship so

[1] Perhaps William Cary of Clovelly (1576–1652), F. H[arrison], *The Devon Carys* (New
York, 1920), facing p. 180, pp. 183–4.
[2] A member of a prominent Devonshire gentry family; b. 1583, son of Sir Thomas
Fulford of Fulford; educated at Oxford and the Middle Temple; knighted 1606. Wood,
Athenae Oxonienses, II, 538.
[3] The disastrous Cadiz expedition of 1625.
[4] Fulford represented Devon in the parliament of 1625. A William Carre esq. was one
of the two members for the borough of St Mawes, Cornwall, in 1626, the other being
a Sir Henry Cary. *Parliaments of England, 1213–1702* (London, 1878), I, 463, 468.
[5] In 1625 twenty-seven English ships coming back from the fishery had been captured
by Barbary pirates. *CSP Dom., Add., 1625–1649*, p. 217.

worthily to signifie vnto mee, that a master of a Shipp being in Southwales, that came from Newfoundland should reporte vniustlie of mee & my good indeuours, and the greate charge that I was as, that yeare when I was at Newfoundland, with a Commission which was sent mee from the high courte of Admiraltie, wherein were divers thinges referred to my care & discretion, for the better reforming & setling of some fitt orders & gouerment amongst such as yearlie trade to that Countrey; and alsoe to vse my best indeuours for the calling home of some erring Subiectes, such as did make mee many large promises towardes my great lost [sic], & hinderaunce received by them in my voyages the yeare before in that Countrey, as also towardes my charge in returning there againe, with their pardons, or notiz therof, that it was graunted, wherein I spent much tyme and a greate deale of money, in hiring of a Shipp, men & victuals at my owne charge to saile there as I did, but could never receive a penney towardes the same from Captaine Manwayring, and also with Captaine Easton prevailed much for the good of all theire voyages; as it is well knowne,[1] But sithence I haue better observed, that some worthie men, that haue had great places of commaund committed vnto theire worthie calling, haue bene alsoe vniustly spoken of by dishonest and some vnworthie persons;[2] Soe as I finde by proofe, what whomsoever shall haue to doe with such a multitude of disorderlie persons as I had, then, and deale never soe vprightlie as I did, yet there will be some dubious Buzzardes that will speake vntrulie of him, though the wiser sorte conceive never soe well of him; For with my foresaid Commission Shipp and men soe hired; I sailed from the North of Trinitie Baie, to the south so farre as Farriland Plantation,[3] & backe againe to the North in all the best tyme of the fishing Season, vnto moste of the Harbours in that Circuite, & setled such fitt orders amongst them, as theie thought good vnder theire handes & seales, which presentmentes at my returne I represented into the high Courte of the Admiraltie, which was there by many worthie men well approved, though towardes all such charge paine & losses in my voyage; there was not any of the fishermen that gave a penney, except it were some of them in 2 harbours that did like the course soe well which I then tooke, did earnestlie entreate mee to come vnto them with my Commission, and they would willinglie give mee some Content towardes my hinderaunce, paines & charge of my shipp,

---

[1] See above, pp. 113–14.
[2] Perhaps a reference to Falkland's own troubles with Adam Loftus.
[3] There was, of course, no plantation at Ferryland in 1615.

10 men & victuals; wherevppon I sailed vnto them, & with all their consentes setled such orders as other Harbours; and theie then afterwardes brought to my Shipp some smale Contribucíon as they list therevnto; which was not able to defraie halfe the losses & charge which I sustayned in comming to them vnto the said 2 harbours, And although divers of them haue yearelie since broken the orders, & spoyled the Harbours, burne [sic] the woodes, & doe what they list there, it lyes not in mee to remedie it, neither could I doe more there, then I did for your Lordships good at my last being imployed there by your Lordshipp, by reason there was such a distraction amongst those which your Lordship had formerlie sent there to plant, and some fishermen before I arived there, as Sir Fraunces Tanfeild may certifie your Lordships if ye please; and as he said to mee, & Iohn Reeves, that after such tyme as Captaine Lenthorpp returned to him againe, that he did often solicitt & laboure with Sir Fraunces Tanfeild that he should quarrell with mee, soe as they both might bring mee out of your Lordships favour; though I am sure that neithe [sic] of them had no more Iust cause so to envie mee, then the least Child in Dublin hath, neither that envious master which your Lordships writes of, though he & some other, haue much abused mee when I was in Ireland,[1] that one should saie that when I had sharked from them, I went awaie; with hatefull worde, there was never any man that did, or could iustlie charge mee withall, for such I am, that my goeing there, with the foresaid Commission, and that I haue beene there twise since to further the said plantation, hath loosted [sic] me aboue 500^{li} besides that I am out about my bookes, that are printed & dispersed the summe of 90^{li} to the printer & 150^{li} of my charge in 5 yeares attendaunce thereon & know not how to recover it againe;

Thus craveing your Lordships pardon to theise my tedious lynes, does most humblie beseech the Continuance of your Lordships lawfull fauors towardes mee that I am much griued to be soe crost as I haue bene; and especiallie by reason that haveing consumed so much of my meanes & tyme as I haue to further the Newfoundland Plantation that now some which I know well doe envie mee should soe vntrulie enforme your Lordship as to saie I had in any respect miscarried my selfe against your Lordship, as to the hinderaunce of any Plantation or fishermen there or elsewhere; &c; Soe with my prayers to God; that the Sumne [sic] of your Lordships vertue may never sett, nor the flowers of your

---

[1] Whitbourne had been in Ireland during the summer of 1625; he had been knighted by Falkland in August. Shaw, *Knights*, II, 189.

Lordships fauors towardes mee maie never wither, the divine grace of your noble hearte maie never decaie. But that your Lordship maie be ever succesful & happie in all thinges, both in heaven and vppon Earth &c I rest

   Exmouth 27th February 1625

     your Lordshipps ever in all dutie and service,
     in what I may to be commaunded/
     Ric: whytbourne:

[*Addressed:*] To the right Honourable viscount of Falkland Lord Deputie generall of Ireland, at his Maiesties Castell in Dublin theise I praye./

[*Endorsed:*] Sir Richard Whitbourne 27° February 1625 Received 1° April 1626 Newfoundland businesse

  14. 13 July 1626 A REFERENCE FOR RICHARD
         WHITBOURNE[1]

Worthy Sir/
This bearer Sir Richard Whitbourne is the gentlmane whome I spake to you for aboue, that you would comend him to my lord[2] from me, you wisht he should come vp as I then told you of his Sufficiencie, soe now I Write vnto you, that I assure my selfe that my Lord hath not a man to comaund a shipp of more escperience and a man that is well acquainted with all the portes in Christendome Wherefore lett me intreat you to shewe him what favour you may & be a meanes to helpe him to a good place and what kindnes you shall shewe him, I will take it as done to my selfe, Iohn Drake[3] comet[h] vp presently whoe will acquaint with all [*sic*] the busines concerning the prisses And this ever restinge

Ashe the 13th of Iuly 1626

     your assured freind to dispose of
      E. Drake

[*Addressed:*] To my Worthy Freind Edward Nicholas Esquire Secretary to my Lord Dukes grace these[4]

[*Endorsed:*] R[eceived] 16° Iuly: 1626 Master Drake of Ashe recommendeth Sir Richard Whitbourne to be a Captaine

---

[1] P.R.O., SP 16/31, 71.   [2] The Duke of Buckingham.
[3] The son, or perhaps the grandson, of Sir Francis Drake.
[4] Nicholas (1593–1669) had succeeded Thomas Aylesbury as Buckingham's secretary in 1625; in 1626 he became clerk to the council and in 1641 one of the secretaries of state. *DNB.*

15. 10 Nov. 1626   RICHARD WHITBOURNE SEEKS EMPLOYMENT FROM THE DUKE OF BUCKINGHAM[1]

And if your Grace be alreadie furnished with such fitt ouerseers, as are to your Graces good likinge so as there is no occassion of your suppliantes imployement therein; Then his humble desire is, that your Grace would be pleased to conferre vpon him some other fitt office as either to be one of your Overseers of the Navie (wherein[2] your Grace shall finde him faithfull carefullie, & iustly to performe such true seruice as your Grace maie anie waie expect from him in that trust.

And if your Grace haue no such fitt place for his imployement, That then your Grace would be pleased to appoynte & constitute him to be Captaine in one of his Maiesties shipps which are shortlie to be imployed at Sea;[3] Wherein your suppliant confidently assureth himselfe by Gods assistance to make his iudgement & valour so knowen, as that hee shall not onelie make good the best opinion that euer the right honourable Lord Deputie of Ireland or anye other noble and worthie parsonage haue had on him, but also approue to your Grace, what hee desireth your Grace might anie waie conceiue of him.

And if your Grace maie likewise be pleased to pervse the true Copie of a Certificate hervnto annexed,[4] which was presented vnto our former late most dread Soueraigne in your Grace suppliantes behalf, by the favourable opinion of the foresaid Lord Deputie, and the then right honourable Sir George Caluert Knight so as his Maiesty might bene [sic] pleased partlie thereby and also partly by both their honours so worthilie certified of your Graces Suppliantes former lief and good behauiour, as that thereby he was put in some good hope his Maiesty would bene [sic] pleased to conferre some fitt reward vpon him towardes his former good endeuours & seruices, as also towardes some great charge which your Graces suppliant was at in bringing of one Thomas Robinson, who was borne at Lynne in Norffolk from a monasterie in the Citie of Lishbone in Portugall vnto your suppliantes home in ye Countie of Deuon.[5] And from thence your Graces suppliant did presentlie vpon his arriuall there write vnto your Graces Secretarie the right worshipfull Thomas Aylesbury of the said Robinson and what hee had related vnto your Suppliant.

---

[1] P.R.O., CO 1/4, 16. Extract.   [2] The brackets are not closed.
[3] Perhaps the fleet which was to be sent to attack Le Havre.
[4] The certificate is missing.
[5] Robinson claimed that he had been persuaded to enter an English nunnery at Lisbon as a secretary and mass priest and that he had spent two years there. In 1622 he published a pamphlet detailing the alleged immoral practices of the nuns. DNB.

And therevpon by order from his late Maiestie your Graces Suppliant brought the said Robinson to his great charge before the right honorable Sir Robert Naunton Knight,[1] then Secretarie to his Maiestie to whome the said Robinson related somuch as hee formerly had to your Suppliant. And the said Sir Robert Naunton did much commend your Suppliant therein, did also forthwith imploye the said Robinson to seeke where hee could finde out anie of such trecherous people as hee had said were come from Spaine & Portugall to doe some mischief vnto the state of this kingdome, but what the said Robinson did therein after your Graces suppliant had brought him to the foresaid Sir Robert Naunton, your Suppliant heard no more of yt, although his honour did then put your Suppliant in some good hope that hee should receiue some fitt reward from his Maiestye towardes his great charge & good seruice in bringing the said Robinson as aforesaid, but as yet your Graces Suppliant neuer receiued anie recompence towardes the same, neither anye answere vnto his foresaid Certificate. By reason that presently vpon presenting the same vnto his late Maiestie by the foresaid Sir George Caluert, your Graces Suppliant was sent for by seueral lettres from the foresaid right honourable Lord Deputie to repaire speedilie vnto his Lordshipp into Ireland, which accordingly your Suppliant did, And therevnto the foresaid Sir George Caluert did also much hasten him, who did then and at seuerall times before, confidently promise your Suppliant that hee would be verie mindefull & ernest to sollicite our said late deade Soueraigne in your Graces suppliantes behalf, whereby to obtayne some fitt reward for him towardes his former good seruices and seuerall great charges which hee had bene at as aforesaid, yet notwithstanding the foresaid Sir George Caluert did nothing therein for your suppliant after hee was gone ouer vnto the Lord deputie of Ireland, nor in some other thinge as hee had formerlie promised him.

Your suppliant humblie desires your Grace maie be pleased to take the premisses into your right noble & fauourable consideracion, as also his seruice which hee presenteth herewith to be euer truelie deuoted vnto your Graces pleasure in what hee may and hee shall willingly attend thereon, so as hee may knowe either from your Grace or from your Graces Secretarie the worshipfull Edward Niccollas whether it shalbe your Graces pleasure to conceiue so well of his former good endeuours and seruices and such good reportes as haue bene giuen of him as that your Grace shall thinke him a man fitt to be in your Graces fauour, So as hee maie liue in hope to haue some reward towardes his former desertes and expence of his time & meanes as aforesaid.

[1] See above, p. 100, n. 8.

And if your Suppliant maie obtaine your Graces fauour so as hee maie haue some fitt place whereby to defraie his expence in attending thereon at your Graces pleasure, hee shall then also be readie to deliuer some other fitt reasons vnto your Grace by what hee hath obserued in some part of his travelles. In what fitt manner his maiesties most hopefull plantacion in the Newfound land and all such of his maiesties Subiectes as shall yerely trade there may be fittly secured from the danger of such enemyes as shall arriue on that Coast to do them wronge, without anie charge vnto his Maiestie as also not to be burdensome vnto such of his Maiesties Subiectes as shall yerely trade there (although[1] by them the charge to maintaine a couple of good shippes and two pinnaces in warlike manner on that Coast should be yerelie defrayed, by whose guard the traders to that Coast maie yerely make a greater benifitt to themselues then as now they durst not do and likewise thereby his maiesties most hopefull plantacion in that Country to flourishe and prosper much better then anie other plantacion his maiesty hath in anie of those westerne partes of the world, and likewise thereby a great benifitt may redound yerelie to your Grace by mayntayninge of such shipps of warre on that Coast, as your Graces Suppliant shalbe readie to deliuer his opinion therein.

16. [LORD FALKLAND'S INSTRUCTIONS TO HIS SETTLERS][2]

To the well affected planters in new fownde lande

first of all I wishe them to plante in the the [sic] most extreme parte of the lan[d] northwestwarde, wheare the bottom of Trinitie Baye & Patentia [sic] baye doth meete to keepe the natiues out from the maine land that lieth towardes the north and north-west; which being Carefullie donne & obserued, they will have the better parte of $\frac{2}{3}$ parte of land of the bignes of Ireland to themselues, in the South and Shouth [sic] east partes of the Ilande, wheare neuer a natiue doth inhabite, Soe that onlie heare they shall have noe more neede but to defend themselues of a foraine enemie which most [sic] be kept out by secureinge the sea Coast & harbours in that parte/

Secondlie to take Care that what nation soeuer doth plant there that they speake onlie the pure Englishe tounge & that they haue but one Religion which being well obserued they will all increase in Amitie and

---

[1] The brackets are not closed.   [2] N.L.W., 5390 D. Damaged.

love & be able in tym[e] to make a braue Conquest vpon the Ilande/

Thirdlie that noe sort of women bee suffred to goe thither but the Englishe & such as have hade good educac*i*on in Englande which will make a good nation in tyme for those will maintaine the language to ther Children & then it is noe great matt*er* of wha[t] nation the men bee soe the women bee Englishe/

fowrthlie I wishe that all those that have proporc*i*ons there doe plante themselues first of all with good store of Cattle such as Cann live in hard grownde, Cattell of Scotlande & the Northerne p*ar*tes of Irelande & some of North Wales I hould wilbee fittest there such as Cann live in the woode & without fodder in the winter and that they onlie of 2 or 3 yeares groweth & in tyme when hey & grasse is provided & the grownde broken vpp then larger may bee sent thither

Some mares & some horses as alsoe swine & good sto[re] of goat*es* most [sic] alsoe bee sent thither/

Those that goe to plant lett them Carie but few peopl[e] with them & onlie such as are Husbandmen w*hich* will [take] paines in the grownde and such as will not live idle & [waste] vittells & Cattell w*hich* should serve for breed for such wil[l] increase but to fast in tyme & therfore of gentreye n[oe] more to be sent thither then soe much as shall bee tho[ught] fitt to Comaunde the husband men/

Lastlie & Cheiflie that none of our planters doe plant themselues amounge the natiues for that is but onlie a drowneinge of our men, But to strengthene our Ile, if we Canne may take some of the young breed of the natiues & bringe them vpp amounge our selues but the[y] most [sic] not be passeinge 5 or 6 yeers olde when wee take them from there parent*es* wherbye they [will] not haue Remembrance of them s[oon]

17. SIR HENRY SALUSBURY'S GRANT[1]

My graunt from my lorde fawklande in new found Land dot[h] Comm*e*nce and begin*e* from the first pointe of the Northerly side of the baye of formosa by a right imm*a*genarye line run*n*ninge from the Easte to the west vnto the bay of Pla[centia] lyinge on*e* the North side of the said lyne bowndinge on*e* th[e] Lord Baltimoores lande/

Alsoe the proportion of lande in Trinitie baye to Comm*e*nce [and]

[1] N.L.W., 5390 D. Damaged. Henry Salusbury (1589–1632) had been educated at the Middle Temple; he inherited the family estate of Llewenni on the death of his father in 1612 and was made a baronet in 1619. *DWB.*

begin*e* by a right lyne beeinge drawne from the poy[nt] of $49\frac{1}{4}$ to run*ne*
duely sowthweste from the North thorowgh the myddest of Trinitie
Baye all the lan[de] lyinge to the Sowthwarde of that baye as it runn[es]
by a right lyne inclusively to the westerly sea/

18. ADVICE ON PLANTING IN NEWFOUNDLAND, GIVEN TO SIR HENRY SALUSBURY[1]

given to S*ir* Henry Salu*s*bury by me Io*hn* Poyntz[3]

Instructions given my m*aste*r Iohn Guy alderman of Bristol[2]
    Ane estimate for the victuals for 8 p*er*sons for a yeare to inhabite
in New found lande

	l	s	d
Sea prov*it*ion only — Bisket 4 hundred weight	3	0	0
beere 6 barrell	1	16	0
driefish 4 C	1	16	0
Sea and lande prov*ic*ion — meale 9⁰ bushe*l*es of good drie wheat to be put up in drie caske	22	10	0
20 barrill of caske	1	0	0
malt 90 bushe*l*es to be put into caske	15	0	0
10 hogsheades of caske	1	10	0
a malt mill			
hops 45^{l} weight	1	2	6
peason 16 bushel*l*es	3	4	0
Beanes for the garden 1 bushell			
butter 4 kinterkins	7	0	0
Cheese 3 hundred^{l} weight	3	6	0
Vineger a kinterkine	1	0	0
Porke 4 C^{li} weight	5	12	0
beefe to be salted 10 C^{li} weight	12	0	0
bacon 6 flitches	4	0	0
sallet oyle 6 gallons	1	4	0
honey two gallons	0	8	0
candles 10 dozen pound*es*	2	0	0
oatemeale groat*es* 4 bushells	0	16	0
A firkin of Aquavitae	1	12	0

[1] N.L.W., 5390 D. Damaged.
[2] John Guy remained an active member of the Bristol city government until the year before his death in 1629. *DCB*, I.
[3] Probably a member of the gentry family of Iron Acton in Gloucestershire. *Trans. Bristol and Gloucestershire Archaeological Society*, XII (1887–8), 153.

a firkin of canarie wine	I	12	0
a firkin of methaglyne[1]	0	16	0
A pecke of mustarde seede	0	10	0
30^{li} worthe of Rice	0	10	0

trenchers, platters, candle stickes
cans, taps, canndells, lanternes,
dishes, bowles, spoones etc
A crocke, a cawdron 2 brasse poundes
a chaffingedish a spice morter/
Sugar
currans
reasons of the sunne
pepper
cloves
mace   to the value in all of 2^{li} worth
ginger   94^{li} 15^{s} 6^{d}
Nutmegs
Cinnamon
Tooles for buildinge and husbandrie
weapons for defence
Netes fishing lines hookes knifes etc
A smith with a paire of bellowes anvill and all other tooles with
iron and steele and some sea coale
Seede for all sortes of garden hearbes and rootes for the kitchen
Two or three heifers of kine & one bull
Two Ramme goates, and 10 femall goates
A boare and a sowe though neuer soe small
To the Southward their is a levell plaine champion countrey voide
of woods patridges and hares and fayre followinge a horse-
backe/

Theise instructions following I receaved from Nicholas Guy which
hath lived in the Bristol plantation in Newfoundland this 16
yeares/[2]

Instructions
giuen to Iohn
Poyntz by the
said nicholas
Guy/

---

[1] A drink made of honey, similar to mead.
[2] Nicholas Guy, who was probably a member of the family of John and Philip Guy
of Bristol, had been at Cupids at least since 1612, when the first English child known to
have been born in Newfoundland was born to him and his wife. Henry Crout's journal,
1612–13 (Nottingham University, Middleton MSS, Mi X 1/66).

att sea	10 tunne of Salt for 3 boates for one fishinge season	30^{li}
	3 sayles for the 3 boates	3^{li}
	3 Roades of Roapes for the 3 boates	48^{li}
	4^0 faddome of small cordage for hallyars & shottes	10^s
	3 breadboxes and 3 flagen bottelles of woode	2^s 6^d
	4 dozen and a halfe of fishingelines	31^s 6^d
	13 dozen of hookes of severall sortes	27^s
	4 splyttinge knyves and 4 gutters	6^s
	3 steeles	
	3 Hatchettes	3^s
	9 maundes for the 3 boates	4^s 6^d
	3 buckettes and 3 boles	2^s 6^d
	3 gymlettes	9^d
att the shoare	A trayne payle a bole and a funnell	2^s
	A kettle	16^d
	wooden platters 4 quarter Canns 4 bread basketts	3^s
	Halfe a hundred waight of Oackame	5^s
	100 weight of pitch	8^s
	2000 of nayles of all sortes	13^s 4^d
	Sawesers and dishes of wood	12^d
	the hire of the 3 boates in fish to the values of	40^s

13 men and a boye for the 3 boates, whereof 9 of those m[en] must be fishers att sea and 4 att land or att shoare, of those 13 you must hier heere in England a header a spilter [sic], the spilter and the header will haue [both] a yeare wages besides meate and drinke and lodging [and] washinge and wringinge the fishinge att Renooze is [many] a yeare better in the fishinge seasone with three boat[es] then it is in fishinge att Bristoll plantation the[re] is too much odds in the goodnes of the fish and much in num[ber] Blacke foxe, beavers, otters, martens, muskrattes [give] a peece to a man and you find hym vittualles or 20^s [wages] theye find their dyet and 40^s a tunne for ye goodes

A shippe of 60 tonne to bee bought will searve 5 b[oates] to transport the fish

12^{li} of powder and 6 dozen of shott will serue a fo[wling] peece a yeare/

Your owne 13 or 14 men with the hier of a master heere will conduct your barke to newefoundland or whether y[ou] will

maintaine a store house with a 100^{li} in provicion and Nicholas Guy will come and bee your tennant[1] an[d] vndertake to put you 120[li] for a 100[li] every year[e]

Every boate takes every fishinge 24000 of fish sold th[ere] for 7[s] the hundred att 120 to the hundred besydes th[e] trayne oyle that will amount from euery boates fish to a tunne and a hogeshead att the least which is now wo[rth] in Bristoll 20[li] the tunne and their in Newfoundla[nd] 12[li] the tunne which is 15[li] the 5 hogesheades 5 [bu]shelles of wheat and as much of malt with 16 bushe[lles] of Pease will fill 18 hogesheades and a barrell which [is] 4 tunne and a halfe and a barrell euery tunne will [cost] 40[s] the carrage / the furnishinge of euery boate w[ith] her implementes att sea & land doeth amount to 15[li and] you must haue a newe supply sent you one euery spr[ing] by some fast freinds that will stand by you with [beef] and wheat and Rye, & pease and apparell and [other] necessaryes for your people for their releefe, oth[erwise] you starve them with wante, and you haue no oth[er] meanes to rayse to pay for this fresh supplye yearly [but by] your fishinge and your servantes to kill rich furres w[ith] their gunnes

14[li] 14[s] 6[d] the implements att sea and land doth amou[nt] vnto to furnish one boate besydes the boate itself you may hier for the estimate of 13[s] 4[d] to be paide

You must haue a header and a spliter one boate and you shall neede noe more for your 3 boates 20[li] per annum their wages, besides meate drinke, washinge & wringing

One mans provisions for sixe monthes	li	s	d	
				Instructions
2 hundred and a halfe of Biskett	1	12	6	given [to Iohn Poyntz] by
2 hogesheades and a halfe of beare	1	05	0	[John]
a kilderkin of Porke	1	08	0	Brooke[2] dwellinge [in]
a bushell of pease	0	03	0	lance street
halfe a hundred drie fish	0	04	0	Bristoll
a butt for the bread	0	03	0	
caske for the beare	0	08	4	
caske for the pease	0	00	8	
for a mans passage out and home	1	00	0	
for a toune fraighte	2	00	0	
	8	04	6	

[1] In 1631 Guy was farming in Carbonear, apparently as a tenant of Sir Percival Willoughby's. Nicholas Guy to Sir Percival Willoughby, 1 Sept. 1631 (Nottingham University, Middleton MSS, Mi X 1/57).

[2] Probably John Brooke, a Bristol merchant and shipowner in the 1620s. P. V. McGrath, ed., *Records relating to the society of merchant venturers in the city of Bristol in the seventeenth century* (Bristol Record Society, 1952), p. 168, and *Merchants and merchandise in seventeenth-century Bristol* (Bristol Records Society, 1955), pp. 6, 124.

CHAPTER IV

SIR GEORGE CALVERT AND THE FERRYLAND COLONY

19. AN ACCOUNT OF SIR GEORGE CALVERT'S INTEREST IN NEWFOUNDLAND[1]

Anno Domini
1620

1623

Avalon
Bounds

Sir George Calvert Knight then Principal Secretary of State to King Iames purchased a part of Newfound Land, which was afterwards in the yeare 1623 granted to him & his heires by pattent from the said King vnder the great Seale of England beareing date the 7.th of Aprill 21° Iac. by which the said Tract of Land was erected into a province[2] & at his Instance called Avalon from Avalon in Somersetshire where Christianity was first received in England

And by the said pattent yᵉ said Province containes all yᵗ Intire portion of Land scituate in newfound Land as afforesaid begining Southerly from the midle part of a Certaine Neck of Land or promontary scituate betweene the two Harboures of Fermose & Aquafort and from thence following the Shore towards yᵉ north vnto the midle part or ½ way over a little harboure called in that regard petit port or petit harboure which boundeth vpon the south part of the plantacion of Sᵗ Iohns[3] Includeinge the one halfe of a Certaine fresh River yᵗ falleth into the said porte of petit harboure & soe tending along the south border of the said Colloney of sᵗ Iohns extendeth it selfe to a Certaine little bay commonly called Salmon Cove lyeing on the southside of the Bay of Conception Includeing the one halfe of the River yᵗ falleth into the said Cove as also yᵉ one halfe of yᵉ said Cove itselfe, from whence passing along the Shoare of the said Bay towards the South & reaching vnto yᵉ bottom thereof where it meets with the lands of Iohn Guy

---

[1] B.L., Sloane MS 3662, ff. 24–5. Extract. The document concludes with an account of the Calverts' involvement in Maryland. While its authorship cannot be established, it is dated 1670 and was probably prepared for Cecilius, Lord Baltimore, for use in his dispute with the Kirke family which he had renewed after the restoration.

[2] See below, pp. 258–69.

[3] In 1617 the area around St. John's had been granted by the Newfoundland company to a group of merchants, including William Payne of London who later became a member of the company's council. In 1627 Payne tried to interest Secretary Sir Edward Conway in buying shares in the lot. Cell, *English enterprise*, pp. 72, 78.

Fig. 5. George Calvert, lord Baltimore

Cittizen of Bristolle named Sea Forrest[1] is bounded with a certain River or Brooke which there falleth into the Sea and from the mouth of the said Brooke ascendeth vnto the furthest spring or head thereof from thence passeth towards the south for six miles together along the borders of the said Iohn Guy his plantacion and there crossing over

---

[1] Despite his break with the company, John Guy did receive a grant of land at the bottom of Conception Bay which he bequeathed to his sons. John Guy's will, 1625/6 (Bristol Record Office, Great Orphans Book, III, 276).

westward in a right line reacheth vnto the Bay of Placentia & ye space of one League within the bay from the shoare thereof hence turning againe towards the south passeth along the harbour of Placentia with the like distance from the shoare and discending vnto newfalkland towards the north and west part thereof strecheth its selfe in a right line eastward continuing the whole southerly lenth vpon the bounds of the said newfalkland vnto the midle part or pointe of the promentary or neck of Land afore mencioned between the Port of Fermose and Aquafort at which place is described and finished ye perambulacion of

Islands the whole precinct And thereby was farther Granted to the said Sir George Calvert all Islands and Isletts y^t are or shall be within tenn Leagues from the Easterne Shoare of the said Region towards the East together with the Fishing of all sorts of Fish

Title The said Sir George Calvert and his heires were by the said pattent Created true and absolute Lords and proprietaryes of the said Province saveing the Allegiance due to his Maiestie his heires and successors. And

Privilidges thereby was further granted to him and his heires all Royall Iurisdictions and prerogatives both Millitary & civill with ye said Province and Islands therevnto belonging To be held of his Maiestie his Heires and

Tenendum successours in Capite yielding and paying therefore to his Maiestie his
Reddendum Heires and Successors a white horse when and as often as any of them shall come into the said Province and the 5th part of all Gold and Silver

1621 Ure which shall be found there In the yeare 1621 he sent one Captain Edward Wynn to be his Governor there who built a faire house & fort

1624 at Ferryland In the yeare 1624[1] he obtained a dismission of the King from his employment of Secretary of State though with some difficulty his Maiestie haveing a particulare Affection to him by reason of his great abillities & integrety. And though he had then declared himselfe a Roman Catholique ordered him to be Continued a Privie Counsellour And at the same time Created him Lord Baltemore of Baltemore in Ireland.

After the Death of King Iames King Charles desiered his Lordship to be Continued a Privie Councellour to him Resolveing to dispence with his takeing the oath of supremacy but at his request gave him leave at Lenth to retire from Court

1627 In the yeare 1627 his Lordship transports [sic] himselfe from England to Avalon being dissattisfied with the Management of his affaires there and haveing passed a Summer Season there returned the same yeare to England & soon after to his Family which was then in Ireland

[1] Calvert resigned in February 1624/5.

In the yeare 1628 his Lordship embarks himselfe and all his Family except his eldest son[1] from Ireland to Avalon he tooke also with him Sir Robert Talbot & Master Willyam Peasely who Marryed two of his Daughters.[2] At which time (there being then warrs betwixt England and France) it pleased God to make him an Instrument to redeeme above 20 Saile of English Shipps there which had been taken by French men of Warr, whereof one Monsieur de la Rade had cheife command and afterwards to take 6 French Ships which were Fishing vpon the Costs [sic], which he sent the same yeare with a great many French men Prisoners into England.[3]

His Lordship finding Avalon by reason of the greate Colds there in Winter to disagree with his Constitucion goes from thence to Virginia in the yeare 1629...

20. August 1621   TWO LETTERS FROM EDWARD WINNE
TO SIR GEORGE CALVERT

A LETETR [sic] WRITTEN BY CAP-taine EDWARD WINNE, to the Right Honorable, Sir *George Caluert*, Knight, his Maiesties Principall secretary: from *Ferryland* in *Newfoundland*, the 26. of August, 1621. Imprinted MDCXXI.

TO THE RIGHT HO-nourable, Sir *George Caluert*, Knight, his Maiesties prin-*cipall Secretary*.

May it please your Honour,
    Vpon the 26. day of Iune, betweene 12. and 1. in the morning we did set saile, & departed from *Plimmoth*; and vpon the 4 day of *August*, (Gods name be praised for it) we safely arriued at *Feryland*. There happened nothing in our ouer-bound passage worthy your Honours leasure of reading. Our passage was somewhat tedious, the which hapned by meanes of much Westerly winds, and not without some foule weather.
    The first land we made was that to the Westward of *Cape de Raze*, and the wind at North-east, by reason whereof our ariuall aforesaid was prolonged by the space of two dayes, in the interim of which time we traueled to and againe to make good that which might maintaine

---

¹ Cecilius Calvert (1606–75), second lord Baltimore.
² Sir Robert Talbot, eldest son of Sir William Talbot of Cartown, County Kildare, married Grace Calvert. The Calverts may have become acquainted with Peasely when he served as clerk in extraordinary to the privy council. J. G. Morris, *The lords Baltimore* (Baltimore, 1874), p. 24; *APC 1621–1623*, p. 466.
³ See below, pp. 279–81.

that outwardnesse towarde our wished Harbour. Hauing the happiness
of a cleere skie all about, & both Coast and Continent without any
Rayne, Fogge or Hazines, they being in these parts the common
attendant of Easterly winds. By this commodity I had the full view
of the Coast betweene (as wee supoosed) *Cape Saint Maries*, *Cape de
Raze*, and *Cape Ballard*,[1] and as farre as *Renouze*, and as we hold alongst
the same I saw (in my meane Iudgment) the pleasantest Sea Cant[2] that
euer mine eyes beheld, for that spacious tract. It is very Champion
Country without any Hill, appearing either within Land, or vpon the
Coast, representing it selfe vnto me like a pleasant Medow, and the
Sea-banke all along of an equall height, and that so indifferent that out
of a floating Boat one may easily throw a quoit vpon the leuell Shore.
Of the fertility of the soyle I can say nothing onely that it is very
probable that much or most part thereof may proue very good with
the help of mans industry, seeming to be void of woods, and the
endowments of Harbours and Roades for Shipping *Trepassey* excepted.

Renouze is a place of great fishinge, and about a league to the
Northward of the same is the Harbour of *Formoze*, thence to *Agnafort*,[3]
another league, from thence to *Feryland* about a mile, & to *Cape Broyle*
another, including *Capling Bay* between both, being ignorant as yet of
that to the Northward of the same. But from *Renoze* to *Cape Broyle*,
for Woods and pleasant Harbours they are most pleasant to behold,
the Sea Cant hereof being vneuen and hilly, yet not extreme, but of
height indifferent, the Inland more enclining towards a Champion, and
by generall consent here, *Feryland* is as pleasant and as profitable a
Harbour as any in the Land. It is endowed with about 100. acres of
pasture land, and as much more of that which is wooddie: all which
lying to the Sea-boord of the beach, which seuers it so from the Maine,
that it is almost an Iland. There is likewise about 200. acres more, lying
close to the Harbour, the which (with some labour) may be made good
pasture land.

The Sea coast to the Northward of *Renouze*, is most capable and
fittest for Wood-land as now it is, but (most destroyed) from the
bottome of the Harbours,[4] and so inwards, for arable and (most)
pasture.

---

[1] Cape Ballard is not marked on contemporary maps, but it is found on English maps
of the late seventeenth century. See H. Harrise, *Découverte et évolution cartographique de
Terre-Neuve et des pays circonvoisins* (Paris, 1900), pp. 312, 313, plate XXII.
[2] I.e. the land bordering the sea.   [3] Aquafort.
[4] A repeated grievance of the settlers was that the annual fishermen destroyed large
amounts of timber.

Both Sea and Land heere swarme (as it were) with benefits and blessings of God for mans vse and reliefe.

The Land here is (without doubt) very fertile, for I haue since my arriuall seene Wheate, Barly and Rye, growing here full eared & kerned, the which had beene accidentally shed out of Salt Mats among Stones & Grasse. Therefore ground of better choise, well manured and fitly prepared, will doubtlesse bring forth plentifull increase, and wherefore there is no iust doubt to be made: for in reason where there is a Summer, there will be a Haruest.

Besides, there are many other inuitements, which (as it were) becken vnto your Honors perseuerance. First the commodity of the Salt, which for vent and making here may fitly and necessarily bee vndertaken. Secondly Hempe and Flaxe for cordage, and thred for necessary vses, as also for Nets and Lines for fishing, Tarre, Iron and Timber in some measure, and places to be had for boords and building, & also for Masts, and yards for Shipping. So likewise Hops will grow here a profitable Marchandize. Also here are two fishing seasons, the the [sic] former for dry fish, and the latter for Cor-fish:[1] wherewith (together with the traine of the whole) many Ships are imploied to the Market & otherwise.

My want of leasure causeth me to omit many things, which otherwise I might haue enlarged, this my seruice of writing.

By the consent and aduise of some of the masters of this Harbour, I am become an humble suter vnto your Honour for the redresse of such abuses, the which (excepte a speedy redresse may be had) wil ouerthrow the whole.

1. And first that Stones or Ballast may not from henceforth be cast into the Harbour, and the Beaches preserued. 2. Secondly, that no man neither burne nor pull downe Stages, Flakes, nor any part thereof. 3. Thirdly that the rinding of Trees may be prohibited, but only such as shall bee felled for necessary vses and needefull behoofes. Fourthly, that all such Woods and Timber-trees so felled, may bee cut close to to [sic] the ground. 5. Lastly, that no man may bee wronged in their Boats and traine-fats,[2] or in any thing else whatsoever. And therefore if this by your Honors fauour and procurement may be had, a prosperous & flourishing time will follow, and all things here will goe on well hereafter, the which *God* grant: And for the which, the said

---

[1] Wet or green fish which the English fishermen made with their excess salt at the end of the season when there was no time for the lengthier drying process.
[2] Barrels for train oil.

Masters humbly pray that large penalties may therin be specified, and first to be proclaimed in *England*. Thus referring all vnto your Honors wisdome and full consideration. Our busines, or rather your Honors now goeth forward apace; the frame[1] is in hand, and almost ready for the rearing; the seller is already diged; al things by Gods grace and blessed assistance shall be performed with al care & diligence, whereof your Honour may be pleased to rest assured, as by the successe of my carefulnesse it shall plainely appeare.

The 5. persons and provision from aboord the *Benjamin*, are safely ariued here the 17. of August, but not without some danger, for I was enforced to send for them in two shallops of fishing Botes from the *Iles of Speare*, 4. leagues from this place.

The place whereon I haue made choise to plant and build vpon, is according to the Letter A in this superficiall draught here inclosed,[2] it being the fittest the warmest, and most commodious of all about the Harbour. And as soone as the house and fortification is fitted and finished, I shall (*God* willing) prepare and fence in a proportion of seede ground, and a Garden close by the house. It may please your Honour not to send any Cattle the next yeere, because I cannot prouide fodder for them so soone, before there bee some quantity of Corne growing, but it may please your Honour to send some Goates, a few tame Conies for breede, as also Pigs, Geese, Ducks and Hens. I haue some Hens already: some Spades from *London* were necessary, if of the best making, also some good Pick-axes, iron Croes, and a Smith, and also such as can brew and bake.

Meale and Malt would bee sent rather than otherwise, being both better cheap & of lesse waste, yet referring all to your Honors pleasure therein, humbly praying you would be pleased to proceed with all cheerefulnes, nothing doubting of a good and profitable succsse [*sic*], for here are are [*sic*] great hopes, and a large Territory for to imploy and receiue many needy people in a blessed and a profitable doing, euen who may liue heere both wealthily and happily.

And withall it may likewise please your Honour, that after one yeere more we shall be able to subsist of our selues by our owne industry, with Master *Iennings* his helpe and furtherance, and that with his profit and content.

I doubt not but that within the compasse of a small time to make your Honour a sauer. If your Honor please, you may defer the sending

---

[1] For the house, which Winne describes in more detail in his letter of July 1622 to Calvert; see above, pp. 196–8.
[2] This sketch map was not printed with the letters.

of a salt Pan one yeere more. *Brigs* and *Owen* hath bin touched with the Scuruie, but are now well recouered but all the rest of vs are in perfect health, I thanke *God* for it.

One Master *Yawe*, Master of a Ship of *Barnstable* (whose owner is called *Strange*) hee did spare mee halfe his Stage; the which did stand me in great steede to put my provision in at the first landing of them. Master *Luxen*, a Master of another Ship of *Barnstable*, hee shewed me much courtesie, & bestowed on me a Hen and 10 Chickens Master *Richard Martin*, Master of the *Blessing* of *Dartmouth*, he gave me a couple of yong Pullets, kind entertainement, and many good turnes. Master *Michael Waltham*, Master of a Ship of *Weimouth*, hee went in person to the *Ile of Speare*, in a Boate of his owne, to helpe to fetch our men and provision from aboord the *Benjamin*, hee hath besides done mee many good Offices, and hath sent mee many presents of Fresh-fish, and his Mate bestowed on mee a good Hen.

My happinesse of preuayling hetherto hath beene such, that all the Masters as well as the common sort throughout this Harbour haue vsed me kindly, and to say truely, I haue not discerned so much as a sowre aspect vpon mee amongst them all.

I haue not beene (and please your Honour) wanting in any thing, which by faire perswasions might produce a good liking of your Honours proceedings: insomuch that (I am perswaded) diuers will stay with me another yeere. Therefore I humbly pray your Honour to entreate Master *Iennings* to send me 3. peeces of Ordnance, a full Saker,[1] a Minion,[2] & lesser peece for our defence, a Drumme, and a Ship Ancient.[3]

And thus with my humble duty remembred, I most humbly cease to trouble your Honour any further for this time, resting,

Your Honours most humble
and faithfull seruant
Edward Winne.

FERYLAND, the 26. of
August. 1621.

Another Letter of the 28. of August, from the said Captaine *Winne*, vnto Master *Secretary Caluert*.

May it please your Honour,
Vpon the 26. of this present I deliuered vnto one Master *Henry Zeny*, Master of a Ship of *Milbrooke*, neere *Plimmoth*, a Packet directed to

---

[1] A small cannon. [2] A small kind of ordnance.
[3] An ensign or standard.

Master *Iennings*, wherein my Letters to your Honirir [*sic*] were enclosed: the Coppies whereof I haue likewise here inclosed, and haue sent the same by Master *Busse*, Master of the *Prosperous* a Ship of *Bristol*, humbly praying your Honour, that I may be furnished with all necessary Tooles and provision of Victuals the next yeare, and if your Honour may, with about the number of twenty persons more, whereof a Surgeon, and a learned and a religious Minister: that then your Honour may be pleased by Gods assistance, not to doubt of a good and a profitable successe in euery respect, and a flourishing plantation, women would bee necessary heere for many respects. Some two miles from this Harbour, direct West, there is a pleasant Champion fit for the Farme, to set forward another yeere. *And thus with my humble duty remembred and recommended vnto your Honour and my good Lady, beseeching the Almighty to blesse your and yours, and so I rest.*

> Your Honors most humble
> faithfull and obedient seruant
> *Edward Winne.*

From *Ferryland*, the 28. of August 1621.

21. 7 April 1623 THE CHARTER OF AVALON[1]

A grant of the Province of Avalon to *Si*r George Calvert and his heires.[2]

Iames by ye Grace of God of England, Scotland, France and Ireland, King defender of ye faith &c. To all to whom these presentes shall come, Greetinge.

Preamble[3]   Whereas our Right Trusty, and Welbeloved Councellor *Si*r George Calvert Kni*ght* our Principall Secretary of State being exited with a laudable, & pious Zeale, to enlarge the extentes of the Christian World, & there withall of our Empire & Dominion, hath heretofore at his Greate Cost purchased a certaine Region or Territory hereafter described in a Country of ours, Scituate in the Westerne partes of ye World, Commonly called Newfound Land not yet husbanded or Planted,[4] though in some partes thereof Inhabited by certain Barbarous people wanting the knowledge of Almightly God. And intending now

---

[1] P.R.O., CO 1/2, 23. Collated with the copy in B.L., Sloane MS 170, ff. 7–14; only significant variations have been noted. The original Latin version of the charter, dated 30 March 1623, is in P.R.O., SP 39/15, 3; copy, Sloane MS 170, ff. 1–6v.

[2] Not in Sloane MS 170.

[3] All marginal notes are omitted in Sloane MS 170.

[4] The charter ignores the Newfoundland company's settlement at Cupids Cove.

to Transport thither a very Greate and ample Colony of the English Nation, hath humbly besought our Kingly Maiesty to giue, Grant and Confirme all the sayd Region with certain priviledges and Iurisdictions requisite for yᵉ Good Government and State of yᵉ sayd Colony & territory to him, his heires & assignes for euer.

Know yee therefore that Wee favouring the Godly and laudable purpose of our sayd Councellour of our special Grace, certain knowledge, & mere Motion, haue Given, Granted, & Confirmed[1] vnto the sayd Sir George Calvert Knight his heires & assignes for ever all that entire Portion of Land scituate within our Country of Newfound Land aforesayd, beginning southerly from the middle p[art] of a certain Necke of Land, or Promontory scituate betwixt the 2. Harbours of Formose & Aquafort, and from thence following the shore towards yᵉ North, unto yᵉ middle part, or halfe way over a little Harbour Called in that regard Petit Port, or Petit Harbour,[2] which boundeth vpon yᵉ South part of yᵉ Plantacion of Sᵗ Iohns,[3] including the one halfe of a certain fresh River that falleth into yᵉ sayd Port of Petit Harbour, so tending all along the south Bourdour of the sayd Colony of Sᵗ Iohns, extendeth it selfe to a certain little Bay Comonly Called Salmon Cove, lying on the South side of yᵉ Bay of Conception including yᵉ one halfe of the River that falleth into the said Cove; as also yᵉ one halfe of the said Cove it selfe. from whence passing along yᵉ Shoare of the said Bay towardes the South, & reaching into yᵉ Bottome thereof it meetes with the Landes of Iohn Guy Cittizen of Bristoll named Sea Forrest, is bounded with a certaine River or Brooke, which there falles into the Sea, and fro[m] the Mouth of the sayd Brooke ascendeth into the furthest spring or head thereof, from thence passeth towardes the South for six Miles together along the Borders of the said Iohn Guy his Plantacion, & there crossing over Westward in a right Lyne, reachest into the Bay of Placentia, and the space of one League within the sayd Bay from the Shoare thereof. Hence turning again towardes the South passeth along the Harbour of Placentia with the like distance from the Shoare, & descending into New falkland towardes yᵉ North & West part thereof, stretcheth it selfe in a right Lyne Eastward continuing yᵉ whole southerly length vpon the Bounds

Geo. Calverts Grant [of] certain Landes in [N]ewfound Land

ye Bounds of it.

---

[1] 'and by this our present Charter for vs our Heires and Successors doe give graunt and confirm'. [2] 'or Petit Harbour' omitted.

[3] About 1620 Calvert had received from William Vaughan a narrow strip of land stretching north from a point midway between Fermeuse and Aquafort to Caplin Bay, see above, p. 21. This charter extended his holding to the boundaries of the St John's plantation which lay within the sphere of the Newfoundland company, see Cell, *English enterprise*, pp. 73, 78.

of yᵉ sayd New falkland into yᵉ Middle part or point of the Promontory or Neck of Land afore mentioned between the sayd Portes of formose and Aquafort, at which place is described, and finished yᵉ perambulac*i*on of yᵉ whole pr*e*cinct.

And all Islands within 10. Leagues of ye Easterne shore of New found Land

Wee doe further give and Grant by this pr*e*sent charter for vs, our heires, and successors, and Confirme unto the sayd S*i*r George Calvert his heires & assignes all and singular the Islandes and Islettes that are, or shall be within ten Leagues from the Easterne shoare of the sayd Region towardes the East.

Ports, Harbours Creeks, soyles [a]nd Woodes &c. The fishing.

With all & singular Ports, Harbours, & Creekes of the sea, belonging unto the sayd Region of the Islandes aforesayd, and all the soylé Landes Woodes, Lakes, and Rivers scituate or being within the Region, Isles & Limittes aforesayd, With the Fishinges of all sortes of fishe, Whales, sturgions and other Royall fishinges in yᵉ Sea or Rivers.

All Mines of Gold & silver

And Moreover all Veines, Mines & delues, asw[ell] discovered, as not discoverd, of Gold, silver, Gemmes and pretious Stones, and all other whatsoever be it of Stones, Mettalls, or of any other matter, or thing whatsoever found, or to be found, within the Region, Isles & Limmittes aforesayd.

All patronage & advousons of all Churches

And furthermore the Patronages and advousons of all churches which (as Christian Religion shall increase) within the sayd Region, Isles and Limittes shall happen thereafter to be erected.

All rightes & Priviledges as amply as any B*i*sh*o*p of Durham.

Together with all & singular the like, and as ample rightes, *I*urisdictions, priviledges, prerogatives, royaltyes, Liberties Immunityes, and franchises whatsoever, aswell by Sea, as by Land, within the Region Isles and Lim*m*ittes aforesayd. To haue exercise, use, and enioy the same, as any Bishop of Durham, within the Bishoppricke or County Palatine of Durham in oure Kingdome of England, hath at any time heretofore had, held used, or enjoyed; or of right ought, or might haue had, held, used, or enjoyed.

[Si]r G. Calvert [h]eires & assignes [m]ade Lords Proprie[to]ur of Newfound [l]and

And him the sayd S*i*r George Calvert his heires & assignes Wee do by these pr*e*sentes for vs, our heires, and successours, make Create, and Constitute, the true, and absolute Lordes, and Proprietours of yᵉ Region aforesayd, and of all other yᵉ Premises, saveing alwayes unto vs our heires & successours yᵉ faith, and allegiance due unto vs.

To haue holde possess and enjoy, yᵉ sayd Region Isles, and other yᵉ Premises unto yᵉ sayd S*i*r George Calvert his heires & assignes, to yᵉ sole, and proper use and behoof of him the sayd S*i*r George Calvert his heires and Assignes for ever. to be holden of vs, our heires & successours Kinges of England in Capite by Knightes service.

And yeelding therefore unto vs our heires and successours a white horse, whensoever and as often as it shall happen that Wee our heires or successours shall come into the sayd Territory or Region.

Paying a white horse to his Maiesty

And moreover ye fift part of all Gold and silver Oare, which within the Limittes aforesayd shall from time to time happen to be found.

ye 5th part of all Gold & Silver Oare found there.

Now that the sayd Region thus by vs granted and described may be eminent aboue all other partes of ye sayd Country of Newfound Land, and Graced with larger Titles. Know yee that Wee of our further Grace certain knowledge and mere Motion haue thought fitt to errect ye sayd Territory and Islandes into a Province, as out of ye fullness of our Royall power, and prerogative Wee doe for vs, our heires & successours erect & incorporate them into a Province, & doe call it Avalon, or ye Province of Avalon, & soe hereafter will haue it Called.

Called ye Province of Avalon.

And foreasmuch, as wee haue hereby made & ordained the sayd Sir George Calvert, the true Lor[d] Proprietor of all the sayd Province aforesayd, Know Yee therefore moreover y^t Wee for vs, ou[r] heires and successours, reposeing speciall trust & Confidence in the fidelity Wisedome Iustice, and provident Circumspection of the sayd Sir George Calvert, Doe Grant free, full & absolute power, by vertue of these presentes to him & his heires for the good and happy Goverment of the sayd Province to ordaine, make, Enact, and under his & their seales to publish any Lawes whatsoever appertaining either unto the publique state of ye sayd Province, or unto ye private utility of perticular persons according unto their best discretions, by and with the advice, Consent & approbation of ye freeholders of the sayd Province, or the greater part of y^m whom for the enacting of the sayd Lawes when, and as often as need shal[l] require Wee will that the sayd Sir George Calvert and his *heires shall assemble in such sort* & forme as to him shall seem best.

Power to make Lawes with ye Consent of the freeholders

And[1] the same Lawes vpon all Men & people within the sayd Province and Limmittes thereof for the time being or that shall be Constituted under the Government & power of him the sayd Sir George Calvert, or his heires, either sayling towardes Avalon from our Kingdome of England, or any other our Dominions, or Countryes, or returning from thence to our Kingdome of England, or any other our Dominions or Countreyes, by the said Sir George Calvert, or heires [sic], or their Deputyes,[2] Leiuetenantes, Iudges, Iustices, Magistrates, Officers and Ministers, to be ordained & appointed according to ye Tenour & true Intention of these presentes, by Imposition of Penaltyes,

power to execute the same vpon all people in the sayd province

---

[1] P.R.O., CO 1/2, 24 is a copy of the charter beginning here.
[2] 'or his heires, or by his or their Deputies'.

Imprisonment and any other Coertion, Yea if it be needfull, and ye quality of the Office[1] require it, by takeing away Member or life, duely to execute.

And likewise to appoint & establish Iudges & Iustices, Magistrates, & officers whatsoever by Sea and Land for what causes soever, and with what power & authorityes soever, and in such forme as to the sayd Sir George Calvert, and his heires shall seeme Most Convenient.

As also to remitt, release pardon and abolishe where before Iudgment, or after, all Crymes & offences whatsoever against the sayd Lawes, and to doe all & every other thinges which unto the Establishment of Iustice, Courtes & Tribunalls, formes of Iudicature, and Manner of proceeding doe belong, although in these presentes express mention be not made thereof.

Which Lawes so as aforesayd to be published, Our pleasure is, and so wee enjoyne, require, & Command shall be most absolute and available in Law.

And that all the Leige people & subiectes of vs our heires & successors doe observe and keepe the same inviolably, so far as they concern them under the penaltye therein contained, & to be contayned.

Provided nevertheless that the sayd Lawes doe stand with reason, and be not repugnant, nor contrary, but as neare as conveniently [sic] may be, agreeable of ye Lawes, Statutes, and Customes of this our Kingdome of England.

And because in the Goverment of so great a Province there may oftentimes arise many suddain accidentes, where in[2] it will be necessary to use the present remedy[3] before the freeholders of the sayd Province can be assembled together to make Lawes,[4] neither will it be requisite in so emergent a Case to Call so many together.[5]

Therefore for the better Government of that Country[6] Wee will, and ordain & by these presentes for vs, our heires & successors doe Grant to and with[7] the sayd Sir George Calvert & his heires, That the aforesaid Sir George Calvert & his heires by himselfe, or by his Governour[8] Officers in that behalfe duely authori[sed] may from time to time, make & appoint fitt & profitable Lawes to be kept & observed within y^t Province[9] aswell for ye preservation of ye peace as for the better

(marginal notes:)
- to pardon offences before or after [I]udgement
- Lawes to be absolute &c
- All people to obey them.
- If not repugnant to ye Lawes of England.
- Sir G. Calvert to make Lawes in Case the freeholders Cannot be Called together

---

[1] 'Offence'.   [2] 'suddeine accidentes doe often happen wherevnto'.
[3] 'apply a Remedy   [4] 'to the making of Lawes'.
[5] 'convenient that instantly vpon every such emergent occasion so greate a multitude should be called together'.   [6] 'ye sayd Province'.
[7] 'grant vnto'.   [8] 'and his Magistrates'.
[9] 'to be ordayned as aforesayd may make and constitute fitt and wholsome Ordinances from time to time within the sayd Province'.

restraint of the people their liveing,[1] and manifest them publiquely to all Men,[2] whom the same may, or doe any where Concerne.[3]

Which Lawes wee Will, and require to be inviolably observed in the sayd Region under such penaltyes as therein shall be expressed.[4]

Provided that those ordinances be made Consonant[5] to reason, & not repugnant, or contrary, but be as neare[6] agreeable to ye Lawes Statutes & Customes of[7] our Kingdome of England.

And also that those Ordinances does [sic] not extend to the right or Interest, of any person, or persons, of or in their Freehold, or to distreine bind, charge, or take away his, or their Goodes, or Chattells.[8]

furthermore that this New Colony may the more happily Increase by the Multitude of people resorting thither, and may likewise be the more strongly defended from the Incursions of Salvages, or other Enemyes, Pyrats, or Robbers, Therefore Wee for vs our heires, & successours doe give and grant by these presentes power Licence and Liberty unto all the Leige people and subjectes both present & future of vs, our heires, & successours (excepting those who shall be forbidden[9]) to transport themselves & familyes unto the sayd Province of Avalon, with Convenient shipping, & necessary provisions, & there to settle themselves dwell & Inhabite, and to build & fortifye Castles, fortes & other places of strength, for the publique & there own private defence, at the appointment of the sayd Sir George Calvert, his heires & assignes. The Statute of fugitiues, or any other statute whatsoever to the contrary of the premisses in any thing notwithstanding.

And wee will also and of our more Especiall Grace for vs, our heires, & Successours, Wee doe strictly injoyne, constitute, ordain, & Command That the sayd Province shall be our Allegiance And that all and singular the subiectes & Leige people of vs, our heires, & successours transported or to be transported into the sayd Province, & their Children there already borne, or hereafter to be borne, be and shall be Denizens, & Leiges of vs, our heires, & successours, and be in all things held, treated,

Marginal notes:
[Th]e sayd Lawes Comanded to be observed If not contrary to those of England
Not to extend to ye taking away any [of] their right
Liberty to all [p]eople to transport [the]mselves (except [t]hose forbidden)
to build & fortify
all transported
or borne there to be free Denizens

---

[1] 'there inhabiting'.
[2] 'publickly to notify the same to all persons'.
[3] 'doth or may any way concerne'.
[4] 'Which Ordinances our pleasure is shall be observed inviolably within the sayd Province vnder the paines therein to be expressed.'
[5] 'So as the sayd Ordinances be consonant'.
[6] 'but so farre as conveniently may be'.
[7] 'Lawes and Statutes of'.
[8] 'and so as the sayd Ordinances be not extended in any sort to binde, charge, or to take away the right of Interest of any person or persons of or in their freeholde, goodes or Chattells'.
[9] 'specially forbidden'.

reputed, & esteemed, as Leiges and faithfull people of vs, our heires & successours borne within our Kingdome of England, and likewise any Land*es*, Tenement*es*, Revenues services, & other Hereditament*es* whatsoever within our Kingdome of England and other our Dominions, may purchasse, Receive take, haue, hold, buy and possess, and them to occupy & enjoy, give, sell alien [*sic*], & bequeath as likewise all Libertyes franchises and priviledges of this our Kingdome freely quietly and peaceably haue and possess occupy & enjoy as our Leige people borne, or to be borne, within our sayd Kingdome of England without any Lett molestac*i*on, vexac*i*on, trouble, or offence of vs, our heires, and successours whomesoever, any statute act ordinance or provision to ye contrary hereof notw*i*thstanding.

to enjoy all Priviledges of England as if borne there.

And furthermore that our subject*es* may be the rather Incouraged to vndertake this Expedition with ready & chearfull Mind*es*, through the hope of gaine, & comfort of Priviledge.

[A]ll that transport [g]oods there to pay Custom*es*

Knowe yee that wee of our speciall Grace certain Knowledg & meer Motion, doe give, and Grant free Lycence & liberty by vertue of these pr*es*ent*es*, aswell unto the sayd S*ir* George Calvert his heires & assignes, as to all other that shall from time to time repaire to Avalon, with a purpose to Inhabite, to Lade and freight there, and into the sayd Province of Avalon by them their servant*es* or assignes from any port whatsoever of vs, our heires, and successours, To transport all and singular their Good*es*, moveable or immoveable, Wares and Marchandizes, as likewise armes & Warlike Instrument*es* offensiue and defensiue, without any Imposition, subsidy, Custome, or any other thing to be payd therefore unto vs, our heires, and Successours, and w*i*thout ye Impediment or Molestac*i*on of vs, our Heires or successours, or of any Officer whatsoever, or farmer of vs, our heires, & successours. Any statute, act, ordinance, or any other thing to the Contrary notwithstanding.

If shipt after leaue of the L. Treasurer

Provided alwayes that before the sayd Good*es* and Marchandizes be Carryed or laden aboard the ships, Leaue be first asked and obtained of the High Treasourer of vs, our heires, and successours or our Kingdome of England, or of the Com*missione*rs of our Treas*ury*, or of 6. or more of the Privy Councill to vs, our heires, and successours, und*er* their hand*es* in Writing.

leaue given y^ou^ to doe it.

To w*hi*ch High Treasourer, Com*issione*rs and Privy Councell of vs, our heires, and successours, or any 6. or more of them Wee haue for vs, our heires and successours given and granted, as W[ee] doe by these pr*es*ent*es* give and Grant power to Grant such Lycences in forme aforesayd.

And because in so remote a Country, and scituate amongst so many barbarous Nations, ye Incursions aswell of the salvages themselues as of other Enemyes, Pyrates, & Robbers, may probably be feared, Therefore wee haue given, and by these presentes for vs, our heires, and successours doe giue power unto the sayd Sir George Calvert Knight his heires and assignes by himselfe, or his Captaines or other his Officers, to Leavy Muster and Traine all sortes of Men whatsoever, or wheresoever borne in the Province of Avalon for the time being to make Warr & prosecute the Enemyes & Robbers aforesayd, as well by sea, as Land, Yea even without the Limittes of the sayd Province, and by Godes assistance to vanquish and take them, and being taken to putt them to death by ye Lawe of Warr, or to saue them, as the said Sir George Calvert his heires & assignes shall thinke fitt.

Power to Leavy Muster & train all men for the defence of ye Province & kill & destroy all opposers.

And to doe all and every other thing which unto ye sayd Charge and Office of a Captaine Generall belongeth, or hath been accustomed to belong, as fully and freely as any other Captaine Generall had ever had ye same.

to be Captain Generall

Also our Will and pleasure is, and by our Charter wee doe give to ye sayd Sir George Calvert his heires, & assignes In case of Rebellion, suddain Tumult, or sedition if any should happen (which God forbidd) either vpon ye Land within the Province aforesayd, or vpon the main sea in makeing a voyage thither, or returning from thence, power, liberty, and authority by himselfe, or his Captaines Deputyes, or other Officers to be authorized under his seale to that purpose, To whome wee also for vs, our heires and Successours, Doe giue and Grant by these presentes full power and authority to exercise the Lawe Military against Mutinous, and seditious persons, such as shall refuse to submitt themselues to his, or their Goverment, or shall refuse to serve in the Wars, or shall fly to ye Enemy, or forsake their Ensigne, or to loiterers, or straglers, or otherwise howsoever offending against ye Law, Custome, and discipline military as freely, and in as ample manner and forme, as any Captain Generall by vertue of his Office might, or hath accustomed to vse the same.

to use Marshall Law[1]

furthermore that the way to Honours & dignityes may not seeme to be altogether precluded, or shutt up to Men well borne, and such as repaire[2] themselues vnto this present Plantacion, and shall desire to deserue well of vs and our Kingdomes, both in peace and Warr & in so farre distant & remote a Country.

Therefore Wee for vs our heires, & successours doe giue free, and

to Conferr Honours

---

[1] 'Marshall law' written in a different hand from the rest of the manuscript.
[2] 'prepare'.

absolute power unto yᵉ sayd Sir George Calvert his heires and assignes, to conferr favour, rewardes, & Honours vpon such Inhabitantes in the Province aforesayd, as shall deserve the same, and to Invest them with what titles and dignityes whatsoever, as he shall thinke fitt, so as they be not such as are at this present used in our Kingdome of England.

to Incorporate Townes

As likewise to Errect and Incorporate Townes into Burroughs, and Burroughs into Cittyes, with convenient priviledges & Immunityes according to yᵉ meritt of the Inhabitantes, & fittness of the places, and to doe all and every other thinges, touching the premisses, which to him, or them shall seeme meete, & requisite. Albeit they be such as of their owne nature might otherwise require a more speciall Comandment & Warrant, then in these presentes is expressed.

those yᵗ Lade Gods [sic] thither shall pay no Custome

And forasmuch as the begining of all Colonyes and Common Wealthes are incumbred with sundry Inconveniences & difficultyes Wee therefore favouring the growth of this Present Colony, & providing out of our Royall Care that those who are burthened one way may be eased another, of our Especiall and[1] mere motion, doe by this our Charter giue and Grant unto yᵉ sayd Sir George Calvert his heires, & assignes, and to all the Inhabitantes & dwellers whomsoever present and to come into avalon aforesayd, Lycence to Import & exonerate, by themselues, & their servantes, factours, or assignes, all whatsoever Marchandizes and goodes that shall arrise of the fruites & Commodityes of the sayd Province either by Land or sea, into any of the Portes of vs our Heires, and Successours in our Kingdomes of England, or Ireland, or otherwise to dispose of the sayd Goodes in the sayd Portes. And if neede be within one yeare after the discharge of the same, to Lade the sayd Marchandizes and goodes againe into the same Ships, or others, and to export the same into any other Countryes, either of our Dominions or forreigne, without paying in any sort any manner of Subsidy, Custome, Tax or Imposition whatsoever, unto vs, our heires & successours in any manner or wise.

Immunity fromCustomes for 10. yeares.

Provided alwayes, and it is our Meaning & Intention, that this our Grace & Immunity from Customes Impositions, and Subsidyes shall continue & be of force for ten yeares, & only to be reckoned from the date of these presentes & no longer, which ten yeares being Expired & Ended, our Will and pleasure is, and wee doe for vs, our heires, & Successours, Grant & ordain, yᵗ the said Sir George Calvert Knight his heires & assignes, and all and every other Inhabitantes & dwelleres present & to come within the Province of Avalon aforesayd may by

[1] 'especiall grace and'.

ymselves or their factours and servantes, Import & unlade, and within the time aforesayd (if they Will) relade & export all manner of Marchandizes, Wares & Goodes whatsoever arising from the fruites and Commodityes of Avalon, into and out of any the Portes whatsoever of vs, our heires & successours. Provided alwayes that they doe pay for the same unto vs our heires, and successours such Customes & Impositions, Subsidyes & Dutyes, as other our Subiectes for the time being are bound to pay.

Beyound which wee doe not intend that the sayd Inhabitantes of Avalon be any way charged

And furthermore of our more ample and speciall Grace, certain Knowledge & meere Motion, Wee doe for vs our heires and successours Grant unto the sayd Sir George Calvert his heires & Assignes, full and absolute power and authority to[1] make Errect and Constitute within the Province of Avalon and Ilands aforesayd, such and so many Seaportes, Harboures, & Creekes and other places of charge & discharge for Ships, Boates, and other Vessells, & in such & so many places, and with such rightes, Iurisdictions & freedomes & Priviledges unto the sea Portes[2] belonging, as to him, or them shall seeme most expedient.

And y^t all, and singular the Ships, Boates & other Vesseles, which shall come for Marchandize and Trade into the sayd Province, or out of ye same shall depart, shall be laden and unladen, only at such Portes, and no other, as the sayd Sir George Calvert, his heires & assignes shall errect & Constitute,[3] any use, Custome, or any other thing to ye contrary notwithstanding.[4]

to unlade only at such Portes as ye Governor shall appoint

Saveing alwayes & ever reserved unto all our subjectes, & the subjectes of our heires & successours of our Kingdome of England, free liberty of fishing, as well in the sea, as in the Portes and Creekes of the Province aforesayd, and the Priviledges of salting & drying their fish vpon ye shoares of the sayd Province, as heretofore they haue reasonably vsed, and enjoyed the same, any thing in these presentes to the Contrary Notwithstanding.

The English to fish any where in the Province or Shoare.

Which Libertyes & Priviledges nevertheless ye Subiectes of vs, our heires, & successours shall enjoy without doing any Injury or notable loss or detriment unto the sayd Sir George Calvert his heires, & assignes, or to the dwellers and Inhabitantes of the sayd Province in the Portes, Creekes, and Shoares aforesayd, and especially in the Woodes growing within the said Province.

ye people there not to Injure ye Wood.

[1] 'absolute power to'. [2] 'the sayd Portes'.
[3] 'as the sayd...Constitute' omitted.
[4] This paragraph is underlined in Sloane MS 170.

And if any shall presume to offer any such Injury and spoyle, he shall thereby Incurre the heavy displeasure of vs, our heires, & successours, together with the danger and penalty which by ye Laws shall be due unto the same.

Grant of the Customes to ye Governor

Wee doe furthermore Will appoint & ordain and by these presentes for vs our heires, and successours, Wee doe grant unto the sayd Sir George Calvert his heires and assignes, that he, his heires, and assignes may from time to time for ever, haue[1] and enjoy all & singular the subsidyes, Customes, and Impositions payable, or accruable[2] within the Portes Harboures & other places aforesayd within the Province aforesayd for all Goodes & Marchandizes there to be laden & unladen.

to Impose no Tax on any Marchandizes

And wee further Will, and by these presentes doe Covenant and Grant for vs, our heires, and Successours, to & with the sayd Sir George Calvert his heires, and assignes, that neither Wee nor our heires, nor successours in any time hereafter will or shall cause to be Imposed any Imposition, Custome or other Taxation, in or vpon the dwellers or Inhabitantes of the sayd Province, or[3] vpon any of their Landes, Tennementes, Goodes, or Chattelles within the sayd Province, or vpon any of their Goodes or Marchandizes to be charged, or discharged within the sayd Province, or within the Portes, Creekes, or Harboures thereof.

all people to obey this Grant

And our pleasure is, and for vs, our heires, and successours Wee charge and Command that this our Declaracion & Grant shall be received, and allowed from time to time in all Courts, and before any the Iudges of vs, our heires, and successours for a sufficient & Lawfull discharge, payment, and acquittance,[4] Comanding all, and singular our Officers, & Ministers, and the Officers, & Ministers of vs, our heires, and successours, and Enjoyning them vpon payne of our High displeasure, y^t they doe not presume at any time to attempt any thing to the Contrary of ye Premisses, or y^t they doe in any sort withstand the same, But that they be at all tymes aiding & assisting as is fitting unto the sayd Sir George Calvert Knight, & to the Inhabitantes and Marchantes of avalon aforesayd, their servantes, Ministers, factours, and assignes, to the full fruition and Enjoyment of the benefitt of this our Charter.

[1] 'haue...unladen' underlined in Sloane MS 170.
[2] 'accruing'.
[3] 'or in or vpon any of the goodes or Marchandises within the sayd Province to be Laden or vnladen within ye Portes or Harbours of the sayd Province' underlined in Sloane MS 170.   [4] 'for...acquittance' underlined in Sloane MS 170.

And if perchance hereafter it should happen that any doubts, or questions, should arise concerning the true sence, or understanding of any word, Clause, or sentence contained in this our present charter, Wee Will ordain & Command, that at all tymes & in all thinges such Interpretacion be made thereof, & allowed in any of our Courtes, whatsoever as shall be Iudged most advantagious, & favourable unto ye sayd Sir George Calvert his heires, and assignes. Provided alwayes that no Interpretation be admitted thereof, whereby Gods holy & true christian Religion, or the allegiance due to vs, our heires, & successours may in any thing sufferr, any prejudice, or diminution although express mention be not made in these presentes of ye true yearly value or certainty of the premisses, or of any part thereof or of any other Guifts or Grants made by vs heretofore, or of any of our pregenitors or predecessours unto the sayd Sir George Calvert Knight, or any Statute, Act Ordinance, provision Proclamation, or restraint heretofore had, made, published, ordained, or provided, or any other thing Cause, or matter whatsoever to the Contrary in any wise Notwithstanding.

In Witness whereof wee haue caused these our Letters to be made Patents, Witness our selfe at Westminster, the 7. of Aprill in ye 21 yeare of our Reigne, of England, france & Ireland, & of Scotland the 56^{th1}
Examined

[*Endorsed:*]   Sir George Calverts Grant of Avalon in Newfound Land April 7. 21. Iacob.

[*in a different hand:*] 7th April 1623
Newfoundland

22. 15 March 1624/5   CALVERT TO SIR JOHN COKE[2]

Sir. It is vnlikely that yo^u haue heard of a journey which I intend shortly godwilling for Newfoundland to visit a plantation which I beganne there some few years since vnder his Maiesties Royall Charter, and whither I haue his licence now vnder his signature to repaire this spring to settle such things as require my presence. To this end I had communication with some owners of a shipp called the Ionathan now in the river and hired her for the transportation of my self and such planters as I carry with me at this tyme. Since I vnderstand shee is stayed

[1] Sloane MS 170 ends here.
[2] Melbourne Hall, Derby, Cowper MSS, Bundle 24. Sir John Coke (1563–1644), commissioner for the navy and master of the requests. In 1625 he was appointed secretary of state in succession to Sir Albertus Moreton. *DNB.*

(my self being absent in yorkshire, and but newly returned) to serve for the king, to which it is good reason that all my occasions should give place: But in good truth Sir, I am by that meanes vtterly disappointed, and yo^u should do me a great favor to cleare her, and her marriners which I should acknowledge both to you and the rest of the Commissioners to whom I beseche yo^u commend my service. The like suite I make vnto you for the Peter Bonaventure another shipp whereof one Sherwyn is Master, with whom I contracted for carrying me over cattle, and the covenaunts are already drawne betweene vs, that he and his marryners with the carpenters of both shippes may be spared for this voyage, and suffered to proceade in this employment wherein I am to vse them, yf his Maiesties service hinder not. I presume Sir so much of your courtesy as I will not trouble you with many words, but tender yo^u an assurance of the hearty affection of

From my howse in	your very loving freind to do
Ch[ ]on rowe. this	yo^u service
15. March. 1624.	G. Baltimore

My Lord Duke hath [illegible] promised me all the assistance and furtheraunce he can give me in this enterprise, as I assure my self whatsoever favor you shall show me herein his Grace will not be displeased with it.

[*Addressed:*] To my honorable freind Sir Iohn Cooke Knight Master of the Requests and one of the Commissioners for his Maiesties Navy.

[*Endorsed:*] 1624. March 15. Lord Baltimore for release of 2 ships Ionathan & Peter Bonaduenture

23. 17 March 1624/5 THE DUKE OF BUCKINGHAM TO SIR JOHN COKE[1]

Sir, I have herein sent yo^u a lettre which I receaved from ye Lord Baltimore, craving ye release of five shipps, wherein I have forborne to give any aunsweare vntill I shall vnderstand from yo^u, whether it will not be inconvenyent or preiudicyall to his Maiesties service to dischardge them: I pray speak with the Lord Baltimore about it, & returne vnto me (together with his inclosed lettre) your opinion what is fittest for me to doe, aswell concerning those shipps his Lordshipp mencioneth to be staid in the west, as these in the Thamis, for I would

[1] Melbourne Hall, Derby, Cowper MSS, Bundle 24.

gladly give his Lordshipp satisfaccion in his request soe farre as I may doe it without hinderaunce to his Maiesties service: And soe I rest Theobalds: 17° Martij. 1624./

Your very loving freind

G. Buckingham

[*Addressed:*] To my very loving freind Sir Iohn Coke knight one of ye Masters of requestes to his Maiestie these

[*Endorsed:*] 1624. March 17 Lord Duke of Buckingham from Theobalds. ships to bee released for the Lord Baltemore

24. 1624/5 REPORT OF CAPTAIN JOHN MASON[1]

If the Navie be not sufficientlie victualled with fish for the whole voyadge, A supplie may best be made from Newfoundland: And to that end on [*sic*] or 2 shipps of the Navie may be Imployed thither accordinge to the quantitie required, (a contract beinge heir made aforehand with certaine fishinge owners for deliverie of ye fish their) and going vnder manned from hence may retourne from Newland to the place whence the Fleet shall be, in August next fully manned with an overplus of men, to helpe to furnish other shipps y^t want. And theis 2 shipps may have from my Lord of Baltimore in their way for the transportation of him selfe and 80 persons and their provisions and som cattell, accordinge to a condition made by his Honour for the 2 shipps called the Ionathan & Peter Bonaventure 400^{li}, in fish their or mony heir; To be gone from hence towards the end of Aprill next, and to be discharged in Newland within 10 dayes after their arival their, which things so effected, the 2 shipps may presently lade fish for the victuall of the Navie, and be with the Navie in August next, and so goe on in their course of service intended

In° Mason.

[*Endorsed:*] The opinion of I. M. concerninge the shipp called the Ionathan, hyred by the Lord Baltimore, and pressed for the Kings service; how she may accommodate both the Kings service & serve the Lord Baltimore 1624.

---

[1] Melbourne Hall, Derby, Cowper MSS, Bundle 24. John Mason (1586–1635) had led a naval expedition against the Redshanks in the Hebrides in 1610. Between about 1616 and 1621 he acted as governor of the colony at Cupids Cove. He had been appointed commissary general, responsible for victualling the Cadiz expedition early in 1625; the following year he became treasurer and paymaster of the English forces. *DCB.* I.

271

25. 30 March 1625   GEORGE ABBOT, ARCHBISHOP OF CANTERBURY, TO SIR THOMAS ROE[1]

Mr. secretary Calvert hath never looked merily since the prince his coming out of Spaine: it was thought, that hee was muche interested in the Spanish affairs: a course was taken to ridde him of all imployments and negotiations. This made him discontented; and, as the saying is, *Desperatio facit monachum*, so hee apparently did turne papist, which hee now professeth, this being the third time that hee hath bene to blame that way. His majesty, to dismisse him suffered him to resigne his secretaries place to Sir Albertus Moreton, who payed him three thousand pounds for the same;[2] and the kinge hath made him baron of Baltimore in Ireland; so hee is withdrawne from vs, and having bought a ship of 400 tuns, hee is going to New England, or Newfoundlande, where hee hath a colony...

26. 7 April 1627   CALVERT TO SIR EDWARD NICHOLAS[3]

Sir I was yesterday an humble suitor to my Lord for the exemption of my ships and men from this general stay, and he was pleased to grant it me, and willed me to find him the names of the shippes as I told you yesternight I pray you Sir lett mee haue your furtherance in the speedy dispence of my warrant, because tyme imports me much, and Sir Arthur Aston[4] stayes onely for it. And for the courtesy you show me in this, or in any other thing that concernes my young plantation, you shall alwayes find a thankfull requitall from

Your very assured freind

George Baltimore

From my lodging in the Savoye 7. Aprill 1627

The names of the shippes

The Arke of Avalon	160.	tunnes or thereaboutes
The George of Plymouth	140:	tunnes or thereaboutes

both now at dartmouth

[1] Extract, printed in *The negotiations of Sir Thomas Roe, in his embassy to the Ottoman porte, from the year 1621 to 1628 inclusive* (London, 1740), p. 372. Roe (1581?–1644), explorer and diplomat; had served as ambassador to the court of the Mughal emperor; appointed ambassador to the Ottoman empire in 1621. *DNB*.

[2] In fact Moreton paid Calvert £6000 for the office. Gardiner, *History of England*, v, 309–10.

[3] P.R.O., CO 1/4, 19.

[4] Probably a member of the Aston family of Cheshire and perhaps the son of Sir Thomas Aston of Aston, Cheshire, and father of the more famous Sir Arthur who died in 1649 defending Drogheda against Oliver Cromwell. *DNB*.

[*Addressed:*] To my very worthy freind Edward Nicholas Esquire secretary to my Lord the duke of Buckingham his Grace
[*Endorsed:*] *Received* 7° *April* 1627
Lord Baltimor to haue his two shippes not to be stayed

27. 21 May 1627 CALVERT TO SIR THOMAS WENTWORTH[1]

SIR,

I am heartily sorry that I am farther from my Hope of seeing you before my leaving of this Towne, which will be now within these three or four Days, being bound for a long Journey to a Place which I have had a long Desire to visit, and have now the Opportunity and Leave to do it: It is *Newfoundland* I mean, which it imports me more than in Curiosity only to see; for, I must either go and settle it in a better Order than it is, or else give it over, and lose all the Charges I have been at hitherto for other Men to build their Fortunes upon. And I had rather be esteemed a Fool by some for the Hazard of one Month's Journey, than to prove myself one certainly for six Years past, if the Business be now lost for Want of a little Pain and Care. At *Michaelmas* I hope to be with you again, God willing. In the mean Time I shall be in a great Fear that your too much Fortitude will draw upon you suddenly a Misfortune, which your Heart may, perhaps, endure, but the rest of your Body will suffer. Believe me, I am so good a Physician in this, as considering the Malice of some Enemies you have, who will provide you Incommodities enough, you cannot long abide it without infinite Peril to your Health.[2] I touch this String still, because I confess it moves me most, and ought to prevail more with you than any Matter of your Fortune, which I suppose cannot be greatly prejudiced. The conquering Way sometimes is yielding; and so is it, as I conceive, in this Particular of yours, wherein you shall both conquer your own Passions, and vex your Enemies, who desire nothing more than your Resistance. If you

[1] Printed in W. Knowler, ed., *The earl of Strafforde's letters and despatches* (London, 1739), I, 39. Wentworth (1593–1641), later lord deputy of Ireland, was an old friend of Calvert's. It was through Wentworth's local influence that Calvert had been elected as knight of the shire for Yorkshire in 1620, the other representative being Wentworth himself.

[2] Wentworth had first angered the Court by his opposition to the Spanish policy. Then, in 1626, he had refused to pay the forced loan which Charles I had demanded. Because Wentworth had been seriously ill in 1622 and 1623, his friends feared that his health would not stand imprisonment. Wentworth ignored their advice. Summoned before the Privy Council, he refused to pay the loan and was sent to the Marshalsea prison in July 1627 and then to confinement in Dartford, Kent. *DNB*; Winifred Gardner, Lady Burghclere, *Strafford* (London, 1931), I, 73–8.

resolve betimes to take this Course, which I would to God you would, it may be yet interpreted Obedience to your Sovereign, and Zeal to his Service; and whatsoever Slackness hath been in it hitherto may be excused by your Friends here, either by Indisposition of Health, or some other Reason, which your own Judgment can better dictate to you than my Advice. I should say much more to you were you here, which is not fit for Paper; but never put off the Matter to your Appearance here, for God's sake; but send your Money in to the Collectors in the County without more ado. Your Friends here are much perplexed and in Fear of you, and none more than I, who know not how I shall be secure of you, being so suddenly to depart, and not in any Possibility to understand how Things go with you until *Michaelmas* that I return. Commend my Love and Service to Mr. Wandesford,[1] when you see him, I pray you: I would write to him in the same Language had I Time. God Almighty keep you both, and grant us an happy Meeting.

Savage, May 21,   Your most affectionate true Friend to serve you
1627   GEO BALTIMORE.

P.S. I go in a good Ship of 300 Ton, with 24 Pieces of Ordnance, with two or three good Ships in Company, so as we need not fear either *French* or *Dunkirkers*.

28. 2 November 1627   A RUMOUR CONCERNING CALVERT'S INTEREST IN THE ST JOHN'S PLANTATION[2]

for matters of Newfoundland I could wish that my Lord himself[3] or some of his did come in for a proportion in the lot of St Iohnes which is well knowne to be the principall prime and chief lot in all the whole countrey in which is great hope of good comodities to be raised and as it now standes the yce being broken and some howses allreddy built it will require no great charge to follow it wishing that my Lord as soone as conveniently he may would adresse his letter vnto Master Iohn Slaynie[4] Governor of his desire for comming into that lot above

---

[1] Christopher Wandesford (1592–1640), a kinsman of Wentworth and also a member of parliament in 1626 when he had joined in the attack upon Buckingham. Wandesford accompanied Wentworth, now earl of Strafford, to Ireland and briefly succeeded him as lord deputy. *DNB*.

[2] Extract, William Payne to Lady Conway (P.R.O., SP 16/84, 13). Payne was a partner in the St. John's lot and had been appointed a member of the Newfoundland company's council in 1618. P.R.O., CO 1/1, f. 123; John Slany to Sir Percival Willoughby, 1 Feb. 1616/7 (Nottingham University, Middleton MSS, Mi X 1/42). Lady Conway was the wife of Sir Edward Conway, one of the secretaries of state.

[3] Sir Edward Conway.

[4] John Slany had been the Newfoundland company's treasurer since its foundation in 1610.

mentioned for my Lord Baltimore at his returne may happily make meanes to get some proportion in that lot of St Iohnes[1]

29. 16 January 1627/8   CALVERT TO SIR JOHN COKE[2]

Sir

There hath beene with me one Master Levett[3] who tells me that having beene a suitor vnto my Lordes of the Councell for some Commission for New England, their Lordshipps were pleased to forbeare giving him an answere, vntill they might vnderstand whether it trenched vpon my plantation or not and that yo^u sent him vnto me for that purpose. I am much bound vnto their Lordshipps for the favor, and do humbly and thankfully acknowledge it, as I do my obligation Sir, vnto your selfe: you may be pleased to lett their Lordshipps knowe that the Colony of New England concernes not me at all; it is farre remote from my plantation which is in Newfoundland, a nearer part of America, by some hundreds of leagues. I would haue wayted on yo^u my selfe but he desires thus much in writing from me. I haue beene diuerse tymes at your lodgings to haue received your commandementes for Ireland, but had not the happynesse to fynd yo^u there or my [illegible] I shalbe ready to serve you in any thing that is within the power of

16. Ianuary. 1627   Your affectionate friend and servant

                                             Geo Baltimore

[*Addressed:*]   To the Right honourable Sir Iohn Coke knight one of his Maiesties principall Secretaryes./

[*Endorsed:*]   1627. Iann. 16 Lord Baltemore concerning New England.

30. 19 January 1627/8   CHARLES I TO LORD DEPUTY FALKLAND[4]

Right trusty and right welbeloued Cousin & Councellour wee greete you well. Whereas our right trusty and welbeloued the Lord Baltimore

---

[1] There is no evidence that Calvert ever tried to obtain an interest in the St. John's lot which bordered upon his own land.

[2] Melbourne Hall, Derby, Cowper MSS, Bundle 29.

[3] Christopher Levett had held land in New England since 1623. On 11 February 1628 he received a grant of money in support of a plantation there of which he was to be governor. *CSP Col., 1574-1660*, pp. 45, 87; John W. Dean, ed., *Captain John Mason* (Boston, Prince Society, 1887), pp. 18, 19.

[4] P.R.O., State Papers, Ireland, SP 63/246, ff. 16–17v. Copy.

holdes by Charter from our deare father of happy memory king Iames, a large Territory and proporcion of land in our Country of Newfoundland, and hath there by vertue and authority thereof with greate charge and expence settled a Collony of our Subiectes and is desirous to proceede with the enterprize, soe as hee may for the better settlement and gouerment thereof with our gratious leaue and good liking remaine there himself in person for some certaine yeares without which hee shall bee discouraged to goe forward, not aduenturing any longer to comitt to the trust of others the managing of his estate there, by whose negligence and otherwise the same hath bin already much wasted as hee informeth vs to his greate preiudice and the hazard of soe good and laudable a worke, Wee therefore beeing noe lesse inclined to fauour and protect the plantations of our good and faithfull subiectes in those remoate partes of the world then was our late deare father and knoweing them to tend much to the honoɩ of our Crowne the enlargement of our dominion and to the good of our people, and beeing well assured by a long experience of the loyall fidelity of the said Lord Baltimore, and of his zeale to doe vs honor and seruice haue licensed him to repaire thither againe in person according to his humble suite made vnto vs in that behalf and to carry with him his wife and family, and such other of our good and Louing subiectes as shall bee willing with him to transport themselues thither; Requiring you that if hee shall desire to passe at any of the portes of that our kingdome not onely to License him soe to doe with the Company that shall goe with him and to carry with him all such prouisions of victualls, Cloth, apparrell Munition, household stuff, and all other carriages and vtenselles whatsoeuer which shall be fitting and necessary for the said plantacion, without any manner of molestacion whatsoeuer to their persons or goodes; but alsoe to assist him with your lawfull fauour in all thinges that may concerne him or the furtherance of the work which hee hath in hand. Giuen vnder our Signett at our Court at Whithall the 19th day of Ianuary in the therd yeare of our Raigne of greate Brittaine Fraunce & Ireland

[*Endorsed:*] Copie of his Maiesties Lettre to the Lord Deputie of Ireland in the behalf of the Lord Baltamore.

31. 7 April 1628 GEORGE COTTINGTON TO SIR JOHN
FINET[1]

Noble Sir/.

I haue bene for the most part in the Country since I had a vewe of
your letter from my lord deputy of Irland, and therefore desyre your
pardon that my purgation from my lord Baltimore aspersion doth come
so late to you. I must fyrst acknowledge my self infinitly bound to
my lord deputy for his present remembrance of me upon your
nomination; and rest obliged to your self for the same recommendation.
Yet on the other syde I am not a lytle ioyed, fyrst that upon your motion
I desyred some proportion of tyme to giue you answere, so lykewyse
that of myne owne accord I sought not this imployment for by these
twoo reasons I hope that noble lord wyll not harbour the least suspition
that I endeauored to surprise his lordship and so betray his trust with
an instrument to serue him/. As to urging my lord Baltimore in
disburthening his conscience of somethinge hee would say of me, teste
mea conscientia it was nothing else but to discharge some rancor of
reuenge conceyued agaynst mee as by the sequell I hope it wyll appeere.
Hee hath pitched upon twoo things (quorum contrarium sole meridiano
clarius) fyrst he entreth Sir Iohn Sedley[2] upon the stage whose affection
(I vowe to God) I euer found so reale towardes mee from the fyrst
day of our incounter tyll this very hour, that were it not contrary to
the lawes of nature I should prefer his fauour, beyond the respect of
those that were bounde to mayntayne me Our beginning first was in
the Uniuersity[3] wher I had the honor to be his tutor, I trauelled wyth
him afterwards twyce into France, our conuersation is at thys tyme
frequent, there has not bene these twenty yeers (for so long hath bene
our correspondence) the least exception taken of eyther part, I am often
wyth him at his house, and he affordeth mee so much welcome as that
I fynde them styll my home. The manner of our parting was thus,
haueng spent nyne or ten yeers with him considering my education
I desyred to better my fortune abroad, and got the opportunity to go
to Sir Francis Cottington being then Agent in Spayne.[4] Sir Iohn Sedly

[1] B.L., Sloane MS 3827, ff. 124–5v. Cottington was related to the diplomat, Sir Francis
Cottington, a close friend of Calvert's. John Finet (1571–1641) was a courtier and diplomat
who, in 1626, was appointed master of ceremonies at court. DNB.
[2] Probably the son of Sir John Sedley of London.
[3] Both Sedley and Cottington were at Magdalen College, Oxford, where in 1612
Cottington received the M.A. and Sedley the B.A. Foster, Alumni Oxonienses, I, 333, IV,
1332.
[4] Sir Francis Cottington (1578?–1652), a diplomat whose career was particularly
associated with Spain and with the proposed Spanish marriage for prince Charles. M.
Havran, Caroline courtier: the life of lord Cottington (London, 1973); DNB.

still desyred my company, but I kept on my purpose and comyng to my lord Baltimore one morning for his letters to Spayne (it was the day after he was sworne Secretary)[1] mention was made of an ancient sute Sir Francis Cottington had to his lordship in my behalfe, and askyng him whether he would accept of my seruice he was pleased to admitt mee into his family, so as I altred my course presuming I had gotten the golden Fleece, but (immane quantum discrepabat) the longer I lyued there, the more I found my self fleeced; I would inlarge my self upon this fyrst imputation but lett this suffise to showe how I left that worthy gentleman, who is ready to testify as muche and muche more when occasion shall be offred.

Now for desertion of my lord of Baltimores seruice how that came to pass, I confesse I know not: Yt is trwe I neuer took absolute leaue of him, neyther was I euer discharged by him. His imployment long before his lordship declared him selfe Catholick, I felt was little or nothing at all for me, during which tyme I discerned and palpably sawe his preparation to a new profession of Religion, whereupon I came but seldome to doo my duty vnto him:[2] But sin fata voluere. When his lordship was in Irland,[3] where many thought he did sett up his rest not to retourne hether, there was a certayne account due to mee upon our fishing aduenture, at Newfoundland (more mony then now I should disburse that way, besydes my aduenture by land which I shall euer account desperat) and seeing others satisfied to the full with an odd neglect of mee, I tooke a legall course and recouered as much as I could by arresting of his ships, these being the last remaynes of our share and at that tyme on the poynt of being sold. This (thoughe I haue not seene his lordship since) yet (as I am informed) hath begotten the breache which together with my religion (incompatible with his lordships) may giue him cause to speake his pleesure of mee. I did his lordship the faythfull seruice I could to my greater loss then gayne, but I fynde an untoward requytall and whereas his characters of mee were sharp: It is fytting lykewyse they should be true, and upon iust ground. I could hereupon dip my pen in vineger and answere by way of recrimination, but calling to mynde he was my master I wyll not be so barbarous, & conclude therefore a tedious discovrse, these twoo inditements being of no greater vitality for truth then (as I take God to wittnes) I haue opened them unto you, what euer his aggrauations were I hope my

---

[1] February 1619.
[2] Some members of Cottington's own family were Catholic, including Sir Francis.
[3] From 1625 to 1627.

lord deputy wyll giue not farther credit to them. I had done well to represent my self unto his lordship in this or the lyke stile but because hetherto I treated no farther then wyth your self I beseeche you lett my lord understand of this my Apology or rather Iustification whose noble partes I shall euer honour, and study to be

April: 7   Your Humble Seruant
  1628/   Geo: Cottington

[*Endorsed*:] Copy of Mr George Cottingtons letter to Sir Iohn Finet Ap: 7: 1628

32. 25 August 1628   CALVERT TO THE DUKE OF BUCKINGHAM[1]

I Remember that his Maiestie once told mee that I write as faire a hand to looke vppon a farre of as any man in England,[2] but that when any one came neare it, they weare not able to read a word: wherevppon I gott a dispensation both from his Maiestie and your Grace to vse another mans pen when I write to eyther of you, and I humblye thanke you for it, for Writing is a greate payne to mee nowe: I owe your Grace an accompte of my actions and proceedinges in this Plantation, Since vnder your patronage and by your fauourable mediation to his Maiestie I haue transported my selfe hither: I came to builde, and sett, and sowe, but I am falne to fighting with Frenchmen who haue heere disquieted mee and many other of his Maiesties Subiectes fishing in this Land: One Monsieur Dela Rade of Deepe[3] with three shipps and 400. men, many of them Gentlemen of qualitie and La fleur de la Ieunesse de Normandye (as some frenchmen heare haue told vs) cam first into a harbor of myne called Capebroile not aboue a league from the place where I am planted, and there Surprising divers of the fishermen in their shallops att the harbors mouth, within a short tyme after possest themselues of two English Shipps within the harbour, withall their fishe & provisions, and had donne the like to the rest in that place had not I sent them assistance with two shipps of myne one of 360 tonnes and 24 peces of Ordnance and th'other a barke of 60 tonnes with 3. or 4 small gunnes in her, & aboue 100 men abord vs in all: These Shipps

---

[1] P.R.O., CO 1/4, 57. Buckingham had been assassinated two days earlier.
[2] The king was far too kind to the appearance of Calvert's handwriting but correct as to its illegibility.
[3] Probably Raymond de la Rade who served as the lieutenant of the de Caën family and protected their monopoly of the St Lawrence fur trade. *DCB*, I.

being discouered to moue by a skowt whom the french kept at the harbors mouth they staid not waying Anchor, but let slip their Cables and awaye to Sea as fast as they coulde Leaving there bootie and 67 of their owne men behinde them on shore for hast: wee gaue them chase but coulde not ouertake them: and that nighte I sent a Companye to fech the 67 men out of the woods, fearing that being well armed as wee vnderstood they weare and then in despiration they mighte force some boates or weake ship, or doe other Mischiefe, and the next morning they weare broughte vnto mee hither, where I haue beene troubled and Charged with them all this sommer Within a fewe dayes after, advertisement was giuen me that Dela Rade was gonne in to the Bay of Conception some 20 leagues to the Northward of this Place and their Committed more spoile, whervppon I sent forth the greate shipp agayne with all the Seamen I had heere and one of my sonnes, with some gentlemen and others that attend mee in this Plantation, but before they came neere him hee was againe freighted by the Vnicorne of London, having first taken divers English Prisoners and Caryed them with him: from thence my shipp and Companye by my directions Consorting with Captayne Fearnes a man of Warre retourned backe to the Southward and in a harbor called Trepasse where Dela Rade first toucht in the beginninge of the sommer, and came from thence to vs, they found 6 French Shipps 5 of Bayonne and one of St Ian de Luz: who had Almost made theire Voyage and weare neere Readie to retourne homewardes: Them wee tooke for the hurte they haue donne vs, and haue sent them now for England, where they shall arive Safelye I hope within your Graces Admirall Iurisdiction and I presume soe much of your wonted fauour as in any parte of this busynes that hath relation to my intrest your Grace will bee pleased I shall bee respected as one of your Sarvantes and that you will pardon all errors of formalitye in the proceedinges: Whether this French gentlemen may retourne agayne when the shipps are gonne I know not: if hee doe, we shall defende this place as well as wee are able: but for the tyme to come, it much concernes his Maiesties Service and the good of that Kingdome in my poore Iudgement that two men of warre att the least mighte bee Continued all the yeare, excepte it bee the winter tyme, vppon this Coast for preservinge of soe many of his Subiectes being all bred Seamen and their shipping and goodes which maye easilye bee donne by a Contribution vppon the fisherye it selfe and it maye verye well beare it without any sensibell burthen to particular men, if your Grace will bee pleased to Intercede vnto his Maiestie in that behalfe and that some principall Owners of the west Countrey maye be Conferd withall to that purpose before the next Spring and the Contribution Imposed heere by his Maiesties Authoritye I haue desired this bearrer Master Peasley, sometyme a servant to our late Soueraigne, whose Company I haue had heere this sommer, to attend your Grace on my behalfe and I humblye beseech you to vouchsafe him Access to your person as there shall bee occasion with fauour and I shall allwayes rest the same now and foreuer

     Your Graces most faithfull and humble servant

Ferryland 25. August

 1628   George Baltimore[1]

33. 25 August 1628   CALVERT TO CHARLES I[2]

In this remote wilde part of the worlde where I haue planted my selfe, and shall indeauour, by gods assistance, to enlarge your Maiesties Dominion, and in whatsoever else to serue your Maiestie Loyallye and faithfullie with all the powres both of my mynde and bodye, I meete with greate difficulties and Incumbrances at the beginning, (as enterprises of this nature commonlye haue) and cannot bee easlie overcome by such weake handes as myne without your Maiesties Speciall protextion, for which cause I must still renew my addresse vnto your Maiestie as your most humble Subiect and Vassall for the continuance of your Princelye fauour to mee and this woorke which I haue taken in hand. Your Maiesties Subiectes fishing this yeare in the harbors of this Land haue been much disquietted by a Frenchman of Warre one Mon Sieur Delarade of Deepe, who with three Shipps and fowre hundred men well armed and appoynted came first into a harbour belonging to mee called Capebroile, where hee surprized divers of the fishermen tooke two of their shipps in the Harbour, and kepte the possession of them vntill I sent two Shipps of myne with some hundreth men (being all the force wee could make vppon the suddayne) in this place where I am planted. Vppon the approch of which shipps neare to the harbors mouth of Capebroile one of them being 360 tonnes with 24 peces of Ordnance the french lett slip their Cables and made to sea as fast they coulde, Leaving for hast both the English shipps behinde them whereof they had formerly possession and 67 of their owne Countreymen on shore whom I haue since had heere with mee prisoners. Wee followed The chase soe long as wee saw any possibilitye of comming vp to them,

---

[1] The signature is in Calvert's hand.   [2] P.R.O., CO 1/4, 56.

but they weare much better of saile and wee weare forced to giue it ouer. The said Delarade hath since donne more spoile vppon other of your Maiesties Subiectes in the North partes of this Land as I was giuen to vnderstand which Caused mee to pursue them a second tyme, but they weare driven out of the Cuntrey by a shipp of London before myne could get thither. Hearevppon being still vexte with these men and both my selfe in my poore fisherie heere, and manye other of your Maiesties Subiectes much preiudiced this yeare by them, I directed my shipp in Consort with Captayne Fearnes a man of Warre then in this Countrey to seeke out some of that nation at Trepasse a harbor to the Southward where they vse to fish. theire they found Six shipps 5. of Bayonne and one of St Ian de Luz whome they tooke with their Lading being fish and trayne and haue sent them for England.

I doe humblye beseech your Maiesties gratious and benigne Interpretation of my proceedinges; where the principall end hath beene to doe your Maiesties Service and to giue mee Leaue vppon this Occation to bee an humble Sutor vnto your Maiestie both for myne owne safetie, and for many thousandes of your Subiectes that vse this Land and come heither everye yeare for the most parte weakely prouided of defence, that by your Maiesties Supreme Authoritye for the preservation of your people being Seamen and Marynors, and their shipps from the Spoile of the enemye (the losse whereof much Importes your Maiesties Service) Two men of Warre at least may be appoynted to guard this Coast And to be heere betymes in the yeare, the fishermen to Contribute to the defraying of the Charge which amongst soe manye will be but a small matter and easilie borne. I haue humblye intreated my Lord Duke[1] to recommend and mediate it vnto your Maiestie on the behalfe of vs all, and doe soe leaue it vnto your Princely Widsome beseeching your Maiestie to pardon this vnmannerly length where with I haue presumed to trouble your patience. God Allmightye preserue your Maiestie with a long Raygne and much happines:

your Maiesties most loyall subiect
and humble servant
George Baltimore[2]

Feryland 25. August
1628

[*Endorsed:*] August 25. 1628.
Lord Baltimore to his Maiestie

---

[1] Buckingham was already dead.   [2] Only the signature is in Calvert's hand.

A relacíon of an attempt by some Frenchmen vpon the Fishery at Newfoundland, and how they were dryven away. And desires twoo shipps of warr may be appointed to guard the Coast and the Fishermen to contribute to it.

34. [1628] DRAFT OF A PETITION [FROM CALVERT TO THE DUKE OF BUCKINGHAM?][1]

Most excelente Prince/[2]
It is not vnknowen to your Grace, and to the rest of his Maiesties most honorable privye Counsell of what Consequence the fishinge in Newfoundland hath been and as yet is to his Maiestie in regard of his Customes, and to our whole nation as well for shipping and mariners as the yearely supply of Comodities Consisting in fysh and trayne Oyle or by the exchanig [sic] from forraine Countreyes, Salt wynes, and other necessaries yealding by Comon Compute neere 300. thousand poundes a yeare for the setling wherof with severall plantacions it pleased the late king of famous memory to graunt a Patent vnder the greate Seale./ But now so it is my good lord, both the fishing fleets and the plantacions, being these as yeat in the infancie, and not able longer to subsist in these dangerous tymes, without some sodaine Course be taken for the preventing of Pirattes on that Coast, do Cast themselves into your Graces protection, and to that end myself being among others a Patentee for that hopefull plantacion doe on there behalf and myne owne humblie sollicite your Countenance and favour, whereby wee maye be furnished with two sufficient Ships on the fishermens Charge to waste and defend them, as the Hollanders yearly vse us, and according to a former Comission graunted by the Privy Counsell with the approbation of his late Maiestie about five yeares past, which happened by a petition exhibited by the Treasurer and Company established in London for the plantacions in that Country,[3] The tymes nowe move & vrgently require it for the savegard of the gaynefull Trade, about which 300. Shippes are yearly occupied and now like to

---

[1] N.L.W., 1595 E.
[2] This is an unusual way to address a duke, though perhaps warranted by Buckingham's extraordinary position at court. Buckingham as lord admiral seems the most likely recipient of such a petition, and the content echoes Calvert's letters of 25 August 1628 to both the duke and the king.
[3] In May 1620 John Mason, the governor of the Cupids Cove colony, had received a commission from the lord admiral to go to Newfoundland in command of a ship of 320 to suppress piracy and restore order in the fishery. P.R.O., SP 12/237, ff. 30–2; the document has been filed with a group of Admiralty papers among the State Papers, Domestic, for the reign of Elizabeth.

fall into greate and imminent danger, This in Duty I make bould to intymate, desiring your Grace, if it seeme expedyent, that as I remayne obliged for many other favours, and for important busyness I may be nominated and appoynted Admirall in the Comission And in my absence that some of my worthy frindes which stand ingaged and interested in the Plantacions may supply the place as Sir Henry Salusbury Baronet Sir Frauncis Tanfild knight, Sir william Vaughan knight,[1] Master Iohn Peale Esquir, Walter Vaughan Esquir,[2] Henry Vaughan Esquire,[3] Iohn Poyntz Esquir

What further good will ensue by these wafting Shippes for the breeding of able Seamen I leave to your wise and noble Consideracion

35. 9 October 1628   THE EXAMINATION OF THE REVEREND ERASMUS STOURTON[4]

The examinacion of Erasmus Stourton gentleman late Preacher to the Colony of Feryland in the Newfoundland had and taken at Plymouth in the Country of Devon the ninth day of October 1628 / before Nicholas Sherwill marchant Mayour of the borough of Plymouth and Thomas Sherwill marchant two of his Maiesties Iustices of peace within the sayd borrough./

The sayd Examinant sayth that he came out of the Newfoundland the 28th of August last in a shipp of London called the Victory and arryved in to this harbour the 26th of September last and sayth that about the 23th of Iuly last was twelve moneths the Lord of Baltamoore arryved in Newfoundland and brought with him two seminary preistes one of them called Longvyll[5] and thother called Anthony Smith[6] which sayd Longvyll returned agayne for England with the sayd Lord and afterwardes in this yeare .1628. my Lord of Baltamoore arryved there

---

[1] William Vaughan was knighted by Falkland in Ireland on 27 July 1628. Shaw, *Knights*, II, 194.

[2] Probably a brother of William Vaughan.

[3] 1587?–1659?, royalist, soldier; sixth son of Walter Vaughan and brother of William. *DWB.*

[4] P.R.O., CO 1/4, 59. Stourton (1603–58), was educated at Cambridge; from 1631 until his death he served as rector of Walesby in Lincolnshire. *DCB*, I.

[5] Thomas Longville (b. 1598), one of the two sons of the anglican, Sir Henry Longville, who became priests. Both were educated at St Omer's college; Thomas was ordained in Rome in 1626. His elder brother, Henry, married Catherine, sister to the first lord Falkland. Lahey, 'The role of religion', p. 504.

[6] Anthony Pole (alias Smith), (b. *c.* 1592), educated at St Omer's college and at the English college in Valladolid. In 1613 he joined the Jesuits. He returned to England in the early 1620s when he seems to have left the Society. He was arrested and imprisoned for a time in 1626. *Ibid.*, pp. 504–5.

agayne and brought with him one other seminary preist whose name is Hacket[1] with the number of forty papistes or thereaboutes where the sayd Hacket and Smith euery sunday sayth Masse and doe vse all other the ceremonies of the church of Rome in as ample a maner as tis vsed in Spayne. And this examinant hath seene them at Masse and knoweth that the childe of one William Poole a protestant was baptized according to the orders and customes of the church of Rome by the procurement of the sayd Lord of Baltamoore contrary to the will of the sayd Poole to which child the said Lord was a witnes./

This Examinant is a Chapleyne of my Lord of Anglesey[2] and is gonne towardes London with a purpose to attend the Lordes of the Counsell as he informes vs./

36. [Dec.? 1628] PETITION OF WILLIAM PEASELEY CONCERNING A SHIP FOR THE DEFENCE OF THE FISHERY[3]

To the Right Honourable the Lords Comissioners for the office of the Lord Admirall.

The humble Petition of William Peaseley on the behalfe of the Lord Baltimore.

Sheweth that whereas your Lordships having nominated the Esperance to bee lent vnto the Lord Baltimore for defence of his Plantacion, and the Englishe fishermen in Newfoundland, against the invasion of the French; Hee doth in all humility render many thanks vnto your Lordships for your Noble disposition to the sayd Lord Baltimore; And knowing that your intendment is to second his Maiesties gratious favour towards him with the assistance of your power, hee doth therefore humbly begg liberty to represent vnto your Noble consideracions the reasons of his excepcions to that shipp. It is most true that the loane of this shipp is a greate argument of his Maiesties and your Lordships speciall favor, and an evident signe of your care for the safety of many thowsand Englishmen, who yearly resort with litle or no strength to Newfoundland, But the Peticioner doth finde that the Esperance requires a greater charge to fitt her to sea then the fraight of another shippe will cost, or at the least a longer time to repayre her, then the

---

[1] Hacket cannot be identified with certainty. In 1630 it was reported that a secular priest named Antonius Rivers had gone to Ferryland with Calvert. Rivers was an alias for Anthony Whitehair and it is possible that Hacket was also an alias. *Ibid.*, p. 505.

[2] Christopher Villiers (1593–1630), brother of George Villiers, duke of Buckingham. *DNB.*   [3] P.R.O., CO 1/4, 61.

necessity of the service doth permitt: For shee hath remayned long in Harbour, not being employd these two last voyages to Rochell, which hath much decayed her, Her sheathing with age and vse is decayd, Her sayles and Cables are eyther vnserviceable or lost, so that shee must bee new sheathed, haue new sayles, Cables & Anchours with many other additions of charge to supply her defect*es*, amounting to aboue 600^{li}. Now the sayd shipp being in this poore Condic*i*on and the time and safety of his Maiesties subiect*es* requiring a speedier assistance in respect of the present preparac*i*on of the Frenche to infest Newfoundland early this next spring, giues boldnesse vnto your Petic*i*oner to conceiue that for these reasons your Lordships will iudge the S^t. Claude to bee a fitter shippe for this purpose, Wherefore hee humbly prayes that yo^u wilbee pleased to giue order for the deliuery of her, that shee may bee made ready, and sent (as is intended) with all speede to that Coast to bee employed for the preservation of his Maiesti*es* right and for the safety of the shipps, estates, and liues of many thowsands of his subiects, resorting thether and depending on that fishing; Besides which motiues, hee doth not doubt of your Lordships fauourable regard of the quality of the Lord Baltimore. For which hee as in duty bound shall dayly pray &c.

37. 13 Dec. 1628 CALVERT IS LENT THE *ST. CLAUDE*[1]

may it please your lordship:[2]

I acquainted his ma*i*estie with the reason my lord Baltimore had to feare that ye french (whome in defence of himselfe and his maiesties subiect*es* he beate ye last yeare at Newfoundland) would this yeare returne for theyr reuenge, and allso with his humble sute that his ma*i*estie would be pleased to lend him a shipp that he might be ye better able againe to defend himselfe./ His ma*i*estie was pleased to graunt the sayd humble request, and Comm*a*unded me to signifie his pleasure vnto your lordship in that behalfe, and in particular he was pleased to say that you might appoynt him one of ye sixe prise shipps shipps [*sic*], which master Nicolas informes me are good and warrlike shipps, and y^t it should be a good one Soe with ye remembrance of my humble deutye I rest

13 december 1628   your lordships most humble seruant
Fra*n*cis Cottington./

[1] P.R.O., CO 1/4, 60.
[2] Richard Weston (1577–1635), first earl of Portland, had become lord treasurer in July 1628. After Buckingham's death he was Charles I's most influential minister.

[*Addressed*:] To the Richt Honourable my very good Lord the lord high Treasorer of England

[*Endorsed*:] 13 December 1628 Sir Francis Cottington for a shipp for ye Lord Baltimore. / The St Claude to be lent to the lord Baltimore for twelue monethes and to be delieuered to Master Leonard Caluert.[1]

38. [Dec. 1628] MEMORIAL FROM CALVERT TO [SECRETARY DORCHESTER][2]

That whereas his Maiesty was pleased at the humble suit of my sonne[3] on my behalf, and vpon your Lordshipps honorable motion to grant me the loane of the S^t. Claude for 6. monethes, that your Lordshipp would be pleased to procure a privy seale to these purposes according to his Maiesties gratious promise.

That your Lordshipp would also be pleased to procure me a letter from my Lordes of the Councell to the Gouernor of Virginia in favor of my wife now there,[4] that he would affoord her his best assistance vpon her returne into England in all thinges reasonable for her accomodation in her passage, and for recovery of any debts due vnto me in Virginia or for disposing of her servantes according to the Custome of the Countrey yf shee shall think fitt to leave any behind her, or vpon any other occasion whenever she may haue need of his lawfull favor. And I shall acknowledge it as a great favor from your Lordshipp

Moreover that your Lordshipp would be pleased to move his Maiesty that [illegible] vpon my humble suite vnto him from Newfoundland for a proportion to bee granted vnto me in Virginia he was gratiously pleased to signify by Sir Francis Cottington that I should haue any part not already granted that his Maiesty would give me leave to chuse such a part now and to passe it vnto me with the like powers and privileges as the King his father of happy memory did grant me this precinct in Newfoundl[and] and I shall contribute my best endevors with the rest

---

[1] Calvert's second son (d. 1649); it was he who led the settlers to Maryland in 1633. The endorsement is in secretary Nicholas' hand. This letter is followed by an extremely rough and partly illegible draft, again in Nicholas' writing, of a privy seal warrant for one of the prize ships to be delivered to Leonard Calvert for twelve months.

[2] P.R.O., CO 1/4, 62. Sir Dudley Carleton (1573–1632) had been given the title of viscount Dorchester in July 1628 and appointed secretary of state the following December. *DNB*.

[3] His son-in-law, William Peaseley.

[4] Calvert's second wife, whose identity is unknown. Possibly he had met and married her in Ireland.

of his loyall subie[cts] to enlarge his empire in those part[s] of the world, by such gentlemen an[d] others as will adventure to ioyne with me though I go not my self in person./

39. [Dec. 1628] STATE OF THE CASE BETWEEN CALVERT AND SOME LONDON MERCHANTS[1]

The Lord Baltimore this last sommer by his owne shipps and servauntes, chased away from the Coast of Newfoundlande Three Frenchmen of Warre with 500 men in them, Recovered diverse English shippes from them, Restored them to their former owners, and tooke 67. french prisoners, whome he kept att his plantacion to his great hazard & charges almost two Monthes. Vppon notice the second tyme that the same french did infest the English in the Northerne parts of the Countrey, his Lordshipp sent his shipp ye Benediction againe, whose Captaine after the departure of the french acquaintes [sic] the Captaine of the Vyctory a man of warre of London, then on that Coast, of his desegne for Trepasse, a harbor in Newfoundlande; in which place he discovered vnto him weere sixe French fishinge shippes of little strengthe.

The Twoe shipps ioyne [sic] and sayle togeather. On the way they make a Consortshipp in writinge that such prizes as they or eyther of them tooke should be devided man for man and Tonne for Tonne/

The Benediction as Admirall enters the harbor first, gaue the first shott to the nomber of 6. or 7., then gives those six french shipps a Broadside, by the terror whereof they quitt the possession of their shipps and make to shoare, leavinge only one man aboard and he hydd amongst the fishe / The Wynde then beinge scant, and the Benediction makeinge a Boarde, was engaged on a lee shoare, from which before shee could free herself, the victory havinge given the French in all but Three shott, beinge the lesser shipp by 150. Tonnes, and having the Wynde larger, boare vp towards the empty shipps, Anchored by them, and with her longe boate boarded some of them a little while before the Benediction came /

In confirmacion of the Consortshipp both shipps devided presently the pilage, man for man /

All the six prizes were afterwards brought into his Lordshipps harbor vnder comaund of his Fort where he might haue kept his owne parte by vertue of his Maiesties Charter /

The Vyctory lost her squadron of shipps by fowle weather at sea,

[1] P.R.O., CO 1/4, 63. Another copy, CO 1/4, 64.

for 12 dayes togeather, duringe which tyme the Benediction spent much labour and tyme in seekinge for them, in staying for them, and in preservinge them from 4. Frenchmen of Warre, that pursued them 2. dayes and brought them safe into Englande /

The Benediction a second tyme preserved Twoe of the prizes belonging to the charge and Care of the Vyctory from a desperat Dunkirker in the Narrow seas, being about to Board them, and had done it, but for the extraordinary Care of the Benediction, whoe forced her away with the expence of about 20. shott, the Vyctory being then att Plymouth /

Since the shipps arryvall at London, the Merchants of the Vyctory, doe Cavill, pretending that the greatest parte of the prises belonges to them, because their shipp Boarded the enemy first, and the Benediction had no letter of Marke: Therevppon to avoyd suite in Lawe it was att their mocion referred to the arbitrament of .4. men /

These men heard both Captaines, with the masters of both shipps, and after Twoe howers debate agreed of an Award, which was, That the Benediction had not broken the Consortshipp, And therefore ordered shee should haue man for man & Tonne for Tonne /

The Arbitratours for the Lord Baltimore signe & seale the Awarde, The other Twoe Refuse, and make frivolous excuses, They havinge themselves in the name of the rest given order for writinge the Awarde /

His Maiestie havinge been made acquainted with this forward dealinge of the merchauntes, was pleased to referre the hearinge & ending this difference vnto your Lordshipp, and the rest of the Privy Councell, whoe are humbly desired to take into their noble consideracion the merritt of the Lord Baltimore in this particular /

By preserving at least 40. or 50. sayle of English from ye french
By chasing them away with his owne shipps & servauntes thereby neglectinge his plantacion & fishinge to his preiudice almost 2000^{li}.
By discovering to the Vyctory the place & strength of those prizes.
By the iust performaunce of her parte in takeing them /
By preservinge them Twyce att sea when the victory had abandoned them /

And therefore it is humbly desired That the Lord Baltimore may haue his parte according to the Consortshipp, and a lettre of Mark antidated, or some other power from their lordshipps to enable him to recover his proporcion /

[Endorsed:] State of my Lord Baltimores cause[1]

[1] CO 1/4, 64, is endorsed: 'Relation of a difference between a ship of the Lord Baltimores, and of the Merchantes of London, about deuiding some French prizes.'

40. 25 February 1628/9   THE PRIVY COUNCIL LICENSES THE EXPORT OF GRAIN TO FERRYLAND[1]

At Whitehall the 25.th of February 1628

Present

Lord Keeper.[2]	Lord Viscount Dorchester.[8]
Lord President.[3]	Lord Bishop of Winton[9]
Lord Priuie Seale[4]	Lord Bishopp of London[10]
Earl of Dorset[5]	Lord Newburgh.[11]
Earl of Salisbury[6]	Master Treasurer[12]
Lord Viscount Wilmott[7]	Master Secretary Coke.[13]

Whereas humble suite was this day made vnto the Board on the behalfe of the Lord Baltimore now remayneing in Newfoundland that in regard of the scarsetie of corne there, and of the greate plentie therof in this kingdome Lycence mought [*sic*] be granted for the buying here, and transporting to his Lordshipp 14 Lastes of Wheate and lyke quantitie of Maulte for the Releefe of those of that Plantacion. Theire Lordshipps vpon consideracion had thereof doe thinke fitt hereby to grant Lycence for the buyeing and transporting of the said quantitie of Wheate and Maulte as is desired. Provided that such person as is imployed on that behalfe shall first pay his maiesties Customes & duties for the same, and giue good securitie not to dispose of any parte therof but for the Releefe of the Plantacion aforesaid. Hereof the Lord Treasurer[14] is prayed and required to take knowledge and to giue effectuall order therin accordingly. /

[1] P.R.O., PC 2/39, p. 106.
[2] Thomas Coventry (1578–1640), first baron Coventry.
[3] Edward Conway (d. 1631), viscount Conway; appointed secretary of state in 1623 and lord president in 1628. *DNB*.
[4] Henry Montague; see above, p. 100, n. 6.
[5] Sir Edward Sackville (1591–1652), fourth earl of Dorset.
[6] William Cecil (1591–1668), second earl of Salisbury.
[7] Sir Charles Wilmot (1570?–1644?), first viscount Wilmot.
[8] Sir Dudley Carleton; see above, p. 287, n. 2.
[9] Richard Neile (1562–1640), bishop of Winchester; later archbishop of York.
[10] William Laud (1573–1645), became archbishop of Canterbury in 1633.
[11] Edward Barrett (1581–1645), chancellor of the exchequer. His first wife was Jane Cary, sister of Henry Cary, lord Falkland.
[12] Sir Thomas Edmondes; see above, p. 105. n. 8.
[13] Sir John Coke; see above, p. 269, n. 2.
[14] Sir Richard Weston; see above, p. 286, n. 2.

41. 9 April 1629   SUPPLIES FOR THE FERRYLAND
COLONY[1]

The ix^th of Aprill 1629. /
In the sainct Claude Regis burthen iij^C tonnes. /
Stephen Bacon Master for Avalon in Newfoundland. /

Captaine Ralfe Morley the assigne of the Lord Baltamoore for the vse
of the said Lordes plantacion there Free of Custom and all duties, by
vertue of his Lordships grant for the space of x. yeres, From oure late
soveraigne Lorde Kinge Iames dates the vij.^th of Aprill in the xxj.^th
yeare of his Raigne as followeth

one hondred quarters of wheate per statute	Cust.	
more one hondred quarters of mault per statute	Cust.	Defaulke
more x. quarters of pease per statute	Cust.	
and x. quarters of oatemeale per statute	Cust.	

42. [1629?]   NOTES ON THE PREPARATION OF FRENCH
SHIPPING FOR RAIDS ON NORTH AMERICA AND THE
WEST INDIES[2]

The french haue Ready at deepe newhauen and homfleur some twenty
sayle of shipes bound for Cannada, the Island of st Christophers and
part for the Newfoundland and all Ready to depart and some twenty
sail of other ships are expected out of brytany & bisky for Cannada.
Captayne Kerke is bound and Readdy to depart wher hee may bee abel
to Renconter and make good his party with them.[3] hee hauing some
six good shipes and three pynnaces all well manned and oth[er]
prouition necessary.

fo^r s^t christoph[ers]: that Is more dangerous If allreaddy o[ur] people
ther are not prouided: or that some speedy sou[cco]ur bee sent.[4]

[1] Southampton Port Book, Christmas 1628 to Christmas 1629 (P.R.O., Exchequer,
Kings Remembrancer, E 190/822/9).   [2] P.R.O., CO 1/5, 3. Damaged.
[3] David Kirke (d. 1654) had led an expedition against the French in 1627; in 1629 he
captured French Canada but it was later returned to the French. In 1637 he was one of
those who received a grant of the island of Newfoundland from Charles I and he
subsequently became governor. DCB, 1; Cell, English enterprise, pp. 113–17.
[4] There were strong rumours that the French intended to attack St. Christophers (St.
Kitts), which was settled by both English and French colonists. In fact it was the Spanish
who attacked and dispersed both groups of settlers. R. S. Dunn, Sugar and slaves: the rise
of the planter class in the English West Indies, 1624–1713 (Chapel Hill, N.C., 1972), p. 119.

fo^r the newfoundland wee haue ther diuers shipes gone for the fishing only beeing In nomber from the west Contry about some forty sayle[1] but all of them for the most part are not prouided for warr but are shipes of small defence: so that except some men of ware be[e se]nt speedyly they may bee surpr[ise]d and taken by the french. It Is sayd that [mor]e shipes of burthen are bound for the newfoun[dlan]d ther to take ther fish of the forsayd shipes: and from thence are bound for the straites If order Could be taken with those good shipes to stay ther for a while till the fishing ended wherby to secure ower shipes which are ther of small forces: It would proue a good seruice and honnour to ower land or In defaut If some 3 or fower men of war Could bee sent to the lord of baltamore wherby to withstand the enrymy. It would much Reioyce the Intrested of the west Contry whoe nowe haue solely ther trade for those partes for fishing

[*Endorsed*:][2] memorial touching ye preparacion of ye French for Canada, terra noua and St Christophers

43. 18 AUGUST 1629   CALVERT TO [SIR FRANCIS COTTINGTON][3]

Sir

In this part of the world crosses and miseryes is my portion; my comforts come from thence where you are, and amongst the rest none greater than to heare of the honor his Ma*ies*ty hath beene pleased to do you in giving you a place at that Table, where of right you ought to have had roome made you long before.[4] God grant you may long enioye it, and reward you for the many favours you have done me. I am so overwhelmed with troubles and cares as I am forced to write but short and confusedly. I hope the trust of those moneyes assigned for my children is now clear out of that Jewes hands of Lincolns Inne, and setled upon you and Sir W. Ashton, and for their mothers sake as well as for myne I doubt not but you will have a care of them. I have sent them home after much sufferance in this wofull country, where with one intolerable wynter were we almost undone. It is not

---

[1] This would have been an unusually small Newfoundland fleet.
[2] By Dudley Carleton, lord Dorchester.
[3] New York Public Library, Arents Tobacco Collection. The letter has been transcribed and published by Laure.ice C. Wroth, 'Tobacco or codfish', *Bulletin of the New York Public Library*, LVIII (1954), 523–34, who identifies the probable recipient as Sir Francis Cottington, one of Calvert's closest friends.
[4] Cottington had been appointed to the privy council in November 1628.

to be expressed with my pen what wee have endured. I must leave it to their relation, who will wayte upon my Lady[1] and you. For this reason I am forced to remove my selfe before another wynter come to Virginia (being the nearest neighboring country inhabited) with some 40. persons in my company, where I hope to lay my bones I know not how soone, and in the meane tyme may yet do the King and my Country more service there by planting of Tabacco, if his Maiesty would be pleased to grant me a Portion of some good large Territory not yet passed to any other with the like priviledges as the King his father was pleased to grant me in this unfortunate place: which I very heartily entreate you to procure me with as much speede as may be least the clamors of wicked people now lett loose with discontment upon this dissolution as that knave Stourton did last yeare[2] may make the suite afterwards unseasonable; and unlesse this Portion be granted me I am utterly undone in my reputation and authority with these people who have putt themselves under my gouvernment. I leave the particulars to be sollicited by Mr. Peasley who is now my sonne in lawe, having married my daughter Anne for the great services he hath done me, and I beseech you the rather in that respect than in whatsoever he shall have occasion to adresse himselfe unto you he may have your trustfull favor, and that you will acknowledge him for your humble and faithfull servant as really he is. I have bestowed upon my daughter his wife twelve hundred pownds for her portion out of those moneyes which are in your hands and Sir William Ashtons and I desire that you would pay it to her or to him, either in ready money yf any of it be in your hands, or by assigning him good bonds for it, and such as are the soonest payable. Land he hath none to make her jointure, but would be contracted to assure that meanes which he hath upon her by such wayes as shalbe reasonably devysed yf God should call him; wherein I shall also entreate you (were it not that your other businesse now of greater weight makes me loth to trouble you) or to ask Sir William Ashton, to take care to see it done. My daughter Helene is 14. yeares of age, and yf a good husband could be had for her I would bestowe upon her as much as her other sisters have had or yf it were 3. or 400. more because 1200.[li] will not advance her much.[3] Out of a little stock there can be but small shares. In the meane tyme I shall desire you that

---

[1] Cottington's wife was Anne, widow of Sir Robert Brett and daughter of Sir William Meredith.

[2] See above, pp. 284–5.

[3] Helen Calvert (b. 1615) married James Talbot of Ballyconnell, County Cavan, Wroth, 'Tobacco or codfish,' p. 532.

forty pownds a yeare be payd her out of the profits of the stock for her present maintenance: With my sonne Leonard I know not what to do, now wee have peace with our neighbors, for which neverthelesse I prayse God, and do not desire warres to maintaine my children upon the spoiles: I pray you let him have fifty pownds out of those moneyes as they can be raysed to bring him hether to me againe and I will provyde for him afterwards as well as I may. My other three yonge sonnes George, Francis, and Henry[1] I have given order shalbe sent to schole, and because I would be free from the contynuall and yearely care of them at this so great a distance of place, I beseech you lett there be delivered to their use and for their present maintenance to my sonne Peasley, three hundred pownds, and they shall neede no more these five years. For the rest of the moneyes (as something will be left) yf it please you to lett my sonne Peasley know from tyme to tyme how they are layd out to the childrens use he will advertise me of it as there shalbe opportunity of sending. I am tyred with writing: Commend my humble service to my Lady. This last wynter hath yielded us not 3. furre scarfs and those not good: so as she cannot be provyded as I wished I have sent her a Naples[2] wastcoat which I desire her sometymes to weare for my sake, and to remember her poore Cosen and servant. Send Iane Barnes to me when she will, and I will take order she shall never be troubled with her more. I must leve my loves alone to my Lord Tresorer[3] my Lord Viscount Wentworth and the rest of my noble friends untill my shippe returne from Virginia: For untill this very day I thought to have went for England myself, and so am overtaken with tyme and busynesse that I can write no more at this tyme, and this which I do is with much difficulty. God Almighty keepe you, My Lady and all your little ones. Feryland. 18. August 1629

Your faithfull servant and Cosen

Geo. Baltimore

[*Endorsed:*] Lord Baltimore from newfound land

[1] The three younger sons of Calvert were born between 1613 and 1617; George Calvert was drowned in Virginia or Maryland in 1634. *Ibid.*, p. 533.

[2] A kind of cotton velvet.

[3] This is the only place in which my transcript of this extremely difficult letter differs from Wroth's; he transcribes it as 'I must leve my letters alone to my Lord President' in which case the reference would be to Thomas Strafford, earl of Strafford, who was lord president of the council of the north. My reading is that Calvert is referring both to Richard Weston, the lord treasurer, and to Strafford.

44. 19 August 1629   CALVERT TO CHARLES I[1]

Most gratious and dread Soueraigne.

Small benefits and favors can speake and give thankes, but such as are high and vnvaleweable cause astonishment and silence. I am obliged vnto your Maiesty for the later [sic] in such a measure as reflecting vpon my weaknesse and want of meritt I know not what to say. God Almighty knowes, who is the searcher of hearts, how myne earnes [sic] to sacrifice my self for your Maiesties seruice, yf I did but know how to employ my endevors worthy of that great goodnesse and benignity which your Maiesty is pleased to extend towards me vpon all occasions; not onely by reaching your Gracious and Royall hand to my assistance in lending me a faire shipp (for which vpon my knees I render your Maiesty most humble thankes) but by protecting me also against calumny and malice which hath already sought to make seeme fowle in your Maiesties eyes: Whereas I am so much the more confident of Gods blessing vpon my labors in these plantations (notwithstanding the many crosses and disasters I haue found hetherto) in that a Prince so eminently vertuous hath vouchsafed to take it into the armes of his protection, and that those who go about to supplant and destroy me are persons notoriously lewd and wicked. Such a one is that audacious man, who being banished the Colony for his misdeedes did the last wynter (as I vnderstand) raise a false and slanderous report of me at Plymmouth,[2] which comming from thence to your Maiesties know-ledge, you were pleased to referre to some of my Lords of the Councell, by whose honorable hands (for avoyding the ill manners of drawing this letter to too much length) I haue presumed to returne my iust and true Apologie to your Maiesty.

But as those rubbs haue beene layd to stumble me there (which discourage me not because I am confident of your Maiesties singular iudgements and iustice, so haue I mett with greater difficultyes and encumbrances here which in this place are no longer to be resisted, but enforce me presently to quitt my residence, and to shift to some other warmer climate of this new worlde, where the wynters be shorter and lesse rigorous. For here, your Maiesty may please to vnderstand, that I haue fownd by too deare bought experience, which other men for their private interests always concealed from me[3] that from the middest

---

[1] P.R.O., CO 1/5, 27. In Calvert's own hand.

[2] Erasmus Stourton; see above, p. 284, n. 4.

[3] In fact Daniel Powell had told Calvert in 1622 that Ferryland had the reputation of being the coldest place on the island; see above, p. 200.

of October, to the middest of May there is a sadd face of wynter vpon all this land, both sea and land so frozen for the greatest part of the tyme as they are not penetrable, no plant or vegetable thing appearing out of the earth vntill it be about the beginning of May nor fish in the sea besides the ayre so intolerable cold as it is hardly to be endured. By meanes whereof, and of much salt meate, my howse hath beene an hospitall all this wynter, of 100. persons 50. sick at a tyme, myself being one and nyne or ten of them dyed. Herevpon I haue had strong temptations to leave all proceding in plantations, and being much decayed in my strength to retire my self to my former quiett; but my inclination carrying me naturally to these kynd of workes, and not knowing how better to employ the poore remaynder of my dayes then with other good subiectes to further the best I may the enlarging your Maiesties empire in this part of the world, I am determined to committ this place to fishermen that are able to encounter stormes and hard weather, and to remove my self with some 40. persons to your Maiesties dominion of Virginia, where yf your Maiesty will please to grant me a precinct of land with such priviledges as the king your father my gracious Master was pleased to graunt me here, I shall endevor to the vtmost of my power to deserve it and pray for your Maiesties long and happy raigne as

> your Maiesties most humble and
> faithfull subiect and servant.

Feryland . 19 . August
    1629.   George Baltimore

Endorsed: My Lord of Baltimore to yᵉ king yᵉ 19ᵗʰ of August 1629

45. 22 November 1629 CHARLES I TO CALVERT[1]

Signed Charles R.

Right trustie & wellbeloued We greete you well, Such is and euer hath beene the estimation We make of the persons of our louing subiects, who imploy themselues in publick actions that tend to the good and glorie of their Countrie, and the advancement of our seruice, as We cannot but take notice of them though of the meanest condition: but much more of a person of your qualitie who haue beene so neare a seruant to our late deare father of blessed memorie. And seeing your plantation in Newfoundland (as We vnderstand by your letters) hath not answered your expectation which we are enformed to take so much

[1] P.R.O., CO 1/5, 39. Copy.

to hart (hauing therein spent a great part of your meanes) as that you are now in pursute of new Countries; We out of our princely care of you, well weighing that men of your condition and breeding are fitter for other imployments, then the framing of new plantations, Which commonly haue rugged & laborious beginnings, and require much greater meanes in Mannaging them then vsually the power of one priuate subiect can reach vnto, haue thought fit hereby to advise you to desist from further prosecuting your designes that way, and with your first conueniency to returne backe to your natiue Countrie, Where you shall bee sure to enioye both the libertie of a Subiect, and such respects from Vs, as your former seruices and late endeauours iustly deserue. Giuen at our pallace of Whitehall this 22. of Nouember In the 5. yeare of our raigne.

[*Endorsed:*] Copie of his Maiesties letters to the Lord Baltimore, as two equall copies were brought to the Lord Viscount Dorchester by the Earle Marshall[1] and the Lord President of the North[2] And by My lord sealed with the signet, the day of the date. 22 of Nouember

46. THE SECOND LORD BALTIMORE DESCRIBES HIS FATHER'S INVOLVEMENT IN NEWFOUNDLAND[3]

Sir George Caluert late Lord Baltimore having purchased a good part of Newfoundland, did for the better goverment and confirmacion thereof, obtayne a grant from his late Maiestie King Iames vnder the greate seale of England dated the 7th of Aprill in the 2jth yeare of his Raigne, and therevpon did at his owne costes and charges send ouer thither at seuerall times diverse Colonies of his Maiesties subiectes, to plant in seuerall habors, mainteyned them buylt howses for them, made fortes for their, and the Fishermens defence, and placed sundry Governours there, as Captayne Winne, Captaine Mason,[4] and Sir Arthur Aston, and other officers necessary for the goverment of the people, and preservacion of the place, And afterwardes transported himself and his famaly thither, intending to reside amongst them for the better safety of that country, against the invasion of the Frenche, who duering the last warrs did infest that place, for which purpose one

---

1 Thomas Howard; see above, p. 105, n. 5.
2 Thomas Wentworth; see above, p. 273, n. 1.
3 P.R.O., CO 1/9, 43. Extract.
4 John Mason was never governor at Ferryland.

Monsieur de la Rade came thither with 2 good shipps and 400. souldje^rs^, who had certainly taken aboue threescore English shipps, and vndone many thowsand Marriners and fishermen, if the sayd Lord Baltimore had not then beene in Newfoundland, and sent against them his owne shipps, manned by his owne Planters at his greate charges and losse; By which meanes hee recovered from the Frenche those Englishe shipps they had then taken, and restored them to their Owners, and the Prisoners to their liberty, and chaced the French from that Coast, and presently after did by his sayd shipps Conduct and guard safely more then thirty English shipps from Newfoundland to England, and preserved them from those Frenche, who expected their returne on the Coast of England. Vpon which Plantacions and employmentes hee disbursed more then 20000^li^,[1] to the great empoverishing of his estate; And then the said Lord Baltimore finding the Country to bee vnfitt for his habitacion, in respect of the great Coldes in winter, did about six yeares since remoue from thence, leaving there a sufficyent Colony, with a Governour, and so continued to his death... And hee [the second lord Baltimore] hath had a purpose likewise to reuiue a former dessigne of his Fathers, which was (with the consent of the Fishermen there) to raise a Custome vpon all the Fishe taken there, for which hee would mainteyne a sufficyent strength, both at sea and land, for their defence, and to conduct them home with safety; Concerning which, there was a Treaty betweene the late Lord Baltimore, at his being in Newfoundland, and most of the Captaines and principall Fishermen frequenting that place, vpon occasion of that service aboue mencioned, done by him there that yeare, and the busines in short time after, was like to haue beene concluded and agreed, had not the late Lord Baltimore vpon his removing from thence, beene hindered by some other occasions from the prosecuting of it for that time...

47. AN ACCOUNT OF CALVERT'S ACTIVITIES IN NEWFOUNDLAND[2]

...Sir George Calvert Knight deceased (who was in his life tyme principall Secretary and one of the then Privy Counsell to the then King Iames) was by a Grant by Lettres Pattentes vnder the greate Seale of

---

[1] In 1660 Baltimore claimed that his father had spent more than £30,000 on the colony. Petition of Cecil, lord Baltimore, to Charles II, [June] 1660 (P.R.O., CO 1/14, 9). 'The Lord BALTEMORE'S Case, concerning the Province of *Avalon* in *New-found-land*, an Island in America', [1661?] (B.L., Egerton MS 2395, f. 310) also contains an account of Calvert's activities in Newfoundland.

[2] Cecil, lord Baltimore's libel against Sir David Kirke, December 1651 (Extract. P.R.O., HCA Libels, HCA 24/110, 329).

England bearing date the seaventh of Aprill in the one and twentieth Yeare of the late reigne of the said late King Iames, and by a good iust and lawfull right truely and fully possessed of and had a good title and power to a certayne part of Newfound Land called the Province of Avalon and of divers Isles and Islandes & Portes Stations and Creekes of the Sea in the said Lettres mencioned...Sir George Calvert had granted vnto him by the said Lettres Pattentes all the Customes Subsidies and Impositions for all goods and merchandizes exported to the said Province of Avalon in all Dutch French and other Shippes or vessels whatsoever, and allsoe all Imposicions and Customes for the stations of the said Shippes within the said Portes Creekes Seas and places in the said Lettres Pattentes mentioned and in such sorte as therein and thereby appeareth...Sir George Calvert did in his life tyme by himselfe and other his Factors servantes and Agentes and at & vpon his owne proper costes & charges duely and in good and rightfull manner make an entry into and enter vpon the said part of Newfound land called the Province of Avalon and of the Seas Creekes and Portes therevnto belonging and adiacent, and tooke the actuall & naturall possession thereof, and was thereof fully and lawfully both civilly and naturally possessed. And the said Sir George Calvert did within the Seas adiacent or lyeing neare vnto the said Province vpon his owne costes & charges build Stations for Shippes and vessells and make & erect harbours and provide vessels and boates for Fishing, and make places for succou͏ͬ defence and security of all manner of Shippes and vessells that came into those partes to Fish, or otherwise to trade and traffique, and therein & thereaboutes layd out & expended divers great & vast sommes of money extending in the whole to about Twenty Thousand pounds of lawfull money of England...Sir George Calvert Knight did in his life tyme make and erect at his owne charges to the quantity or number of One hundred Fishing boates, and likewise divers stages out from the Land vpon the Seas for the dryeing and makeing of the fish (after the same was taken) in the said Seas Creekes and Portes in or neare adioyning to the said part of Newfound-land or province of Avalon aforesaid, Every of which Fishing boates were sett out to Sea in those partes to take Fish and did in fishing yeild vnto him the yearely proffitt of Fifty Forty thirty or at least twenty poundes per boate,...Sir George Calvert being so rightfully and peaceably possessed of the͏ said premises and fully possessed thereof and every part thereof did depart this Life in or about the moneth of Aprill in the yeare 1632 leaving behind him his Sonne and heire the said Cecill Lord Baltamore...

48. A FISHERMAN REMEMBERS CALVERT[1]

...hee hath by times as master and mariner vsed the trade of Newfoundland for theise fourtie yeeres last or thereaboutes, and thereby well knoweth that there is a place or bay called Fermoose in Newfoundland, and another place harbour or Bay therein called Petit Harbour, and that betweene the aforesaid harbours, place or bayes of Fermoose and Petit harbour there are situat and being theise places or bayes ensuing, that is to say, Aquafort harbour, Ferriland harbour, Caplin Baye, Cape Broyle, Ile Despere, Mouneapple Bay, Wittlesea Bay and Baye of Bulls, all which harbours are lying and being on the Easterne sea of Newfoundland. And he further saith that Sir George Calvert late Lord Baltamore (By such as hee imployed herein) built the chiefe Mansion house at Ferriland within the Province of Avalon in Newfoundland in the partes of America, and that this deponent knewe Captaine Edward Wynne who was sent thither as Agent or deputie for the said Sir George Calvert late Lord Baltamore about thirtie yeeres since, and there resided as his agent for diverse yeeres. And this deponent alsoe knewe Sir Arthur Aston, who alsoe resided there for diverse yeeres, as agent likewise for the said Sir George Calvert late Lord Baltamore: And deposeth that the said Sir George Calvert Lord Baltamore was afterwardes there alsoe himselfe with his wife children and familie, all which hee knoweth because hee this deponent was there present the respective persons there in the qualities and imployment aforesaid, And hee well knoweth as he saith that the said Sir George Calvert late Lord Baltamore was at greate costes and chardges in making fortes and platformes and providing of ordnances and amunicion for them within the time predeposed there and also in making provision for diverse people or persons by him transported thither to settle a plantation...

49. NEWFOUNDLAND SETTLERS REMEMBER CALVERT[2]

The Examinacion and deposicion of Anne Love inhabitant in Ferriland taken before us Commissioners at the Mansion house[3] in Ferriland August 31th: 1652.

To the third shee saith the said Sir George Calvert came here at his

---

[1] Deposition of Robert Alward, 29 March 1652, in the case of Baltimore against Kirke (Extract. P.R O. HCA Examinations, Instance and Prize, HCA 13/65).

[2] Extract and abstracts. Maryland Historical Society, Calvert Papers.

[3] The stone house built for Calvert and occupied by Sir David Kirke in 1638.

owne proper cost and charge – and was lawfully possessed of the said Province of Avalon and provided alsoe ships and boates for fishing, and made alsoe places of Succour and defence for Shipps and vessells that came into those parts to fish or otherwise to trade and traffique and does beleeve by the Iudgments and report of people he expended the summe of Twenty thousand pounds

To the fourth she saith the said Lord Baltemore built a shippe called the Anne and divers boates but the quantitie shee knoweth not, and alsoe built divers stages for makeing and dryeing of fish, and also sett forth and imployed the said quantitie of boates in takeing of fish, but what profitt hee gott by them shee knowes not, nor any thing else contaned in the article.

Examination and deposition of John Steevens taken at Ferryland, 24 August 1652

He does not know of any imposition collected by Calvert from the fishermen. He agrees that Calvert set forth war ships and fortified the harbour of Ferryland and that he kept boats and built stages to use in the fishery.

Examination and deposition of Amie Taylor, taken at Ferryland, 24 August 1652

She claims that Calvert spent £1,700[1] on improvements at Ferryland and that he built 150 fishing boats as well as stages, but she does not know how much profit he made.

Examination and deposition of Philip Davies, taken at Ferryland, 24 August 1652

She is not aware that Calvert ever had any power to collect an imposition from the fishermen. She heard the second lord Baltimore say that Calvert had spent not more than £1,200 at Ferryland. Calvert had no more than 20 boats and some stages but she does not know who built them nor how much profit was gained from the fishery.

Examination and deposition of John Staughton of Capelinge [sic] bay, 31 August 1652

He knows that Calvert did not spend more than £1,800. Calvert did buy and build boats and build stages and he employed 32 boats in the fishery but Staughton believes that he suffered losses in the fishery.

[1] The settlers' estimates of Calvert's expenditure should be compared with the more than £20,000 which lord Baltimore claimed that his father had spent. See above, p.298.

50. 25 February 1636/7   TRINITY HOUSE PRONOUNCES SETTLEMENT IN NEWFOUNDLAND A FAILURE[1]

Now Right honourable Lordes as wee are not Fishermen soe wee professe our ignorance in the trade and business of fishinge cann [sic] therefore say little to [the purpose] only this wee cann say from the mouthes of others that as yet none of all th[e adventurers] which haue attempted in the Nufoundland to settle there to liue, and draw[e] others to them, never thryved, the Lord Baltimore Captaine Mason, Master Guy of Bristoll, and other men ingenious and of excellent partes, yet wearye[d] and soe removed...

[1] The warden and assistants of Trinity House to the privy council (Extract, P.R.O., CO 1/9, 41. Damaged).

INDEX

Nicholas, Sir Edward, 14, 237n., 241, 243, 272–3, 286, 287
North-East Passage, 234
North Falkland, 41, 211–13, 225, 236; conditions of settlement at, 214–15
North-West Passage, 126–7, 234
North-West Passage company, 38
Nova Scotia, 35, 89n., 224

Old English, 37, 38–9, 43, 45, 48, 50
Old Perlican, 77
Orpheus Junior, *see* Vaughan, Sir William
Ortelius, Abraham, cartographer, 90n.
Oxford University, 16, 18, 20, 26, 27, 28, 46

Parkhurst, Anthony, 3, 26, 29
Passage Harbour, *see* Bull Arm
Payne, William, of London, 250n., 274n.
Peale, John, 284
Pearson (Percevall), Bartholomew, settler at Cupids Cove, 69, 83, 87, 88
Peasley, William, son-in-law of Sir George Calvert, 54, 253, 281, 285–6, 287, 293, 294
Peckham, Sir George, 48
Penguin Island, *see* Groais Island
Percevall, Bartholomew, *see* Pearson, Bartholomew
Percy, George, 33
Perlican, 73, 87
Petit Harbour, 250, 259, 300
Pirates, 8, 12, 24, 81, 114, 115, 116, 135, 162, 183, 207, 283; *and see* Barbary pirates; Easton, Peter; Mainwaring, Henry
Placentia Bay, 9, 12, 30, 34, 36, 52, 72, 73, 84, 117, 151, 207, 245, 252, 259
Plancius, Petrus, cartographer, 90n.
Plymouth, 22, 51, 81
Poole, William, settler at Ferryland, 285
Portugal, 24, 33, 111, 127, 142, 156, 165, 167; *and see* Newfoundland fishery
Powell, Daniel, settler at Ferryland, 52, 54, 196, 198, 295n.; letter to Calvert, 198–200
Poyntz, John, 246, 247, 284
Prowse, Daniel W., historian, 23, 35
Purchas, Samuel, 8, 26

Quodlibets lately come over from New Britaniola, *see* Hayman, Robert

Rade, Raymond de la, 252, 279, 280, 281–3, 298

Raleigh, Sir Walter, 23, 57, 115
Ramusio, Gian Battista, 229n., 235
Rastell, John, 3, 18
Renews, 8, 13, 24, 25, 34, 36, 62, 77, 81, 196, 203, 207, 214, 215, 236
    description of, 41–2, 152, 208–11, 254
    as site for colony, 151–2, 170, 209–11
    settlement at, 22, 23, 58
    supplies for settlers at, 222
    fishing at, 210, 211, 248, 254
Robin Hood's Bay, 212
Roe, Sir Thomas, 272
Rowley, Thomas, 12, 69

Sack ships, 1, 148
Sackville, Edward, earl of Dorset, 290
St George's Bay (St Peter's Bay), 12, 33, 34, 117, 118
St Jean de Luz, 282
St John's, 52, 112, 250, 259, 275
    settlement at, 51, 259n., 274
    as site of colony, 62, 151
    fishing at, 95
    mermaids at, 194–5
St Kitts, 291
St Lawrence (river of Canada), 92, 98, 118, 119
St Mary's Bay, 34, 117, 207n.
St Peter's Bay, *see* St George's Bay
Ste-Croix, 6
Salmon Cove, 60, 250, 259
Salt, 63; cost of, 142, 230–1, 234; made in Newfoundland, 167, 171, 179, 230–1, 234, 255
Salusbury, Sir Henry, of Llewenni, 44–5, 245n., 284; description of his grant, 245–6; receives advice on planting, 246–9
Sanford, Alexander, of Lime, 62
Savage Harbour, *see* Dildo Arm
Scott, Sir John, 13, 89
Scurvy
    at Cupids Cove, 9, 62, 80, 88–9
    at Ferryland, 55, 257
    treatment of, 80, 89, 93
Scurvy grass, 62, 70
Sea Forest, *see* Guy, John
Sedley, Sir John, 277
Settlement, *see* Aquafort: Cupids cove; Ferryland; Harbour Grace; Renews
Ships
    Abraham of Plymouth, 51
    Anne, 301

308